HOT FOOT

Walter Knox's Remarkable Life as a Professional in an Amateur World

By David Town

FriesenPress

Suite 300 – 852 Fort Street
Victoria, BC, Canada V8W 1H8
www.friesenpress.com

Copyright © 2014 by David F. Town
First Edition — 2014

Cover art by Keltie Town

All rights reserved.

No part of this publication may be reproduced in any form, or by any means, electronic or mechanical, including photocopying, recording, or any information browsing, storage, or retrieval system, without permission in writing from the publisher.

ISBN
978-1-4602-4462-3 (Hardcover)
978-1-4602-4463-0 (Paperback)
978-1-4602-4464-7 (eBook)

1. Biography & Autobiography, Sports

Distributed to the trade by The Ingram Book Company

Table of Contents

Introduction 1

1. Who *is* this Guy? 4

Growing Up

2. Learning the Ropes 16

3. A Big Time Amateur 30

4. The Workingman's Sporting Tradition 45

5. The Elites Take Over 52

6. The Late Blooming Freshman 65

7. The Adventure Begins 74

The Hustling Years

8. A New England Adventure 90

9. The Wild and Wooly West 94

10. Once More for Harry 107

11. Barnstorming 116

12. The Athletic Wars, 1907-1909 133

13. 1906: Amateur Records, Dirty Dealings and Duping the "Coon" . 141

14. Getting in on the Ground Floor 162

15. A Magnificent Day, Except For… "The Photo" 171

16. A Tour of Michigan 183

17. Inner Turmoil 193

18. California Here I Come 206

19. Prospecting 224

The Highland Games Years

20. A Working Professional 236
21. Olympic Coaching Controversy 253
22. The Stockholm Olympic Games 268
23. Scottish Tours and Disappointments 286
24. Finally, Respect and a Legacy 309

The Prospecting Years

25. New Directions 320

The Coaching Years

26. Another Tour of Olympic Duty 336
27. The Antwerp Olympic Games 352
28. Putting Ontario on the Right Track 364
29. Developing Olympic Champions 386

Retirement

30. Some Final Flings Before Retirement 406
31. Epilogue 424

Appendix 1. Walter Knox's Personal Best Performances 432
Appendix 2. More Walter Knox Quotes on Athletics 434
Appendix 3. Walter Knox Life Timeline 438
Citations and Notes 448
Acknowledgements 497
Bibliography 501

Introduction

Today it is not uncommon to see an Olympic champion track and field athlete living a pretty good life. With multi-million dollar advertising contracts, appearance fees in the tens of thousands of dollars, significant prize money at the biggest events and the fawning support of athletic wear companies, the top athletes can set themselves up comfortably in life. The days of the "amateur" track athlete are over for the very best of them.

But imagine a Usain Bolt, or Donovan Bailey, or any other dominating sprinter of this era, if they had lived back in 1905; would they have been so successful, so motivated, if competing without all the trappings of success? Athletics was truly amateur in that era; there were no sources of income, no advertising contracts and, worst of all, the over-bearing sports governing body spent the majority of its time investigating accusations of professionalism by individual athletes. Athletes were rigorously forced to remain poor.

The amateur-professional debate in Canada was at a crescendo 100 years ago. The sports administrators, appalled that hockey, baseball and boxing athletes were corrupting sport by accepting money to play, determinedly held the amateurs in the Olympic sports to stringent codes of conduct, aimed at protecting them from the insidious influence of money. A star athlete was to keep his sporting endeavours a "hobby" while he prepared himself for a real career.

So what were the top track and field athletes to do, especially those who felt they should be able to make a living from their physical talents? There was but one choice: the seedy world of professional matched racing.

An underclass of low profile runners, operating outside the realm of the amateur sport governing bodies, toured North America, setting up matched races in far-flung towns off the beaten path. These races offered big stakes, often a year's wages for a workingman. Private wagers in saloons and hotels then supplemented the matched race stakes, generally tripling the cash outlay (and potential profit) by the professional runner. This was a dangerous way to make a living, given the high stakes and rampant boosterism for a hometown hero, especially when the touring pro deceptively ran under an alias with a false backstory. Many runners were beaten up and crippled after being found out.

Academically, much has been written about the great amateur-professional debate of that era, of who argued what, of the attitudes and cultural mores involved, of the social impact sport was beginning to have on society. It is well-worn ground. But what is decidedly absent in the academic record is a comprehensive description of the day-to-day life of the professional hustler.

The touring pros were secretive by nature. Because they had to assume false identities to be able to set up matches, they were ever vigilant in sailing under the radar. They never allowed their true stories to be written down, especially by newspapermen (who obligingly turned a blind eye, given the spike in circulation the spectacle of a big matched race could provide). Newspaper reporting of big matches generally downplayed the likelihood of assumed names. It was only after the professional runner had won his race, collected his wagers and high-tailed it out of town that newspapers acknowledged the possibility that the winners had misrepresented themselves, further exciting their paper-buying customers.

This book takes us along with Walter Knox (aka "Johnson", "Renwick", "Wilson", "Kennedy", "Davis", "Newton", etc.) on his adventure as a professional hustler: the drama, the danger, the audaciousness. It is a rare, full-length biography of a sports hustler of that era. Knox, in the twilight of his life, jotted down his story for posterity but never published it. The only copy of his notes was found buried in the personal papers of Harold Hale, a prominent newspaper publisher, stored in the public library in Knox's hometown of Orillia, Ontario, long forgotten. The story is remarkably accurate as compared with the newspaper clippings of the day.

More than just an athlete of the caliber of Usain Bolt or Donovan Bailey (he did, after all, unbelievably break the world record in the sprints, the shot put and the pole vault, three diverse events requiring completely different skill sets), Walter Knox was a fascinating and indefatigable person who packed several more lives into his years after his hustling days were over, lives that were just as interesting: Olympic coach, three times; gold miner; developer of high school athletics in Ontario; early proponent of women's athletics long before that was socially acceptable; champion wrestler in the days when that was a dangerous sport; legend in Scotland as "The Canadian" on the tour of their Highland Games and of course "World All Around Athletic Champion" in 1914.

This is Knox's story as he told it, based on his notes but corroborated by independent research. Almost all the dialogue in the book directly quotes Knox's own writings, keeping the flavour of the personality he chose to see remembered. After 50 years of keeping his hustling exploits a secret, even to his closest confidants, this proud and stalwart man felt the need to leave a legacy. In 1914, at age 36, that need had driven him to the world title after a career spent in secrecy. Then in 1939 (and supplemented in 1950) he decided to record his life story, his true legacy that remained unpublished until now.

His was a life lived to the fullest. It is a life worth remembering.

David Town, May 2014

1

Who *is* this Guy?

He was short and non-descript. Quietly and unobtrusively, he slipped into the pool hall in Oakland, California, picked up a cue and began pocketing balls. His grizzled, workingman's hands deftly handled the cue. At thirty-one years of age, his mop of short brown hair was thinning and the faint wrinkles around his eyes had begun to betray his life in the sun. No one took any notice of him as he sized up the situation, and that's the way he wanted it. It was the start of September 1909.

Of course, all the attention was focused on the back room where Jack Johnson, the great black heavyweight champion boxer, was getting his rub down after a training session. As his entourage kibitzed, Johnson slowly recovered his gregariousness. The pool player, quietly minding his own business, took it all in, looking for his opportunity.

Jack Johnson, a magnificent, powerful black man, six foot two and 210 pounds, had held the World Heavyweight crown for a year and a half, the first black man to hold it. Since his stunning win, the campaign had been on to find the "great white hope," a white man to win the title back and put the big, uppity, black Johnson in his place. He was here in San Francisco training for one of those fights, the current great white hope being local hero Al Kaufman. Johnson had dominated every boxer presented to him, his brash style and big mouth backed up by supreme talent and a killer instinct. Kaufman was not anyone Johnson was too concerned with.

Johnson was notorious, not just for his dominance in the ring, but even more for his lifestyle. He lived the high life, flagrantly flaunting the unwritten Jim Crow conventions that kept blacks subjugated, safe behind the veil of his celebrity. He even married a white woman. That lifestyle just stoked the flames in the search for the man who would put this "coon" in his place.

Johnson's ego was legendary, and it got him into trouble often. It was about to happen again that September day.

Our pool player, meanwhile, was watching and listening. He had been told that Johnson thought himself a fast runner and was willing to put his money on the line to prove it. After an hour in the pool hall, it was clear that getting a match race with Johnson, the self-inflated *nigger*, would not be too hard — and his money easy to fleece.

So, here was an opportunity. Our man, Walter Knox, a small, compact man from rural Ontario, casually let it be known that he had done a little foot racing.

Rolling a ball down the table after a game with one of Johnson's hangers-on, he boasted, "I can run faster than that ball was going". That perked up some ears.

His opponent, seeing a chance to ingratiate himself with the champ and maybe make a little money in the process, blurted out, "The big fighter in there thinks himself a fast runner too. In fact, Johnson challenged another guy to a race just a few days ago, but that race never came off."

Of course, that's what Walter had been told the day before, but he wasn't about to let on here.

"You should see the big fella do his road work. Then you'd see what sprinting really is!"

"That big stiff?" Walter yelled, making sure the whole room heard him, "I can beat his head off!" [1]

As expected, that got Walter invited into the training rooms, where more of Johnson's handlers waited to talk to him.

Facing a handful of black men, some lounging way back on their chairs against the wall, one standing imposingly with his arms crossed over his chest, Walter was asked, "How far do you run?"

Without hesitation, Walter replied, "Anything from 100 yards to 10 miles." Knowing Johnson wanted to sprint, it was a safe bit of calculated bravado.

"Well, Johnson will take you in a sprint!" came shooting back.

Twenty minutes later, they all assembled in the back gambling room where Walter for the first time felt the full, imposing presence of the brash, dominating Jack Johnson. Both sides were looking for some easy money. Johnson was, by all accounts, a pretty good sprinter with his lightning reflexes and powerful physique. He towered over Walter, a five foot eight, 147 pound shrimp.

As for Walter, well, he knew what he was doing.

Johnson studied him. Walter could practically hear what he was thinking. Everybody was out to get the champ, but he always managed to put them in their places. This guy looked like just another one of those dime-a-dozen pool hall layabouts with a chip on his shoulder and something to prove.

There was the briefest moment of silence as the two men sized each other up. Walter stiffened his spine and met the gigantic boxer's gaze steadily.

Then suddenly, as if to break the tension, Johnson started the negotiations. "What's all this talk, white boy, about you being able to beat me in a foot race?"

"I can do it and I'll prove it!" Walter played up the chip-on-his-shoulder role to good effect. "You a runner? I don't think you can get out of your own way!"

"Well, money talks…" Johnson flashed his big, white grin. Chuckles broke out around the room. Here was the chance he'd been waiting for, a chance to prove he was as good a runner as he was a fighter. He was a magnificent specimen and had a magnificent ego to match.

"I'll run you 200 yards for $200. And if you don't like it, hush up," challenged Walter, fully aware that Johnson's cancelled race that week was over that distance.

Johnson's eyes narrowed. Apparently he'd just realized this guy was serious.

Walter saw that the hook was set; now he had to reel him in, get him to put up some forfeit money. Nothing mattered until money was laid on the table.

After a little more squawking, the match was set: They'd use Johnson's training course on the road out back, 240 yards from post to post, for $300 a side, winner-take-all. This was quite a bet, at a time when a workingman was doing well to make $500 in a *year*!

Walter reached deep into his pocket, pulled out a wad of cash and slapped $150 down on the craps table as forfeit money. Then he glared at Johnson.

Forfeit money sealed the deal. Each runner would lose his forfeit if he backed out of the race. This was the moment of truth.

Johnson, without a word, nodded to one of his handlers, who slowly peeled himself out of his chair and took a few steps over to a large mahogany desk. Opening a drawer, he pulled out a moneybox and set it on the desk.

But before he could open the box, the door to the rub down room flew open. Every head in the room swivelled toward the opening. Walter had no idea who it was, but he did know everyone in the room, including Johnson, showed him respect. It only took him a few seconds to surmise the man was Johnson's manager, Billie Little. Little strode right over to Johnson's side.

Slamming his palm down on the craps table and looking the champ straight in the eye, Billie said, "Champ, you've got a fight in 10 days that means thousands. I'm not letting you take a chance on hurtin' yourself for a few hundred!"

Walter held up his hand. "I'll make the race a week after the fight."

That comment was ignored as Little glared at Johnson, their silent communication drowning Walter out.

The handler at the desk quietly put the box back in the drawer. Walter clenched his fists in frustration; his easy money was evaporating right before his eyes. He stuffed the wad of cash back into his pocket. Little left the room mumbling, satisfied the monkey-business was all taken care of.

Walter waited until the door closed behind him before he turned to the champion. This wasn't over yet. "Johnson, I often heard you were a quitter, and now I believe it!"

The easy-going smile melted off the big black head, replaced by a glare. Not many men could keep their legs from weakening under his withering scowl. The flea was about to be flicked. He shot a glance toward the closed door before turning back to Walter.

"You watch your mouth, white boy. You want a race? I know someone who'll wipe the track with you over 100 yards! And let's make it *$1000*!"

Now that was the payday Walter was looking for. It mattered little to him who the race was against. He slapped his $150 down on the craps table again. Locking stares with Johnson, he waited for the deal to be sealed.

Johnson didn't nod at his handler this time, as expected. He clearly wasn't about to cover the forfeit. He'd have to contact the other runner first.

Walter snorted in contempt and reached for the cash. "Well, you sure are yellow! You've quit again, and if it wasn't that you're going to fight Kaufman in 10 days, I'd take a punch at you myself, but I wouldn't want to hurt you!"

That was too much. Without warning, Johnson lunged over the table at Walter. Thoroughly frustrated at being hamstrung by his manager, and provoked by this snarky little punk, he lashed out the only way he knew. But Walter, his senses always on high alert for danger, reacted quickly. Evading Johnson's reach, he demonstrated his sprinting skills as he scooted out the door and down the street*. The race never came off. ²

Who was this little man who was so audacious as to threaten the great Jack Johnson? Who would have $300 or $1000 to so easily bet on a mere running race? He didn't look like a great athlete with his diminutive size, especially not a sprinter, an event usually dominated by large, powerful men. He looked, well, ordinary.

Walter Knox as he appeared in 1909 decked out to race.
Courtesy of Orillia Museum of Art and History

---

* *Twenty years later, when Knox was coaching youth athletes in Ontario, he often taught that a boy needs to be able to fight or run. If he can do one, he doesn't need to worry about the other!*

Walter Renwick Knox was a professional runner. And a good one. He was the consummate professional track and field athlete at the turn of the twentieth century. In a time when track athletes were strictly held to be "lily white" amateurs, Knox made a good living off his physical prowess. And as was common in those days, he successfully jumped back and forth between the amateur and professional ranks.

But more than that, Knox was a shining example of everything that was wrong with pre-World War I athletics. The amateur associations, the Olympic Committees and the college officials all held the pros in utter contempt. In their eyes, professional athletes had sold out to the gamblers and the seedy characters who manipulated sporting events for their own personal advantage. The world of professional track and field, in fact, all pro sports, bred betting and match-making, which led to deception and cheating, and finally to mercenary athletes who had no moral fibre.

Spurred on by unscrupulous handlers, these scurrilous hustlers were believed to hold a win-at-all-cost attitude above sportsmanship and fair play. Professional sports were seen as the purview of the common man, aggressive, opportunistic men of low morals. True amateur sportsmen competed for the love of the game and to demonstrate and improve their Victorian manliness. Moneyed competition was corrupting and immoral, or so the Puritan sports leaders said.

Yes, Walter Knox *was* a professional. He did run for money and he did bet extensively on himself, often with wealthy backers to help him work the gambling community. But he was not the vile man the Olympian idealists held him out to be. He was simply a pragmatist. Opportunities existed to make a living off of his abilities, and he was going to take advantage of them. Many pro track athletes *were* the shysters reviled by the purists, but some pros, like Knox, had a moral sense, and refused to indulge in the dirtiest of tactics or associate with corrupt professional gamblers. Knox was a capitalist. He was happy to take advantage of other people's weaknesses. If they were of poor judgement, were over-inflated, unrealistic or even corrupt themselves, he felt no lack of honour in relieving them of their money in an agreed upon matched race.

His tight grasp on morality loosed as his reputation as a sprinter grew and no one would race against him, or at least *bet* on a race against him. He then had to resort to the oldest of tactics: running under assumed names in scattered locales where he would not be recognized. The pragmatist in him told him this was the only way to make his money and that this was a buyer-beware world. If the other poor fellow was dumb enough to race him for money without knowing his background, well, too bad for him. And there were lots of those self-inflated rubes out there. This form of deception never seemed adverse to Knox's moral code; it was the moral code of the matched racing world and Walter felt no pangs of conscience when in that world. Outside that world, though, he was as upright as could be.

At the turn of the twentieth century, the rigid amateur rules and the organizing bodies' total lack of provision for professionals actually *drove* many athletes to the hustling underworld. Knox is a perfect example of this. Given the choice of competing as an amateur and watching the associations and gamblers reap the financial rewards of your efforts, or turning to the hustling underworld where good money could be made, if dangerously, many athletes like Knox saw no choice at all. Making a good living was hard; why not use your talents to your own advantage?

Amateur athletes "outed" as professionals, often for the most trivial reasons, had nowhere to turn athletically in the majority of sports. Most just retired. Only a few sports accommodated professional athletes (hockey, baseball and boxing being the standard bearers). A champion athlete who wanted to continue in competitive sports honestly as a professional could only turn to those few pro sports available. Often he was far from the best athlete in his new sport.

The most sensational example of this, Jim Thorpe, the greatest all round athlete in the U.S. at the time, was stripped of his Olympic gold medals in track and field after officials found out he had played a little semi-pro baseball two years earlier. He gave up track and became a journeyman professional baseball and football player, scrounging for a living until well past his prime, and dying in poverty. Walter Knox, the pragmatist, wasn't going to go down that road.

The amateur athletic associations, in aggressively defending their "lily-white" rules, kept the sports underworld flourishing before World War I. The disbarred amateurs, fodder for seedy promoters, kept the old, rural matched-race tradition in sport alive, and the gamblers happy. If they really wanted to rid the world of the seedy side of athletics, the amateur associations could have set up a system to share the proceeds of sport with the athletes, as hockey and baseball did. In taking the high road, the associations assured the low road would flourish and that there would be no middle road. A century on, after much angst and uproar, the middle road is the mainstream in most sports, for better or worse.

Later in his career, Knox experienced this middle road of regulated professional athletics, and saw first-hand how sharing the wealth was working. He went to Scotland to compete in the professional circuit of athletic events in the Highland Games and found his niche. Here he could compete and make a living with a healthy conscience, with no middleman promoters or backers. Here he became what he always claimed to be: an honest competitor.

When he retired in 1914, his rivals in Scotland lauded him as a gentleman and a sportsman.

Knox is one of the few who took the seedy, underworld of sport route and survived to be welcomed back to the amateur world. He became a highly respected and sought-after coach; parents were proud to say their boys had been instructed by the great Walter Knox. He came to be held up as a paragon of health and character.

However, the long road back to respectability was not an easy one for Walter Knox. Those skills learned on the hustling circuit, including the suspicious, calculating and devious attitude he had developed, were not easily put aside. It is clear he never really did.

He had gone all the way down a dissolute path, sniffing out the money in athletics and pursuing it. He had learned how to search out matched racing opportunities, how to negotiate a match, and how to ensure its fair execution. He became adept at soliciting bets in saloons and hotels, and at collecting his winnings after the race, no mean feat in those times.

Finally, he learned how to identify who to trust to help him, from point men making the initial contact, to wealthy backers who could work the gambling community, to men who would stand with him if things got rough. And after all that manoeuvring, he then had to be able to offer up bald-faced lies with a straight face to fool the self-righteous amateur associations into allowing him to enter their meets. These were skills the amateurs could hardly comprehend.

To survive in the matched racing world he had to be tough. He had to be shrewd. He had to be better than the other guy.

And if you *were* all of that, as Knox found, it could be a wonderful adventure.**

** There was an epilogue to his confrontation with Jack Johnson. Johnson went on to defend his world heavyweight title for six more years, crushing the greatest (but past his prime) white hope, Jim Jeffries. His cavorting in the white man's world and then marriage to a white woman led him into troubles with the law. Threatened with arrest under the Mann Act (transporting women over state lines for immoral purposes) he fled to Europe where he continued his title defenses, though in increasingly shabby circumstances, and continued the rebellious high life normally taboo for black men. Walter Knox and Jack Johnson met again in London, England in 1915, 6 years after their first encounter. Walter, riding on the top of a bus, saw a sign on a theatre advertising Jack Johnson's appearance there every afternoon. Walter got off at the next stop and went in to say hello; to his surprise, Johnson remembered him. They had a quick laugh over the whole race affair and Johnson invited Knox up to his room to talk. Walter politely declined and quickly left, not wanting to associate with the black man who had married a white woman, a scandalous thing in those days. As Walter pointedly commented, "he had his white wife with him".[3] Knox was a conservative, somewhat racist man, typical of the time, and had a hard, conventional attitude towards cultural mores.[4] Walter's not so subtle slight to Jack Johnson undoubtedly left a frown on the big man's face for a second time.

Growing Up

2

Learning the Ropes

Right from the beginning, Walter Knox had trouble putting down roots. He was born January 27, 1878, the fourth of five children. His father, William Knox, was a 37-year-old mill worker. William moved his growing family from Listowel, Ontario, where Walter was born, to Brampton and then to Toronto, all in Walter's first year. That would be home for the next nine years before the moves started all over again.

These were boom times in Ontario. The province was rapidly growing and industrializing out of its recent homesteading past. The vast forests were being harvested and cleared at a spectacular rate; farmland was becoming prosperous and the rising tide of industry was looming. As the dominant community in southern Ontario, Toronto became the center of this industrialization and its population swelled, doubling in 15 years to 86,000 in 1881. There was work for those who wanted it, and William Knox wasn't afraid to chase the good jobs.

Walter followed his older sister (Mary) and two brothers (John and William) to the Brant Street School when he was six years old. Little Isabella would join them four years later. It was here that Walter first took interest in sport.

At age seven, he joined his brother and the older boys in games of leapfrog. The other seven-year-olds lacked the agility to join in, but Walter easily kept up with the older boys. When the school held some races and games at St Patrick's square, these older boys dragged Walter along. It was an inauspicious start in the world of athletics. Halfway through his race, he was so far behind he stubbed his toe on purpose and fell, taking himself out of the competition. "This was the case of a quitter," Walter would later say, "but it never happened again to me as I made up my mind I would always run to the end of a race no matter how far behind I was."[1]

William Knox, Walter's father
Courtesy of Claudia Courtney

That summer Walter got the chance to practice his running. The horse-drawn streetcar would come up from King Street and police officer Archibald would clamber down near Walter's house to start walking his beat. Walter and his pals would lie down on the lawn opposite the car and look for Archibald's feet to step off the car. That was their signal to start calling him names and taunting him, starting the race. Off the boys would fly around the corners of John and

King and Peter Streets, darting up alleyways and over fences with the red-faced officer Archibald in hot pursuit. Walter was never caught. When he was older, he would claim, "That was the foundation of my running later in life." There would be no quitting in those races!

Those shenanigans on the street also presaged a streak in Walter's personality that resisted authority. Later in life he became very independent, getting his back up when told what to do. He almost reveled in the forbidden challenge: don't go there it's too dangerous. In his adolescence this attitude took him into the street gangs of Orillia, in adulthood, to the frontier towns in the west and the mining towns in Northern Ontario.

It wasn't until a year after his first race that he got his chance to test himself again, at a Sunday school picnic in Aurora. Both Walter and his brother Willie decided to enter the athletic contests. This would result in Walter's first prizes in sport. First place in the standing long jump (ahead of his older brother) and second place in the 100-yard dash (behind his brother) garnered him a rubber ball and a pop gun. This experience was a little more encouraging.

Soon after, in 1887, William Knox and family were on the move again. They relocated up to the frontier, Fesserton, Ontario, on the southern tip of Georgian Bay. This was lumber country, where the largest stands of virgin white pine stood nearest to Toronto and right on the lake route to Chicago where the demand was voracious. The lumber industry was booming, and experienced mill hands like William Knox were in demand. His employers, Brisley and Woods of Toronto, sent him to be the foreman at their new sawmill there. Eleven-year-old Walter started helping out in the mill, learning the shingle making trade, a skill that kept him steadily employed after his mid-teens.

Moving the boisterous boys to the country gave them room to spread their wings. But even more fortuitous for William Knox's family was the strong tradition of sport, especially track and field, in and around Fesserton. A great world champion lived right there, shot putter George Gray, along with his two Canadian champion brothers, John and Joe. Just a quarter mile down the road lived their cousin Harry Gill, soon to be the North American all-around athletics champion. Jake Gaudaur, the world champion sculler, and his brother Charlie, a top notch wrestler, lived in nearby Orillia. That nearby town even had a championship lacrosse team that had recently toured Australia. Taunting policemen for sport was replaced by emulating these larger-than-life heroes.

Jack, the oldest Knox boy, took advantage of the piles of loose sawdust at his father's sawmill to take up pole vaulting. All he had to do was chop and whittle down a likely sized sapling and he was ready to go. Jack was soon winning most of the vaulting prizes at picnics all around the area. Walter, at age 11 or 12, tried to emulate his older brother and carved himself a pole out of a cedar tree. "I remember when I vaulted 5'11" I thought that was a wonderful jump," he recalled. But his vaulting career ended abruptly when the pole snapped on him one day and nearly ran him through. It was a while before he tried that event again.

Within the year William again moved his family, this time to the Leach farm in nearby Coldwater. The 13, 15 and 17 year old boys built up their physiques running the farm while William ran the nearby mill. The Leach farm just happened to sit right next to the Gill farm. Harry Gill, just two years older than Walter, was already making a name for himself in athletic contests. Harry and the Knox boys would meet on the side of the road halfway between their farms to practice running and jumping. Jack and Harry were serious; they traveled to all the picnic competitions in the region cleaning up on all the prizes. Walter was still too young to go with them but he soaked up their experiences.

Walter's first entry in the open division (as opposed to the boy's races) finally came at the 24th of May games in Coldwater's Lovering's Grove in 1893 when he was 15. Walter's older sister Mary was dating Leonard Leach at that time. As Leonard was a cobbler,

Walter had him make a pair of spiked running shoes for this competition, thinking they would win the race for him. On the grassy fields or dirt tracks where the races were held, the traction the spikes gave could be a big advantage. The other boys in the race that day were in tennis shoes or bare feet, making Walter all the more obvious in his fancy shoes. So when he came dead last in the 100-yard dash he was embarrassed, and put those fancy shoes away, not to be seen again any time soon.

In those days there were really only two big sports competitions held regularly every year in any rural community: the holiday fairs on May 24th and July 1st. There were no real track and field organizations hosting meets in the rural areas. These picnics were a big deal, with worthwhile prizes to entice entrants and rampant betting, heavily favouring the hometown hero. Walter's loss here at this big event, in his fancy shoes, was a high profile debacle. He was too discouraged by this embarrassment to run any more races and turned his attention elsewhere.

Shot putting caught his eye. Every Saturday night, like they did in so many rural communities all across Ontario, boys would congregate at the four corners of nearby Fesserton to test their mettle in games and physical stunts of all sorts. One Saturday, inspired by a recent shot put championship win by George Gray in Toronto, the boys tried their hand at a rock putting contest. Walter "took part in the shot putting, willing to try anything on account of not being much good in the running" as he said, and was beaten by four feet by Thomas Johns, "who had never tried anything much in the sport line".[2] A failure again, Walter decided not to go to town for the next three weeks. But he practiced putting the shot every day after obtaining a small iron ball from an old engine at the Leatherdale Iron Works.

After working the farm one day, Walter walked the mile and a half to Lovering's Grove near the wharf on the Coldwater River to watch big, amiable George Gray work out. Walter was too small to heft Gray's 16 pound shot, but he did retrieve it for him, rolling it back. In return he got some coaching from the world champion, pointers to work on at home. George Gray, though smaller than the other great shot putters of his day, was able to go undefeated in a 17 year career by perfecting his "graceful and effortless" technique.[3] He changed the sport of shot putting and, as he had done with Walter, happily shared his secrets with his rivals.

The fourth week, Walter returned to Fesserton and the shot putting contest. This time, with sharper technique, Walter *beat* Thomas Johns by four feet. None of the local boys would ever beat him again in the shot put.

Even at that early age, Walter could not accept defeat or a humbling. He wasn't prone to instant revenge, and wasn't about to force an issue and take another humbling, but he wasn't one to forget either. He bided his time and prepared for the right opportunity to return the favour. He learned to choose his fights and to make sure the odds were in his favour. Technique and preparation were critical, he realized, and could overcome the superior size and strength of his adversaries. George Gray had proved that. For a small man like Walter, this was an important lesson. One that would serve him well in the coming years.

Then the Knox family was on the move again. William relocated yet again to Orillia, 20 miles away, first to Bond Street then to Gill Street. Orillia in 1893 was a bustling industrial community of almost 4,000 people, prosperous from the lumber industry and known as the most progressive industrial town north of Toronto. At the time, Orillia was only 20 years removed from its wild frontier past of lawlessness and brawls and rampant drunkenness. While the righteous civic leaders had succeeded in taming the town (mostly due to the lumber industry moving north to Muskoka), there was still an undercurrent of boisterousness in its culture. The dominant temperance movement forced the bars out of town and Orillia officially became "dry" in 1906, 11 years before the rest of Canada,[4] but the predominant blue collar factory workers still just had to cross the bridge to the bars in Atherley to get their booze. In the civic leaders' minds, this community energy, this boisterousness, was the "Orillia Spirit", an unfettered can-do optimism that they could succeed at anything they put their collective minds to.[5] For the local boys, it was just unfettered energy, and that often meant trouble.

The boys who met at the corners in Orillia were not very interested in athletics and Walter dropped out of the sports world. He began hanging out with the south ward boys well into the evening, often getting into trouble. The north and south ward gangs, separated by the railway tracks that divided the town, defended their turfs. When one group crossed the tracks, a brawl usually ensued. Walter's father finally had to forbid him from crossing the tracks to the north ward except on Saturday nights.

After a summer of this volatility, the boys started transferring their aggression into sport. Walter remembered it all starting accidentally. He and a few of his friends wandered north of the tracks to the foot of Mississaga Street where some of the north ward boys were doing some jumps, physical stunts like the boys in Fesserton had done. Given a chance to have a go at it, Walter beat one of their best jumpers. That led to an inevitable brawl as Walter and his buddies fought their way home. Soon there was a return engagement when the north ward boys came south of the tracks to challenge them to another jumping contest, which again ended in a fight. These encounters began to be more frequent and soon the fighting stopped. It became a running and jumping rivalry, not a fighting rivalry. With the end of the brawling, Walter rediscovered his interest in athletics. But that summer when he was 16, he learned the hard way how to take care of himself.[6]

His older brother Jack had kept up with the pole vaulting and continued to win prizes at local meets. When he returned from a meet in Toronto in 1894 with a big gold medal as Ontario champion, Walter was impressed and decided he was going to get one of those for himself. He started back to serious training, especially in the pole vault, his brother's event. He'd meet some other south ward boys at the stave mill near the train station and practice jumps of all kinds in the sawdust pits. By then, Walter and his brothers had started learning the sawmill trades at his father's mill in earnest. After their day's work he and Jack and Will, and many of their friends, began congregating in front of their house on Gill Street to practice, after they dug jumping pits and starting blocks there.

Walter Knox at age 16, 1894
Courtesy of Orillia Museum of Art and History

During those years in Fesserton, Coldwater and Orillia, from age 13 to 17 especially, Walter's schooling was "haphazard", as he put it. He never did make it to high school. He worked the family farm one year and spent many hours in the sawmill learning to run the shingling machine. Even "as a kid in short britches" he was particularly adept at feeding and stacking the shingles, so there was a job for him whenever he wanted it and his summers were spent at the mill.

School, like his mill work, never interfered with his running, jumping and throwing practice: sports were exciting, spelling and arithmetic were not.

In preparing his life story in the late 1940's, Walter wrote a closely typed, 30 page, legal-sized manuscript with almost no punctuation and disjointed grammar — essentially one run-on sentence. He had beautiful handwriting, the hallmark of a public school education, but virtually no composition skills, a subject learned in high school. With considerable understatement, Walter said, of him and his brothers, "competition was our meat!"

It is apparent Walter revelled in bringing puffed-chested lugs, twice his size, back down to earth. Reading his notes, one can almost see the subtle smirk and glint in his eye after humbling a farm boy 50 pounds heavier than himself. School paled next to this invigoration, and besides, he had a career on the shingle machine well under way.

Jack Knox, 1899. Four years older than Walter, Jack inspired him by winning an Ontario Championship pole vault crown.
Courtesy Orillia Museum of Art and History

Jack Knox's silver medal from the Canadian Championships in 1895, the year after his inspiring gold medal at the Ontario Championships.
Courtesy Orillia YMCA

With that re-discovery of sport as a 16 year old, it was off to all the local competitions for the next few years for Walter, organized fair events on May 24 and July1 but also other picnics put on by churches, the unions, the Orangemen and others, in places like Washago, Jarrat's Corners, Sebright, Hawkstone, Brechin, Waubashene, Midland, Penetanguishene, Coldwater, Uptergrove and Beaverton. All small communities within 30 miles or so that they could hop a train to get to, sitting in a boxcar or between cars.

By 1896, Walter's abilities began to be recognized. He could jump. He wasn't always the fastest runner as he was still figuring that out, but he could leap. Standing or running, long jump, triple jump, high jump, even pole vault, he was becoming unbeatable. For that reason, he and his friends were not always warmly received when they showed up at a competition.

At Jarrat one day, they wouldn't let him enter the hop, step and jump event after he won the 100-yard dash. The organizers said it wasn't fair for their boys, after working in the fields all day, to have to compete with these city boys who didn't have to work. He cut a

Learning the Ropes — 25

deal with the organizers; he'd do a standing jump while everyone else could do a running jump. When Walter still out-jumped the locals, he was barred from entering any more events![7]

At the First of July games in Washago, the organizers announced that everybody was welcome except (specifically) the Knox brothers; this was right on the bill advertising the contests. It seems they wanted their good local athlete named Geno to win the prizes. When the crowd noticed Walter and his brothers Jack and Will (of course they showed up!) doing jumping demonstrations across the road by the hotel, they raised a ruckus, demanding to see them compete. Walter won three events and took second in three more that day.

In some of the towns, it became rather serious. At Hawkstone, Walter and George "Shorty" Hern showed up for a set of contests. The village blacksmith's son, a local celebrity, was expected to beat all comers in the shot put. When Walter easily won that event, the crowd started getting upset, likely because a lot of money had been bet, as with all sporting events in those days. It got worse in the hurdles race. Walter, running just ahead of the local favourite who was crowding right behind him, cut the boy's leg with his spikes in leaping over the last barrier. The crowd burst into an uproar when the boy fell, "bleeding like a stuck pig". Walter crossed the finish line first, and then kept right on running, hurdling the fence and scooting away with men and boys in hot pursuit! That was the end of that meet.

Shorty Hern sensed the brewing fight too, but had the audacity to go collect Walter's prizes—a leg of lamb, a pound of tea and an umbrella—and meet up with him in back of the hotel where they hid out for a few hours. Later, when all was clear, they made their way to the railway and jumped aboard between two cars and headed for home. What Walter pointedly remembered about that whole affair, curiously, was that he broke the umbrella jumping on the train and had to throw it away. He lost his prize, and that mattered, even a useless thing like a silk umbrella.[8]

Then there was Sebright. By now Walter and his buddies were getting a little cocky in their successes and had purchased themselves a set of "classy track suits". When they arrived at the field, the local boys, who by all accounts were pretty good and expected to take most of the prizes, got their backs up and tried to have them barred from the meet. The judges saw no reason to bar them, but the large crowd started talking. It was clear they were not popular.

During the warm-up, the Orillia boys saw that the locals had some talent and decided Shorty Hern and Blair would take them on in the running races and Walter would concentrate on the jumping events. The first race, the hurdles again, was a close one with one of the locals looking like he'd take it. But when one of the Orillia boys got off course and spiked the local boy, cutting his leg, it set off an uproar. As Walter later related, "it was the cold shoulder from then on".

While the officials were still dealing with the hurdles commotion, Walter trotted out to compete in the first jump, the standing broad jump. The local boys had practiced jumping with hand weights and were pretty adept with them. When they showed up with their dumbbells, Walter objected and they had to set them aside, turning the spectators even more against the outsiders.

After Walter won, someone yelled out, "He can't beat 'em with weights, and here's $20 to say he can't." Amid the clamour, the Orillia boys huddled up and managed to pool together $20 to take the bet, knowing Walter had used dumbbells too and was just as good with as without them. When Walter did beat him, likely his first money prize in a matched contest, things started getting hot. It was clear these out-of-towners were no longer welcome.

Badly outnumbered and confronting a very hostile situation, the boys decided it was time to get out of town as fast as they could. Since they knew making a break for it would only ignite the powder keg, they split up, one getting the horses and democrat ready, one collecting their things. Walter was assigned the task of buying sandwiches for the 20 mile trip home. Over at the dance stand, Walter bought a stack of sandwiches and quietly made his way off towards the horses.

Suddenly a big fellow grabbed him from behind and spun him around. "You're under arrest!" the burly policeman hollered, accusing him of stealing the sandwiches. As he began dragging him away, about 100 spectators followed along, happy to see Walter put in his place. Pleading his case was useless in the commotion. When Walter finally was able to stop the policeman and insist he ask the lady at the stand whether or not he had paid, he was ignored. Fortunately, a few friendly people in the crowd came to Walter's support and cowed the policeman into at least talking to the sandwich lady.

Grudgingly, he dragged Walter off to the dance stand where the issue was quickly put to rest by the lady who "told him plenty", calling them all "big fools". Walter was released and headed home to Orillia as fast as he could go.[9]

Sport in those days, even at this local level, was not for the faint of heart. Of course, not all competitions ended in threats and fisticuffs, but people always had to be ready because often they did. The spectators had significant vested interests in the outcomes of the events; local pride demanded it and a lot of money was going to change hands as a result of it. An outsider who showed up the local hero put himself in a bad position, as Walter had learned with the street gangs of Orillia. The crowds could be more intimidating than the competitors, providing a real sense of danger because brawls and donnybrooks were still relatively commonplace in those days.

Back then, when travel was difficult, local pride was a much stronger force than today. Not being aware of what the outside world had to offer made the top local anything seem better than it necessarily was. The best example was the resident athlete. To farmers who had never traveled more than 20 miles from their farm, the biggest, strongest, fastest local farm boy looked like a giant-killer and hometown pride could blow his reputation out of proportion. When a little outsider like Walter Knox showed up and humbled him, and cost one of those farmers a $5 bet, it could get a little hot under the collar. It was humiliating for the farmers to realize how naïve (or gullible) they had been and often someone had to pay the price of their misdirected aggression. An undertone of violence was ever present for outsiders who were too brash, too cocky, too good.

This was the lesson Walter was learning in those teenage years. Go, win, but don't rub it in, and always make sure you have your escape route planned.

3

A Big Time Amateur

By 1899 Walter was 21 years old and happy with his situation in life. He had steady work on the shingling machine at the mill, hockey in the winter, lacrosse and baseball in the summer, and track and field competitions every few weeks in the warm weather. His growing reputation as a top-notch athlete increased his self-assurance. Now respected as one of the better workers at the mill, he had stability in his career path and made more than a dollar a day, a comfortable wage then. But as far as his track and field went, he felt he had outgrown this "small time" kid's stuff. He knew his marks weren't too far behind the top athletes in Canada and the States, and he wanted to make that next step into the top class sports world.

That spring life intervened. Erastus Long, owner of Orillia's E. Long Manufacturing Company, had just developed a new shingling machine with refinements that increased output. He approached Walter, who had been working on one of the new machines that winter, with an offer. Calling him "just about the smartest shingle man in town", he asked Walter to move up north to Verner where one of those new machines was being installed on a trial basis. If all went well, several more would follow. He offered an increase in his pay, but Walter's first concern was the opportunity for track and field there. He trusted Mr. Long, who had been a pretty good shot putter in his day too, when he described the strong sporting tradition up north. After a chat with his family, he was off on the start of a lifetime of travels.

It turned out Verner was nothing more than a whistle stop and four corners halfway between Sudbury and North Bay, 200 miles north of Orillia, all rock and bush and tough lumber camps. But there were lots of sporting opportunities, just as Long had said. Walter arrived with a respected reputation as a shingler, the expert come to demonstrate the new machine, but failed to impress anyone with his reputation as an athlete. These were big, strong working men, proud of their physical prowess, and he was a soft kid from the city.

The sport there was football (soccer), but one look at the rough and tumble play on the gravelly field told Walter he wanted no part of it. Not given much choice, he finally relented but played in relative safety as goalkeeper. He played lacrosse there too, but stayed on the fringes, passing the ball quickly to keep from being aggressively cross-checked. The game, as Walter described it, was mayhem. Every day after work, and after football practices with the team, Walter would get in some track practice in a small clearing in the bush. By the end of the summer he was scarred with black fly and mosquito bites.

For the Verner football team, the big game was to be at the July first picnic in Sturgeon Falls, a larger town 15 miles away. Given the hot rivalry, the game itself was anti-climactic as Verner won easily, but what caught Walter's eye was the bill of track and field events offered afterward. As in many small towns, especially in these remote areas, there was a celebrity local athlete, Kinch, who routinely won all the events at these meets. This was a situation, coming in as the unknown giant-killer, that Walter felt right at home in and relished. As Walter related, Kinch "strutted" onto the field and then skulked away after only three events, losing to scrawny, 145 pound Walter Knox in the 100-yard dash, pole vault and hop, step and jump. No more was seen of Kinch that day.

Two weeks later Walter made the trip to Sudbury, then a mining town in its infancy, for an athletics meet. This was his first experience with "finagling", as he called it. One of the local boys, out to impress his girl, approached Walter and offered him the first place winner's money if he would let him win. In those days the small rural towns always had small cash prizes for their sports days, and no one thought anything of it. Because no one in these remote northern locales would likely ever have anything to do with the organized sports scene in the civilized parts of the country, these cash prizes were at little risk of being reported, opening one up to accusations of professionalism. After winning five other events, Walter magnanimously came second in the shot put as agreed.

By mid-summer the mill in Verner was slackening its work schedule, giving Walter a little more time off. He used it to concentrate on perfecting his pole vault technique with an eye on contending at the Canadian championships in Toronto in the fall. At the time, jumpers used stiff wooden poles that did not bend the way modern poles do, and they landed in sand pits, resulting in many turned ankles. Practice, both in leaping and landing, was critical to success. In late August Walter cleared ten feet in practice, a mark competitive with the best jumpers in the world, the world record being 11' 8". He knew he was ready to step up to the major competitions now.

On September 22nd, 1899, Walter Knox strolled out onto the Rosedale athletic grounds for the Canadian track and field championships. In the pole vault there were several strong competitors, most notably Irving K. Baxter of the dominant New York Athletic Club, the American champion. Irving Baxter was a high jumper, but had a pole vault best within a foot of the world record. He was the man to beat. Walter, as much as he wanted to win, wanted to study Baxter's technique, to see what he could learn from a top vaulter, too. Walter had developed his technique by emulating his older brother and figuring it out by trial and error. Were there subtleties he was ignorant of?

In the end Walter improved his personal best, remarkably, by half a foot, clearing 10'6" and losing to Baxter by a mere two inches to take the silver medal. He had pushed one of the best in the world to his limit.

Walter's silver medal from the Canadian Championships in 1899.
Courtesy Orillia YMCA

This was an early demonstration of one of Walter's strongest attributes: when it came down to the crunch, he performed. He was never prone to "nerves", was never intimidated and never second-guessed himself. He had confidence because he never entered into a contest he wasn't prepared for. If he was in it, he was in it to win. And no one won without preparation. For eight weeks he had dedicated himself to the pole vault, so when he walked onto the Rosedale field he knew he would not, could not, be humiliated. In his mind he was a force to be reckoned with, even though no one else had ever heard of this mill worker from the wilds of northern Ontario. In an age when the science and training for sport was in its infancy, an athlete who prepared thoroughly had a big advantage. This Walter intuitively understood.

In the spring of 1900, Walter was working and training in Parry Sound, on the shore halfway up Georgian Bay. Their July first sports day was going to be competitive, with several local athletes of ability entered. Walter trained for a few weeks with these runners and jumpers and always seemed a stride slower and jumped a shade shorter than them. No one in the know really gave him a chance. At the meet though, Walter won the 100-yard dash, then the hop, step and jump. Then he won the broad jump and the shot put, sending the whole squad of local athletes down to defeat in their own events, one after the other. It was another learning experience.

As Walter explained, in training "the others all tried to do their best and I was always behind them." They soon found out "I kept my best for the day of the games." In other words, the locals pushed too hard competing against each other in practice day after day and had lost their edge by the big day. Walter saved himself, letting them win in practice while concentrating on perfecting his technique. On the day of the meet he was rested and sharp. Many times in the future he would use the same tactics, pushing his competitors to over-exert themselves in training so as to get cocky about beating him. Then he showed his real stuff when it mattered. How psychologically deflating it was to be out-done by someone you had bested every time in practice!

From there it was off to the July 14th Ontario Championships in Toronto, the same meet from which his brother Jack had brought home the gold medal for pole vault in 1894, the medal 16-year-old Walter was inspired win too. The boat from Parry Sound chugged down the coast on July 12th, to dock in Midland, the railhead. From there he'd have a day's visit with his family in Orillia, then on to Toronto.

Walking from the docks to the train station, Walter noticed the bills in the shop windows for some athletic contests in the park, part of the Orangeman's Day celebrations. He slipped his spiked shoes into his pocket and headed for the park. Once there he decided to enter 3 events but saw that there were cash prizes, something that would professionalize him and make him ineligible for the provincial championships in Toronto if someone reported him. The amateur code, strictly enforced by the Canadian Amateur Athletic Association (CAAA), governed the provincial championships. Any financial reward received for anything to do with athletic activities was strictly taboo and would lead to an immediate lifetime ban from amateur sport, a heavy price to pay.

Faced with the dilemma of either protecting his amateur status or winning a few bucks on a lark, Walter recalled in his writings that he thought, "Aw, what the hell."[1]

Walter Knox, the independent man who saw nothing wrong with winning a few bucks, entered the meet on the spur of the moment as "Johnson", the first of many times he would use an alias. It was a huge risk. If anyone pointed him out to the CAAA as a pro his career would be over. Why take that risk for a piddly local meet? It wasn't like this was in the forgotten north; these people could very well appear at the championships in Toronto, in the crowd or as competitors. But Walter, by nature, didn't like being told he couldn't do something, and he didn't agree with the draconian amateur rules anyway. His maverick side, his independent, libertarian streak, bubbled up. He followed a well-worn tactic in "amateur" sport and hid his identity. Here, for the first time, he was about to discover the complications this attitude could bring him.

Midland was 30 miles from his home town of Orillia, and he felt safe he could compete incognito. However, just before the meet started an excursion train from Orillia pulled in with a load of spectators for the day's excitement. When the first event was called and the name "Johnson" announced he could hear the buzz in the crowd. Walking out to the track, Walter heard someone in the crowd quietly say, "Hi there Walter." They clearly knew who he was, but no one gave him away. One man even came up and said "Hello Johnson-Knox, I won't give you away." This was the father of the Washago athlete, Geno, who tried to have the Knox brothers banned from their meet three years earlier.

Walter instinctively knew how to win the crowd over and keep his cover. His competition in the shot put was Ron White, the idol of the Midland sports scene. He was a superior athlete and fully expected to have his way at these games. Walter, in his rolled up pants and shirt sleeves, deliberately laid off on his first put, throwing well short of White's mark. The Orillians in the crowd saw the opportunity he was giving them. The betting money began to fly as the Midland crowd was confident in their man and the Orillians were happy to take their bets, backing Walter. On his second put, Walter put up a mark White, in his fancy track suit, couldn't touch, winning a lot of money for the Orillia crowd. There was no way they'd blow his cover now and have to forfeit their winnings.

Walter won two more events then hustled out of town and home to Orillia, no doubt enjoying the coup he pulled.

Two days later, July 14th, 1900, he was in Toronto for the provincial championships. He only entered the pole vault, the event he felt he could win. Just before the meet started it was announced that there were several names that would be called out of people who had been competing for money and would be protested. Isabella, Walter's sister, and her boyfriend, Byron Bellamy, were in the stands, quite aware of Walter's recent exploits. "Well, you've finally got caught," Byron assumed. They sat nervously waiting for the names to be called, as did Walter. But his name was not on the list. No one had ratted him out. For some people that moment would have been enough to scare them out of ever pulling a stunt like that again. Walter likely just smirked, like the street-smart kid he was.

Walter's competition in the pole vault was a familiar face to him, Ab Gray of Coldwater, younger brother of George Gray, the world record holder in the shot put. IK Baxter was not at this meet for a re-match with Walter as he was busy in Paris winning two Olympic gold medals (in the pole vault and high jump). Walter jumped 10'6" for the win, with Gray second. That was 4 inches higher than his older brother Jack could do; Jack, who had recently won the Canadian championship (in 1898, vaulting just over ten feet). Now Walter had a championship of his own, and the gold medal to prove it.

Walter's Ontario Championship gold medal from 1900.
Courtesy Orillia YMCA

Heading back to Parry Sound, he reversed his route, stopping briefly in Orillia to rub his win in to his brother. In return, Walter received a good scolding for taking such a stupid risk so close to the championship, flirting with being outed as a professional. Isabella, his younger sister, especially delivered the admonishment. Interestingly, as Walter reported the anecdote, they scolded him for taking the risk, not for being deceitful.[2]

Back in Midland, waiting for the northbound steamer, Walter ran into Ron White of all people, who asked him to show him how such a little fella threw the shot put so far. Down to the railway yard they went, where they threw the shot put for a little while, striking up quite a friendship. Then they walked uptown again towards the dock. Along the way White introduced Walter to a few of his friends as "Johnson".

But when one storekeeper got that introduction he replied, "What! Are you trying to have some fun with me? Don't you think I know who this fellow is? He's Walter Knox from Orillia!" The storekeeper had grown up in Orillia.

White, chagrined, had certainly heard of Walter Knox, but he had never met him. He had only competed against Walter's brother Jack and Harry Gill over the years.

As the storekeeper laughed at the deception, White said, "You won the pole vault in Toronto a few days ago. That's why you were "Johnson" at this meet! Well, that's a good one on me, I wished you'd told me before I introduced you to my friends here!"[3]

Walter said the locals had a good joke on White for some time after that. But no one ever reported Walter to the CAAA. It was all a wink and a nod. Walter was now a star athlete the whole region took pride in as one of their own. When he succeeded all the locals could puff up their chests a little, like they did with world champions George Gray and Jake Gaudaur before him. Walter would rely on this wink and a nod from the locals many times over the next 10 years when he could easily have been outed as a pro or have an alias blown.

Later that summer, 1900, Walter was back in Orillia training with Harry Gill down at Couchiching Beach Park. Gill ("slow spoken, plodding Harry" as Walter called him), was at the apex of his athletic career. On July 5th he had won in spectacular fashion the North American Championship in the all-around event, 10 different events all in one day, setting a meet record that would stand for five years. This win brought him standing with the Ontario AAA as one of their representative athletes, and money to cover his travel costs to major competitions. His big win also brought him offers to coach several US college track teams, which he would do at the University of Iowa in the fall.

Harry and Walter, after doing their drills one day in September, got to talking about the Canadian Championships in Montreal that weekend.

"Why don't we take a shot at them, Walter?" Harry casually asked, an embarrassing question for Walter even though he decidedly wanted to go. After hemming and hawing a little bit he finally blurted out he just couldn't afford it. A trip to Montreal was expensive. Gill wasn't to be put off.

"Let's flip a coin for it, heads we go, tails we don't."

The fluttering coin came down heads and it was decided. Knowing he could get some reimbursed later by the OAAA, Harry scraped together a little money, but Walter was in a spot. They hustled uptown and found a few representatives of the Orillia Lacrosse Club who agreed to sponsor Walter by passing around the hat. It was to be a frugal weekend for both of them.

Unable to afford a sleeper, they sat up all night on the train. They arrived in rough shape but felt better after a little breakfast and a rest in a cheap hotel room. They awoke groggy and late at 2 in the afternoon, with a streetcar ride clear across town awaiting them. Standing in the cold drizzle at the streetcar stop chilled them to the bone. The trip was not going well at all.

When they arrived at the Montreal Amateur Athletic Grounds, just in time, Walter overheard a familiar voice in the next change room. It was Irving Baxter, the American who had just barely outjumped him the previous summer. "My nemesis" Walter called him. Baxter, fresh off his Olympic victories, was saying, "This should be easy today, I only have that fellow Knox from Orillia to beat".

Then more bad news. Neither Baxter nor Walter had brought a vaulting pole with them, expecting them to be provided by the host club. The organizers had to race off and get one from McGill University, which turned out to be too short, only 10 feet, six inches long, and hard to handle. But at least it was a level playing field with Baxter stuck using the inadequate pole too.

The rain stopped by the time the meet got under way but it was damp and cold. Two thousand people packed the stands anyway. Walter had trouble getting going and knocked the bar down on his first two attempts at only 8 feet, 6 inches. Could the weekend get any worse? But then, on his last try, he made it over and finally got rolling.

After Walter cleared 10 feet even, Baxter knocked the bar down. He insisted on taking all three of his jumps then and there to avoid waiting in the chill air. That was not according to the rules, but with an Olympic champion on their hands the officials let him get away with it. When Baxter knocked the bar down for the third time, Walter finally felt he had evened the score with him. Baxter acted like he couldn't believe it and asked Walter if he could take another jump.

"Sure, you can jump all day if you like, now that I have the championship tucked away!"[4]

Walter was then given a chance to take an exhibition jump and cleared 10'2" on his first try, putting "a glum look" on Baxter's face as he retreated to the dressing room. Walter was elated. As he passed by Baxter's dressing room he mockingly called out, "There's just that Knox fellow to beat", and then had to duck as a shoe whizzed by his head![5]

Gill failed to win any event, taking two silvers and a bronze and falling in the hurdles. That day it was Walter Knox who was the star for Orillia, representing the Orillia Lacrosse Club. It would be his only Canadian Championship gold medal.

Gill, after that disappointing performance, made up his mind to take the coaching job in Iowa. That would professionalize him, as soon as he was found out. In the eyes of the amateur associations, receiving money for coaching was just as bad as receiving money for competing. You were being financially rewarded for your skills in sport. This moved by Gill is significant as Walter saw a top athlete in his prime, a good friend and confidante, decide to go the professional route. Being an amateur champion wasn't paying any bills and bills *could* be paid on the proceeds of sport.

In the spring of 1901 Harry Gill returned home to Orillia after the Iowa track season ended. He and Walter settled into preparing for the Pan American Exhibition games in Buffalo on June 16th. Harry felt confidant no one would have heard of his stint as a coach in far off Iowa.

Gill was excited to repeat his North American all-around championship win, as this meet was the designated setting for that competition. Now more confident in his abilities in the other events at this level, Walter was also interested in trying his hand at the all-around but opted out, not wanting to have to take on Gill. He asked Harry to withdraw; he'd surely be protested, and besides, the competition wasn't very strong and Walter felt he could win it, but Gill was set on competing. Walter was always in it to win; the idea of losing to even a great champion and friend like Harry Gill was adverse to him. Instead he decided to enter the junior pole vault, shot put and long jump contests.

Then, as the meet was about to get under way, Gill was called out as a professional. Someone had blown the whistle on him. It was the end of his amateur career. At this late date Walter was not allowed to put himself into the all-around contest and he had to stick with his original entries.

In the 16 pound shot put contest, Walter put up some convincing throws without over-extending himself. He wanted to stay as fresh as he could for the pole vault, the event that mattered to him and he felt he could win, and a gold medal in the shot put could be costly. His easy 39'9" toss won him the silver medal. It also kept him in the junior meet. At this competition a win in any junior event moved the athlete into the senior ranks for the rest of the meet. In the vault, he won comfortably at 10'4" just as the shot put results were being announced. Had he gambled and won the shot and hoped the vaulting would be over before the results were announced, he would have lost out by just minutes and been disqualified (he felt he held back about two feet in the shot and could have easily won).

As it was, he pinned a gold and silver medal on his chest, although he was now ineligible for the long jump. Not getting in on the all-around competition was a big disappointment though. Adding up his points for his likely scores would have put him on top.

"By golly Walter, I'm sorry I was so bull-headed." Harry apologized.[6]

Soon after the Buffalo meet Walter was on the move again. His father had gone to work for a lumber company in Montreal and was now being sent to manage a mill in Newfoundland. This mill had just installed one of Long's new shingle machines and Mr. Long approached Walter to join his father out there to demonstrate the machine. So it was "off to the other end of the world," as Walter said. This turned out to be the roughest and most backward place he had seen yet. He headed home at the earliest opportunity, but not until after one sporting escapade.

A local store clerk was an amateur boxer who had made a habit of roughing up all the locals. He spent days trying to taunt Walter into a few rounds and when he was ignored thought Walter was afraid of him. Finally one day, with a "flip remark", he tossed the gloves to Walter in front of a room full of men and insisted on a little sparring. It was an offer Walter couldn't refuse. It wasn't long before this clerk was sitting on his behind thanks to a Knox glove to the chin.

Flustered and angry, he lunged back at Walter like a windmill, throwing all caution to the wind. "It was no trick at all to finish him off," Walter recalled. "This time when he hit mother earth he stayed there!" The store owner thanked Walter for taking him down a peg and later Walter heard the gloves were put away for the rest of the summer. His days on the streets of Orillia had paid off.[7]

Walter also jotted down this note on his stint in Newfoundland:

> "*During this time I was called upon to take the place of a doctor for any of the men who were injured. I amputated three fingers and fixed a very badly crushed hand. My surgical instruments were a good pair of shears and a jack knife and I made a couple of good jobs.*"[8]

Obviously Walter had the assurance and courage many other men would not have been able to muster.

One final event helped shape Walter's thoughts that summer. On his way home from Newfoundland, he looked up Tim O'Rourke, one of the top shot putters in Canada then, at his hotel/saloon in the St Lawrence Market in Toronto to catch up on events in Ontario. Tim said a couple of his friends from Cleveland were in town and would enjoy a shot putting demonstration by them. Walter overheard his phone call to them that went more along the lines of "come on over and watch me put it to him". This was not to be just a demonstration, Walter realized. O'Rourke, a 220 pound strong man, did not realize that Walter, 149 pounds dripping wet, had been throwing better than ever in practice that summer and was quite surprised when Walter gave him a good trimming with all three sized balls. He had backed Walter into a corner and paid for it.

This event was a bit of an epiphany for Walter. On the train home to Orillia he came to a conclusion. In his own words:

> "*Beating O'Rourke in itself was stimulating to my*

confidence in myself, but it raised some considerable doubt also. Here I was endowed with better than ordinary physical ability but what was it getting me, or more properly, what would it get me? The more I thought it over the more I came to the conclusion that as an athlete, being a high grade shingle cutter was more to the point." [9]

That fall he dedicated himself to his sawmill career, still working out for the fun of it, but only competing in two meets in all of 1902, at local picnics in Parry Sound and Orillia, where his most remarkable win was in catching the greased pig! Just as he was coming into his prime, 23-year-old Walter Knox, the pragmatic capitalist, decided not to waste his time on track and field.

— 4 —
The Workingman's Sporting Tradition

To appreciate Walter Knox's life up to this point, and even more what was to come, one must understand the societal forces at play. The world of athletics at the start of the twentieth century was molded by two colliding cultures: the rural workingman's and the urban elite's. When it came to sport, these two worldviews were diametrically opposed. Because of his athletic abilities, Walter Knox was drawn into a sporting environment in crisis, pulled between two extremes with absolutely no middle ground. He had to choose sides. His choice, not surprisingly, was not to choose.

The administrators, organizers and regulators of the growing athletic world were the middle and upper classes. They designed the rules to suit the leisured classes and to promote their vision of manly sportsmanship. The ones this group clashed with, the ones they were trying to suppress, were the promoters of the rural, workingman's traditional sporting ethic, and their blood sports, matched races and gambling events. It was a class war with the elites asserting their control over the common man's traditions, all in the spirit of bettering society.

Early in Canada's history there was little sport. Establishing and maintaining a pioneer life took up all one's energies, and people lived in relative isolation on their farms. But at social gatherings friendly competition did occur. Theirs was a form of masculinity, "that valued physical strength, recourse to violence, danger and a certain wildness among youth."[1] Men raced their horses, boys ran footraces and wrestled, and feats of strength were contested. And, of course, wagers on the outcomes were integral to the whole tradition. Sports historian Frank Zarnowski described these events as "a local, impulsive sport."[2] But organized sport, whether team or individual, was largely unknown in the early 1800s.

The state of early physical contests is described by historian Kevin Wamsley: "the drinking and fighting that often accompanied barn-raising and harvesting bees in rural areas, and the contests of strength and skill, boxing and wrestling, which pitted townships against one another, were considered offensive by some but revered by others."[3]

The first popular sport was horseracing. "Well bred horses were valuable in agricultural society and it was only natural for men to show off their horses at holiday races," historian Nancy Bouchier wrote.[4] By the 1820s, crowds of up to 60,000 would show up for a big horse race in the US and the gambling money would fly. This was the impetus for the first organized footraces. With all the people in the crowd hankering to place wagers, it soon became common for footraces to be staged after a horse race, sometimes spontaneously, sometimes as a promoted draw for bigger crowds.[5] Of course, in Upper Canada there would not be such large crowds, no community would even have 60,000 people for several decades, but the horse races did draw crowds and the idea of footraces would have quickly spread to the northern colonies. Soon foot races were being promoted on their own.

Betting was legal then and bookmakers abounded. It only took until the 1830s, though, for the spectators to catch on to the race fixing that inevitably developed, particularly with footraces, which were obviously more susceptible to fixing than horse races. Interest in foot racing ebbed and flowed in the 1830's as rumours of cheating came and went. But people still showed up for races, cheering for their local favourites.

In Canada, then still a collection of rural colonies, the traditions of sport grew out of that culture. At social gatherings, men would cheer on their friends and local heroes in many sports, from catching greased pigs and feats of strength to boxing and wrestling to running, jumping and throwing events. The gambling associated with these sports was the traditional working class recreation.[6] Historian Colin Howell went so far as to say, "Gambling was more popular than the sports themselves... (and was) associated with the speculative nature of frontier life."[7] In running, standard distances for races slowly emerged and a system of handicapping, where one runner would start a certain negotiated number of yards behind the other to level the playing field, developed to encourage wagers. Historian Alan Metcalf put it this way, "Central to all indigenous working class sports was money and gambling... Sport was not a vehicle for the demonstration of social qualities; it was for victory itself."[8]

Even in the small towns this sporting culture developed, as historian Lynne Marks explained. Young men with few alternative amusements, little money and no comfortable home to relax in, clearly enjoyed hanging out with friends on street corners. Small towns had problems with the "loafers" and "loungers" who were often drunk. Gambling was popular with these men and they were the supporters of the cock fights, horseracing and running races.[9]

Of course, the big draw for gamblers was the matched race, a challenge put forward to a runner of reputation for a wagered prize. The rumour of a race for $25 a side, winner take all, could draw a considerable crowd where many more wagers could be taken. A shrewd operator could make a tidy sum. Over the middle decades of the 19th century the matched race culture flourished.

Track and field (or athletics) found its origins at the same time, emerging at the holiday festivals starting in 1845, the first year of the Victoria Day, or May 24th, holiday. Local communities organized holiday fairs with dances, parades, speeches and a wide variety of contests from three-legged races to pie judging. At these fairs (and soon the Dominion Day July 1st holiday and the August 1st civic holiday) locals could compete in running races of all distances and many throwing and jumping events. The list of events varied with each fair but gradually some standard events developed, like the 100-yard dash and the long jump.

Small cash prizes were offered to encourage participation in the advertised list of events. Most organizers found it easier to award cash than to arrange for trophies. The middle class and wealthier contestants, though, preferred a "tangible" trophy they could display as a badge of manhood, since they didn't need the money. It was the working class, who saw their small entry fee as a wager on their own success, who relished the monetary pay-off for winning.[10]

Though not as prominent as in the big promoted matched races, gambling was still common at the fairs. Professional gamblers, says Nancy Bouchier, lived on the fringes of fairs, festivals and horse races.[11] Over the first two decades of holiday fairs, the athletic events gradually replaced the horse races in popularity and relegated the nags to the agricultural fairs, while attracting the gamblers to the runners. Bouchier has pointed out that these serious gamblers were looking for an advantage in their wagers, "secret information" about a "sure thing", in contrast to the sportsman, who risked his money strictly on the certainty of his own judgment.[12] The gamblers became a corrupting influence on the competitions.

Soon many holiday fairs in Scottish regions began hosting Caledonian Games. Having crossed the Atlantic with Scottish immigrants, the Caledonian or Highland Games included a relatively standard table of athletic events, from tossing the caber and heaving the heavy stone to the whole range of running and jumping events. As well, they staged dancing and piping contests and many other Scottish cultural traditions. The cash prizes offered at the Caledonian Games were larger than the typical fair prizes, making the Games more popular with the athletes. At the time they were the closest thing there was to a standard track and field meet.

Athletics began to change in 1853 when the New York Clipper newspaper began keeping the first "record book" for athletic events. The idea spread rapidly. Sports began to be covered regularly in the press, raising the profile of the athletes and spreading the word of athletic feats. It became rather profitable to be an athlete if you were good enough. Reputations were invitations to matched race challenges where wagers could earn an athlete and his backers significant profits. And as Zarnowski states, "In 1850 there was no stigma attached for people at any social or economic strata in accepting a prize for their efforts."[13]

By 1860, the culture of sport was settling into the Canadian persona. It was rough-edged and could be violent, far different than what would be seen just 25 years later, but it was established as part of the culture. Many church-goers and temperance crusaders objected to the whole culture as a breeder of vices, but the mainstream man, who now had a little time on his hands and lived in a little larger community, enjoyed the thrills sport provided. Sport became spectator-driven. Larger and larger events were promoted, driven largely by gambling.

However, a growing resistance to the whole sporting culture was brewing. By the time of Confederation, lobbying for restrictive drinking and gambling laws had begun, spearheaded by the growing temperance movement. The first federal anti-gambling laws were passed in 1876. These laws, however, only governed public behaviors; they had no jurisdiction over private events like matched races and prizefights, and they had little effect on the rural sporting tradition. The laws passed were created primarily to develop a "rational" workforce to serve economic interests[14], that is, to prevent workers from destroying themselves with alcohol and poverty so the farms and factories would keep the economy humming. Reigning in sporting contests was not the main goal of the new laws. The authorities enforced those laws to stop the rowdiness and self-destruction of drinking and gambling, not to stop the sporting contests that facilitated the drinking and gambling.

The sport that developed then was a young man's domain, not a boy's. In the 1850's in Ontario, physical education in schools was non-existent. Honest work around the house and farm was considered the only necessary exercise. No mention of physical education in schools came until the School Act of 1875 when teachers were allowed to incorporate games into the curriculum at their own discretion.[15]

In the 1870s, the boys themselves began organizing teams and games at Ontario schools and even started playing interschool games in Ottawa and Toronto in 1877.[16] The schools didn't get involved in the organization of teams until 1885. After physical education became mandatory in Ontario public schools in 1889, training for boys consisted only of calisthenics and military drills, aimed at developing "discipline" and "obedience" in the boys.[17] For girls, the physical endeavors in school were calisthenics to prepare them for motherhood.[18] Competitive sports like track and field were not promoted in high schools in Ontario until the 1900s. With this lack of formal encouragement for boys to compete it is no surprise athletics was a man's game in the mid-1800s.

Walter Knox, born in 1878, would not have been exposed to athletics in the schools, and makes little mention of it. He grew up in the rural sporting tradition, learning physical stunts at crossroad meeting places and testing himself at holiday fairs. Graduating from the children's races to the adult contests at the fateful holiday games at Lovering's Grove in 1893, he would already have been familiar with the intensity of adult competition. At the fairs he would have been exposed to the gambling life from a very early age to the point where it was an accepted part of any contest. There was always money on the line in these races and they were to be taken seriously. Of course, the races were always taken seriously because the competitor's self-esteem, his reputation as a man of physical prowess, was always on the line.

5

The Elites Take Over

The rural sporting tradition, which had become well ingrained in Canadian society, became a target of the moral upper classes by the 1870s. There was a vocal temperance movement and a growing anti-gambling trend in Ontario at that time and these vices were seen, justifiably, as endemic in the sporting culture. Between 1870 and 1884 the campaign against the tavern sports and matched races built to a climax.

The elites (wealthy landowners, professionals and men in positions of power) and the bourgeoisie or middle class (wealthy merchants and businessmen) looked down on these aggressive, uncouth common sportsmen from their comfortable perches. They were attracted to the British traditions of manliness and civility. Sport, if done at all, was a vehicle to show one's character, to exercise sportsmanship and to demonstrate one's civilized values. The crude win-at-all-costs nature of the rural sports was anathema to them.

In the late 1860's, the urban elites began to form their own sporting clubs. Cycling, rowing, and pedestrian (running) clubs, as well as baseball, lacrosse and hockey clubs, became more common in large and small towns. Initially the clubs were there to promote the sports, but they quickly became vehicles to mold the sports. How the game was played (fairly, showing hardiness, self-restraint and team work) became more important than who won. This was the opposite of how sport was run at the holiday fairs, especially the team sports. It was the demonstration of civility, even chivalry, which mattered. Even in the smaller towns where there wasn't a large enough leisure class to support an elite club, the new club set up by the bourgeoisie would be at least middle class and followed the tenets of the elite big city clubs.

For 20 years, these two sporting traditions evolved side by side, the holiday fair sports, rival town teams, matched races and blood sports operating in the rural areas on the one hand and the club teams in the urban centers setting up exclusive leagues and individual sporting contests on the other. Each grew more extreme in their views and actions, and especially in their attitudes towards the other.

The dividing line between them was class. The upper classes disdainfully barred any workingman with his immoral and aggressive attitudes from their sporting events. The working-men in their rollicking tavern sports and competitive challenge contests thumbed their noses at the snobby elites and their intrusive rules and codes. While the elites haughtily disapproved of the vices associated with the tavern sports, it must be noted individual club members were, hypocritically, familiar sights at the matched races and fist fights of the 1860s and 70s, placing their wagers along with the working men.[1]

The elite clubs, leading the charge to civilize sport, became flamboyantly pretentious. Starting in the late 1860s, sporting clubs organized to provided equipment and facilities such as rowing sculls, bicycles and club houses for their members' use. By 1880, however, they had become as much haughty and snobbish social clubs as sports clubs. Often several clubs in the larger cities (cycling, rowing and football for example) would amalgamate and pool their resources, building lavish clubhouses with gymnasiums, bowling alleys, playing fields, billiard tables, libraries, pianos, and luxurious social rooms.[2] Full-time managers were hired to oversee the day-to-day operations.

Hefty membership fees or referral requirements strictly limited membership. Those considered the "wrong people" were kept out. Often the clubs were allowed to manage the town's fields, stands and playgrounds, and tightly restricted who had access, further limiting the common man's sports. People were arrested and prosecuted for staging footraces without permission on the supposedly public fields.[3] Facilities were often closed on Sundays for "religious reasons", again limiting the common man's access on their day off. Members of the elitist clubs were not allowed (and likely didn't want) to compete with the athletes outside the membership who didn't abide by their rules and codes of conduct, and who, it was thought, had the unfair advantage of the fitness gleaned from physical work every day.

By the 1890's, many of these athletic/social clubs were going bankrupt. Expanding into dining rooms, Turkish baths, rifle ranges and sleeping rooms, the clubs became decadent in their elitism, and costly.[4] Many clubs resorted to renting out their facilities before going under. The lavish Toronto Athletic Club, with its indoor pool, indoor tennis courts, gymnasium and lavish clubhouse, went bankrupt and closed in 1894.[5] By then, though, the elites had found another vehicle to assert their dominance over sport and its culture, and the social clubs became marginalized in the sporting world, hence their decline.

The rural sports became equally extreme. Still the venue for local men and boys to test their abilities in friendly competition, the rural sports too often succumbed to the manipulation of promoters and scam artists. By 1880, baseball had become overtly professional, with players being paid to play. The tavern sports of prizefighting and cockfighting flourished into the 1870s when laws were finally passed to control them. In track and field, the main events into the 1880s were still the holiday sports days, supplemented by sports days put on by unions, churches, fraternal organizations and factory owners on other weekends. Top athletes learned to tour these events and make a living through side bets and matched races. By the 1880s, these professional athletes had extended their tours to many urban centres in the US to find enough competitive opportunities. Groups of professional athletes took to touring together, anonymously, for mutual support.[6] With the advent of sports boosterism in the newspapers, it became easier for these highly skilled athletes to find and, under assumed names, fleece local stars.

One such hustler, starting in 1879, was Alby Robinson of Woodstock, Ontario.[7] An outstanding runner, he'd spend the summer looking for racing opportunities all across southern Ontario, becoming adept at working a community for wagers. Intentionally winning or losing a close race at the fair would lead to a matched race for a small wager. Enough of a delay was planned so he and his backers could work the gambling community for bigger bets before he would win the rematch and collect his winnings.

It was routine to travel and compete under assumed names, often against others doing the same. Robinson remembered, "When big stakes were up on specially matched races contestants were bought and sold, bought again and re-sold again. Timers and trainers were tampered with and surely there existed no honor among thieves." Sometimes there were not enough track meets organized, necessitating long breaks in his summer, "so recourse had to be had to the working up of special opportunities." A carefully selected local man would be taken into confidence as an accomplice. For several weeks Alby would play the role of his hired man, becoming familiar around town and known as a bit of a runner. A local hotshot runner would be "worked" in this fashion until Alby's "employer" could set up a highly promoted matched race. The accomplice would work the town for wagers and the winnings would be split. Walter Knox would use this very tactic later.

Alby Robinson captured the essence of the professional's life:

"Around these humble trials of speed, what stories could

> *be woven wherein conceit, over confidence and over estimation, high spirits and enthusiasm, frantic efforts to get in on the good things, secret whisperings of the knowing ones, quiet tips, secret bets, hero worshipping of the favorite son, the quiet evolution of the "working up", the tense and breathless waiting at the finish, the putting up of the novice gambler's last cent, the borrowing of money to get in on the chance of a lifetime! Here surely was a time when opportunity was rapping his knuckles on everybody's door."* [8]

Surely the crassness and dishonesty of the rural sporting life was no better than the elitism and intolerance of the club sporting life. Through the 1870s, these two cultures clashed and moved farther apart. The clubs were "bewildered" when rocks were thrown through their windows, club dogs were poisoned or bicycle spokes were sawn through.[9] Likewise, the rural athletes roiled at their barring from public fields and ostracism from the club facilities.

In the 1880's, the elites started to take control. Considering themselves the natural leaders in society, they took it upon themselves to set up athletic associations (AAA's or Amateur Athletic Associations), cooperative legislative bodies that would oversee groups of clubs in a variety of sports. Of course, the main legislative rules were meant to keep the rural sporting culture marginalized.

The most dominant was the Montreal Amateur Athletic Association (MAAA), founded in 1881 when the Montreal snowshoe, lacrosse and cycling clubs merged to acquire an athletic grounds and clubhouse. Three years later the MAAA spearheaded the formation of the Amateur Athletic Association of Canada (AAA of C), an association of other like-minded urban clubs across Canada. Its goal was to combat professionalism in sport, especially the track and field athletes making a living on the tour of Caledonian Games and holiday fairs, degrading athleticism with their matched races and gambling.[10] By 1890, most towns along the Montreal-Toronto corridor had formed their own AAAs, affiliated with the AAA of C. The Caledonian Games rapidly disappeared as the AAAs took over the holiday fair games, replacing cash prizes with trophies.[11]*

The AAA of C created the framework for sport, defining rules and eligibility requirements that were biased towards urban centers and the cultural mores of the elites of society. It endorsed "respectable" sport as promoted by churchmen, educators, social workers and the upper classes.[12] It endorsed "public order" versus "undisciplined street play", "commercial prosperity" as opposed to "absenteeism, drunkenness and wanton self-interest". To many of the elites in this era of reform, this attack on the crude and immoral forms of street sport was serious business. It was about civilizing society.

The AAA of C required each member association to host a track and field meet every season under its strict jurisdiction and to support their national championships every year (there had never been a national championship prior to this). The standardized events, standardized tracks, careful timing and record logs introduced by the AAA of C allowed events to be compared nationally. This organization boosted the popularity of track and field tremendously, and in doing so allowed the AAA of C to legislate the rules under which athletics would operate. Needless to say, athletes from the rural sporting tradition were to be excluded. And that was the trick, to find ways to exclude them. Thus began in earnest the amateur/professional debate in Canadian sports, which was to culminate in the "athletic wars" of 1907-09, at the peak of Walter Knox's career.

Right from its start in 1881, the Montreal AAA's key tenet was the definition of amateurism. Up to that point, professionalism was

---

* *Interestingly, and demonstrating its frontier nature, there is no record of an AAA in Orillia during Walter Knox's career, even though, at the time, it was a progressive sports-minded town of over 6000 people located just 75 miles from Toronto.*

defined by profession (hence the word) and, therefore, class; professionals were men who worked at a job that gave them an advantage in competition with the leisured upper class athletes. For instance, the strength and agility manual labourers gained on the job was a decided advantage over a landlord or engineer in a jumping or throwing competition .[13] In 1870, an amateur was a "novice" and a professional was "skilled".[14] But as working hours shortened and the opportunity for working men to take up sport grew, the leisured classes were elbowed aside by the surge of working men partaking in sport, making a new definition of professionalism necessary.[15] Sometimes a workingman who gleaned no advantage from his profession still put the club athletes down to defeat. Obviously the definition of professional was not working from the upper and middle class perspective. A new definition, codified by the MAAA in 1881, based professionalism on money and profit from sport. The official AAA of C definition of an amateur in 1884 set the battle lines:

> *"One who has never competed for a money prize, or staked a bet with or against any professional for any prize, or who has never taught, pursued, or assisted in the practice of athletic exercises as a means of obtaining a livelihood."*[16]

It was a negative definition, stating what an amateur was not, and never stating clearly what he was. This was overtly exclusionary, as no attempt was made to define the ideology of amateurism itself.[17] But it was crystal clear now; competing for money was the defining feature of a professional. It was assumed that "when money enters into sport corruption is sure to follow", an ideology never applied to other professions such as medicine or engineering.[18] In hindsight, it is clear the original target under attack was the drinking and corrupting gambling culture associated with the professional sports culture, not necessarily the idea of competing for money itself. Whatever the intent, now the central feature of the rural sporting tradition, wagering, excluded those athletes, and anyone who happened to race against them, from the AAA of C and their now dominant track and field meets.

After 1884, to compete in an AAA of C meet (and in the Montreal-Toronto corridor that included all the holiday fair games) you had to belong to an affiliated AAA club. That meant you had to have been given an amateur card declaring the club had investigated your amateur status and deemed you "clean". Generally, local officials knew who was who and would not grant a card to an athlete they knew had raced for money. Class was a big indication. In 1887, the Toronto AAA had 250 applications for their amateur card but granted only 180.[19] Many top athletes from the holiday fair games era were now shut out of the new AAA of C meets.

Right off the bat, the AAA of C dominated track and field, due to their organizing and standardizing of competitions. But it also had jurisdiction over 19 other sports and had more trouble with them. Between 1885 and 1905, the amateur rules were amended many, many times to tighten them up and to deal with loopholes exploited by the team sports. The legislation became more and more draconian. This made it harder and harder for rural athletes like Walter Knox who grew up in a frontier town, to adhere to the rules when the only sporting opportunities were at the holiday fairs, which were still thriving away from the Toronto-Montreal corridor. He never talked about the "amateur rules" but always, derisively, the "lily-white amateur rules".

Team sports like hockey, lacrosse and baseball had already begun paying their players by 1884, the year the amateur rules came into effect. It started at the holiday fairs where team games pitted rival towns against one another. Rowdy boosterism thrived as the honour of the town was at stake. It didn't take long for "ringers" to be brought in to help avenge losses, and soon mercenary players who were paid to play. When leagues started to form, the local athletes in smaller towns couldn't compete with the larger town teams and the hiring of top athletes became commonplace by the 1880s. Just look at little Kenora, Ontario, isolated north of Lake Superior, winning the 1907 Stanley Cup in hockey before it was taken over by the professional National Hockey League; half the team were paid mercenaries. In sports such as baseball, hockey and boxing, where the masses accepted pay-for-play athletes, those sports went overtly professional and ignored the AAA of C and its rules. However, the masses never supported professionalism in track and field as openly.[20]

By 1900, the CAAA (the re-organized AAA of C) was spending most of its time investigating alleged cases of professionalism.[21] But the AAAs never attained total hegemony over sport.[22] The working class sporting tradition continued in spite of the AAA's best efforts to eradicate it. Matched races continued to thrive in rural and out of the way places, especially where the AAA of C had little influence. In a rural country like Canada with many frontier towns, a man's worth was often measured by his physical prowess. Spontaneous matches of strength, speed and agility were a natural extension of that culture. Walter Knox, for example, grew up on the border of these two worlds, learning the ropes at the holiday fairs untouched by the AAA's but close enough to Toronto to vie for their amateur championships. The working class sporting tradition was still an enduring culture, even in the face of the overlords of the AAA of C. Of course, the many athletes who were denied amateur cards became a breeding ground for this culture.

For all its good intentions, the AAA of C made the fundamental mistake of never understanding the motivations behind the working class sporting tradition. In the world of the lower classes, money came and went easily; it was something to be used, not accumulated, that was the nature of rural life.[23] Life was speculation, investing your meager resources in ventures linked to your physical work like farming and small business. This class of athlete saw sport as a "workplace"[24], an opportunity to invest and make some money, no different than anything else in their lives. Working class athletes weren't just crass and immoral mercenaries, prone to cheating; they were "speculators", investing in themselves for a quick payoff. "The win-at-all-costs attitude", commented sports historian Bruce Kidd, "The culture of training and practicing, the scientific analysis of technique and the specialization of these rural athletes is just an expression of their reward-oriented approach to sport".[25] Sport, beyond recreation and braggadocio, was a kind of "self-help" — a chance to get ahead, to make a little quick cash.

The supporters of the AAAs, on the other hand, were the proponents of "muscular Christianity". This cultural value "held that the physically developed man, tempered and guided by Christian morality, was better positioned for a successful life".[26] They felt that "the playing of sport for its intrinsic values and for building character was the basis for amateurism". Hence, living manly, morally upright lives, with a patriotic sense of duty to both God and the country, was the goal of life and sport was a means to develop that. Winning and losing? Pshaw! That meant nothing if you didn't have the manliness and character to play the game honestly.

To appreciate the cultural differences between the rural and elitist camps, just look at the attitudes towards referees. The AAAs often felt, self-righteously, that there was no need for them since every player was duty-bound to call his own fouls and transgressions. The players were held responsible for making the game fair. In the matched race world, on the other hand, the runners relied on their trusted seconds to negotiate the terms of the race, right down to whether holes for starting blocks could be dug. A supposedly neutral referee, usually a town official or hotel keeper, always held the stakes and oversaw the seconds as they negotiated, making sure the event was carried out as agreed. He was the one who announced the terms of the race to the wagering crowd and the newspapers. He was also the one who could call "all bets off" if he saw a transgression of the agreed upon rules. The referee was crucial to that sporting tradition.

The rural athletes and the AAAs might as well have been living on different planets. But strangely, they shared many of the same values: manliness, fairness, perseverance, courage. It was the over-riding ideology on each side that manifested those values in completely different ways. Take fairness, for example, a central value to the AAA athletes who were guided by Christian morals such as the golden rule. The working class athletes were also committed to fairness, believe it or not, but went about it very differently. A runner had a lot riding on a race (both in dollars and ego) and was not about to be played for a sucker. The terms of a matched race were scrupulously negotiated and refereed, but, of course, you always played to win too, angling for any advantage you could get. Anything not explicitly negotiated was allowed. Being the gentleman and playing nice would likely lose you your $5 stake, probably leaving you hungry for a day or two. So you did what you had to, constrained to follow the negotiated rules by the risk of violence against cheaters by the rival or the wagering crowd (not to mention the loss of your forfeit money).

On the frontier, life itself was a gamble and every decision you made was overlaid with a valuation of how it could help you get ahead. Getting beaten up or crippled, always concerns when deceptively running under an alias, were risks to consider. Matched racers were always acutely aware of how fair a contest was and wouldn't enter into one if there was a chance it wasn't on the up-and-up. The dishonesty of aliases and the bribing of judges were part of the ever-suspicious, buyer-beware nature of the negotiations — you chose to race me, if you're not happy with the outcome, too bad! The highfalutin AAAs and their rules and unwritten codes were mocked on the frontier, if anyone thought about them at all. The only rules that mattered were the ones negotiated that day. But those rules carried a lot of weight.

Accepting financial reward for sport was the defining difference between the two camps. A Christian athlete would never stoop to that "vice", as far as the AAA leaders were concerned. For the rural athletes, financial reward was a way of life. That difference wedged the two camps apart, separated the civilized upper classes from the uncouth working men.

Likewise, a sense of duty divided them. The AAAs promoted the sense of duty to society and to the game. The idea of "becoming a better citizen, developing character" was instilled in athletes by focusing them on their duty "to the good of the game". The rural athlete only considered what was good for him. Is this venture going to "get me ahead", whether financially, in reputation or just in fun? The game, the match, the contest, it was just a negotiated tool to get ahead, like investing in a business venture. There was no "duty" involved, no higher principle.

The AAAs were part of a social movement devoted to "civilizing" and "lifting up" society. They were kindred spirits of the temperance and anti-gambling crusaders. Sport, being so popular a pastime by the turn of the century, was seen as a major front in the battle to eradicate vices. The zealotry of the AAA leaders was not much different than that of the temperance crusaders like Carrie Nation with her keg-splitting hatchet.

Sport, then, in 1900, pitted rural capitalism in the extreme against urban socialism in the extreme. With the definition of amateurism in use, there was no middle ground; it was utterly black and white and defined by money.

Walter Knox was clearly in the rural, capitalist camp, looking out for number one, but he was shrewd enough, or proud enough, to see the advantages of staying in the amateur loop. Not only did the amateur meets feed his competitive drive to prove he was the best, they got him coaching, they got him an education, and they got him experience, three things that were useful to him as he tried to "get ahead". But the actual "getting ahead"? That came from the working class sports. That earned him the money he was able to seed into further speculation that eventually allowed him to retire in comfort. No amateur ever did that through sport.

6

The Late Blooming Freshman

Walter Knox spent 1902 working at a shingling machine in Parry Sound and Verner, and spending a short time back home in Orillia looking for a less taxing career. Still attuned to the athletics world, though no longer a part of it, he heard through the grapevine that his old friend, Harry Gill, had gone back into coaching in Wisconsin. In fact, Harry had contacted a couple of up-and-coming sprinters from his old hometown of Coldwater about competing for him at Beloit College, offering them a college education. When they both declined his offer, Harry tracked Walter down in Verner and gave him a call.

At almost 25 years of age, Walter was a dubious prospect as a college freshman. But after two weeks of negotiations, he agreed to visit the college in Beloit, Wisconsin, about 100 miles northwest of Chicago, just to talk, when Harry offered to pay his travel and expenses.

In January of 1903, Walter boarded the train for Wisconsin, not at all convinced it was a good career move. Beloit College was tiny, well under 1000 students, and a "Christian College", not a selling feature for Walter. The track team competed with the larger established schools of the Big 9 conference but was not competitive enough to even be entered into the conference championship meet. Furthermore, Walter had not even *gone* to high school, let alone finished it! How could he be considered for a college position? But Harry Gill was insistent, and was determined to land Walter as a freshman athlete.

Walter sat down with track coach Gill and college head coach Jack Hollister after his campus tour. They offered free room and board in addition to free tuition and books. Walter, remembering his initial negotiations with Harry Gill, responded with, "But where does the 'kick back' come in?" He had a successful career in the sawmill; why should he give that up? He had no intention of being a volunteer student athlete.

Hollister then sweetened the deal. All college athletes could apply to have their expenses reimbursed by the college, including the actual costs of college life as well as trips away from the home campus. All Walter had to do was submit his bills to the alumni association. Here's the rub, he was told. Before submitting your bill, add a digit or two, turn $8 into $18. Make sure you're happy.[1]

Walter's response? "It first caused me a twinge of conscience but as time went on I got real careless with the way I could throw those digits around." A top athlete could get away with it; scrutinous eyes would look the other way if he was bringing glory to the school. Here, Walter believed, was a gravy train that made suspending his shingling career acceptable; he just had to perform up to expectations.

Walter Knox the pragmatist also saw the opportunity to get an education ("being handed to me on a platter") and selected courses that might help him down the road: horticulture, veterinary science, penmanship, bookkeeping and commercial law. His lack of high school was a stumbling block though, and he had to enroll in Beloit's preparatory school. Here were a group of Midwest farm boys who didn't have the opportunity to graduate high school, earnestly trying to get ahead. Walter found himself not with boys, though, but with men, some his own age, a re-assuring surprise, and set himself to studying as much as training.

When it came to track and field, Walter was rusty and out of his element so he was glad to put himself into Harry Gill's hands. He trusted Harry and respected his abilities. Harry's first move was to turn Walter into a sprinter. "You can beat anything they can put up against you in Wisconsin." Harry knew Walter's innate talent was as a leaper—pole vault, high jump, long jump—and wasn't going to ignore those events, but was simply going to add the sprint to Walter's repertoire. His running style was unrefined. Harry felt he wasn't getting everything out of his spring-like legs that he could.

In no time Harry had him doing 75 and 100-yard sprints in better times than Walter thought he had in him. Harry was showing the coaching expertise that would bring him legendary status over the next quarter century. In July 1902, Walter had raced his older brother Jack over 100 yards at the park in Orillia, losing to him, even with a five yard head start. The next summer, after four months of training under Harry Gill, they raced in the park again, this time from an even start. Walter won decisively. Harry knew what he was doing, and Walter listened.

The first track meet of the season for Walter was a prep school meet against two other high schools. Walter, in his first event, set a new shot put record for Beloit College. More importantly, Walter won the 200-yard sprint with ease. Harry then arranged an exhibition race with the three other Beloit college sprinters and again Walter won easily. No one knew who this new "kid" was and coach Gill connived to keep it that way. Scant attention was paid to him in the papers as Gill endeavored to keep Walter's sprinting a secret until the Central Championship meet.

Next the Beloit team competed at an open meet in Milwaukee. Harry refused to enter Walter in the sprints, still keeping him under wraps. He did win the pole vault and the shot put, though, and probably would have won the sprint too, if given the chance.

The coach of the Milwaukee Athletic Club, impressed with Walter's performances, approached the Beloit team and secured permission for Walter to compete for his athletic club team when Walter wasn't representing Beloit College, thus securing him a coveted AAA amateur card. Two weeks later, Walter joined the MAC for an indoor meet in Chicago.

Walter won the pole vault and then walked over to compete in the shot.

Walter Knox in 1903: Small but strong with a full head of hair.
Courtesy Orillia Museum of Art and History

A big fellow from the University of Illinois, a 200-plus pound shot putter who dwarfed Walter at 147 pounds, sidled up to coach Harry Gill, who accompanied Walter to these MAC meets. "What's that kid doing in the shot put?" He smirked. "It's a shame to have him go against fellows the size of the rest of us."

"He's a conceited little rooster," Gill told him, playing it up, "and this is as good a place to take some of it out of him."

Walter put the 16 pound ball over 40 feet for the win, humbling those over-inflated strongmen who were weak on technique. Not only that, his throw was surprisingly close to the new world record of 45 feet set just two weeks earlier by Walter's old neighbour and mentor George Gray, another under-sized veteran of the shot put who knew something about technique. Harry Gill knew Walter reveled in that kind of underdog victory and egged the big boys on to their own demise.

Two weeks later, Walter was back in Chicago with the Milwaukee Athletic Club for an indoor competition at the 16th Armories. A little bit of practical joking almost got him disqualified before the meet even started. The hall was packed with 3000 spectators, with the athletes competing up on a stage. As the shot putters took their places on stage for the warm-up, Walter surreptitiously smuggled an indoor baseball into the stack of iron balls. With his first practice throw, he "accidentally" launched a magnificent throw right into the crowd, sending scores of spectators scrambling for cover as the baseball bounced around the seats.

The officials were not amused. This crass violation of the ethics of amateur sportsmanship was indignantly condemned and loud and heated arguments ensued. In the end, Walter was allowed to compete. Good thing, because the commotion surrounding the shot put paled in comparison to the excitement his performance created.

Walter only placed third in the shot because it was a handicapped affair. He had the longest throw, but had to give away 6 and 7 feet to the next men to level the playing field. He had an equally big handicap in the pole vault but won anyway with a magnificent leap of 11 feet even. The indoor world record was 11' 1 ¾" and Walter was offered a try at it. He sailed over the bar at 11' 2" without even grazing it and left the stage oblivious to the argument behind him. One of the judges questioned the measurements and demanded a confirming measure of the height. A University of Chicago athlete held the world record and the locals were not keen on a rival Milwaukee athlete taking the record away. During the measurement, the bar fell down. Without the confirmation the record was deemed invalid. It was the first but not last world record score Walter would not get credit for, and it was one that legally should have been recognized.[2]

It had been a busy winter for Walter, doing his prep school classes and having to do some college classes as well to make him eligible for the college track team. He took all the classes seriously, taking advantage of the opportunity he'd been given. Between Beloit and the Milwaukee Athletic Club, he was also competing almost every weekend. But now it was time for Beloit to cash in on their investment, as the outdoor season got under way.

First up was a duel meet with the University of Wisconsin, a competition Wisconsin took as a warm-up for their more important meets. Harry Gill decided this was the place to introduce the world to Walter Knox, the sprinter. Wisconsin had a black man, George Poage, who held the Wisconsin state 100-yard record of 10 seconds flat. Poage was a remarkable man, a respected trainer of the school football team, the substitute coach of the track team, and soon to be a university graduate with a degree in history. He was also an Olympic double bronze medallist in 1904, all as a black man at the height of the Jim Crow era.[3] But for Walter Knox, he was just the sprinter to beat in the Big 9 conference.

Harry Gill said he was beatable, if Walter could be a few feet ahead at the 50 yard mark. Poage was a strong finisher so Walter would have to be in the lead. But Walter, ever confident, was sure he could win. He considered himself a strong finisher too; he just hadn't had to show it yet, all his races being easy wins so far. And he had already run 10 1/5 seconds in one of those wins. Here was his first real test.

After a win in the long jump, Walter trotted over for the 100-yard dash. He knew Poage was known for his "flyers", jumping the gun, and couldn't let him get away with one here or it would be all over. Lining up at the start he heard, "On your marks, get set" and then saw Poage explode out of the blocks. Walter didn't move, which made the jump obvious and forced the starter to call Poage back. On the second start, the same thing happened again, except this time Walter went after him and the starter let them go. At 40 yards, Walter was already two yards behind. Walter later wrote about his thoughts as the race was in progress, "Am I going to be beaten by a coloured fellow?" This was answered by, "No coloured fellow can beat me!"[4]

Harry Gill turned away, commenting his boy was beaten. When he turned back at the 80 yard mark, the two racers were even. At the finish, Walter was ahead by a foot and "slow, plodding" Harry was jumping around as no one had ever seen him do before! Walter later commented that when he caught Poage at the 80 yard mark, he could see the other runner fading and just put him away. The time was 10 seconds flat, tying the state record.

Wisconsin coach Kilpatrick came storming over yelling, "Where'd you come from Knox? You're a professional and I'm going to look into your past and by the living God if there's anything that won't square up I'll protest you!"

Walter just smirked. "Go ahead. Use a microscope, brother, but it won't do you any good except to give everybody a good laugh, which they are getting this afternoon over the good lickin' your team is taking from the little college of Beloit!"[5]

Keeping Walter's sprinting a secret worked; they caught Poage by surprise.

With that victory, Beloit had a fair chance of winning the meet, a stunning upset of a major university by a tiny Christian college. The last event was the pole vault, which Walter won as expected, bringing his total to four wins for the day. The meet hung on whether Beloit's second man could beat the Wisconsin pole vaulter. He couldn't, and the meet was lost by just half a point. Still, that stellar team performance got Beloit invited to the Big 9 conference championships. Walter thought to himself that the championships would be the stage to really show his stuff.

It was not to be. The next week he sprained his ankle badly in a small duel meet, costing him a full week of training. He decided to enter the 100 at the Big 9's anyway and got through to the finals, placing second in his heat to the Michigan Meteor, Archie Hahn, the fastest man in America. In the finals, Walter was leading at the 75 yard mark when his ankle totally gave out and he stumbled to a fourth place finish. Hahn finished in 9 4/5 seconds.[6]

Frustrated, Walter returned home to Beloit to nurse his ankle; the college season was over for him. A few weeks later, the Milwaukee Athletic Club invited him to compete at their regional championships in Detroit. Still sore, Walter went and placed second in the 100, pole vault, and shot put (which he purposely lost to a teammate who asked Walter to let him retire on a winning note). He was in the middle of the hammer competition when the coach came running over, out of breath. He had just tallied the scores to find out a victory in the final relay would win them the meet. His relay team had missed the train so he was cobbling together a high jumper, a half miler, a hurdler and Walter, a sprinter, for the 4x440 hurdles relay.

"The race is about to start" he yelled. "Get out there!"

So out Walter scooted, in his heavy throwing shoes (no time to change them!) onto the soggy cinder track, passing on his final hammer throws. The first runners had already started the race. Walter got to the track for the third leg of the relay just as the second man was coming into the home stretch. His soggy shoes felt like lead and the second place team quickly passed him, kicking up cinders in his face. Walter backed off to clear his eyes, but soon saw the leader starting to fade. With 150 yards to go, he took off after him, splashing through puddles on the track and over the hurdles in his heavy throwing boots, and passed into the lead with 90 yards left to the hand-off. The final MAC man held the lead Walter had provided him, giving Milwaukee the relay win and the meet championship. Walter's finishing kick to re-take the lead likely won them the race.

With that race Walter's arrangement with Milwaukee ended, and with the Beloit semester over he was done with any obligations in the mid-west. He had graduated from the Beloit prep school and now had a high school equivalency diploma tucked away. With those invigorating months behind him, he headed from Detroit up to Sault

Ste. Marie, Ontario and another athletic opportunity. Even though steady work was beckoning again, the athletics bug had returned. Four months under Harry Gill's instruction had turned him into a top ranked sprinter. Walter was anxious to test his new wings.

7

The Adventure Begins

Sault Ste. Marie was a sporting hotbed in 1903. Their July 1st sports day, a Caledonian Games, drew athletes from all over eastern Canada, mostly due to the larger than usual prize money offered. However, in the previous two years, a pair of brothers from Ottawa, Sandy and Harry Quinn, had dominated the meet, taking most of the prizes and effectively discouraging local entries. The organizers were actually considering canceling the meet in 1903 for lack of entries.

Someone close to the organizers, whom Walter identified only as an "old time friend", contacted Walter in Wisconsin about entering the meet in "the Soo". This friend offered him a job at the lumber mill in exchange for taking the Quinn boys down a notch. The real lure was that an underdog like Walter, if he could keep his reputation quiet, could set up a betting bonanza for those in the know, given the Quinns were seen as unbeatable. Walter was happy to oblige. Steady work, a chance to humble some blowhards and a windfall betting opportunity to boot; why not?

So in mid-June of 1903, Walter Knox set off for the Soo to start his adventure in the workingman's world of competing for profit. He had been invited by the Milwaukee Athletic Club to go to New York for the United States All-Around Championship, but declined in favour of the Caledonian Games in the Soo and the potential wagering windfall it offered. Obviously Walter made a decision that summer to test his mettle in the gambling underworld of sport, where the money was, rather than at the amateur AAA-sanctioned meets. He chose adventure and profit over prestige and reputation.

Walter reported to the Clerge Paper Company in Searchmont, about 20 miles northeast of the Soo, where he was given a job on a shingling machine. It was an ideal setup for him. This was, as Walter said, "about as wild and woolly as lumber camps went in those days". Isolated out in the bush with a bunch of rednecks like that, it was easy to hide his college exploits. But it was also ideal for training purposes. Several men there felt qualified to take a shot at the big games in the Soo and had cleared a makeshift field where they would practice. Walter joined them every day, but was careful not to "let myself out" for fear of word of his ability getting around and ruining the betting prospects. He even took an alias, Bill Bailey, to throw everyone off the scent.

Four days before the July 1st games, he finally met up with his friend in Sault Ste. Marie to discuss their gambling arrangements. He was told Quinn money was being thrown all over the place. Walter told him to take any and all bets, confident he could win most of the contests. It didn't take long for suspicions to arise, when so much money suddenly started going against the Quinns. Soon rumours spread that the great unknown was actually college star Walter Knox. This didn't discourage the gamblers, so dominant were the Quinn boys. The money still flowed.

Walter's unnamed friend had told the organizing committee that he was bringing a couple of athletes to town to give the Quinns their come-uppance. Walter ran into the other athlete the night before the meet, while walking along the main street in the pouring rain. It was his brother Jack!

"What are you doing here?" Walter blurted out.

"The same thing as you. So you're the Bailey that has both sides of the border talking."

"What name are you sailing under?" Walter asked.

"I hadn't given it any thought up to now," said Jack. "But I guess from now on I'll be Jack Bailey!"

So it was to be the brothers Quinn against the brothers Bailey.

As luck would have it, they ran into the Quinn boys that evening. Both of them were high on their chances to win the 100-yard dash, though Sandy was the faster of the two. Walter quickly realized they didn't have any idea of his ability. The Quinns were a rowdy pair and the discussion grew a little heated; Walter, in true workingman's fashion, offered to settle the argument with a $25 bet on the race. They jumped at the offer.

About an hour after they parted ways, the Quinns hunted the Baileys down again and bluntly started fishing for information about Walter. They must have heard the rumours. Eventually they offered another arrangement. The $25 bet would stand, but if Walter did win the next day on the Canadian side, he would agree to let Sandy win at the next meet, July 4th in the American "Soo". The merit to this arrangement, Quinn pointed out, was the potential for a re-match at some later date where there would be lots of excitement in the betting parlours. Walter agreed.

Torrential rain continued to fall all night on June 30th, causing the Canadian meet to be postponed for a week, so Jack and Walter headed across the border for the July 4th meet in the American Soo. This called the whole arrangement into question. Walter didn't really know how fast Sandy Quinn was, and was reluctant to throw the first race to him. Walter now suspected that if he threw the race in the US, the Quinns would give him "the double cross" and renege on the deal by trying to win in Canada too. Wanting to protect himself, he took Jack and went to clarify the deal with the Quinns.

"Do the arrangements still stand?" demanded Walter.

"Sure. I'll go out and win here and you take the Ontario race on the 8th."

"Then," Walter declared, "When we run on the 4th, make room for me for second place as I don't intend to finish farther back."

"Take what you can get," came the belligerent response.

"Do you mean that? If there isn't any room for me to take second, I'll take first and make you like it!"

"Try and do it!" was Sandy Quinn's parting shot.

As with so many set arrangements, a monkey wrench was thrown into the affair. Walter told Jack just before the race that he was going to take Sandy Quinn out very fast and see what he could do from there. Halfway down the course, Quinn found his hands full with a dark horse on his other side. Markle, from Hamilton, was pressing him too. Thinking Walter was going to let him win, Quinn started an elbowing war with Markle, taking as much as he was giving. Walter hung in with them then spurted to win the race, seeing no way to finish between them. Quinn just edged Markle for second place.

Sandy Quinn was boiling mad. When Walter went on to win the 220-yard sprint, the standing and running broad jumps and tied Jack to win the high jump, it only made it worse. Quinn, no slouch as an athlete, did mange to beat Walter in the running hop, step and jump though, to ease the pain a little.

Then they all moved back to the Canadian side for the July 8th games. Just before they left the US, Walter and Jack were accosted by a newspaper boy who bawled out, "Here come the Bailey boys. Take off your false whiskers you Knox brothers!" Taken aback by his accusation and wondering how anyone knew, Walter and Jack hurried across the border, hoping to keep their identities concealed a little longer. The newspaper reports of the American meet listed Walter as "Knox", not "Bailey". This was a risk for his amateur standing, not to mention his return to Beloit College and the Milwaukee AC next year.

Back at the field in Canada, the Knox brothers ran into the Quinns every day in training. Walter actually warmed up to them, describing them as "just a pair of rollicking bully-boys who looked on life as a lark." Walter could relate to that.

Around town the scuttlebutt was that the Quinns had held back on the US side. The betting was still brisk, with the most money riding on which athlete would win the greatest number of first place finishes. The Quinns were all-rounders and still seemed a good bet.

When asked by his gambling friend if he still had it in him to win, Walter replied, "Name any event and I'll win it!" He was then informed of the appearance of Dan MacDonald, a stonemason from Owen Sound, who was outstanding in the shot put. At over 6 feet and 220 pounds he towered over Walter.

"You don't mean to tell us that you think you can top him?" Walter's friend asked.

"Let me see him make one put and then I'll tell you whether I can beat him or not."

So, on the afternoon of the big Caledonian Games, Walter had the uncertainty of Quinn hustling him in the 100, the pressure of so much money riding on his winning the most first place points and the challenge of contesting the shot put against a gigantic and worthy opponent. It could be an interesting day.

First up was the 16 pound shot put. His gigantic opponent proved to be strong in body but weak on technique and Walter immediately told his friend to take any bets offered, especially when Walter shanked his first put, looking a little amateurish. Walter's second put sailed 41 feet, 7 inches, a foot past his rival's, and no one could come close to that. At the time, anyone who could heave the heavy ball over 40 feet was considered in the first rank of throwers and MacDonald's 40' 9" first put was a superior effort as well.

Then they hoisted the 12 pound balls. Walter offered to bet he would win by over three feet but there were no takers. Everyone now knew what he was capable of. But even Walter was surprised at what he did next. His shot put sailed 55 feet, 4 inches, just 2 inches shy of George Gray's world record! It was the longest throw Walter would make in his whole career.

The officials thought something must be wrong, re-measured the throw and even sent the ball into town to be weighed, only to find the shot put was actually two ounces overweight. It was truly a magnificent performance.

MacDonald was no slouch either. His put of 53' 9" was not far behind Walter's (someone should have taken the bet). MacDonald won the 56 pound weight throw, the caber toss and the hammer throw handily, all with outstanding marks.

Walter kept up the pace all day, winning 11 first place prizes and one second; he purposely lost to Sandy Quinn in the 200-yard dash, allowing Quinn to save face with one win. He put up many more strong marks too: 20' 11" in the long jump, 44' 3" in the hop, step and jump, and 4' 6" in the standing high jump among others. In many of the events, Sandy Quinn wasn't far behind as he was an outstanding athlete in his own right. All 12 events were carried out in just 5 hours, on the "hottest day of the season", with hardly a chance for Walter to catch his breath in between.

In front of 1000 spectators, Walter had one of the outstanding days of his entire career. "The greatest day of its kind the Soo has ever seen!" the local paper trumpeted.

Sandy Quinn's later reputation only emphasizes what an achievement Walter realized that day. A newspaper report in 1918, while he was recovering from his war wounds, described Quinn as "one of the greatest all-around athletes in the Dominion. Walter Knox was, in fact, about the only track and field star who excelled Alex's (aka Sandy's) marks for all around efficiency".[1] He went on to win the Canadian Police Championships in 1904, '05 and '06 and won events in many different parts of Canada. During the First World War, he won citations for bravery and was wounded twice on the Somme.

As in the American Soo, the local Canadian paper listed Walter as "Wm. Knox" in the meet results, not the "Bailey" name he registered under. His risk of being outed as a professional increased, only tempered by the fact that the Soo was such a far-flung rural backwater, isolated from the centres of AAA sport.

At the end of the day, Walter tallied up his loot: he had a set of razors, an ice cream freezer, a lawn mower, a large ornately framed picture of someone he didn't know as well as $125 in prize money (out of the $200 in total up for grabs). The cash prizes alone amounted to a quarter of what he could earn in a *year* as a shingler.

On top of that, he had his side bet earnings. In his writings, Walter rarely confessed to how much he wagered on himself, though it is apparent it could be a substantial amount. He had, after all, shown up at Jack Johnson's pool hall with several hundred dollars in his pocket. Often he didn't have much ready cash to bet, but when he did, he wouldn't hesitate to risk it. Most of his wagering was done through intermediaries, like his unnamed friend in the Soo, and these business arrangements were kept very secretive for obvious reasons. Generally, in this business, a runner's backer put up a gambling stake and split the winnings with the athlete who did all the work of winning.[2] Walter's backer did all the betting in bars around town and at the track, allowing Walter to keep his nose clean and prepare for the competition. It was a very successful venture for Walter in every aspect, though he found "most refreshing" the thanks he got for putting the Quinns in their place.

Walter left the Soo and headed right into a storm at the sawmill. Hauled into the foreman's office for a scolding he felt he didn't deserve, Walter refused to be cowed by the tirade. As a result, he earned the respect of the foreman, who liked the sort who stood up for himself. So when the foreman called Walter aside one day to warn him of trouble brewing out in the bush camps, Walter listened. As advised, he quit on the spot, took his pay packet and headed south. Three weeks later the bush crews, looking for better pay, stormed into camp and went on a rampage. When the unrest spread to town, the city officials had a troop of militia sent in from Toronto who finally quelled three months of carnage. Walter was given a lucky break, and it wasn't the last time he would retreat from other people's arguments. Later, he often preached keeping your nose clean and out of trouble, even if it meant looking less than heroic. It was a pragmatic workingman's attitude: look out for number one first.

His next step was to plunge all the way into the depths of subterfuge for profit. He had dabbled at misrepresenting himself in Midland and the Soo to keep his amateur status, but now he was about to enter into an arrangement that was blatantly about deception for personal gain. He was about to become an out-and-out hustler.

Up in the Soo, his brother Jack told him about a "phenom" in Peterborough who had broken 10 seconds in the hundred. It seemed that this runner, Dave Belland, had double-crossed one of his backers, George Stevens, a local businessman who was steamed and wanted revenge. Stevens had approached Jack to come for a match race so he could win some of his money back. Jack wrote back that the best he could do was 11 seconds flat, but he knew someone who was much faster and could put Belland in his place. Jack promised to approach Walter.

Jack and Walter met up with Harry Gill in Orillia to discuss the situation. They had never heard of Belland, the "phenom". Harry convinced Walter there could be no unheralded backwoods boy who could hope to beat him. So off the three of them went to meet with Stevens in Ashburnham, just outside Peterborough.

Stevens "was no dummy when it came to rigging a match race", Walter admitted later.

The businessman told them, "This fellow Belland is so stuck on himself that we may be able to get a five or ten yard handicap. Especially if he thinks he has an easy mark to handle."

His plan was to let Walter work around his farm for a few weeks where he could be passed off as some hick from the woods who can run like a deer. Once word gets out about him Belland would come to them.[3]

With a little trepidation, Walter agreed to the plan. He wasn't worried about his ability to beat Belland. He was worried that there was more going on here than Stevens, a pretty slick operator, satisfying a grudge. Still, Walter went ahead with the plan, carefully monitoring every aspect of the scheme with Jack and Harry's help.

Walter's role was easy: look like you're working a little and enjoy the fine cooking and soft bed in Stevens' big farmhouse. Every afternoon he'd run some sprints down the road, very publicly attracting attention. It had been most of a month since the meet in the Soo and Walter was thankful for the practice time to sharpen up.

A few nosy neighbours started showing up out of curiosity and word quickly spread about the runner at the Stevens place.

Who is he? Bill Bailey.

How fast is he? Somewhere between "fleet and lightning"!

It wasn't long before a handful of city folk showed up one day who Stevens knew were from the Belland camp. If Walter were recognized, the jig would be up. They waited a few days to sense the result of Belland's assessment, and hearing nothing to challenge them, felt confident the whole plan could be pulled off.

The next step was to enter Walter in the Labour Day sports contests in the city park. Warned not to overplay the hick act, Walter lined up for the 100-yard dash with 9 other runners. Three, including Belland, wore sharp-looking track outfits. Walter was dressed in a pair of Stevens' trousers, "6 inches too big at the waist and 2 inches too short", but with his professional running shoes to show he had raced before.

Walter had a big challenge from another farm boy for last place, 20 yards behind Belland. Then he scurried home and out of sight, letting Stevens go to work.

Stevens was a well known backer of runners, with a reputation for a keen eye. He fumed around the grounds, chastising the miserable performance of his man. In short order he had a match race set up with Belland, and Walter was to get a six yard head start to boot!

Then he made it clear he had $1000 to bet on his man and he'd be at the Oriental Hotel at 8 p.m. to take any and all bets. Stevens did know his way around the matched race community.

The Oriental Hotel was the sports hotbed in Peterborough, and the proprietor, George Graham, often acted as stakes holder. At 8, the race agreement would be signed and the forfeits of $100 a side would be given to Graham. After that, the betting free-for-all would begin.

Around the supper table back at the farm, it was agreed that Walter should steer clear of the hotel lest someone recognize him and blow the whole deal. So Stevens headed off alone. But not long after, word was sent back for Walter to get down to the post office right away. There Stevens informed him that he had been identified. Graham had been chatting up a commercial traveller who was an enthusiast of running of all types, "nuts about foot racing", as Walter later described him. He had come to town when he heard the rumour of a high stakes foot race. Graham had the traveller show Stevens a newspaper clipping from the Milwaukee Sentinel with a beautiful photo of Walter above the caption, "the fastest sprinter in the US".

Walking back to the farm, commiserating about the botched plan, Stevens casually informed Walter that the fast time Belland was famous for was "screwy". His sub-10 second 100-yard time was really over an 85 yard course. Walter, on hearing that, declared he was all for marching back and making Belland "put up or shut up". But he left town as was prudent, instructing Stevens to follow up on Walter's threat with Belland.

Back in Orillia, a telegram was waiting for Walter. His Milwaukee AC coach wanted him to come back for a track meet there. Walter hopped on the train to the mid-west, competed uneventfully and, 10 days later, was back on a train to Montreal with the MAC team for the Canadian Championships. He had an uninspired meet, placing second in both the shot put and the pole vault. But worse was his 4th place showing in the 100, which was won in only 10 1/5 seconds. In his notes, Walter later remarked, "I knew they would be watching to see how I did, from Peterborough, so I didn't try to make a showing."[4] He had a long memory and a determination to come out on top of any dispute, even if that meant purposely losing a Canadian Championship. He had his eye focused on Belland. Walter, embarrassingly, had been caught in a lie and forced to skulk out of town. But this wasn't what got him riled up. It was Belland's fraudulent claim to a sub-10 second 100 that had to be exposed. Walter had to return the embarrassment; his pride demanded it.

On the train home from Montreal, Walter had an argument with Walter Liginger, the MAC coach, about his expense account. He had traveled a long way on the train and had living expenses the club would reimburse, but they were nitpicking his claims. No doubt Walter was padding that account as he was used to doing at Beloit College. Again we see the depth of Walter's animosity when crossed. He swore he would never represent Milwaukee again. The next summer, 1904, the Chicago AC contacted Walter about representing them at the Olympic Games in St. Louis to challenge the great Irishman Kiely in the all-around competition. When Walter asked for his release from the Milwaukee AC, they insisted he compete at the Olympics for them and refused to release him to Chicago. In a fit of pique, Walter just skipped the whole event rather than put on a MAC jersey again.[5]

Back in Orillia in late September, Walter wrote to Stevens about a possible match race with Belland on even terms. Stevens answered that the Belland people had been gloating over Walter's poor showing in Montreal and would welcome that match. But Stevens wanted no part of it; he was still living down that summer's embarrassing fiasco. So Walter dispatched his brother Jack and a friend, Jack Coulson, to Peterborough to negotiate the match.

The terms ended up as $500 a side with a $150 forfeit if either side backed out.[6] These were very large stakes, a year's salary. Belland, after hearing Walter came fourth at the Canadian championships, must have felt confident to lay down that much money. Walter's team made one critical mistake, though, in allowing Arthur Rowntree to be named referee. He was a typical "small town sport", as Walter said, a gambler, with his hand in many pies. Walter had warned Jack about steering clear of Rowntree, but as owner of the Turf Club Park, the ideal setting for the match, he forced his way into the match.

The forfeit money was placed in the hands of Dr. Bradd, who put it in the bank. Unbeknownst to Jack, Rowntree had himself, as referee, made a co-signee of the deposit, and controlled its withdrawal from the bank.

The race was set for the last Thursday in September and a trainload of Orillians made the trip to see Walter run and to pick up some easy money.

Walter said he had never felt more confident on the day of the race, feeling he had Belland beaten even before the gun when he saw how nervous he was. On top of that, he was a stutterer, "and you could kid the living daylights out of him about that," Walter found out, and undoubtedly did.

The race was anti-climactic. Belland false started and was called back by starter Harry Gill, who then penalized him one yard for the second start. Walter said, "I could have made a terrible sucker out of Belland but finished a good six yards ahead of him, without any effort."

A tremendous cheer rose up from the Orillia section of the crowd, roughly half of the spectators, as the two judges at the finish immediately declared the race fair.

Suddenly Rowntree appeared on the track, waving a paper and declaring "all bets are off!" The crowd was stunned into silence as he continued, "The race was fixed. All bets are hereby declared off."

The crowd, predictably, went berserk! Fights broke out all over the place. The crowd rushed Rowntree, but being "a scrapper of no mean proportion" he held his ground before taking a terrible beating.

In the midst of all this, Walter hustled up to Belland and demanded, "What's the big idea? You were either beaten or you were not. What's all this howl about it being a fixed race?"

"I was beaten fair and square," he stuttered. "This is all Rowntree's doing. He's cooked it up by himself and I don't want any part of it!"

The next day, the two Jacks went around to Dr. Bradd to collect the forfeit money. Rowntree claimed that Belland had lost on purpose and thus forfeited the race. He had supposedly run a 100 in under 10 seconds, and here Walter beat him in a time of 11 ¼ seconds. He must have thrown the race, Rowntree had deduced. Walter wanted the $150 forfeit money. Here's where Jack found out Rowntree controlled the bank account and that he refused to hand over the money.

Storming into Rowntree's hotel, they found him in bed with a massive black eye and "a face that looked as though it had gone through a sausage grinder."

But he contemptuously repulsed them saying, this race "smells to high heaven and shows some fixing went on somewhere. Now git out!" He was accusing Walter of being in on the fix. "Take it to court," was his final answer.

Jack did. Two months later, the court ruled that both sides had agreed in advance that the referee's ruling would be final, and found in favour of Dr. Bradd, whose name was on the bank account. Jack had to pay court costs, making the whole venture a total loss.

Lost in all the turmoil of this event was the fact that Dave Belland was, in fact, a superior runner. He represented Canada in the 100-yard dash at the 1908 Olympics in London. He had a very poor showing there, losing badly in the first round, but was a good enough runner to make the team. And Walter had beaten this able rival, no trouble at all.

Walter's bad summer was not about to improve. Beloit College got in touch with him after his hustling fiasco in Peterborough and informed him he was not invited back to school. Then he was contacted by a man named Bob Harrison in Toronto who wanted to set up a race.

Walter was unaware, unusual for him, that Harrison was a promoter who specialized in taking up-and-comers down a peg. A hustler. He proposed a match race in Barrie with Taylor from Montreal for $100 a side. Harrison knew the whole town of Orillia would show up in nearby Barrie for this race after the excitement in Peterborough.

Walter got nervous after a couple of friends said they saw Taylor run and it looked like a set up. "That was confirmed as soon as we started running," Walter said. He finished a couple of yards behind him and the Orillia townspeople got fleeced of their wagers, mostly by Harrison, though the betting had been slow after word got out before the race how fast Taylor was. "Taylor" turned out to be an alias, although the man got away without being identified. Walter only said, cryptically, "It took me quite a while to find out who he was, but I did, and it salved my wounded pride somewhat when I found out who my opponent really was." He never disclosed that name in his book or notes.

The big money, Walter learned the hard way, was in racing other professionals, if you knew how to work the mark, as Harrison had worked him.

At this point Walter did some more soul searching. In his own words:

> "*I had convinced myself I belonged in the first flight of sprinters; I had no doubt as to my pole vaulting abilities; in the shot putting angles I knew where I stood, and as for the "in between" sports I had been able to better than hold my own. In other words, I had something that the average human hadn't, which could be turned*

into account or which could be nursed along for my own personal satisfaction. Could I tap "returns" or should I merely go along taking the pickings — which had been mighty slim in my recent adventurings — as they came my way. I had jeopardized my amateur standing to an unwarranted degree and was waiting for the blow to fall from that quarter. Things were in a muddle. I was at the cross roads and it looked as though, for once, I had lost my sense of direction." [7]

Walter went back to the shingle mill in Orillia to ponder his future.

The Hustling Years

8

A New England Adventure

It only took two months for an opportunity to present itself that helped Walter make up his mind on his future. It came in the form of a letter from George Sanders, a past acquaintance from another interesting episode in Walter's life.

Back in 1902, when Walter gave up sports for the shingling trade, he spent a little time working in Tommy Goffat's barber shop at the foot of Mississaga Street, looking for an easier way to make a living. This George Sanders was a stranger to town who would come into the shop every day to get a dollar bill changed. Walter started to get suspicious when, with his change drawer getting low, he couldn't interest Sanders in trying the hotel across the street. After confronting him as some sort of scam artist, Walter was taken into confidence. Sanders was a detective looking for someone passing lead quarters in the area. Many coins changed hands at the barbershop, and he was investigating the problem, looking for leads. When slugs did start appearing in his till, Walter set to helping him, ultimately exposing a Coldwater counterfeiter, "Yankee Jack" O'Connor, who was sent to prison for a few years.[1]

Later, up north, Walter helped Sanders again when Sanders went undercover as a prisoner in a jail in order to root out some excise law fraud artists. Walter acted as his intermediary, passing his mail in and out of the jail.

Now, less than a year later, just after New Year's 1904, the letter came from Sanders asking Walter to come down to Southbridge, Massachusetts to help with another investigation.

With no better prospects, off Walter went. Sanders immediately got him a job in an optical factory, and a week later a promotion to foreman. That put him in a position to help. Sanders was investigating the loss of thousands of dollars from the factory that no one could figure out. They had narrowed it down to the gold room; a room Walter now had access to as a foreman. Gold was disappearing somehow, but months of observation had failed to crack the case and Sanders was brought in. Walter was to be his inside man.

Sanders figured the gold was being "sweated", gold dust ground off coins and secreted out in very small quantities. By process of elimination, Walter fingered a likely suspect, a burly, bearded fellow. With a little ingratiating banter, Walter was able to strike up a friendship, and when they discovered a mutual interest in sport, an invitation to the man's house. From there it took no time to catch him shampooing his hair and beard and saving the water to filter out the gold dust. Walter cracked the case. In all, he had spent a few months working at the optical factory.[2]

Thinking he had found a sleuthing partner, Sanders proposed another case, spying for a man who wanted a divorce. That was going too far for Walter and he cut his ties with Sanders. Fingering a criminal was one thing, spying on a cheating wife was another. That was not how Walter wanted to spend his life.

It was back to sport, his fall back profession. The Southbridge YMCA recruited him for its track team and off he went on a series of uneventful meets around Boston, working his way back into shape. A friend, Tom Keane, soon had Walter thinking of bigger and better events, more lucrative affairs. Together they started molding Walter's sporting reputation to take advantage of some professional races later in the summer. Walter went on the win some, lose some routine, looking good, but not too good.

At one meet, he got into a heated argument when another contestant wanted to change the hop, step and jump event to a hop, hop and jump. Walter flashed the official program that listed the hop, step and jump, swaying the judges in his favour. After winning the event, Walter challenged MacDonald, his rival, to a hop, hop and jump match he wanted, for $25, and won that too. Unfortunately, all that did was etch Walter's memory in MacDonald's mind.

The next event was an AAA sanctioned meet the Southbridge Y team entered. The officials there used professionals to help spot other pros, like Walter, trying to enter this amateur meet.

Of course MacDonald, one of the pros, spotted Walter. "Let me remind you of the 25 smackers that you took away from those who tried to beat you with 2 hops and a jump. That was 'money won', wasn't it?" he accused.

Walter, seeing the writing on the wall, had to think fast. He was about to lose his amateur standing and be professionalized forever. Word travelled fast between the Amateur Associations.

He remembered Harry Gill mentioning MacDonald as a top flight leaper and deflected the question, saying, "You know Harry Gill the all-around champion? I've heard him speak often of you as an old friend and a mighty hard man to beat in almost anything."

Suddenly they were talking about past meets and building camaraderie.

"So you're the fellow from Gill's home town that he told me so much about. Well, don't say anything about my holding you up and go in and get as much as you can!"

When he wanted to, Walter could turn on the charm. Throughout his career, he often deflected animosity by changing the subject and flattering his adversary. Walter left a trail of people behind him who happily gave him the wink and a nod, helping him in his schemes and calling him a friend. And this as a non-drinker in a world sloshed in alcohol. How much easier it would have been for him to ingratiate himself over a few beers? Walter learned how to do it on charm alone.

Within the week, Walter was on the train home to Orillia. New England hadn't offered up many opportunities, just one close call.

His short stay in Orillia during the summer of 1904 was notable for his baseball exploits. Baseball was the hot sport that year and Orillia had formed a team. On Walter's appearance in town, he was eagerly recruited. He only played a couple of games, but left a remarkable impression.

The main reason he agreed to join the team, he said, was to see what his speed could do on the base paths. In his initial at bat he swung wildly at the first pitch to back up the fielders then bunted the next pitch down the third base line. By the time the ball was scooped up, he was on first base. He then stole second and third and scored on a short hit. Next time up, he got on base and then stole second, third and home to score again. Finally, Walter completed a triple play that the locals would talk about for years. When a sharp hit sailed just over the pitcher's head, Walter leaped up and snagged it at second base, putting out the batter. Then, by tagging second base and throwing to first, he put out the runners who had raced from those bases on that sure hit. It was one of those heads up and athletic plays that is long remembered in any town.[3]

But that was the end of his baseball career in Orillia. Within days, he was on the move again, this time to the lucrative gambling fields of the far west.

9

The Wild and Wooly West

Like any young man of his age, Walter was finding his way. A shingle mill career would provide steady, predictable work that would support a family but not much more. But it was dull and strenuous. Walter was looking for something better. What kept presenting itself was the lucrative world of matched racing. Betting on yourself in this cut-throat business was unpredictable and risky, but at the same time, for someone of Walter's temperament, also exciting and stimulating. On the hustling circuit he would get to do what he loved, compete, but not wear out his body, as the mill would have done. He would be working on his own terms, not a foreman's, and his destiny would be entirely in his own hands. He would also reap all the rewards resulting from his own ability, whether as a fast runner or a shrewd negotiator. Likewise, all the misfortune, and it could be considerable misfortune, would land on his shoulders too. In the end, of course, it was a high stakes life. It could be very, very lucrative or literally deadly. As an independent, confident man-of-action, the matched racing world, though risky, sure looked like more fun.

So Walter finally decided to commit to hustling as a career, and set off for the frontier where big, strong men were anxious to put their reputations, and money, on the line; where physical strength was of paramount importance; and where people didn't know or care about the Amateur Athletic Associations. The west was full of lumber towns, mining towns and rural backwaters. People there were like the ones he grew up with in Hawkestone, Sebright and Washago, susceptible to the over-inflated egos of small town heroes. Walter was going to tour those towns and make his fortune… and have a good time doing it.

Walter had been corresponding with Walter McClelland, his old foreman from a mill stint he did in Huntsville, Ontario, who had repeatedly insisted he had to come to British Columbia. He was working for the Orillia Slocan Lumber Company in Slocan, BC, owned by the Lavalle brothers of Orillia. McClelland gushed about the opportunities for shingle cutters out west, a year round booming business. He also pointed out that every other man there thought he was a top notch athlete and, more to the point, was willing to back up his boasts with bets that would amaze easterners. Walter had shied away from his wild stories in the past, but now was ready to see if the west was really as outlandish as McClelland had said. It was.

Early in August, Walter reported to the mill in Slocan, deep in the mountains between Calgary and Kelowna, where his shingle cutting expertise was welcomed. But Walter had just spent the better part of four months in the optical factory in Massachusetts and had lost the toughness in his hands a lumberman needs. He took to wearing cotton gloves until his palms had toughened up again. Ten days into the job, one of the bulky gloves caught in the dog of the cutting machine, pulling his hand into the iron shredder. This was the bane of all mill workers, so many had nubs and stumps for fingers. Walter, reflexively yanking his hand out, managed to limit the damage to the last knuckle of his index finger.

Here, in this moment of crisis, Walter's true persona emerged, with the silent, calculating, yet charismatic patina scraped off. At the hospital, Walter's deeply guarded and distrustful nature emerged, his obstinate determination that only he could make decisions regarding his personal well-being, his self-centredness. He had seen many stumped fingers in the mills and how a surgeon could botch a job. Walter, in no uncertain terms, laid down the law for the doctor, dictating how he wanted his finger amputated and sewn, arguing with the doctor about how it should be done. As Walter had performed a few amputations himself in Newfoundland, he was, at least in his own mind, an expert. The doctor, over Walter's objections, and probably for good reason, insisted on putting him out with gas. But Walter's stubbornness trumped the doctor's advice and, in the end, Walter watched the job and supervised the sewing. If someone was going to scar Walter's body, he was going to do a first class job of it![1]

This whole episode of the world's most difficult patient left the doctor with an anecdote he "gleefully" told. After the job was done, Walter defied the doctor's recommendation to lay off the sports for a while, even advising the doc to "mortgage the hospital" to bet on his winning the upcoming Labour Day sports contests. Obviously taken with Walter's bluster, the doctor did bet and won $50 while enthusiastically regaling people there with the story of how Walter had bossed him around on the stitching job.

Back at the mill, McClelland had let a couple of other men he trusted in on Walter's sporting abilities. The four of them pooled $1800 to bet on Walter, swollen, stumpy finger and all. If nothing else, Walter was one tough cookie. He came to BC to compete and compete he would.

The name "Walter Knox" was pretty familiar by now to anyone who was in touch with the sporting world, thanks to the boom in sports reporting in the papers. So Walter decided to go by the name "Renwick" while he was in BC. "Everybody was doing it," Walter later related. "Aliases were thicker than fleas on a dog's back."

Two top athletes were known to be entering the Labour Day games. One was a pole vaulter of some reputation, but the other, more important figure, was Kirby Douglas, who had entered the 100-yard dash, and who considered himself the fastest man in B.C. . Supporters of those two athletes brought all the betting money

Walter's group could cover. Walter said, "British Columbians were the bettingest fools I had ever met up with!" Renwick, the unknown mill worker, was only of note because of the money laid down on him, mostly by his own little cabal.

Walter later explained the logistics of hustling. The athlete brought the talent, the sure win; his backers put up the money and arranged all the bets, at the field or in the saloons. After the race they split the proceeds 50-50. Walter didn't have to put up any of his own money, though he could make his own side bets and keep those winnings for himself.[2]

Walter had no trouble beating Douglas in both the 100 and the 220. He then easily won the pole vault, 100-yard hurdles and running and standing long jumps. In the shot put, Walter's hand was throbbing too much (undoubtedly from gripping the vaulting pole) so he putted the shot with his left hand. He still took second place. After the first event, the 100, the gambling money dried up for Walter's backers. No one wanted to bet against him after that drubbing of Douglas, the star sprinter, but the betting damage had already been done. Walter had carefully kept out of sight until called to the marks in the 100, playing the role of the unknown of no consequence. Douglas and his backers hadn't had an opportunity to size him up until the race was over.

McClelland was so elated with their betting success that plans were immediately made for a trip to Sandon for their sports day five days later. This little mining community was a 20 mile boat ride followed by a 15 mile horseback ride up into the mountains. On the way, Walter and his four betting partners joined up with a couple of fellow travelers who had heard over the telegraph wires of a "dark horse" who had made quite a mark in the Slocan games. Walter, having a little fun, quietly pointed out McClelland, who had never done an athletic turn in his life, as the Slocan wonder boy. Soon after their arrival in town, McClelland, unaware of Walter's prank, was startled by the attention he was getting from the townspeople, but soon warmed up to his newfound notoriety and played it up. His lumpy, clumsiness would only encourage the betting against Walter.

Harry Gill had taught Walter the technique of sprinting. Few people could match his explosive start.
Courtesy Orillia Museum of Art and History

The little group lucked out again in that there was a top notch athlete in Sandon too. This Nicoll had bettered 42 feet in the hop, step and jump, a respectable leap. The betting money started to flow again until the real Walter was spotted, scaring off any more bets. Walter won his three events and the group quickly headed back over the mountain that same day, cash in hand.

Meanwhile, the residents of Nelson, BC were ruminating over the loss by their man, Douglas, to the upstart shingler, Renwick, in the 100 at Slocan. They sent word to Walter's group back in Slocan that they had a man for a match race over 100 yards on whom they "would bet all the money in Nelson".

Up until now, Walter had found the pickings out west pretty

straightforward and lucrative. He had likely pocketed well over $1000 for just two events so far, double what he would have made in a year at the shingle mill! In these last couple of events of the season in BC he was about to find out how matched racing really worked.

The Nelson gamblers had brought in WW "Big" Smith of Fort William, Ontario, who was living in Rossland, BC that summer. He was a sprinter of the first flight. The match race was set up for October 21st in Nelson, $500 a side over 100 yards. McClelland and his partners were able to drum up another $1200 in side bets in the saloons, the support around town split equally between these two men of reputation. Walter was identified in the paper as "Walter Renwick Knox of Orillia, acknowledged to be all-around champion of Canada".[3] Just before the race was to start, gamblers were offering two to one on Smith, making him the favourite with the crowd.

By 2:30 p.m., the racecourse down the main street of Nelson was lined with spectators, people who had come by boat and train from neighbouring towns. A high-profile matched race like this was a spectacle in this world of limited entertainment opportunities. The local paper billed it as "the best race ever seen in the country."

At the gun, the runners burst away evenly but then Walter immediately hit soft ground and fell a good two yards behind. Racecourse conditions were never predictable in these towns. They could be uphill, downhill, hard, soft, straight or curved; each runner inspected and agreed upon the course and had to accept whatever problems arose. That was the matched race ethic. So tough luck, Walter just had to make up the lost yardage. And he did, passing Smith just before the finish line to cross first by about a foot and a half, by Walter's estimation. The three judges, in a split decision, declared Walter the winner, but then suddenly one of them changed his mind and declared for Smith. The crowd, most not in a position to see who had won such a close race, was split on who they thought had won. Smith, based on a two to one decision, took the victory and the $500 purse, and his backers won the side bets. It was a big loss for the

Slocan crowd, not to mention Walter.

Not one to be taken advantage of, Walter pressed for answers as to why the decision had been changed. None of the judges would talk until a full year later, when it was too late to do anything about it, although Walter continued to press for justice even then. That next summer, the swing judge told him, "he bet his money on Smith and in his excitement gave me (Walter) the race then thought about the money he had on Smith and changed it as quickly as he could."[4] Welcome to the wild west. Incidents such as these make it easier to understand why the proper and moralistic eastern elites of the AAA's were intent on eradicating the matched race world.

The Slocan crowd clamoured for a rematch, pooling together $2000 for a purse to entice Smith before the day was out. But Smith and his crowd could not be cajoled. Walter took this as acknowledgement of their lack of faith in the judge's decision. Though the betting on a re-match would be massive, they didn't want to risk losing the enormous purse they would have had to match.

Even more telling, the Nelson crowd switched its allegiance to Walter! Charley Walmsley, the saloonkeeper and sports promoter in Nelson, took Walter aside and convinced him to move his base of operations to Nelson, some twenty miles south of Slocan. This would mean giving up his job in the Slocan mill. Walter, appreciating the increased opportunities for big paydays in a larger community that had totally embraced the betting mania, made the move.

Right away a match race was offered, brokered by Walmsley. Feelers had been put out to Fred Mitchell of Fernie, BC, a small village 150 kilometers west of Nelson, near the Alberta border. Mitchell, a tailor, was a runner of dubious reputation (he'd been "laughably" beaten by "Big" Smith a year before) but was backed by a rabid betting crowd.

Mitchell was, as Walter put it, "a sure thing sport", meaning he was apt to fix races to make the event a sure thing.[5] Predictably,

Mitchell soon appeared in Nelson to size Walter up and propose a deal. He intended to give the Nelson crowd a good trimming by bribing Walter to throw the race. The heavy betting would be on Walter, the local star, so more money could be made if Walter threw the race than if Mitchell did, was the argument. He was obviously experienced at this type of thing. In fact, the town of Fernie had a reputation for dirty dealing. Intimidation and gunplay were a part of life there and, in fact, two men had recently been gunned down in a poker game in that town.

Walter put Mitchell off, saying he'd have to think it over, then ran straight to Walmsley. He was advised to "agree to anything that the Fernie coot or his backers want, but go out and win the race when it is run!"

So, although he never revealed what his price was, Walter duly reported to Mitchell the deal was on, and prepared to put his neck on the line by double-crossing him.

The race was set for $500 a side with a $250 forfeit, to be run November 10th in Nelson. The Nelson Fire Chief, proposed by Mitchell's crowd, was agreed to as stakeholder, to collect and hold the forfeit money and then collect the rest of the stakes on race day.

In the week leading up to the race, over $2500 was wagered in the saloons around town, with Walter as the favourite.

The typical Fernie shenanigans began the night before the race. Mitchell sent word to Walter that there was a "new angle" in their agreement and that he was sending two friends over to discuss it with him as he obviously couldn't come himself without raising suspicion. So Walter went for a walk with these two fellahs who casually led him to the slaughterhouse on the edge of town before they got down to business. Their business was pure intimidation.

Without warning, they grabbed Walter and jammed a gun into his ribs growling, "Listen Renwick, Knox, or whatever your name is. We're not going to stand for any monkey business in this race. You run it the way it has been agreed or you'll be a dead duck before the sun goes down tomorrow!"⁶

White-faced and shaken from the experience, Walter hustled straight to Walmsley for support.

"Run it out on them," he directed, "We'll take care of anything they'll do."

"That's all very fine," Walter replied, "but I'm the one who has been promised a dose of lead, not you!"

"Don't be scared Walter; with the whole of the Nelson police force with their money up on you, they're not going to stand for anything that the Fernie bully boys can cook up."

Walter was putting his safety into Walmsley's hands. He had to trust him, a thing he was not inclined to do, especially in his first dealings with him. But he was in deep now and had little choice.

On the morning of race day more warning flags went up when the Fire Chief who was holding the stakes backed out, saying he wasn't willing to do it any more. Obviously the Fernie thugs had gotten to him and he was scared. A lieutenant in the police force took over the job and collected the rest of the stakes. He now held $1000, the reward for the winner of the race.

Soon after the stakes were collected, a few Fernie men approached the police lieutenant in Walmsley's saloon and talked him into having lunch with them. As they got up to leave, Walmsley jumped over the bar and joined them declaring, "I'll go along with you. The lieutenant has my money as well as yours, and if ever a copper needed some protection I think this is the place." A big bruiser of a man, Walmsley stuck to the policeman like glue the rest of the morning, making sure he wasn't talked out of the money, as commonly happened in matched racing. As was typical, Walmsley, as Walter's backer, had put up the $500 stake and would split the winner's share with Walter 50-50. He was looking out for his own interest as much as Walter's.

A large crowd had gathered in town by noon and lined the racecourse at the Nelson recreation grounds. Several warm-up races for $10 a side were staged by local athletes, one with the local Member of Parliament falling flat on his face to the great amusement of the crowd. There was a buzz of energy and anticipation through town not seen in a long time. Bets of up to $400, a year's salary, were being placed on the big race.[7] "A prominent hotel keeper", likely Walmsley, bet $550 on Walter, giving two to one odds.[8]

Finally, after three in the afternoon, the main event runners lined up on the field. Mitchell and the Fernie crowd were sure they had the race in the bag. Walter, who knew otherwise, nervously eyed the crowd where he spotted the gunman from the night before waiting in case of a double cross. Would Walmsley and his friends really be able to protect him?

To make matters worse, Walter was caught by surprise when he found out it was to be a "mutual consent" start, something he had never seen before. There were two starting lines five yards apart. Any time that both runners were between the two lines the race would be on and the starter would fire the gun. Being up at the forward line could give you a five yard head start but crossing the back line running could send you zooming past the stationary man. It was a cat and mouse game Walter wanted no part of. When Walter started to complain, Walmsley shook his head. He assured Walter that the starter had his money on him and would make sure Walter wouldn't get taken advantage of.

So the two runners started jockeying, in the starting position, out of it, for about eight interminable minutes, according to the paper, before the gun finally went off, with Walter a yard behind. At the 80 yard mark, Walter edged ahead and finished no more than a foot in the lead. It was a close call for the three judges who were split on their opinions. As they wrangled, the crowd started getting upset; a lot of money was riding on their decision. The Fernie "bully boys" sensed they had to take matters into their own hands and started to move into action. But they had not reckoned with Charley Walmsley. Each of the Fernie thugs had a Nelson policeman or Walmsley supporter shadowing him. As they stepped onto the field, moving to rush the judges, they were nabbed and put out of commission. The gunman headed for Walter at the finish line, but he had taken no more than a few steps when "Big Hank", a Nelson gambler with a decided limp, brought his "cane", actually a small sized club, down on his head, knocking him out cold!

When the Fernie crowd began shouting that the judges had illegal bets down on the race, the judges, wisely, announced that they would declare the winner at six o'clock in Walmsley's saloon, when cooler heads were prevailing. The three judges, the runners and the stakes holder retired to discuss their decision calmly in private. The police lieutenant stakes holder, also wisely, deposited the $1000 prize in the safe at Walmsley's saloon for safe-keeping during that meeting. Good thing, too, because the Fernie boys immediately invited him over for a drink, and slipped him a few knockout drops, looking to grab the cash he no longer carried. He almost died that night from the drugging.[9]

Walter, nervous, changed hotels that afternoon and stayed out of sight.

At six o'clock, the judges, by a two to one vote, declared Walter the winner and awarded him the prize money. The Nelson gamblers immediately scrambled to collect their bets. Livid at the double cross but leaderless after the arrests at the race, the outnumbered Fernie men had no choice but to pay up. However, they would not forget this back-stabbing.

Mitchell found Walter that night and invited him out for a friendly drink. Having seen enough of that crowd for the day, Walter declined, assuming his drink would be doped too. The next day, seeing how organized the Nelson group was against them, the Fernie men left town.

The lesson for Walter, given the intimidation and dirty tactics, was the value of a backer. Walmsley had proved a loyal partner who saved his bacon and saw the event through to its lucrative end. Wandering into a town like Fernie alone and trying to set up a match race would have been suicide, Walter now realized. He needed a negotiator, someone who knew the terrain in a community and someone who would be there when muscle was needed. Walter was impressed with Walmsley and appreciative, calling him "a diamond in the rough".

A week later, Mitchell re-appeared in Nelson, looking for Walter. He wanted a re-match, and to try again to arrange for Walter to lose to really make a killing. Walter wanted no part of it. Then Mitchell proposed a race in Cranbrook, halfway between Nelson and Fernie. It would still be a good betting proposition, seeing as they had finished so close in Nelson. This time Walter agreed, but only if it was "on the level". They'd run 100 yards for $500 apiece with a $200 forfeit.

Walter never said why he was willing to deal with these dangerous Fernie gamblers again. He'd been truly shaken by their first encounter, and they obviously were out to get even. It may be that he bent on making his fortune and Mitchell was the only match runner around who could draw the betting crowd. And Walter did have an audacious streak; he was willing to take risks. So he decided, for whatever reason, to step back into the hornet's nest, dismissively calling Mitchell "a glutton for punishment".[10]

By the time Walter and his backers made it to Cranbrook, Mitchell was already there, laying the groundwork, Walter assumed. He insisted Walter pay the remaining $300 to the stakeholder early which, of course, Walter had no intention of doing. He waited until the very last minute, and then said he'd only put his money down after he saw Mitchell's money. Mitchell wouldn't produce it, and probably never intended to, hoping to abscond with Walter's money through an "arrangement" with the stakeholder, as they had tried to do in Nelson. Walter called the race off and claimed the forfeit. Having laid his own groundwork in anticipation of more shenanigans, he had an injunction placed on both Mitchell and the stakeholder for "scare purposes", showing he had the authorities on his side. It didn't take long, as Walter said, to break Mitchell and his backers, and he took legal claim to their $200 forfeit. Half a year's salary in the shingle mill made without breaking a sweat, not a bad day's work.

But the Cranbrook crowd wanted a race. They put forward an Ottawa man, Hummel, who claimed to be the champion of Ontario. Leery, but content Hummel was no real threat, Walter made the match for $80 a side over 100 yards, even giving Hummel a four yard head start.

It had been snowing all week, but no sooner was the match announced than a gang of men set to shoveling the course down the main street, excited there was to be a match race after all. It was no contest, "I could have beaten him by 15 yards," Walter said.

Even that late in the season, there was an appetite for one more race, a drubbing of Percy Wilkinson in Rossland for $50. But the betting was sparse, even giving away a head start and odds of two to one. Walter was becoming too well known.

Over the winter months, Walter and Charley Walmsley had time to put their heads together to plan for the spring season of 1905. Walter had learned a lot. Most significantly, he understood that racing unworthy opponents did not yield profits. To make the effort and risks worthwhile, he had to race first class runners. He decided to seek them out and to ignore the riffraff like Wilkinson and Hummel. Trouncing ill-equipped upstarts was spreading his reputation and scaring off future betting prospects. The locals in Nelson, no strangers to the matched racing world, introduced Walter to the term "hot foot": someone who only ran high stakes races, seeking out the fastest opponents who could draw the highest payoffs.

Walter was now a "hot foot".

10

Once More for Harry

While Walter and Charley Walmsley waited for the warm, dry weather to arrive and bring opportunities to pursue matched races, Walter received a letter from his old friend Harry Gill. Harry had left his coaching job at Beloit College for bigger and better things at the University of Illinois. His team was mediocre, he said, but one more good sprinter could make the difference. He invited Walter, at age 27, to go back to school for a term. With no better prospects until the warm weather arrived, it sounded like more fun than the shingle mill.

Walter, after a season on the frontier hustling circuit, had forgotten about the restrictive world of the Amateur Athletic Associations. He had freely broken their rules in so many ways: he had competed for money; he had bet on himself; he had associated with gamblers; he had raced against professionals; he had run under an alias. Any one of these infractions, if discovered, would professionalize him for life. But now here he was, trying to enroll in university as a lily-white amateur. The game was really on now. He was taking that gigantic ethical step over the line, misrepresenting himself to the university officials more blatantly than ever before.

At Beloit he felt he had only been dabbling in small time hustling which should really be over-looked. He was just playing around; he didn't really feel the ethical tension. But now he had made the conscious decision to make as much money as he could running and had actively pursued those opportunities. He had gone way over the line, and he knew it. To enroll in the university he'd have to lie through his teeth. Harry knew it too, but collaborated with him and set up an appointment for him with the university dean for a special, and highly unusual, mid-term admission.

In early April, Walter arrived in Urbana, Illinois. He had been warned that Dean Clarke was no pushover; he'd be suspicious of this extraordinary admission set up by the athletic director. Walter went into the dean's office nervously and felt the full brunt of his glare as he let Walter talk without giving any indication of his impression of him. "His eyes seemed to bore right into you and through you," Walter later exclaimed.

Then the questions started. Why so late in registering?

"Well, my Dad is a farmer up in Ontario and a horse kicked him and broke his leg which held me on the farm until he could get around again."[1]

Won't you be needed even more now at seeding time?

"That's all been taken care of."

On and on the inquiries went, rapid fire, as the dean looked for a contradiction in his story. But Walter never flinched, he said, and finally it came to this: So you're an athlete, what's your specialty?

"Track".

How good are you?

"I made a pretty good showing at Beloit two years ago but don't know how I will pan out at such a big university as Illinois."

A twinkle appeared in the dean's eyes, Walter said, at that statement. "So you're Knox of Beloit, I guess you'll make good all right." Clarke no doubt remembered how Walter had single-handedly led tiny Beloit College to a near defeat of his great rival the University of Wisconsin.

Then, as the conversation continued, the dean pulled out the admission papers and started filling out the forms. Obviously he had more than a passing interest in sport and understood why the coach wanted him, even at this late date. Walter's credentials as an amateur enrolled at Beloit so recently must have deflected any suspicion that he could be a professional. Walter's exploits in the remote lumber towns of BC, while notorious there, were unknown in the civilized world.

Admission papers in hand, Walter scooted over to the athletic building to report to the coaches.

"How'd you make out?"

"Dean Clarke certainly is a tough nut to crack… but he gave me this card which will allow me to enter next year."

Walter smirked as he watched the two coaches' jaws drop. They grabbed the card but said, "We ought to warm that fanny for you!" when they realized Walter was just pulling their leg.

His couple of months at the University were unremarkable. His professors were clearly instructed to give him an easy ride. He coasted through classes in horticulture, agriculture and veterinary science and didn't bother studying, even had fun playing practical jokes on his classmates while his professors turned a blind eye to his antics. At the semester's end, a few of the professors contacted Walter saying they'd be happy to help him along again in the fall semester if he returned.[2] Someone there had a lot of pull.

The Dean showed up at a few practices to check out his abilities, and clearly indicated he knew there was some misrepresentation going on but, like so many other people in Walter's wake, gave him the wink and a nod and played dumb.[3] The officials in the AAA's and college associations were officially severe in their promotion of the amateur sport culture, but apparently rules were bent and blind eyes were turned when personal interests were on the line. Walter, to no one's greater surprise than his own, got an amateur card! That, I'm sure, would have amused him no end.

Walter competed in four meets before the conference championships in Chicago. There he managed only second place finishes in the sprint, the high jump and the shot put, but with Harry's coaching Walter had found the knack for the hurdles and won that event. In those meets, Walter's scores were of a superior caliber but not his best: 100-yard dash in 10 and one fifth seconds, shot put at 41 feet, 6 inches, pole vault at 11 feet, long jump 22 feet.

Harry's gamble had paid off; Walter scored a lot of points for the team at the conference championships, establishing Harry's credentials as a top coach. The gamble of bringing in a professional could have cost him his job and career; instead it solidified his position at the university and set him on his way to a historic coaching career there. Over the next 30 years, his Illinois team won 19 conference championships. In 1920, he placed enough strong athletes on the US Olympic team that they could have won the Olympics by themselves! During World War I, Harry was integral in the formation of the NCAA, the National Collegiate Athletic Association, a massive, multi-billion dollar enterprise for today's universities.

In 1918, Harry, dissatisfied with the quality of athletic equipment available, started his own company and developed many innovative pieces of apparatus that became the standard: the ash javelin, flexible aluminum vaulting poles followed by carbon poles, the L-type rocker hurdles that didn't break your knees, the standard discus, and the portable starting blocks. Harry's U of I track team was able to use his innovative equipment to their advantage, something the other schools were slow to pick up on. The Gill Athletics company is still around today and is the official equipment supplier to the US Track and Field Association. Had Walter screwed up his admission interview, who knows where Harry would have ended up? Certainly not in athletics; a coach who so flagrantly flouted the amateur rules would surely have been suspended, and in those draconian times suspension was always for life. Knowing Walter so well, Harry must have been confident in his ability to pull off this bit of subterfuge. It worked out well for him... and gave Walter something to do until the spring hustling season started.

In June of 1905, Walter headed home to Orillia for a quick visit before his adventure continued. It was an all day and night train ride from Urbana, Illinois to Orillia, but Walter only stayed there for a few days before he was off again. He liked to touch base with his family and would continue to do so for years, but the athletics season was starting and he was anxious to head back out west where the action was.

An old Orillia friend, Jack Cameron, had sent a letter to Walter at his parents' home, telling him he could set up a good race in Port Arthur, Ontario. So off Walter went in mid-June of 1905 for the first race of what he hoped would be a long and fruitful hustling season.

In Port Arthur, Walter found his friend Cameron was somewhat lacking in match-making experience. He had made overtures to Alf Cooper of nearby Fort William but couldn't get a significant commitment out of the cagey runner or his retinue. Knowing Walter's reputation was a deal-breaker, Cameron had set up the match under the name W. Johnson, but could only squeeze a deal for $25 a side out of Cooper's camp. When Walter arrived on the train a few days later and sized up the situation, he decided this was a race to "chalk up to advertising", that is, to lose to increase the likelihood of bigger profits in the next race. A "hot foot" doesn't want to dominate, doesn't want to build a reputation as being unbeatable. So he lost the race, but only by two feet. You want to be competitive to draw future matches, but also beatable. Walter remarked that this race "doubled" Cooper's reputation. Walter saw dozens of faces in the crowd who knew who he really was and would be sure to spread the word about who Cooper really beat![4]

Then it was on to Nelson to see what his backer, Charlie Walmsley, had cooking. Walmsley was in high spirits, having gotten "a whale on the end of his line"! He had started working up a match for Walter with Tom Morris of Spokane, Washington. Morris was a top flight sprinter who had won the Chicago World's Fair 100-yard dash for professionals in 1893 and a World's Championship Sweepstakes in Indiana in 1903. He had defeated some of the best men in America. This was a big fish, but one past his prime. Morris was 37 years old. He had run 10 seconds flat in the past and felt he still could, being in "splendid condition", as the papers reported.

Now this was a match for a "hot foot": A beatable runner of big reputation and big money backers.

Walmsley had sent his side-kick, Bob McTavish, on to Spokane where he was readying the Morris camp to come to terms. Those negotiations gave Walter a little time to train and sharpen up after his travels. He used the Nelson Dominion Day Games as a warm-up, winning the 100, 220 and the pole vault, then hung around Nelson training before hopping the train to the coast when McTavish said the time was right.

Walter was happy to be back in experienced hands again. McTavish had laid down solid groundwork for the match. Walter dutifully showed up in Spokane with a big mustache and pants fully two inches above his ankles, a poor farm boy newly arrived in the big city. The Morris camp was told he was Walter Renwick, a prodigy who hadn't run a single race until the last year when he beat several good sprinters around Nelson and now felt he had the world by the tail. The negotiations were difficult and took some haggling, and all the while Walter had to play the rube, agog over the sights of the city.

It is interesting the negotiations took place in the Spokane Amateur Athletic Clubhouse. This was a matched professional race they were planning, anathema to the Amateur Athletic Union in the US. This club must have been one of the lavish men's clubs sidelined by the AAU in favour of the stringent rulebook approach to controlling amateur sport. In spite of its name, this club, in being a party to this race, was in no way supporting those amateur codes. It was likely one of the hold-over, stodgy old boys clubs that had developed in the

1880's but were now in decline, marginalized as a focus of amateur athletics by the AAU in the States and the CAAA in Canada. But from Walter's perspective, it demonstrated that the Morris camp came from money. They belonged to the stodgy old boys club. Perfect.

The race was set for $250 a side, over 100 yards, to be run at the Interstate Fairgrounds on Thursday, August 4th.

Several hundred people lined the track on race day but the betting was disappointing. Walter's backers could only get $300 in side bets. Still, a worthwhile race when the $250 winner's stake was added in.

When the gun fired, Morris got off to his famous lightning start, but Walter was right with him. Morris pulled ahead when Walter hit a patch of soft ground, but at the 80 yard mark Walter was passing him comfortably. Not wanting to beat him too badly, to protect any future matches, Walter pulled up a little to make it a close race, only to feel Morris surging at the same instant. As any sprinter will tell you, it's terribly difficult to accelerate after you've let up a little. Walter bore down but they crossed the line evenly. The judges declared a dead heat and, after a fiery debate with both camps, called for a re-run on Saturday, two days away. All bets were to be held over until then.

This suited Walter just fine. He felt confident he would win and now had two more days to weasel some more bets out of the Morris crowd.

What followed were "a most hectic two days", as Walter put it, while he posed as the poor country boy gawking at the big city. A couple of locals offered to show him the town. When they took him to a bar, Walter, a tea-totaller, declined, saying, "Paw made me promise I'd leave the liquor alone. That's the only way I got him to let me come down here."

When the same pair showed up Friday to continue the tour, Walter knew he was being buttered up for a deal of some sort. Walter was not going to throw the race, but saw this as an opportunity to fatten his wallet by double crossing the other side. McTavish was leery of the idea; afraid they might rob or even cripple him.

Taking McTavish's warning to heart, Walter took his personal bankroll, $2200, and buried it in the cellar of a friend's house. He had been carrying it around with him all week!

Sure enough, his tour guides turned out to be Morris bully boys, who eventually offered him $500 to throw the race.[5] Walter played them along for a while before he finally said, "Of course, you'll have to give me the money now to clinch your proposition".

Naturally they refused, and the negotiations continued until they got fed up and tried strong arm tactics. Luckily, McTavish had insisted on two of his men shadowing Walter. With the knowledge that backup was right there, Walter stared the thugs down and they parted ways glaring at each other, no deal made. One of those bodyguards was a wrestler named McMillan who was good enough to have had a match with the world champion. He became a close friend to Walter and taught him the ins and outs of wrestling, very successfully as it turned out.

Next morning, race day, the race fixers spread word that Walter was no rube from the backwoods. With no reason to carry on the charade, off came the mustache and out came the nice clothes and running gear. The race was set for 2:30 so the spectators could gravitate to the baseball game across the street at 3. The crowd was double what it had been on Thursday, but the new betting did not materialize. The Morris money had dried up.

The race itself was no contest. Walter won by three yards, with a time of 10 seconds flat.

Walter and McTavish, representing Walmsley, split the total haul of $550. This had to be disappointing, given Morris's reputation and moneyed backing. To make matters worse, Walter was outed in the newspaper by a Rossland man who identified him as Walter Knox, giving many details, some true but most off the mark. In the end, this boosted Walter's reputation when it came to attracting the very best professional runners who also saw the financial benefits of racing other top flight runners. But it also meant Walter would have to keep using aliases if he hoped to continue hustling lesser talents.

Of course, it also risked his amateur standing, though that meant very little now that he was committed to the professional world. But, then again, Walter liked to keep his options open, so this could turn out to be an inconvenient turn of events.

11

Barnstorming

Now, late in the summer of 1905, Walter struck out on his own. He decided Alberta was the place to go; his reputation, as Renwick, was too hot in BC. Alberta was booming. Settlers had been pouring onto the Canadian prairies since the CPR railway was completed in 1885. Thousands of homesteaders, actively courted by the federal government, had been cultivating the prairies for over 20 years; their supporting villages had begun growing into towns and cities all along the railway lines.

Adding to the boom, the closing of the American frontier in 1890 drove hundreds of thousands of Americans north of the border where good, free land was still available. Both Alberta and neighbouring Saskatchewan became provinces on September first, just after Walter arrived. Here again Walter could find boisterous communities of farmers, cowboys and working men itching to prove their physical prowess and even more eager to wager on someone else's. Even better, the iconic Mounties notwithstanding, the booming population kept the west under-policed and open for business for gamblers. And with no upper class to speak of, there were few prying eyes for the Amateur Athletic Associations. This was matched racing country.

Walter decided to go it alone now, leaving Walmsley's steady support behind. He needed to seek out opportunities that Walmsley just couldn't manage from his base in Nelson. The Fernie experience, demonstrating just how rough it could get, had taught him to keep his guard up. Walter talked about his mind being "at a steel taut tension most of the time" that summer with decisions having to be made on the spur of the moment.[1]

He was going barnstorming, from town to town looking for matches, living by his wits. By now he had fully developed his attitude of *caveat emptor*, buyer beware. In his writings he felt no guilt over assuming aliases and overtly trying to take his marks for all he could. "Let me repeat," he later wrote, "I am not defending myself, for, according to my reasoning, it needs no defense".[2] If someone freely agreed to a match and put his money down, that was his business. Buyer beware. Walter wasn't going to let him have any free information and was, with no pangs of conscience, going to mislead him any way he could. The goal was to maximize his profit.

It was to be a busy summer and fall: nine towns, holiday track meets, matched races, and even novelty events that all won him some money. In each new community he had to surreptitiously scout the lay of the land and find a way to set up a match. Finding local supporters was critical to working his mark and exploiting the gambling community. All the while he had to keep in top shape, without anyone seeing him practice. This was the hustling world, and every day Walter had to seek out the rougher edges of town to make his money. Constantly watching your back was part of the lifestyle.

Leaving Spokane in early August, he headed to Lethbridge, Alberta, in the heart of the dry prairie, some 800 miles by train away. A fair there with a special 100-yard dash for a $50 cash prize caught Walter's attention. As he suspected, it attracted a better than average field of runners. He had little trouble winning the race, and was careful to win by just a nose. After the race, Walter approached the second place finisher, fishing for a matched race. His mark was only interested in a fixed race, though, and didn't appear to have much backing, so Walter dropped the idea and moved on.

He headed to Michel, BC, situated one hundred and fifty miles back up the CPR rail line. The town had organized an afternoon of sports and games that looked interesting. Up through the Crow's Nest Pass and just into the mountains of BC, Michel was only 20 miles from the infamous Fernie, whose star runner Walter had double-crossed a year before and whose supporters had threatened Walter with a gun. Surely he must have had trepidations traveling to that vicinity.

Remember, Fred Mitchell made the trip back to Nelson a week after Walter had double-crossed him, to entice Walter into a rematch in Cranbrook, only to be out-witted again and relieved of another $200. To appear just 20 miles away in a well-publicized games was asking for trouble. Men on the frontier had long memories and Walter had made many enemies in Fernie. Why take that risk? Walter never commented on it but it is an indication of his brazenness. Not that he was courting trouble; he did come to town under a new alias. Likely, knowing his calculating nature, he saw this as the best opportunity around and expected he could skip town before any trouble-makers from Fernie would catch on that he was back.

Trouble found him right off the bat. Just after checking into his hotel and barely having set his bag on the bed, a knock came at the door. It was the owner, demanding he pay in advance. He accused Walter of checking in under an assumed name, which he had, Walter K Wilson, and insisted he wasn't going to be stiffed again after some patrons had skipped town without paying their bills already that week.

Walter, as was his wont, deflected trouble by taking the initiative and responding with, "You have a safe down below. Suppose you put this away for me and give me a receipt." He then handed the dumbfounded proprietor $1200.

That broke the ice and the two struck up a friendship. The hotel man said someone in the bar, obviously a Fernie man, had recognized him as Renwick. Walter confided to his new friend that he was indeed Renwick, the man who had been burning things up in Nelson. In return, Walter was directed to the most likely mark in town, a stuffy and arrogant Englishman who believed himself to be nigh on unbeatable in a sprint. He was entered in the games and that's where Walter could make his move. Walter had found his backer.

At the games, Walter won the high jump and the hop, step and jump events. Then, in the 100-yard dash with the Englishman, he was careful to win by the thinnest of margins. Having sized up his mark, Walter got the expected response: The Englishman blamed the judges and crowed that Walter was lucky to have won. Playing the indignant, rightful winner, Walter offered— no, threatened—to beat him again, and even give him a five yard head start. The Englishman jumped at the bait.

The match was set for $75 a side and the hotel man was able to lay down a couple of hundred dollars of Walter's money in side bets. Easy money. His backer, pleased with his cut of the winnings, invited Walter to stay on for a couple of weeks free of charge. The Fernie thugs hadn't shown up, but Walter wasn't about to wait for them and quickly moved on.

Around this time, Walter made a visit to a dentist to give himself another tool in his scheming arsenal. He had lost a big front tooth and wore a false white one on a bridge. He asked this dentist to give him a second false bridge he could put in, but this time made of gold.[3] Now when Walter wanted to run and be inconsequential, he would wear the plain white tooth. But when he wanted to be remembered, he'd pop in the gold tooth and smile all the time. He could be gregarious, garish, annoying Walter or receding, placid, inconsequential Walter more effectively now. Undoubtedly the Englishman saw the condescending, gold-toothed Walter.

In Michel, Walter was contacted, as Renwick, by the secretary of the miner's union in Frank, Alberta, inviting him to come as the star attraction of their benefit sports day. Based on his reputation in Nelson the previous summer, the union no doubt believed his presence would increase attendance. The miners were in a protracted strike and money was being raised to support them. So Walter hopped back on the train for the 30 mile trip back across the provincial border to Frank, a tiny mining community at the foot of the Crow's Nest Pass. Walter was indifferent to the strike but he did smell a betting opportunity.

The union secretary met him at the train and whisked him away to discuss the meet. He asked Walter to tick off the events he thought he could win and Walter, of course, ticked off most of them, including the shot put.

The secretary shook his head at the shot put tick saying, "We have a big miner here named Boyd that you'll never be able to beat. He's good."

As to the pole vault, he said, "There's a young fellow here from the States who thinks he's good. He'll give you a tussle unless you're real sharp."

That brought on this arrogant response from Walter, "Do you want to know how sharp I think I am? Can you find me someone who can do some betting for me?"

"Certainly!" was the enthusiastic reply, as the union secretary smelled a money-making opportunity.[4]

And off they went to the bank on the main street, of all places, and strode right up to the bank manager's office. The bank manager, a most unusual choice, and a couple of his clerks became Walter's betting agents, and they seemed to know their way around that business.

Boyd the shot putter was a real physical specimen, just as Walter had been told, well over six feet and two hundred pounds. His first put was over 39 feet, easily out-classing the rest of the field. On Walter's first throw, he fell in an amateurish way, giving the bankers an easy time getting bets down. Laying off his second put kept the bets coming. Then, on his last throw, Walter sailed the iron ball 41 feet 7 inches.

Boyd was dumbstruck, and told Walter so while shaking his hand. "You're the best shot putter I ever saw!"

The "swanky young squirt from the States" did not take his come-uppance as gracefully. Walter feigned difficulty clearing each height in the pole vault, and when he finally beat the youngster, nasty words started to fly.

As the situation heated up, Walter finally shot at him, "You think that mark is hard to make, do you? I'll tell you what I'll do. I'll bet you $20 I can go over a full foot above that!"

Out came wallets all around and Walter covered all the bets. The bar was set at 10'6", now a routine jump for Walter, and over he sailed.

Was Walter putting a puffed shirt in his place, as he had loved to do back in Orillia, or was he just working the mark? Normally he refused to show what he could do, to protect future prospects, but here he seemed intent on putting an exclamation mark on the argument. Either way, he probably picked up an extra hundred dollars in this display.

The bankers were jubilant with their part in the day, and showed their appreciation by taking care of his expenses, including another week in the hotel if he wanted. Walter left town $200 the better.

Blairmore, famous for its hot sulfur springs, was just a few miles down the road from Frank. With no prospects lined up, Walter headed there to spend some time soaking and enjoying the scenery.

One afternoon, Walter noticed a small crowd forming in front of the hotel and sauntered over to see what was going on. There a big strapping fellow was putting on a heavy weight throwing demonstration.

After watching for a while, Walter sidled over to him and said,

"You throw a nice stone. I can throw a weight myself. Maybe you and I could make a match and a few dollars for both of us."[5]

He was suggesting a fixed match whereby they'd set up the contest, garner bets from among the crowd heavily weighted towards the agreed upon loser, the brawny local hero, then split the proceeds when Walter beat him. They could net a tidy sum from the betting crowd.

Walter's offer was met with a good bawling out and an insulting accusation of "Crook!"

Surprised and hot at this dressing down, Walter retired to the bar to cool off.

The affable bartender quickly took Walter's side, telling him how much he despised the braggart and would do anything to "take" him. "What gets me so sore at him is that he is always looking for marks. He pulls out a big wad of bills and slaps it down on the counter when he thinks he has someone he can overawe and wants to bet the pile that he can throw the stone farther than him or anyone else." Of course no one who ever took him up on the challenge could beat him; it was calculated braggadocio.

"Listen," Walter said, seeing his opportunity, "If we can get him into that mood, grab his money quick and say you have a man that will cover it."

Then they sat down to wait. The braggart came into the bar every day, larger than life and telling the world, but no money was slammed down.

On the third day, after a friendly heaving competition on the lawn with a tourist, he came in waving his wad of cash, declaring, "I can put the stone or the shot farther than anyone and there's my money to say so!" as he threw a roll of bills on the bar.

The bartender had his hand over the cash almost before it was put down, and Walter immediately stepped up, announcing he would cover the full amount, which turned out to be around $200!

The man remembered Walter and snarled, "You tried to

proposition me."

"Yes," Walter shot back, "in a joking sort of way. But now this isn't talk. My money's up and so is yours."[6]

The braggart insisted the match be then and there, so out onto the lawn they marched where a 12 pound shot put was produced. Walter then proceeded to beat him by a full two feet, and pocketed his wad of cash.[7]

Walter did not use any delay tactics to make time to work the crowd for bets, as he normally would have. This was more about putting the braggart in his place, to avenge his holier-than-thou insulting attitude. Even though Walter, by soliciting a fixed match, earned that type of condescension, he could never understand it. In his mind, everyone should want to make a little cash. It would all be good fun. He was so entrenched in the matched racing world now that he could rationalize any tactic he used to make a little money. To belittle Walter based solely on his casual suggestion was uncalled for. This guy was a blow-hard and asked for it. No more justification was needed. The frown on his face as Walter pocketed his wad of cash was all Walter wanted.

After the match, Walter let it be known that he could run a little too, if anyone wanted to take him on. Someone did. A short, squatty "foreign" fellow who ran the fruit stand across the road, challenged him to a sprint as a joke, but only if he "would make his weight", which was about 200 pounds.

Walter put him off, but got to wondering if it could be done. So he went to a quiet field and strapped on 50 pounds of sandbags, one on his chest and the other on his back. Running like that "was no trick at all" he found, so off to the fruit stand he went. The proprietor was up for the race and they agreed to 50 yards at 202 pounds. The poor fellow came in a full 10 yards behind Walter, huffing and puffing.

After finishing his R and R in Blairmore, Walter set his sights on the upcoming day of sports in Golden, BC, 130 miles due north.

Golden lay just inside the Alberta border, but a circuitous day-long train ride away. Before Walter even started on the trip, a letter came for him from the secretary of the miner's union in Golden. He invited Walter ("Renwick") to those very games in order to arrange a matched sprint with a mysterious runner who had arrived in town claiming to be the champion of BC. It was to be a "double mystery"; Walter brought in to hustle the hustler.

The secretary met him at the train station and whisked him away to a stately brick house where they discussed the arrangement. Just like in Michel, Walter would get a chance to size up the competition at the sports day then decide if a matched race was worth working up. Walter was directed to lay low in the house all week, only coming out to train at night. He was to be just another inconsequential runner.

The secretary investigated this mystery runner, Leslie Grant, whom Walter had never heard of or seen.

Walter showed up for the sports day in his long pants, rolled up to the knee. In the 100, he quickly sensed Grant was "laying off" so it was no problem to win the race by a nose. Walter still had no idea what he was up against, though Grant didn't run like a 10 second flat man. Finishing the day, Walter won the 220, broad jump and hop, step and jump events. Then Grant approached him.

It didn't take long for him to get down to business, proposing a fixed race. Walter played the rube, but in the end agreed to the fix. Grant had a backer who would bet heavily on him, but he proposed a double cross whereby Grant would let Walter win and they'd split his backer's money and any other bets on Walter. As Walter said, "He was a sure thing runner who worked both ends against the middle".

So they set up the match for $100 a side to create interest, and the miner's secretary worked the town for bets on Walter. The race was a mismatch; Walter had to slow down to make it look good. "This fellow couldn't do a hundred in under 11 seconds!" But Walter took his half of the proceeds and left town.[8]

While in Golden, Walter received an urgent telegram from Charlie Walmsley, to get back to Nelson right away. He had a big matched race coming together for him. After this small stakes racing, Walter would have welcomed this news from his trusted friend. Walter didn't linger and hopped the train for the long journey down through Alberta and back through the mountains to Nelson.

By now it was getting into mid-September but the cool air didn't dampen the appetite the gamblers had for a big event. After some wrangling, the match with a sprinter named Monroe from Phoenix, BC was finally set for mid-October at $500 a side. That gave Walter almost a month to settle into some real training. Walter called this one of those "can't lose affairs", happening in his home base with both Walmsley and McTavish included as officials. None of those precautions were necessary though as Walter easily won in a slow time of 10 and 4/5 seconds. Again, Walter saw the advantage of having an operator like Charlie Walmsley working for him. This was big money that turned out to be easy pickings.

So when Walmsley asked Walter to hang around a little longer to see what would develop from a promising nibble he'd had from Vancouver, Walter listened. This runner's backer refused to identify his charge, no matter the prodding. It would be a match with an "unknown" again, just like in Golden. All Walter knew was that his opponent was a "champion of some sort" and his backer feared that if his identity was discovered the Nelson crowd would dry up. It all sounded like a dangerous risk but Walmsley put up the $150 forfeit and invited the mystery man to Nelson for the race.

The long, thin and lanky runner was HW Ferguson, an unknown to Walter, but obviously someone who knew what he was doing on the track. He was a better than average sprinter, Walter surmised, someone who could give him a run for his money. The gamblers, with a long, boring winter around the corner, laid down their bets lavishly on this event, likely the last bit of excitement for quite a while. This looked like a close race, and that got their adrenalin flowing.

The match was set for mid-November in Nelson. Race day, deep in the mountains, was frigid and windy, brutal conditions for half-naked sprinters. Walter used a special rub-down preparation on days like this that would "leave a glow for minutes afterward". He liberally rubbed down his bare legs with the liniment, pulled on his heaviest long johns and then his trousers before walking onto the track. Given the conditions, the starter quickly called them to the mark. Both men pulled off their trousers. Ferguson was bare legged. Walter, in his long johns, took a little jog down the track and back to warm up then sat down to laboriously peel off the underwear. All the while skinny Ferguson stood at the starting line in his bare legs, slapping his arms and jumping up and down in an attempt to keep warm as the wind whipped over him. By the time Walter finally came to the marks, Ferguson was chattering and rattling. It was no contest. Ferguson never even got going; "miserable" was how Walter described his showing.[9]

Through chattering teeth, Ferguson grumbled that he could still win under normal conditions. "Any time, any place" Walter shot back. That time would be the next summer.

In his month and a half in Nelson, running two 10 second races set up by Walmsley, Walter probably netted close to double what he could have earned in a year at the shingle mill, even after splitting the profits with his backers. The rewards certainly justified the risks and the pangs of conscience, not that Walter seemed to have many of those.

Even in mid-November there were still foot races being staged in the west. Walter caught wind of a race in Maple Creek, a small town in the new province of Saskatchewan, just across the Alberta border. "The bettingest town I ever got into!" Walter later said. A local speedster had just lost a close race to an "unknown" who took a pile of loot from the betting crowd. Walter thought there might be an opportunity to get a match with one of the two runners there.

Not wanting to arouse suspicions, Walter booked a train ticket to Swift Current, the next town past Maple Creek, so he could arrive in town from the east. "Renwick" was known all across the west by now, and steps had to be taken to hide his identity. He registered at the local hotel as "WR Wilson", newly arrived from Winnipeg.

The owners of the hotel, a couple named Stearn, were very friendly. Walter spent a few days in their company getting his bearings in the town, without mentioning running at all. It was Mr. Stearn who, after three days, brought up the subject of the recent race. It seems the local hero, Regan, the assistant station manager for the CPR, had been coming on and would have won the race in another stride or two. After making the train switch, Walter had probably walked right past Regan after arriving in town. Eventually, Walter mentioned he could run a little too. He even went so far as to say he'd be curious how he would stack up against a real runner, even for a small wager, say $25, just to make it interesting. In no time Regan came walking into the hotel lobby.

Regan questioned Walter closely about where and when he had raced, and against whom. Walter had all his answers ready. Regan was cagey about strangers and said he'd need something to offset his disadvantage of racing an unknown. "Give me four yards and I'll give you a race."

"Well, I know nothing about your running ability any more than you know about mine. Four yards are a lot to give away. Still, you can't lose much, neither can I, and for the pure sport of it, I'll try," Walter casually replied, setting the bait.

On a very cold day, they met on the track over a hundred yard course. There was very little betting; the crowd was shy after their recent losses to an unknown. This time Walter made no delays, giving Regan no excuses, and the gun fired as soon as possible after they left the warm confines of the buildings. Regan won by just a foot. But Walter came back yammering about being cut off and insisted he had actually won the race himself! He got really worked up and excited and spluttered out, apparently without thinking, "Why, I'd give you nine yards start and bet you $250 that I could beat you!"

The crowd, as expected, heard the challenge and a dozen voices rang out, "Do you mean that? Say it again."

Walter drew back, feigning that he regretted his outburst. The crowd urged him on, sensing a killing to be made. Walter delayed, saying he was freezing and that he'd have to warm up so he could think. Back inside, just as he expected, Regan confronted him and Walter allowed him to hold him to his word. A match in 10 days for $250 a side was agreed to. The trap had been cleverly set.

Ten days gave Walter plenty of time to get in some good training. After a couple of workouts, a young nineteen year old kid asked if he could join him. Seems he once thought he had some speed but had put on some weight and hoped Walter would help him burn it off. It turned out he was pretty good, and with a little of Walter's coaching began to really go. Walter would give him outlandish head starts on the icy roadway and run him down but by the end of the week had to cut the advantage way down. It worked well for both of them. Then came the shock.

At their last practice together, the kid said, "Tomorrow will tell the tale and no one around here thinks you are anybody else than Wilson from Winnipeg, but I know who you really are."

"Is that so? Well, who do you think I am?" Walter asked, wondering which of his many aliases would come back.

"You're Knox from Orillia!"

Caught off guard but coy, Walter responded, "What makes you think that?"

"I come from Peterborough and I saw you run Belland there."

Uh-oh. Walter's heart dropped. "And now I suppose you're going to spill the beans?"

"Why should I? I have a few dollars to bet and I know who I'm going to bet it on!"

It was the old wink and a nod again. Walter's ace in the hole was always his ability to win someone a little money. Out here no one cared about who he really was, as long as they were in on the con. Walter was an opportunity to those in the know. Luckily there was no one out west who really cared about the ethics of professionalism and the Amateur Athletic Associations either. In Montreal or Toronto, if Walter was identified running matched races, let alone pulling a con like this, he'd undoubtedly be reported immediately, opportunity or no. The sporting elites had vowed to eradicate Walter and his ilk. But this was not Montreal or Toronto, and this kid was not part of the sporting elite.

After setting the match, Walter had wired a friend in Spokane to come to Maple Creek as soon as possible. This fellah, McMillan, his bodyguard in Spokane, had been manager for the World Champion middleweight wrestler, and was a pretty good wrestler himself. He knew the betting world better than anyone Walter knew. Maple Creek was ripe for the picking, but Walter couldn't do it alone. The Stearns at the hotel were clearly in Regan's camp. With a week to go before the race, Walter's backer showed up and, with Walter's money, went to work all over town.

Race day, a warmer early December day than usual, Walter showed up at the track early to check things out. The handicap start lines caught his eye.

"That's the longest dragged out nine yards I ever did see," Walter declared.

The race referee handed him the measuring tape and told him to measure it himself. But Walter knew all about "short" and "long" tapes, where an inch per foot was added or subtracted on the tape.

"Thank you," he said, "but we'll use our own. In that I have to run over it I am entitled to know if it's right or not."

Taken aback, the referee sheepishly responded they might have made a mistake. It turned out the nine yard head start was actually eleven yards![10]

As he knew he could, Walter won the race by one yard after

making up the nine yard deficit. The extra two yards they had tried to tack on would have cost Walter the win. As it was, Walter had to go all out to take the race.

After the race, a man named Jim Baxter came up to Walter and asked if he had any idea of the time he had just run. Then he handed Walter his stopwatch that showed 9 2/5 seconds. The world record for the 100 was 9 3/5. (Remember, this race was run in December on the prairies; it was cold and the ground was frozen, making the time all the more remarkable). Walter didn't argue with him but he knew amateurs could have itchy trigger fingers.[11]

But Baxter, no amateur, had been the backer for the "unknown" who had beaten Regan just before Walter did. Was Walter interested in a race with him? Baxter offered to set up the race as Walter's backer after seeing his phenomenal performance in Maple Creek. Allegiances followed the money in the west. The other runner was good, but Walter was better. Baxter was changing horses.

Within a couple of days, he had set up a meeting with this still unknown runner's handlers over in Medicine Hat. These gamblers, confident in their man, were excited about a race, and even proposed a whopping $500 a side stake. Baxter kept Walter's identity under wraps, calling him his backwoods cousin just come to visit; they made the two hour train trip back across the Alberta border along with "the better part of the betting population of Maple Creek". The backers were ready to sign, but their runner insisted he had to see his competition first. After arguing back and forth, Baxter finally called for Walter, to placate his mark. Sure enough, it turned out to be Leslie Grant, the "sure thing" runner Walter had fixed a race with in Golden, BC a couple months back. One look at Walter and the race was off; no offer of a head start would convince him to run.

Meeting Baxter wasn't a total waste though. Back in Maple Creek, Walter spent some time with him and they struck up a friendship. Baxter was a follower of the sprinting world, keeping up to date on developments. What he suggested to Walter would shape his career down the road. The "greatest race in the world", he said, was the Powderhall Sprint in Edinburgh, Scotland, the closest thing there was to a world professional sprinting championship.

Held every New Year's Day, the best runners from Europe and around the world participated in the handicapped betting event. Every entrant was evaluated on past performance and the judge's estimate of their ability, and spotted a handicap of a certain number of yards head start on the "Scratch" runner, the fastest man. This ensured a close finish and wild betting. Over the 130 yard course, some runners would be spotted a 25 yard head start! After a series of heats, the handicaps were adjusted and a final race of the top eight men was run for the championship. The prize money of 50-100 pounds was, given the worldwide renown of the race, only just enough to attract attention; it was the prestige that drew the best runners. The Powderhall was first run in 1870 and by 1905 a stadium had been built for the race that had been used for the British AAA athletic championships for years.

"That's the race for you. Why don't you put in your entry?"

Walter had no interest in traveling all the way to Scotland, wherever that was, just for a race and politely declined.

Baxter even offered to make the entry for him. Walter had no objections to that, but never intended to go. Baxter kept sending Walter's entry (as Walter R Stearns) to the Powderhall year after year, long after they had parted ways. He was a running enthusiast and just wanted to see Walter go there and win, to be a part of history; he had that kind of confidence in him.

Maple Creek was a long way from Edinburgh, and Walter's last race of the season couldn't have been more different than the elite Powderhall Sprint. Walter was flirting with the lowest reaches of the running world, novelty races, when he raced an opponent he had never faced before. One day, a rancher bet him he couldn't outrun his horse. Not knowing anything about racing a horse, Walter told him to come back in a few days so he could think about it. Seeking expert advice, he walked out to a rancher friend's spread to get the lowdown.

"Over 50 yards? The horse will beat you."

"How about with a turn at a stake?"

"It will beat you and run you down." His friend demonstrated. His cowpony could turn around the stake as fast as a man.

Playing around, they determined that Walter had a reasonable shot at winning over 35 yards around two stakes, with the horse running a different course than Walter.

When the rancher returned a few days later, Walter accepted his bet and dictated the course he and his friend had devised. Walter won by three feet but the pony would have taken him in just a couple more strides.

Then came the big snows and the foot-racing season was over.

12

The Athletic Wars, 1907-1909

While Walter had been away adventuring in the west, storm clouds had been forming in the amateur athletics world. Events there were going to make his life more difficult and force him to venture even farther afield.

Since the 1880s, the sporting elites had been wrestling for control of sport, doing all they could to eliminate the rural sporting tradition of matched races, blood sports and the gambling and violence associated with them. They chose the issue of money as their battleground, declaring it illegal to receive any financial rewards for athletic endeavors, or even to associate with anyone who did. In most individual sports they had been widely successful. Athletics, swimming and most Olympic sports became firmly under the control of the Amateur Athletic Associations through their organization and standardization of the sports. Others, though, like skating and cycling, still had a parallel professional branch developing independently of AAA control. Rowing, especially, had a blatantly professional side.

But it was the team sports that caused most of the headaches. The AAAs were formed too late to control baseball, hockey, lacrosse and rugby, sports which, because of their wide popularity, had already started down the road to professionalism. Even against the AAA's best efforts, the pay-for-play athletes found opportunities to enrich themselves in these burgeoning sports. There were always opportunities to get paid to play outside the amateur venues if you were good enough, and the local amateur teams were under pressure to bend their rules to accommodate professionals when gate receipts began to grow and that income became too important to lose.[1] After 1900, the debate was obviously coming to a head, which resulted in the "Athletic Wars" of 1907. The battle for control between 1907 and 1909, "a period of unbelievable chaos"[2], had a direct impact on Walter Knox and his athletic career.

The elites in the AAA movement held a central tenet that money was corrupting to sport. Athletes who had any contact with professionals ("prostitutes" was the term often used) were "tainted" in their eyes.[3] Sport for profit would inevitably lead to cheating, the antithesis of the moral uprightness the purists strived for. The elites said they abhorred men who, like Walter, made sport their business, missing the irony that they themselves, as successful businessmen, made money their prime consideration in whatever their work endeavors were.[4] Sport was the only exception to their capitalist rule that making money was good. It was a remarkably hypocritical position. They claimed that sport as work would lead to cheating and race fixing, then violence, ignoring the fact that violence and race fixing were not unknown in amateur sports, no matter how pure the elites professed it to be.[5] Historian Ronald Smith has claimed "there simply is no evidence that an amateur is more virtuous or heroic than a professional, just by being an amateur".[6] And sport historian Alan Metcalf has said, "the real reason for the amateur's distain for professionals lay in a complex of deep-seated and perhaps sub-conscious values within the aim of the movement itself".[7] Amateurism, in more liberal circles, was beginning to be seen as a curious relic of Victorianism, an albatross around the neck of Canadian sport in the evolving Edwardian age.[8]

Nowhere was this elitist value system more apparent than in

sport's treatment of blacks, natives and other ethnic groups. The AAA's war was with professionals, as a surrogate for the crass and aggressive workingman as a class; but non-whites, no matter how "pure" they tried to be in their participation in sport, were never given the same consideration as whites either. It wasn't a "professional" issue; it was really all about class.

In 1900, blacks were, as a matter of course, seen as "morally inferior" and not allowed to compete with whites.[9] Tom Longboat, Canada's greatest distance runner at the time, is a prime example of how the elites' conservative values affected his ability to compete. He, as a native, was singled out for attention when he began winning big races in 1906, and was almost routinely called out as a professional, being suspended by the CAAU twice in 1907, only to be re-instated both times. A challenge over his eligibility for the 1908 Olympics was the turning point in the Athletic Wars. Though the AAA's fundamental mission was to eliminate the professionals, their prejudiced Victorian value system was just as much a part of their operation, whether they admitted it or not. Here we see the class war laid bare. The lower classes, the working men, were being marginalized just as the blacks and natives were, but indirectly through attacks on their sport-for-profit tradition.

It was a very complex and complicated time in Canadian sport, governed by a group who could only see black and white based on their deep-seated value system.

If they had only looked, they could have found a current example of professionalism working if governed properly. The Amateur Athletic Union in the US was just as draconian as the Canadian version, but the American college system was not. College sport was initially student-run. The students saw the potential for revenue by charging admission, money that could support their programs. When, for example, in the early 1890s Harvard College refused to allow the football team to charge admission, the students simply moved their game to Boston.[10] It didn't take long for the colleges to see the cash cow for what it was, and by the early 1900s stadiums were being built and scholarships were being offered to outstanding athletes.[11] Likewise, the colleges turned a blind eye to student-athletes like the great Jim Thorpe playing summer baseball for pay, and started to hire professional coaches like Harry Gill, both flagrant violations of the amateur code.[12] Compromising and governing the professionalization of sport worked there under the guise of education. It could be done. The games were fair, the athletes honest and just as virtuous as any others. But winning did become more important than the amateur code.

In 1898, when the battle to eliminate the professionals was stalling, the AAA of C reorganized itself into the Canadian Amateur Athletic Union (CAAU), claiming jurisdiction over 17 sports including the increasingly commercialized and popular sports teams. The new organization set even higher standards for amateurism. But claiming jurisdiction didn't necessarily transfer into control. Prestigious trophies such as the Stanley Cup in hockey and the Minto Cup in lacrosse were controlled by trustees outside the realm of the CAAU, and they paid only lip service to the amateur code, being more interested in the gate receipts. Over the next few years, amendment after amendment was added to the amateur code by the CAAU to combat the growing pressures to use or compete against pay-for-play hockey and lacrosse players. The situation became "ludicrous", and policing almost impossible, for the AAA teams who wanted to vie for those cups.[13] This amateur/professional subterfuge could not continue.

The new amateur rules, created to stop the exploiting of loopholes by the teams, were applied universally to all sports, including athletics. The amateur/professional schism became more and more draconian. Hence Walter's disdainful use of the "lily-white" adjective whenever he talked about the amateur rules.

In late 1906, the crisis in amateur sport came to a head in Montreal. After 1900 some sport leaders said the inevitability of professionalized team sports should just be accepted and the amateur rules liberalized for them.[14] This idea of allowing professional hockey and lacrosse players within the AAA system was hotly debated.

Sport was booming in the decade of 1900 – 1910 in Canada, in lockstep with the population and industry, both of which doubled.[15] Team sports, especially, caught fire and many felt the general capitalist attitude in society was inevitably going to overwhelm the sports world.[16] Others insisted the rules needed to be even more strictly enforced, given the pressures.

The Montreal Amateur Athletic Association (MAAA) forced the issue in 1905, when its "pure" lacrosse and hockey teams had become uncompetitive. The MAAA asked the CAAU for an exemption from the amateur rules for their lacrosse team, on the threat of the MAAA withdrawing from the CAAU. The MAAA was the dominant club in Canada and generally carried a block of Quebec AAA votes with it, even though conservative Toronto was the biggest power base in the CAAU. The CAAU relented and gave the exemption, but only for the lacrosse team. Amateur lacrosse players could now play with or against professionals and still maintain their amateur status, but could not accept any remuneration themselves. But a year later, when the MAAA was lobbying to have the exemption extended to its hockey, rugby and football teams too, the exemption was rescinded in a dramatic vote at the annual general meeting of the CAAU. The vote blatantly revealed the liberal Montreal vs conservative Toronto schism in the CAAU. Five months later, the MAAA followed through on its threat and withdrew from the CAAU saying "it was better to recognize the professionals openly than to continue under the various disguises as has been the practice over the past three years".[17] It took a block of Quebec AAAs with it and they formed their own rival association, the Amateur Athletic Federation of Canada (AAFC), on February 1st of 1907. The war was on.

The CAAU said "gate receipts and championships were being put ahead of the amateur principle on the road to the ultimate extermination of amateur sport".[18] Iron-fistedly, they declared all AAFC athletes to be professional, even the runners, cyclists and swimmers who had nothing to do with the hockey and lacrosse leagues. Then the CAAU began to campaign and organize aggressively. In every province, smaller towns were encouraged to set up AAAs in affiliation with the CAAU. In 1907, the CAAU had 37 affiliated AAAs representing 479 sports clubs. One year later it was double that![19] The AAFC, on the other hand, settled quietly into their Quebec base, only extending themselves to form a loose affiliation with the AAU of the US.

This situation was no better for amateur sport than what had come before. While teams were confused and torn by mixed allegiances and athletes deprived of their competitive rights, sports leaders remained intransigent.

Again, Tom Longboat, the great Indian runner, was the flashpoint. In selecting the 1908 Canadian Olympic team, the Canadian Olympic Association (COA) negotiated a truce between the CAAU and the AAFC for the betterment of sport. The two rival organizations agreed they would both defer to the COA in rulings and challenges regarding the Olympic athletes. Both associations sent athletes to a common Olympic Trials meet (the first one for Canada) and the winners were selected to the team, regardless of their amateur affiliation. The COA accepted Longboat as an entry in the marathon.

Both associations accepted the COA's jurisdiction and got along amicably until ten days before the Games. The American AAU had been making noise about Longboat's previous suspensions for professionalism in the US, but the Canadian organizations, led by the COA, had remained silent, as agreed. Suddenly the AAFC, apparently trying to build a bridge politically with the Americans, put forward a challenge to the COA regarding Longboat's eligibility, a clear breach of their contract. The British Olympic Committee, the games host and ultimate arbiter, was called on to mediate and ultimately allowed Longboat to run (though he didn't finish the race in the stifling heat).

It was the beginning of the end for the AAFC. The press turned against them. Pleas for peace within the Canadian sports world became persistent. The CAAU egged the press on and clearly stated that only if the AAFC dropped its rule exempting its teams from competing with and against professionals would the CAAU consider negotiating a merger.

Finally, in November of 1909, the AAFC gave in and the two bodies merged again into the new AAU of C. The war was over. The conservatives had won. There was to be no brokering with professionals in Canadian sport, sport had been "rescued" from professionalism.

The AAU of C drafted an even more draconian amateur code (if that was even possible). The same negative definition of an amateur in use since 1884 was re-stated: an amateur never took money, competed with professionals, wagered or promoted sports events. They added in a new caveat, "Any athlete guilty of the above can never be reinstated". Then they specifically stated that an amateur could never compete with or against a professional or in a game where admission was charged and could never use an assumed name. Clearly it was a rescinding of the AAFC rules. The definition was full of the word "never". Nowhere did it actually say what an amateur was, just what he was not.

There were several far-reaching effects of the end of the Athletic Wars. First was the formation of overt professional leagues. The Stanley Cup in hockey was replaced by the amateur Allen Cup for AAU of C teams. The Minto Cup in lacrosse was replaced by the Mann Cup. The old cups were seen as money-making mediums controlled by mercenary promoters, and expelled. Hockey promoters seized the moment and the professional National Hockey League was the end result.

Second, as sports historian Bruce Kidd has pointed out, the new amateur code worked very well up to 1930 for those who championed it, acting to place an effective limit on the amount of time and energy top athletes had to devote to training, allowing them time to prepare for a post-athletic career.[20] Sport was successfully kept recreational as opposed to professional in spirit. As a result, after a very successful showing at the 1908 Olympics, Canadian athletes began to steadily fall behind the rest of the world. Canada was one of the last jurisdictions in the world to continue banning from amateur competitions sports instructors, phys. ed. teachers, playground leaders and YMCA instructors.[21] It would take an about-face on some of the tenets of amateurism in the 1920s to re-establish Canada's position as a player on the international sports scene, starting with the hiring of full-time professional coaches around 1920. Walter would be in there on the ground floor as a professional coach.

But most importantly for Walter was the massive penetration of the amateur ethic into Canada's frontier reaches. Up until then, amateur sport was mostly limited to the Montreal-Toronto corridor. Small towns all across the country now had officials linked into the over-bearing central authority, eyeing athletes and controlling competitions. Hiding his professional antics was going to get harder and harder for Walter. The holiday fair sports days were to quickly go the way of the Caledonian Games. Winning a couple of bucks in a sprint at the Victoria Day games could now very easily cost you your amateur card. Most athletes didn't need those games any more anyhow; the AAAs were organizing track meets on regular schedules where standard events and official records made the small time fairs seem backward. They would go back to what they originally were, casual fun days, and the real athletes both flocked to and were stuck with the amateur meets, the only game in town. The era of the itinerant, hustling athlete was entering its twilight.

13

1906: Amateur Records, Dirty Dealings and Duping the "Coon"

Just after Christmas in 1905 Walter, after a quick visit with his wrestler friend McMillan in Spokane, hopped on a train and headed back to Orillia for a visit. He hadn't seen his older brother Jack in a long time or his parents in almost a year. Meeting up with Jack would change his life, just as meeting Baxter and learning of the Powderhall Sprint would. From both men he tucked away an idea, an opportunity, for future reference.

In the meantime, Walter's mind was still squarely focused on track and field. Late in January of 1906, he picked up a Toronto newspaper to find a picture and long article about Ed Archibald of Toronto who was claiming to be the Canadian champion pole vaulter. After looking up the results of past Canadian championships and making inquiries with sports authorities, Walter, as he suspected, found no one had topped the vaulting record he set in 1900. (Walter did not seem to be aware William Halpenny had cleared 11' 5" at Summerside, PEI the previous July, bettering Walter's mark by several inches. Walter was only digging up the results of the previous few Canadian championship meets). In Walter's mind, his higher leap trumped Archibald winning the last Canadian Championship. These long fawning articles about Archibald were a "slap in the face" to Walter's pride.[1]

So Walter wrote to the Toronto Central YMCA, which Archibald represented, and issued a challenge to him. Not only was this a test of Walter's supremacy in the vault, it was a test of his amateur status. The Central Y, staunchly allied with the Amateur Athletic Associations, would never allow a professional to compete there. If they were willing to allow Walter to compete, he would know all his professional exploits out west had gone undetected in central Canada. As Walter well knew, there were any number of opportunities for the Canadian Amateur Athletic Union to have found out about his professional activities. He had been identified by name in the Sault Ste. Marie newspaper in 1903 when he put the Quinn boys in their place. He had his name and details of his life in Ontario outlined in the Spokane paper in 1904, exposing his use of an alias after beating Tom Morris in a high stakes matched race. In Peterborough, a foot racing enthusiast had identified him and produced a picture of him to prove it, ruining his carefully planned hustling of Belland. Even the 19 year old kid in Maple Creek had identified him but kept his mouth shut so as to make a little cash. Any one of these cases could and should have been reported to the CAAU. The rescinding of his amateur status would have been an open and shut case. The CAAU, though, if it had looked Walter up, would have found his registrations with Beloit College, the University of Illinois and the Milwaukee Athletic Club, his participation in the 1900 Ontario Championships and Canadian Championships, and even the Pan American Exposition Games in 1901. He did have solid credentials as an amateur too. This would be the test.

The Y contacted Walter and said they wouldn't be able to set up a matched competition as it was against the AAA rules, but would offer him an invitation to compete in their indoor athletic meet that weekend, three days hence. Archibald was entered in the pole vault already.

Walter was successfully back in the amateur world!

That afternoon, Walter hopped on the train to Toronto and was practicing in the Central YMCA gym by evening. He had kept in good shape and just had to sharpen up on his technique. He'd be ready for the weekend competition. His friends tried to dissuade him, advising him to wait for a better situation and time to prepare properly, but Walter was confident and knew he'd be heading out west again soon. The time to put Archibald in his place was now.

The next day, while practicing, a friend mentioned that Archibald was sitting up in the stands watching. Walter then proceeded to knock the bar down at the lowly height of nine feet six times in a row before clearing it. Archibald was overheard saying he'd "show him how to vault". You can just see Walter's smirk. Another puffed shirt about to be humbled.

On Saturday, the first event up for Walter was the 12 pound shot put, and there was another top ranked shot putter there Walter couldn't resist taking on. Harry Giddings, another smaller man at 160 pounds but with good technique, threw out a superior put of over 42 feet on his first attempt. Walter laid off, sizing up the situation. But on his next put he sailed it a full two feet past Giddings best, within a few feet of the world YMCA indoor record! That was that, and now on to the main event.

Giddings went right over to his friend Archibald and warned him what he was up against. That only helped Walter by putting Archibald on edge.

When the vaulting competition started, Archibald easily cleared the lower heights but then knocked the bar down on his first try at nine feet.

Walter, in a very friendly way, sidled up to the 21 year old Archibald and casually said, "Don't get too excited about that, we'll give the crowd a good exhibition and do around 11 feet."

Of course Walter, a self-assured 28 year old, knew Archibald had never cleared eleven feet. He was playing with his head, as he had learned to do so well on the hustling circuit.

Archibald cleared nine feet on the next try but never got over nine feet six inches. Walter did, but didn't attempt anything higher. Now that he had avenged his honour as the best pole vaulter in Canada he saw no point in laying all his cards on the table. Besides, Archibald was a good vaulter; they may meet again. In fact, they would, at the Canadian Championships the next summer, 1907, when Archibald had improved considerably.

The Central YMCA officials were impressed with Walter and invited him to join their athletics team (and issued him a coveted amateur card). They even organized another meet in a month's time for Walter to show what he could do with some practice. Archibald, in a fit of pique, left the Central Y for the West End Y. Neither he nor Giddings showed up for the meet on March 3rd.

Walter showed up ready for action. He was sharp after four full weeks of training. His 12 pound shot mark of 49' 4 ¾ inches was a new indoor YMCA world record! He followed that up with a vault of 10' 9 ¾ inches breaking the American YMCA indoor record.[2]

Basking in the glow of his spectacular performance, Walter was approached by a man in the audience. He represented the post office, he said, which had been collecting money to send Archibald to the Olympic Games in Athens, Greece that summer. "Do you think you could beat Archibald outdoors?" he asked.

"Were you at the meet a month ago when I took him to camp?" Walter shot back testily, frustrated people wanted to talk about Archibald on his big day. "Well, that answers it! What are you so nosy about?"

Apparently the post office now wanted Walter to go to Athens in Archibald's place. "If you are a better man than Archibald then we want to send you!"

Though they had already collected $250, it was barely enough to cover transportation and accommodation. Walter turned them down. It would have cost him money for meals and entertainment, and to ask them for spending money like that would have professionalized him, making him ineligible for the Olympics or any other amateur meet. The better course was to head west to make some money instead of spending the whole spring on one meet that would cost him money. After two weak Games in 1900 and 1904 the Olympics hadn't gained the prestigious reputation they would after the hugely successful Games in London in 1908. It wasn't the drawing card it would be in just a few years.

Archibald did go to Athens but the train conductors in Italy lost his pole. The replacement pole provided for him in Athens snapped on one of his first jumps, almost impaling him, and left him a nervous wreck. He tied for last place, clearing only one height. Just before the Games he had been clearing 11 feet in practice and likely would have won a medal. He did win a bronze medal in the 1908 Olympics in London and that summer cleared his lifetime best of 12' 5", just four inches short of the world record. The man Walter had defeated was no slouch.

By early April 1906, Walter was "out west" (he didn't ever say where) and ran a race making "a nice sum of money". Having achieved that end, he started having second thoughts about the offer to go to the Olympics in Athens.[3] But that ship had sailed, literally. The Athens Games were to be held at the end of April and Archibald was already aboard ship for Europe.

So it was on to Vancouver where he heard about a May 24th athletics meet in Nanaimo, BC. Nanaimo was directly across the Strait of Georgia on Vancouver Island, a 60 mile ride by steamer. In his pocket he had a letter of introduction to the proprietor of the best hotel in town. But Walter opted instead to check into a small out of the way inn where he could remain anonymous. Not only did he have to hide the name "Knox", now he had to hide the name "Renwick" too, his reputation in that guise was so great all across the west. At the best hotel in town, where all the tourists and businessmen stayed, he could easily have been spotted and lost his opportunity for gambling profits. He checked in as "W Wilson" of Calgary.

Walter found just what he was looking for in Nanaimo. Another sprinter of ability was entered in the games, one who would be itching to set up a match with him. It was HW Ferguson, the man Walter had left shivering and chattering on the starting line six months earlier in Nelson; the man who swore he could beat Walter under normal conditions.

At the starting line for the 100-yard dash at the holiday games, Ferguson made no sign that he recognized him. So Walter let him win and stumbled in dead last thinking, "If that's the way you want to play the game, so can I." Immediately after the race, Walter aggressively challenged both the top two finishers to a match race for $50 a side.

Not long afterward, Ferguson's emissary hunted Walter down and a match was made for one week's time, June 1st. It was for a trifling stake, but Nanaimo was a gambling town and Walter was able to lay down bets that made the event more than worthwhile. Ferguson was a local Vancouver runner who garnered strong support after defeating many capable challengers. "Wilson" was just another in the string of pretenders to their champion's crown. He sure didn't show anything at the holiday games.

Walter laid low in his hotel for the week. With the betting going so well, he didn't want to blow it by being spotted by someone who had seen him run before.

A couple of days before the race, Walter began to feel unwell and put it down to indigestion. But the night before the race was a bad one and Walter woke up distressed. His head was pounding and the world was spinning so badly he couldn't walk for falling over. Staggering over to the mirror, he fell, but crawled to the door when he heard someone walking down the hall. Pulling himself up by the doorknob, he crashed into the hall in a stupor.

"What's the matter, pal?"

"Get me a doctor quick," blurted Walter, flat on his back, "I'm dying!"

"Or pickled." remarked the man, "Nanaimo squirrel whisky is powerful stuff."

"Honest, man, I need a doctor and need one fast."

"Too early for them," the man replied, more earnestly, "I'll see if the druggist is open across the street." And off he went.

Shortly, the Good Samaritan came back. He had described Walter's symptoms and had brought back the druggist's preparation. It mollified the headache and steadied Walter enough to get dressed and down for some toast and milk to settle his stomach. He couldn't keep that down even a few minutes.

Staggering down the street like a drunk, vomiting several times, Walter managed to find a doctor's office. He was the first patient there and was led right into the consulting room. The diagnosis was ominous: iodine poisoning. Someone had slipped colourless iodine into his food.

It all became clear to Walter then. He remembered seeing one of Ferguson's handlers in the kitchen of the hotel several times that week. He had thought nothing of it as he was the son of the grocer who supplied the restaurant. Routine deliveries. Walter had stayed out of his way to avoid any confrontation. But he and the Chinese cook were too chummy, Walter remembered thinking, and now he knew why. They both probably stood to make quite a bit of money when Walter had to forfeit the race a few hours from now.

The doctor, a sports enthusiast himself, offered to help. He sent a boy to pay Walter's bill at the hotel and then took him to a quiet room in the very hotel Walter had rejected as being too high profile. The owner and the doctor were good friends. Under the doctor's care, Walter rejected any thought of forfeiting the race. In his own words, "I decided I had a score to settle with those who had drugged me. If, I concluded, I feel better in a couple of hours, I'll go out and give Ferguson the damnedest race he ever had from a dopey easy mark!"[4]

Just after noon he got up, wobbly and pasty, but determined. By sheer will he got himself out to the Caledonian Grounds track, still in a bad way. Even a small misstep would easily land him on his rear end. Walter, apparently, didn't have a backer here; he did his own negotiating, but now had to pick someone to be "his" judge, something he had planned to do the day before. Ferguson had already picked one of his henchmen. A stoic Walter looked around and pointed to a minister in the crowd, with his white clergyman's collar, thinking a religious man at a matched race must be a real sportsman and would want to see a fair race. Surprising both of them, the minister agreed to represent Walter. Walter was then able to quiet himself while the minister took care of the details.

This was a desperate gamble by a man desperate to win.

There was no posturing here, no head games, just grim, straight ahead determination. Walter wanted to get this over with and leave no room for second-guessing the result. He had no stomach for a melee after the race.

With a large crowd of four to five hundred heavily invested in the outcome of the race hooting and yelling, Walter made sure of the decision, winning by three or four yards in 10 2/5 seconds. "I never started away so fast in all my life. I went like a bullet and was in deadly terror lest one of those staggering dizzy spells would hit me."[5] The newspaper report said he didn't even have to extend himself, finishing "in an easy manner" looking over his shoulder.[6] Had Ferguson even nudged him he would have gone down, so unsteady were his legs. Walter, as he knew he had to, took the lead right off the start and didn't give him the opportunity.

Ferguson went right to the reporters and accused Walter of being a "ringer" from the East, running under an assumed name to pick up some easy money. Walter, also talking to the reporters right after the race, was all business in spite of his swooning head and wobbly knees, challenging any local sprinter to a match, offering good handicaps. It's like both runners said the same thing. Then he headed right back to the hotel to recover.

But the Ferguson supporters were not good losers. Walter and an acquaintance were caught at the hotel and "ganged". Walter only remembered coming to on the steps of the hotel with bruised knuckles, a pounding headache and a messy black eye; his friend was in worse shape. All anyone could tell him was that he had put up a good fight.

Well, that was enough of Nanaimo. Walter, presumably after collecting his winnings, was on the first boat for Vancouver in the morning.

During his week in Nanaimo Walter had issued a challenge in the Victoria and Vancouver newspapers that spread all over BC.

"I will take on any man in British Columbia for any one or all of the following events for any sum he wishes to name: 100-yard footrace, running long jump, hop, step and jump, pole vault, putting the shot."

He signed it "W Wilson". This was not the first time he had done this. From Port Arthur, on his way out west a year before, he had issued a public challenge in the Winnipeg paper, hoping to find a match as he passed through. In Nelson, he issued another public challenge to any runner in British Columbia. Nothing came of either challenge. The newspaper article described Walter as a small man, under 150 pounds, but one who "understands the running game thoroughly". He "not only uses his feet but his whole body is in action when he runs".[7] It quoted Walter as saying, before their race, that while Ferguson is a good runner he does not know how to use his body and that he "could make him four yards faster in his 100-yard sprints in two weeks".

Getting off the train in Rossland BC, deep in the mountains, Walter met up with some of his Nelson friends who confronted him with this challenge. They insisted "Renwick" had to challenge this upstart, "Wilson", to an all-around match. They were adamant he had to take this brash braggart down a peg. Finally, to shut them up, Walter had to confide that he, "Renwick" was in fact the upstart "Wilson" and he had no intention of taking himself on!

Giving up on that idea, one of them set about negotiating a match for him in Fernie against a runner named "Davis". It was clear "Davis" was an alias but he offered a $200 a side stake and Walter, as "Renwick", took it. Returning to Fernie was not so dangerous this time; they seemed to have forgiven him for double-crossing their man, Mitchell, 18 months earlier and even took Walter in as one of their own. Again, in the west, allegiances followed the money. Walter was the best bet to win some money, no matter who he raced. Walter beat Davis by two yards, netting a tidy profit in the betting-mad community. He never found out who Davis really was, though he was an accomplished runner.

Almost immediately after that race, the Fernie crowd set up another match for Walter. They arranged for Tom King to come there from Winnipeg for a hefty stake of $1000 a side. King and his retinue arrived in mid-July and after posting his forfeit money began dickering about setting up a fix. As Walter could attract the heavier betting, king's side wanted him to agree to be the loser.. Walter wanted none of it, so King and his followers pulled up stakes and left town, leaving their $250 forfeit money behind for Walter. Easy money. The press report, after a big buildup for this match, was scathing, making King out to be a cowardly scam artist. It was salve to Walter's manly ego, especially when the same paper had lambasted Walter in an identical way just a year earlier.

Walter now hopped aboard the train to his hometown, Orillia, back in the east. He wanted to compete in the Penman Games there, one of the better amateur athletic meets in Ontario that year. But he also wanted to continue the discussion with his brother Jack about events unfolding in Northern Ontario. He met up with Jack in North Bay, in the wilderness five hours north of Orillia by train. Jack, bubbling with excitement, convinced him to spend a day with him on a side trip to Earlton, 100 miles north of North Bay, where he was situated. It was a big inconvenience as Walter was anxious to get home, but Jack was over the top with enthusiasm and Walter just couldn't say no.

Jack had taken a free land grant from the government in recognition of his services in the South African Boer War. He and Walter wandered around his land where he was taking timber off for the mill. But that's not what they were talking about. There was a gold and silver rush in that area in 1906. Stories of fortunes being made overnight were rampant. Jack was set on going prospecting, getting in on the ground floor, and wanted his little brother to join him. He had a bad case of "gold fever", and he gave it to Walter. They made plans to stake a claim and get rich.

But Walter had plans too, and continued on to Orillia the next day, leaving Jack to scout out a likely claim. What Walter had to offer was a little capital to get supplies and property. There were still opportunities to fatten his bank account and come back to Earlton later in the fall to help Jack once he had found the right stake. So it was on to Orillia and more competition.

The Penman games were an annual competition set up by the YMCA, this year hosted by the Orillia Y. A valuable shield, donated three years earlier by Dr. John Penman, would go to the athlete garnering the most points in 10 different track and field events. A magnificent trophy would be awarded to the highest scoring YMCA team. It was a closed event for YMCA athletes only, and runners, jumpers and throwers from Y's all across the province showed up. Walter had already entered as a member of the Central Y team in Toronto and was the headline athlete in the local paper. Curiously, even though the Orillia YMCA hosted this event, it didn't have a formal athletics team organized until the following summer, after their modern building was finally erected with a gymnasium available to exercise in[8].

"Walter Knox, world famous athlete" was the moniker the Orillia Packet trumpeted leading up to the meet. Ed Archibald, the reigning Canadian Champion pole vaulter, whom Walter had just humbled, was entered for the West End Y. Bobby Kerr, who won a gold and bronze medal in the sprints at the 1904 Olympics, and was the reigning Canadian 220 yard champion, was entered from the Hamilton Y. Another athlete entered, the distance runner Don Linden, had also just returned from the Olympics in Athens where Archibald had broken his pole. In all, there were 100 athletes entered, all top notch. Even Harry Gill, Walter's old friend and coach, was to be there to put on a discus throwing demonstration, probably recruiting for the University of Illinois team. The Penman shield and the magnificent Penman trophy were on display all week in William Frost's "Diamond Hall" jewelry store on the main street, Frost being one of the driving forces at the Orillia Y.

The big event went off on the hot afternoon of Aug 9th at the Oval grounds in Orillia in front of an enthusiastic crowd. First up for Walter, in front of his proud but aging parents, was the 12 pound shot put, the same event he had broken the indoor world YMCA record in just 5 months earlier. His put of 44 feet won the day but was 8 inches short of the Canadian record. Given another try for the record, Walter sent the iron ball flying 49' 6 ½" for a new Canadian record! The old record had been held by Giddings, the same man Walter had beaten at the indoor meet at the Central Y in the spring. In second place was veteran athlete W Madill of New Zealand, a massive man on tour of Canada, who specialized in the hammer throw. This was another example of 145 pound Walter using speed and technique to defeat a man close to 100 pounds heavier.

Walter followed that up with a third place in the 120 yard hurdles, a third in the 12 pound hammer throw and a win in the long jump (20'11") before lining up for the 100-yard dash. There were three top sprinters entered, Walter, Kerr and Worthington, a medalist at the Canadian Championships. Walter won his heat with Worthington in 10 2/5 seconds, slightly uphill and into a wind. Kerr won his heat in 10 4/5 seconds. Before the final, Kerr pulled Walter aside with a proposition: Let him win here so that when they met again at the YMCA Athletic League Championships in Hamilton a month hence the betting prospects would be much better and they'd split the killing made when Walter won there[9]. (Even at lily-white AAA meets there was still rampant betting in the crowd, just not as overtly as at matched races. The runners, though, had to stay well clear of it. Historian Nancy Bouchier commented, even though it contravened both the rules and the spirit of the AAAs, considerable evidence says there was betting, even by AAA members, at amateur events[10]). As Walter said, "they paid me well to do this".[11] So well, Walter later said, Kerr wasn't able to recover that cost in bets in Hamilton.[12] The whole payoff was a total loss for Kerr. Using the excuse that he was tired from the long jump, Walter let Kerr win, but not without first taking him out fast to see what he could do, before fading at the finish. The winning time on the poor track was 10 seconds flat. Walter was confident Kerr was his for the taking next time.

Then came the pole vault. Archibald was a no show, but two other superior vaulters were there, Reeds and Cameron. All three easily cleared the bar through the nine foot heights, eliminating the other competitors. Reeds and Cameron both cleared 10' on their first try but Walter missed. Then he knocked the bar down again on his second try. This was a routine jump for Walter; he must have been unnerved. His third, and final, attempt was thankfully successful and the bar was raised again. Clearing 10'8", Walter eventually won the event and was asked to attempt the Canadian Record height of 11'0". These were not the best conditions, it was windy and the pole he was using had a poor point (there was no "box" or hole in the ground to plant the pole into as there is today, the vaulters relied on the sharpened point of the pole to grip the dirt), but Walter cleared the bar on his first try to tie the record that had stood for 10 years. But after five hours of steady competition, Walter was exhausted, and only at the urging of William Frost did he attempt a new record height. It was one step more than he could do on that long day.

But what a day! Three wins, a fixed second and two third placings, all against top flight competition, won Walter the coveted Penman shield and a re-affirmation of his greatness in the eyes of his hometown, not to mention the wider athletics audience. Walter was back in the amateur mix, a force to be reckoned with.

Walter spent the next few weeks trying to drum up a matched race, to no avail. There were eight weeks between the Penman Games and the YMCA Championships in Hamilton on Oct 6th and Walter wanted to make the most of that time. Having been away from the Ontario scene for so long, he thought there would be opportunities for him. Finally, near the end of August came an interesting proposition.

Down in Corry, Pennsylvania, just 25 miles from Lake Erie near the harbour town of Erie, was a Negro runner who considered himself a world-beater. This was a running hotbed, with several athletic clubs in that small town alone. Henry Batson was the star runner in the Negro club and 50 of his supporters had each contributed $10 to a pot, challenging anyone to try to beat him. There was a $500 prize waiting to be snatched, though it wouldn't come easily.

A matchmaker in Corry, "Mr. Weston", contacted Walter about setting up a match. It was the best opportunity Walter had found, so he agreed to let Weston start the negotiations and headed across the border. Corry, Walter was assured, was a betting town. There was money to be made; and that's exactly what Walter found when he got there. The town was "race mad", the townspeople talked of nothing else and the newspapers went all out in their enthusiasm.

Rumours about the match flew. One newspaper reported,

> "There are reports on the street that the young man who calls himself W Wilson of Batavia NY is none other than

Arthur Duffy, the world's champion at short distances, but they have long wanted to match Batson with Duffy or a man just as good so if Wilson wins fairly he can have the money without a murmur."[13]

Others suggested Walter was the Milwaukee Meteor, Archie Hahn, the great college sprinter Walter had pushed to a sub-10 second 100 while at the U of Illinois (when Walter was hobbling on a sprained ankle). All these rumours only heightened the excitement around town and pushed the betting to wild levels.

Walter's training had hardly started when he was informed a spy was scrutinizing his every move at practice. A local saloonkeeper, whose bar was the hub of the Corry sports scene, had sent a man down to hide under the bleachers to watch Walter's training sessions, stopwatch in hand, and listen in on the conversations afterward. Walter's spies found anything that was said at the track was spread around the bar.

Here was an opportunity.

"I'll tell you what to do Walter," Weston devised, "Give him a sprained ankle to report back to his boss!"

They rehearsed a little after dark then at the track next morning, after making sure the spy was in his hideout, Walter went into his act. His handlers argued with him against making a speed trial, claiming his training was not far enough advanced. Walter played bull headed and insisted on the timed sprint. Out came the watches, both above and below the stands, and Walter took to his marks. Exploding down the track, he suddenly bowled over as if shot, apparently wracked with pain. Weston and the handlers actually carried Walter off the track to the stands, right above the spy.

"What in the world happened, Walter?" Weston asked.

Walter groaned. "I must have hit a soft spot or a hole."

"Better get him to a doctor as fast as we can," one of the handlers said.

"Better protect yourselves," whimpered Walter, "I'll never be able to get back my speed now. Get some bets down on Batson as a hedge."

They whisked him off to the hotel, scolding Walter for being so blatant.

When the saloonkeeper himself put down a $300 bet on Batson that afternoon, Walter's camp knew they had swallowed the bait hook, line and sinker. Walter lay low, but when he was seen out of his room he used a cane. His training was now done on a back country road well after dark (where he could have sprained an ankle for real stumbling around in the dark).

Soon after the "accident", a surprise visitor to his room put Walter on the defensive. It was the Chief of Police. After a little small talk, he came to the point. He had $300 saved as a down payment on a house and was willing to risk it on this race. How bad was Walter's injury?

Suspecting another spy, Walter put him off, saying he was going to test his sore ankle in a couple of days and would let him know then. The fellow seemed sincere but Walter wasn't one to be caught unawares.

Here was a nice, thorny issue for a council of war. In the end it was Weston who made the decision. Bring the Chief of Police in on their side; trust he would aid and abet their scheme. If he was on the level, he had a lot to gain and could be a valuable ally after the race. Weston was worried. Just outside Corry proper was Sugar Grove, the Negro encampment where Batson lived. A huge contingent of Batson supporters was sure to be at the race and could get ugly if their subterfuge was discovered. Having the Chief of Police on their side could be important.

Right on the heels of this dilemma came another. Walter had been leery of this whole setup from the start; the situation seemed too good to be true. He had sent a telegram to Tom Keane, his backer during his sojourn in Boston in 1904, inquiring as to Batson's reputation. Now his reply came back: Batson was no lily-white amateur. He had a history for "pulling fast ones that was almost as black as himself."[14]

"Don't take him as an easy mark and don't race him unless you are in tip top condition." he warned. "That's his game. To make himself look as though he's easy meat but get him in a race and he'll show you a pair of flying heels!"

That telegram sobered Walter up.

Soon after, the Chief of Police returned as directed. Walter laid his cards on the table with trepidation, saying he'd never been as fit in his life, then held his breath for the Chief's response. With a grin, the Chief, in no uncertain terms, made it clear he was no friend of Batson's camp. Whether due to racial prejudice or past underhanded dealings, it was conceivable to Walter and his camp that the Chief was on the up and up. Satisfied he was going to double his money, the Chief left "pleased and laughing". The next few days of betting would reveal if he was really on side or not.

It didn't ease Walter's nerves any either, when the official stakes holder, William O'Rourke, suddenly asked to be excused, and a hotelman had to take his place. That was always a sign that some underhanded tactics were being used.

Race day, Saturday, September 15th at 5 p.m., finally came and Walter nervously watched the huge crowd assemble. Spectators were charged 25 cents a head admission with half the profit going to rent the Fair Grounds field and the rest to the winner. Batson arrived just as he'd been described, a fine, strong fellow, built like a runner, obviously well educated in technique. Walter knew he was in for a race. What he didn't know was whether Batson had any shenanigans planned, although Walter suspected he did.

Batson wasn't an intimidated black man either. After Walter false-started Batson, "the coon", as Walter referred to him, admonished him, "You needn't be in such a hurry, white boy."[15] Walter was dead serious now.

At the second start Walter hit his stride perfectly, taking the lead after just 10 yards and never looking back. He won easily by 4 yards with a time of 10 seconds flat.

All his fears of being played for the sucker were put aside by his pure ability and determination. When the race was on and the stakes were high, Walter, as he so often did, let his feet do the talking. Batson was a serious opponent. It looked for all the world like a set up. All Walter could do was out-perform Batson, to not let his machinations, if there were any, matter. In these situations, Walter had a wonderful power of concentration and the ability to focus all his powers on performing. Like a caged tiger, Walter took matters into his own hands when the cage was opened.

That night the Chief of Police visited Walter and offered him some of his winnings. Walter refused but they had a good laugh over the whole event. The Chief could now start building his house.

Walter headed back to Canada with close to $1500 in winnings in his pocket.

The final competition of the season was the YMCA League of Canada Championships in Hamilton on October 6th, three weeks after the race in Corry. The YMCA was a significant player in the sports world then, separate from but closely allied with the AAAs in spirit. Physical development had been a core fundamental in the Y mission for decades and it had developed the best facilities and coaches in most communities. The YMCA wasn't interested in developing sports specialists but did develop top-notch athletes in every field of sport all across Canada.[16] Many of the top athletes from across Canada and a few from international locales, like Madill of New Zealand who would break the world YMCA hammer record here, were entered. Walter entered five events.

It was a miserable day at the Britannia Park field in Hamilton. It poured rain from dawn to dusk. The track was pooled with puddles and the field became "the muckiest kind of muck", according to the paper. Demonstrating the importance of the event, a "goodly crowd of spectators", the paper reported, about 100, braved the elements to watch the contests from under the protection of the grandstand roof.

First up was the 16 pound shot put. In spite of the puddles in the throwing circle and the slippery iron ball, Walter put out a heave of 41' 9", almost three feet past his nearest competitor, for the win and a new Canadian YMCA record.

The long jump venue was a comical mess. The runway was under water and the pit a sea of mud. The jumps, needless to say with the slippery footing, were not of superior quality, but Walter managed to win with a leap of 19' 6 ¼", a mere ¼ inch ahead of the second place man.

Then came the showdown with Bobby Kerr in the 100-yard dash that the crowd had been waiting for. They both won their heats on the soggy cinder track. Then, as agreed in Orillia, Walter won the final. Walter lined up for the final jogging, without any rest, straight over from the long jump pit where he "had had a bad fall". Under these miserable conditions, running around the curve and through puddles, he still put in the impressive time of 10 1/5 seconds, winning by just a yard. The paper reported that Kerr was "unfortunate" to get off about a foot behind Walter who then "pocketed" him, or as another paper reported, "stepped into his course, and Kerr had to take several extra steps to get around him". When he finally freed himself, the paper said, he was gaining and would have won in "two more strides".[17] There was always a way to save face in a fixed race, but it is significant Kerr never protested. The papers raised no suspicions of a fixed race, or the questionable fact that Kerr never protested. Walter later chuckled that there was hardly any betting action (likely due to the small, miserable crowd) and Kerr's take of Walter's winnings was far less than he had paid Walter to lose in Orillia! Walter won on both ends of that arrangement.

In the hammer throw, Walter surprised even himself by placing second behind the mammoth Madill of Australia. Walter squeaked out the silver medal over the next best Canadian by four feet but was fully forty feet short of Madill's mark, a new YMCA world record.

Finally, at six o'clock, the pole vault competition started in the teeming rain. A jumper by the name of William Halpenny from Montreal, who had placed fourth at the 1904 Olympics and had cleared 11 feet that year (and 11'5" in 1904), showed up with his own pole, painted in red and white candy stripes. Six other jumpers appealed to the referee to be able to use his special pole as well and were allowed to, over Halpenny's serious objections. But not Walter. All he said was that he'd "never handle that thing", and furthermore "would beat him out with any old pole".[18] The striped pole reeked of self-important pride, was too flamboyant, and only served to get Walter's hackles up.

Three men cleared 10' 4", Walter, Halpenny and Cameron, who had given Walter a run for his money in Orillia. But Halpenny couldn't clear 10' 6" that day. Both Walter and Cameron continued on to best 11 feet. By then it was seven o'clock and getting dark. With the rain still teeming, they both failed at 11' 2", then again at 11' 1". It was no use, the conditions were deteriorating with the light and the event was stopped. The officials declared the winner would be decided by a coin toss. "Tails," Walter called, and it was. Walter got the gold. Both men had tied the Canadian YMCA record at 11 feet.

With four gold and one silver medal, Walter won the prestigious Spalding All-Around Trophy with 23 points to Kerr's 13. But even that trophy couldn't have been as important to him as a hot shower at the end of that miserable day!

After six months back in the amateur world, Walter had set five YMCA records (the YMCA kept their own list of records set by athletes representing YMCA teams, separate from the official AAA records reported in the newspapers): the world indoor 12 pound shot put and American indoor pole vault records, as well as the Canadian outdoor 16 pound shot, pole vault and 12 pound shot records. "Knox" was now as famous in Ontario as "Renwick" or "Wilson" were out west.

But now it was time to take care of his gold fever. As planned, he headed north, in October of 1906, to join up with Jack to get their piece of the gold and silver rush, fully expecting to make their fortune.

14

Getting in on the Ground Floor

Jack Knox, Walter's oldest brother, spent a year in the military fighting in the Boer War in South Africa. After expectations of a brief policing mission to tame the Boers, the war was going badly for the British and men across the empire rallied to her defense. Donald Smith, aka Lord Strathcona, a fabulously wealthy Canadian businessman now situated in London, England, offered to form and finance a cavalry regiment to aid the cause (the last individual to ever do this). In January of 1900, he began recruiting 537 cowboys, Royal Canadian Mounted Policemen and other hardy, fit men to ride the herd of 599 horses he acquired. These hardened men required limited training and sailed for South Africa in March of 1900. Selected to lead the regiment was Sam Steele, Canada's most famous Mountie, who had ridden west with the original founding troop of RCMP in 1874 to police the west. Steele was born and raised near Orillia, and through that connection Jack likely found his way into Strathcona's Horse.

Strathcona's regiment fought many pitched battles and won many honours but was remembered mostly for their reputation as skilled scouts: daring, wily and adept at working in isolation on their own initiative. Jack sailed home with the regiment at the war's end in January of 1902, receiving regimental medals from King Edward VII himself on the way. It was a short but intense tour of duty for Jack, and after it was all over he was entitled to a free land grant from the Government of Canada in recognition of his service. That's how he ended up in Earlton, in Ontario's far north, learning the lumber industry.

When Walter spent a day with him in July of 1906 tramping around Jack's timber property, Jack had likely been there for a season or two. He would have spent some time after returning from South Africa to consider his future and then scout around for an appropriate location to take his land grant. Remember he showed up in Sault Ste. Marie in July 1903 to help Walter put it to the Quinn brothers and made no mention of his move north to Earlton then. The whole application process for the land grant would have taken months. During that time, he would have made contact with the experienced lumbermen in Orillia to learn that end of the trade. He had grown up, like Walter, working in the lumber mills his father ran so he knew what to do with the timber once it had been cut down; now he was learning how to set up the logging operation. It was likely 1904 or 1905 before he actually started any type of operation in Earlton.

But events overwhelmed him almost as soon as he got to work.

North of Lake Temiskaming was a clay belt of arable land with huge stands of white pine where Jack took his land grant. By 1900, the small settlements that had developed in the region possessed enough commercial interests to justify the building of a railway to connect them to civilization. In 1903, the Toronto and Northern Ontario railway (the T & NO) stretched the 100 miles north from North Bay to the Temiskaming region.

A bold fox, one day, inadvertently set off a chain of events that transformed the region forever, far more than the railway ever would. That fox stole one of the railway navvies' lunch. When Fred LaRose threw his hammer at it to get his lunch back, the resulting chipped rock revealed a vein of silver. Soon there were headlines all across Canada of the discovery that was eventually to produce 460 million ounces of silver, more than all the gold taken out of the Klondike in the last big prospecting rush less than a decade earlier. LaRose, seeing his opportunity, ended up a millionaire.

The big silver rush didn't start until the spring of 1905, but swarms of prospectors, some experienced, most raw greenhorns looking for the get-rich-quick windfall, flooded into the Cobalt region 15 kilometers south of Haileybury that spring. A tent city developed there in typical hodgepodge fashion as men threw up shelters and raced to the bush as fast as they could to stake claims and get digging. Rumours of men picking up $15,000 of loose nuggets in a day were rampant. The hangers-on arrived too, the bootleggers, provisioners and con men who also saw their opportunity to make their fortunes. In the end, 13 major mines flourished after buying up and consolidating staked claims, making their owners millionaires. They paid their miners $3.25 a day to dig up the silver, far more than the $1.25 a day Walter could get as an experienced shingler. The veins of silver here were long and straight and pure, money just waiting to be scraped out of the ground.

In 1906, the Cobalt mine stocks were the talk of the New York stock exchange. As the prospectors sold out to larger mining interests that consolidated into major mining operations, stock in those companies was offered to investors. In New York City, mounted police had to clear the streets of excited investors who were obstructing traffic in their frantic efforts to buy shares from curbside brokers.[1] In 1908, the Temiskaming region was producing 9% of the world's silver! But it was exhausted rapidly, mostly by 1912, though operations straggled on until 1930. The petering out only led the prospectors farther afield and resulted in the Porcupine gold rush of 1909 and the Kirkland Lake gold rush of 1912, just 80 and 150 kilometers north of Haileybury.

The state of the hysteria is documented in Stephen Leacock's *Sunshine Sketches of a Little Town*, his humourous satire of small town Ontario life in 1912. Leacock, writing about characters in Walter's hometown of Orillia, devoted a whole chapter to Jefferson Thorpe, the barber who became rich speculating in Cobalt silver and then lost it all. Though a fictitious story, it captured the excitement and urgency of the silver boom. "All day in the street you could hear men talking of veins, and smelters and dips and deposits and faults, — the town hummed with it like a geology class on examination day."[2] This was true wherever people had money to invest.

Jack Knox, perhaps as early as 1904, was in Earlton, 45 kilometers to the north, pulling down trees while all this was going on. Coming into Haileybury for supplies in the spring of 1905, he couldn't have avoided the excitement of the big silver rush. Being isolated in the bush far to the north, he might have picked up the odd bit of scuttlebutt earlier, and undoubtedly he would have noticed the increased demand for his lumber as Cobalt and Haileybury began to grow, but in 1905 he was swept up in the boom as thousands of southerners poured off the train in Cobalt and headed into the woods. That's when he caught the fever. It took until the next year, 1906, after Walter agreed to help him, for Jack to head off prospecting seriously, just in time for the next silver rush, the one started by the legendary Jack Munroe.

Jack Munroe was one of those larger-than-life characters bred on the American frontier. Born in Cape Breton, Nova Scotia in 1873, he traveled to the US mid-west and the mining camps in Montana. He learned the mining trade both by studying geology at university and by spending his summers working in mines or prospecting in the hills and mountains of the far west. But he became famous for his athletic abilities. He starred on championship football teams and was renowned for his size and great strength. When the great Jim Jeffries, the world champion heavyweight boxer (and Great White Hope after Jack Johnson won the crown), passed through his mining camp one day in 1902, Munroe made his reputation.

Champion boxers made a good income traveling through small

towns putting on demonstrations and sometimes offering to take on all comers for a fee. In front of a crowd of 1500 miners, Munroe took him up on his challenge that no one could last four rounds with him. Jack knocked the overweight Jeffries down in the fourth round and was skillful enough to deflect the withering counter-attack, landing enough blows to not only survive but be declared the winner of the fight, collecting $500![3]

News of the lowly miner who knocked down the invincible Jim Jeffries spread like wildfire through the west and burned in Jeffries' craw. Munroe started training as a fighter, getting good instruction, and became a real contender for the heavyweight crown after beating several top-rated boxers. Jeffries pursued him, demanding a chance to redeem himself, claiming he was badly out of shape in Montana. When Munroe was finally groomed enough, he accepted the challenge in California in 1904, creating national excitement when the papers announced the World Championship fight. It was a horrible mismatch. Jeffries pummeled him, winning by technical knockout in just the second round.

Munroe retired from the fight game after that humbling and landed in Cobalt in 1905 to get in on the silver rush. His geology background gave him a huge head start on the greenhorns and he staked a few successful claims in the region. He also started promoting boxing and wrestling as a diversion for the weary miners. He was integral in building a Sport's Palace in Cobalt to bring professional boxers there for bouts. Munroe created opportunities for locals to show their toughness with the gloves on and soon was promoting wrestling and other events as well, a significant turn of events for Walter. Munroe was likely the largest man in Cobalt both in physique and in reputation by 1906.

In the spring of 1906, Jack Munroe, sensing he had exhausted his prospects in crowded Cobalt, made the decision to move on to a new territory, a move that started the next chapter in his legend. He and four partners, grubstaked by a local wealthy miner, paddled

50 miles northwest up the Montreal River to serene Elk Lake. Grubstaking prospectors was a common practice by the mine owners of "Millionaire's Row" living along the shoreline in Haileybury. They used men who couldn't afford to stake themselves to do the prospecting for them, thus earning a share in whatever discoveries they made. To avoid having to take on a silent partner in this way, Walter, after catching "gold fever" from his brother, went back on the hustling circuit that summer of 1906 to earn a grubstake for him and Jack. Like the veins of silver in the region, the Knox boys had a long and straight and pure vein of independence in their backbones and had no intention of taking on a silent partner.

Munroe and his partners, including wrestling champion Joe Acton, set up camp on this secluded lake near the one settler who was eking out a living there. Elk Lake was 15 miles long and a stone's throw wide, really just a widening of the river, but spectacularly scenic. That one settler was going to be appalled at what was about to happen in his remote paradise. Soon Munroe spotted the tell-tale quartz deposits indicating silver, and they staked a number of claims that ended up being in the heart of a massive series of silver deposits. When they traveled back to Haileybury in December, 1906, to register their claims and get their ores assayed, the rush was on. Jack Knox followed the crowd and got in on the ground floor, staking some reasonable claims around Elk Lake either that winter or in the spring, when the real rush began.

Prospecting was a hard life. Living in a tent in forty below weather was a challenge even for the hardiest of men. It took experience to get anything accomplished outdoors. The snow crusted and stuck heavily to boots, due to the innumerable and unavoidable bogs and streams creating hidden wet areas. Where the water was flowing, softening the crust, many a miner suffered frostbite or worse, trudging home with a soaked foot. Snowshoes were a necessity as prospectors tramped into the bush all winter looking for likely claims, trying to outrace the greenhorns who would inevitably show up with the warm weather. The prospectors had to navigate unbroken trails, thick underbrush and fallen trees to get to the treacherous, icy rocky ledges, where the rock could be examined for mineral content, to do their work. All supplies had to be hauled into Elk Lake by canoe, up rapids and over three portages, until freeze-up in mid-November, when it became a 50 mile trudge. Along the way, there was one abandoned lumber camp that provided a cabin to shelter in. It would have been reminiscent of Jack Knox's camp, abandoned for the dream of rich silver veins. Only a few adventurers followed the Munroe group back up to Elk Lake that January of 1907, but Jack Knox was very possibly among them, or at least with the first out in the spring.

It was bitterly cold that winter. There was no thermometer, the Munroe group recorded on January 13, "Very cold, Neil's face froze several times. We had to watch each other at all times to keep from freezing".[4] Jack Knox, though hardened from the war and two years cutting timber in the bush, would have had a very hard time bushwhacking on his own. He never mentioned any partner but Walter.

It had taken the world almost two years to react to the Cobalt silver strike. They were not caught unawares this time at Elk Lake. The Montreal River route became a highway in the spring of 1907 as prospectors raced to get their claims staked. The rush intensified when a load of silver arrived in Haileybury in May. Twenty-five canoes a day were leaving by then. In the summer of 1907, a branch line of the T & NO railway reached within 25 miles of Elk Lake, cutting the trek there by half. In 1908, a boat service made it even easier to access. The trip involved four different steamers and three portages but was easier than canoeing or walking, especially when carrying silver out.

Thousands of miners pitched their tents along the shores of Elk Lake that summer, a new tent city, and the moonshiners and their blind pigs followed. Even faster than in Cobalt, a semblance of a town developed and services like stores, banks, doctors and entertainments began to pop up. This was largely due to Jack Munroe's leadership. He had staked all the land where the town developed and made a fortune selling lots off to businessmen. Munroe, the wealthiest and most respected resident, became the first Reeve of the newly incorporated township, essentially mayor of Elk Lake, in 1909.

Walter, fresh off his hustling of the big Negro Henry Batson in Corry, Pennsylvania and the big track meets in Orillia and Hamilton, hopped on the T & NO railway and met up with his brother Jack in Cobalt in October of 1906, just before the Elk Lake rush started. In the four months since Jack first dragged him up there to see his land grant in Earlton, Walter had pocketed a bankroll of over $1500 (that we know about) from his sporting ventures. Meanwhile, Jack had been maneuvering through the crowded Cobalt prospecting region looking for unstaked areas where he could get to work. There were slim pickings left as Jack Munroe had concluded. But Jack Knox was getting experience and learning how to prospect. When Walter showed up, they would have had to make some decisions about their mining future; obviously Cobalt wasn't going to be the place to get rich. But as every other prospector there knew, it was inevitable more silver or gold would be found; one just had to be in the right place to get in on the bonanza. In December, Walter headed back to Orillia, now Jack's "silent partner" having grubstaked him (though he would have kept a good portion of his wad to seed his next season of hustling). Jack was to keep poking around, while Walter waited for his call to join him to dig up whatever claim he could stake in the next big rush.

Less than a month after Walter headed south, the next rush was on. Jack Munroe had shown up in Haileybury just as Walter was leaving, with a pouch of silver and a sheaf of maps for the claims he was registering around Elk Lake. The race was on, and Jack was there, in the right place at the right time, with Walter's cash in his pocket! Thousands of other frustrated prospectors were there in Cobalt too; now it was a matter of who could get out there first in the forty below weather. Jack would have sent a letter off to Walter in Orillia telling him where he was going, and then made arrangements to leave as soon as he thought feasible. The mine owners of Millionaire's Row immediately grubstaked their own teams who got off to a real advantage. It was one of these teams that sent the first shipment of silver, mined around Elk Lake before the snow even melted, back to Haileybury in May, 1907, that started the big rush. Jack couldn't wait for Walter, and would need more money anyway, so he headed off alone and Walter went off to make more money in the hustling season of 1907, expecting to join up with Jack and get down to work in the fall.

15

A Magnificent Day, Except For... "The Photo"

In January of 1907, as Jack was trembling with the news of the Elk Lake strike, Walter was home in Orillia with his parents. He had been contacted by friends on the west coast about a university coaching job available in Portland, Oregon they said he was perfect for. Walter, not particularly interested but always keeping his options open, let them make inquiries for him. The officials at Forest Grove University, upon reading his qualifications, indicated the job as coach of their sports teams was his for the taking.

But before Walter had even decided if he was going to take the job, a letter arrived in Orillia from Archie Hahn, the Milwaukee Meteor, who had beaten Walter in the 100 final at the Big 9 conference meet, with a deal to consider. He had heard of Walter's opportunity and said he had the same "sure" offer to coach at the Montana Agricultural College in Bozeman, Montana. This job offer was not exactly what he was looking for, but he was attracted to the Forest Grove job. Hahn was a recent graduate of the University of Michigan, a university man, and he wanted to stay at that level. Walter was more of a workingman; he'd be a better fit at the agricultural college, Hahn suggested. Would Walter like to switch? The result was that they each declined their offers and highly recommended the other in his place. It worked.

So in February of 1907, well before the hustling season started, Walter headed west to become a coach. When the college president flattered him at his reception, Walter set to work with "a will and determination to make my presence felt". Walter was well aware coaching was against the CAAU amateur code. But he had flaunted that code so often in the west, it didn't seem to concern him. What he didn't understand was that the Athletic Wars had just started, with the Montreal block of AAAs forming their own Federation in competition with the CAAU. The resulting rapid expansion of the CAAU into every part of Canada in 1907 meant there were many more eyes observing and reporting on professional activities all across the country. Walter probably felt this small, out-of-the-way college was never going to be noticed by the CAAU. He was wrong.

Hahn dropped in on Walter in Bozeman on his way to the coast and ran a few exhibition races with Walter and his charges as a show of thanks to Walter. The college president even gave the students a half day holiday to attend the exhibition by the former world record holder.

Walter's first order of business was whipping the baseball team into shape. In recent years they had taken some beatings, but with focused instruction, they improved in 1907 and began winning their games. The local newspaper described Walter as "particularly up on team play", and Walter put his two best athletes at shortstop and behind the plate where quick thinking and agility were most important.[1] Individual players began having their photos taken for the papers, and after they beat the big University of Montana, a team photo was printed in the paper with Walter front and center as coach. That photo was to be his amateur undoing, a matter-of-fact, routine photo in a backwoods American newspaper.

Walter's athletic career almost ended that spring in a freak accident after one of these big baseball wins. In the rally after a game on the Bozeman campus, an anvil was "fired" in some sort of celebration and flew through the air to hit Walter square in the thigh! The paper said Walter had "severe bruises" and was lucky to have no broken bones.[2]

Walter's track team had an undefeated season too. It was evident that not only was Walter a student of the science of sport, he could communicate his knowledge too. Not all top athletes can coach. Being able to excel at an endeavour doesn't mean you know why you excel or that you can impart that knowledge coherently. Given the sudden success of the baseball and track teams (not to mention the dominant women's basketball team) it was apparent Walter was a top notch coach.

With the end of the school year in May, Walter decided to head home to Toronto for the Canadian Track and Field Championships. His time in Bozeman had allowed him ample opportunity to get in top shape and he was confident he could win a number of events. Walter left Bozeman "blithe and gay" with a promise to return the next spring to take up where he left off. The college athletics season nicely filled the spring months before the hustling season started and Bozeman was a fine place to prepare. He had been paid $350 for less than 4 months' work.

The CAAU Championships were a one-day affair to be held at Hanlan's Point on Toronto Island June 8th. All the great athletes associated with the CAAU were entered, but only one Montreal club (the Gordon AC) was represented; the rest were bound to their affiliation with the new AAFC, the Quebec-based rival organization created to start the Athletic Wars in Canada. In Walter's events, most of the best athletes in Canada were entered: Bobby Kerr in the 100, Ed Archibald in the pole vault, big Tim O'Rourke in the shot put and Cal Bricker in the long jump, all Canadian champions, all in their primes.

After the competition, the newspaper remarked that there "was a good deal of hard feelings between Knox and Kerr, Bricker and Archibald and he was determined to give them all a beating".[3] Now in his prime, at 29 years of age and in "perfect condition", as one paper reported, Walter saw this as his opportunity to put it to his rivals and really show them who was Canada's top athlete. Walter had that type of ego and tended to show disdain and little respect for his rivals. As the quote above shows, they were not too well disposed towards him either. Walter was adept at playing "head games" before a race, an important skill in the hustling world where winning was all that mattered. But in the amateur world, that kind of behaviour was frowned upon and created ill feelings. While Walter was quick to make amicable and long-lasting friendships with those who could help him, he just as easily burned bridges with competitors who were in his way.

Walter arrived in Toronto a day before the championships and did a light workout at the Central Y, the team for which he would be competing. After doing his turns, Walter was surprised to find that Coach Crocker himself would be giving him his rubdown; Crocker needed some quiet time to talk to Walter as he had some bad news. A challenge to Walter's amateur status was going to be made in the morning, he said, by the president of the West End YMCA.

One of the baseball players Walter had coached at Bozeman had a close friend on the West End team. He had proudly, and innocently, sent him the picture of the winning baseball team, with Walter front and center listed as the coach. Walter was spotted instantly; he had a notorious reputation at the West End Y.[4] Of course, as everyone knew, coaching was a breach of the amateur rules; you were receiving financial compensation for your athletic expertise and that made you a professional. The West End Y had made inquiries and the president of the Montana Agricultural College in Bozeman had dutifully sent a letter saying that he had, indeed, paid Walter $350 to coach the college's sports teams that spring. There were further allegations that Walter had competed under assumed names on more than one occasion but those were only supported by hearsay evidence. The West Enders didn't need that to make their case against Walter anyway, the coaching was enough to professionalize him. He was going to be called out as a professional in the morning.

But then Crocker informed him that he could still compete under protest. Until Walter had his hearing, he could compete, but wouldn't be awarded any medals until a decision was made.

"Get in there and show them what you can do! It may be your last chance to show them," Crocker urged.

The West End and Central YMCAs in Toronto had a bitter rivalry. Crocker knew Walter wouldn't be able to score points to help him win the meet but he could score personal points with the West End coach by putting it to his athletes. He knew Walter would feel the same way. Walter remarked that around the West End Y he "was poison", and there were "great gleams of glee" around that Y while the investigation was going on.

Walter, for his part, felt no ill will towards the people calling him out. He had resigned himself to that fact he would be called out one day. He only regretted he never had the chance to win a big all-around title: Harry Gill kept him out of the North American championship in Buffalo in 1901 and the Milwaukee Athletic Club blocked his entry to take on world champion Kiely at the Olympics in 1904. Now Crocker broke the news that he had planned to send him to the North American All-Around Championships that summer in Jamestown where, he said, no one was close to the scores he could put up. (In actual fact, in setting, shattering, the amateur world all-around record that summer, American Martin Sheridan posted marks that would have split the events 5 each, given what Walter was able to do at that time. It would have been very close, except Sheridan didn't enter the 1907 North American Championship. Walter would have won easily as Crocker said, with a reasonable performance[5]).

Walter wrote he "had no regrets about capitalizing on what gift or ability I had been endowed... I had my fun as I found it."[6] But now he felt he owed his "old friend" Crocker something. "He wanted a good score run up for good old Central? Why not?"

So, at the Canadian Championships, where Walter was entered in six events, he was going to show the world how good he really was. It was his last chance.

Saturday was a beautiful day, "perfect weather" the papers reported. Over 7000 spectators took the ferry ride to the Island Oval field to see the big event. It was the largest event ever in Canada, according to the sports reporters, and efficiently run, a cutting salvo in the Athletic Wars since the renegade Montreal AAA was the traditional host of the Canadian Championships.

Right on schedule, as Walter prepared for the first heat of the 100-yard dash, the protest of his status was flashed. After some discussion between Coach Crocker and the officials, the meet carried on as expected, with Walter under the dark cloud of professional accusations.

Walter would run in the first heat alongside Bobby Kerr. He had proved to himself he could beat Kerr in Hamilton last summer in the rain, even though the race was fixed. Some sports writers had brushed Walter off as a fluke or claimed his win only resulted from the "cheap talk" on the starting line. This was the big test for the both of them; Kerr's Canadian Championship was on the line.

Of course, now that Walter was professionalized the betting prohibitions were off too. His brother Will, no stranger to the gambling world, was in the crowd, and he had Walter's wad of cash to work with. Walter was as intent on making a profit as he would be at any other contest.

The sprint and hurdles races were run on the "greensward of the center field", that is on the grass field. Needless to say, this was much slower than a cinder track would have been, and duly affected the times.

In this first race, an elimination 75 yard sprint to establish the line-up for the two semi-final heats to come, Walter uncharacteristically jumped the gun. The starter bawled him out and set him back a yard for the next start. Walter and the starter had a short jawing match before they settled down again. As Walter said, "I was establishing to everyone that Kerr had one yard advantage, and, forcing the starter to be on his toes to send us away on even terms."[7] Well, that's what Walter told the reporters after the race. Years later, he confessed he had a bet down that he would beat Kerr by a yard in the 75 heat and was announcing to the gambler in the crowd the stage was set for the bet.[8] Walter won that race with a strong finish, in spite of Kerr's taunts he was a sloppy finisher. Message sent, bet won.

They matched up again in the first 100-yard semi-final heat. Kerr won that race by a foot in 10 3/5 seconds. Sebert of the West End Y won the second heat in the same time. More chatter came from Kerr about Walter's weak finish. Kerr was trying to give Walter a taste of his own medicine; resentment lingered over Walter's treatment of him last summer. Those in the know considered Kerr a sure thing in the 100. He had won 39 straight races that year since his last loss, to Walter, in the rain, in Hamilton.

Newspaper photo of Walter (left) narrowly losing to Bobby Kerr (center) in the semi-final race at the 1907 Canadian Championships.
Courtesy of Orillia Museum of Art and History

Then came the big final. Standing side by side behind the starting line, Kerr and Knox looked remarkably similar: both were diminutive for champions in a strength event like sprinting. At 5' 7", Kerr was one inch shorter than Walter, and 5 pounds lighter at 144 pounds. But both were lean, fit and confident, though Kerr was four years younger at 25 years old and lacked Walter's receding hairline. There was no love lost between the two star attractions, and everyone could see it. Bystanders told reporters that Walter got Kerr's nerve at the starting line by growling, "I'll beat you today, Kerr!" They were both off fast at the gun but Walter pulled away in the final yards to win by a yard, putting Kerr and his chatter to rest. The time was a slow 10 2/5 seconds, but fast given the soft, slippery racecourse. The Olympic champion was no longer the best, even in his own country. After that, Kerr didn't enter his specialty, the 220.

Next up was the running long jump. Walter's competition was Cal Bricker of the West End Y. Twenty-two year old Bricker, the Canadian Champion, would go on to win the bronze medal at the Olympics the next summer in London and a silver four years later in Stockholm. Walter wrote he had nothing against the talented Bricker, but as a West Ender, Bricker was intent on beating Walter. Again running on the grass, Walter won with a leap of 21' 8". Another Central Y athlete, George Barber, came in second at 21' 4" with the past champion, Bricker, third at 20' 10". Walter commented that Bricker was capable of leaping just as far as he was, but always seemed to falter under pressure. No doubt Walter helped him feel the pressure here.

The pole vault was the most popular event of the afternoon with the crowd. Every cleared leap elicited a roar of approval. The vault, with its stiff 12 foot poles, was always a novel spectacle the audience appreciated as the athletes risked injury every time they dropped those 10 feet to the sand pits. The crowd was treated to a close competition that day.

Only three athletes cleared 10' 8", Walter, Cameron of the Central Y and Ed Archibald of the West End Y. Remember, Archibald was the Central Y star when Walter first showed up in Toronto a year back, specifically to embarrass him on his own turf. Archibald immediately left Central for the West End Y in a huff after that humiliation. He had represented Canada at the Athens Olympics and now had cleared well over 11 feet in practice. He was Canada's star pole vaulter and would be for years to come.

With the bar raised to 11' 1", just above the Canadian record height of 11 feet, only Walter was successful in clearing it, and this in spite of a badly sprained thumb that made gripping the pole painful. It was his third win of the day. However, when officials re-measured the bar to confirm the new record, they found it was only 11 feet, so Walter had only tied the Canadian record again. Cameron and Archibald had to jump off for second place (really the gold medal, given Walter's questionable status) and Cameron won, this time clearing 11 feet and tying the record as well. Walter did not try to raise the record as he probably could have, given the heights he had cleared at other (unofficial) times; there were more fish to fry on that busy day. Unknown to Walter, at the Canadian Championships held by the rival AAFC in Montreal that summer, William Halpenny, user of the infamous candy-striped pole Walter had so disdained in Hamilton the year before, cleared 11' 5 ½" to set the new Canadian standard. This was one of the most competitive events in Canada.

Next up was big Tim O'Rourke, the dominant shot putter from Toronto, representing the Irish Canadian Athletic Club. Six years earlier, when Walter was returning from his short shingling stint in Newfoundland, he had dropped in on O'Rourke while passing through Toronto. O'Rourke had tried to embarrass Walter in a shot putting exhibition only to learn the hard way how quick and tough Walter was. Walter never forgot slights like that. This was their first (and last) meeting in an athletics meet. O'Rourke, at least six inches taller and 80 pounds heavier than Walter, was the heavy favourite. But once they got down to business, it was no contest as O'Rourke could only post a weak effort of 34 feet with the 16 pound ball. Walter, still less than 150 pounds dripping wet, came up with an impressive 41' 1" effort to win in decisive fashion. News reports said O'Rourke's effort was "away off colour" and otherwise he would never have lost. But Walter's put was as far as O'Rourke had ever done, and not even up to his own standard.

Walter met O'Rourke again that day in the hammer throw. It was the one bad mark on Walter's day. He failed to register a throw, fouling out each time. O'Rourke got his moment in the sun here.

Finally there was the discus, one of Walter's weaker events. The favourite was Latremouille of the Toronto Police Athletic Club, a six foot, 190 pounder, though O'Rourke was entered too. Walter's throw of 105' 1" won the day against 99' 1" for Latremouille and 97' 6" for O'Rourke.

Five events, five wins, all against the best there was in Canada in their specialties. Not only that, Walter competed in many more events than any of his opponents and had to overcome the fatigue that went along with his busy day too. There were only two Canadian Records set in the whole meet: Walter's pole vault and a 5 mile run by Coley of St. Catherines. Though conditions were perfect, the performances were not as outstanding as expected, mostly due to the poor facility (it was a clay track, much slower than the modern cinder tracks at other fields). Walter put up strong marks in all his events, but none were personal bests. Mostly he was there to beat the competition, and he did.

Newspapers across Canada initially highlighted Walter as the star of the meet then later reported the professional allegations overshadowing his efforts. "Canada's Greatest All Around Athlete", "The greatest all-around athlete Canada ever saw", "Knox Dominated", "The all-around Canadian champion cleaned up"; the reports were very positive and hyperbolic. Over the next few days, reports of Walter's professionalism hearing were equally sensational, and added fuel to the amateur-professional debate raging in sporting circles across the country. Still, they didn't tarnish the admiration of his pure athletic performances.

Walter's final comment, scribbled in his own hand 40 years later in the margin of his typed notes, was a sad, "five prizes but I didn't collect any of them".

Later that week, the YMCA League of Canada, who had jurisdiction over the championships as host, held the hearing. Presiding over the meeting was, ominously, NJ Stevenson, President of the West End YMCA, the organizer of the championships. He was also the person who had laid the charges against Walter! The newspaper reports said there was little discussion and no hesitation as Walter was expelled from the amateur ranks. They had the photo with his title as coach and the letter from the college president saying he had been paid. The rules were abundantly clear: a lifetime ban from all amateur sport. That was that.

Central's team championship was revoked in favour of the West End Y. Without Walter's contribution, Central lost by a mere 4 points.

Then, the very next day, a new accusation arose, as reported in one paper. Walter was to be charged with criminal perjury. The accusers (likely West End Y officials) claimed Walter had signed an affidavit almost two years earlier that was on record at the Central YMCA, declaring he had never done anything to breach the amateur code. It was stated the Central Y requested this before they would give him an amateur card when he first arrived in Toronto. Furthermore, the accusation continued, there were allegations, made at the time, that Walter had run under assumed names prior to his signing that affidavit, which was also on record at the Central Y, but ignored. The Central Y denied all the allegations, said the spurious claims of running under assumed names was just hearsay and rightly ignored, then threatened reprisals against West End athletes. The paper reported "there may be a police investigation" of the perjury charges.[9]

For his part, Walter denied ever signing an affidavit, and in all likelihood, never would have. He was meticulous in protecting himself and surely would have tried to talk his way out of signing a legal document he knew was a blatant falsehood.

It was all "a shot in the dark", as Walter put it, and amounted to nothing; more posturing between two rival YMCA teams.

Before leaving town on June 15th, Walter left one parting shot when he talked to reporters:

> *"I am going to Boston to compete in the semi-monthly professional games. I want to tell all of you before I leave that there are two or three more* YMCA *men who cannot take that amateur affidavit. What about the West End pole vaulter who competed at Uno up in New Ontario last summer where money prizes were put up? There are a couple of runners up there who have taken money too and, by the way, certain West End officers are pretty busy these days offering good outside men soft jobs in town to come and wear their colors."* [10]

Of course he never went to Boston. This meet was always just a prelude to the hustling season.

16

A Tour of Michigan

Being professionalized took a monkey off Walter's back and seemed to change his attitude. He no longer had to worry about what the snobs in the AAAs were thinking, no longer had to avoid opportunities for fear of being outed. He was going hustling and was going to make as much money as he could. But he became more brazen and cavalier too, hurting his ability to draw out matches. This was a problem since he and Jack corresponded regularly so he knew his brother was making progress at Elk Lake, putting pressure on Walter to get a wad of cash together so they could expand Jack's operation in the fall.

Walter headed to a proven sports betting ground at the July first holiday games in Sault Ste. Marie, where the Quinn boys were still holding court. Walter won nine events there. The betting probably wasn't as brisk as it had been four years earlier, given Walter was a known commodity now, but there would have been a decent take over that number of events, especially since the Quinns were as dominant and popular as ever.

Then, on the recommendation of a well-known "sport", or gambler, named Barr, Walter passed up on the meet in the American Soo to travel to Bessemer, Michigan, near the south coast of Lake Superior 400 miles to the west, for their July 4th games and better betting prospects.

Who did he find on the entry list when he got there but Archie Hahn! They had a good visit. Archie teased Walter about getting the better of their job switch. It seemed that the Forest Grove University faculty Hahn worked for actually put academics ahead of athletics and frustrated many of his initiatives, where Walter's Montana Agricultural College faculty heartily supported the sports teams, even canceling classes for big sports events. Archie said he was relieved when the term was over and he could get out of there. But Archie, a lawyer who never practiced law, went on to a long, successful career as a track coach, excelling at Princeton and Virginia and eventually writing the "the bible" of sprinting texts, *"How To Sprint"*.

Archie asked what Walter's plans were for the summer and Walter said his friend, Barr, was taking him on a tour of Michigan looking for matched races. Archie, a Michigan native, discouraged him, claiming the matches were tough to come by, the betters were tight-wads and the locals were rough, tough men. Faced with two opposing viewpoints of the prospects for hustling, Walter opted to follow the gambler Barr.

First up were the July 4th games in Bessemer. A local hotshot, Charles Williamson, was entered against Walter and Archie. They let him win the 100-yard dash. Then, in the 50, the starter let him off with a false start. Archie set off to run him down but fell a yard short. Walter held back again, but went into action as soon as the race was over. Storming up to the officials, Walter lodged a loud and angry protest about how the local man was getting favourable treatment. It was "bald-faced" he yelled belligerently. That gathered a crowd. Archie, sensing trouble, backed away, leaving Walter to his doom.

Then Walter yelled for all to hear, "I can beat him by two yards in 50!"

The crowd jumped at the challenge, waving their wallets in the air. A few of the locals got nasty and Walter took a swift kick to the shins. Walter glanced up to see the I-told-you-so look on Archie's face, but then, red-faced and determined, he followed through on his provocation. Coiled taut as a spring, he cowed the crowd with a show of bravado, looking for his assailant and staring down the loudest loudmouth in the crowd. It was a huge risk as he could have taken a beating, but it worked; a match race was set up with Williamson for July 13th, 9 days hence, and the wild crowd was ready to put their money down against this upstart hothead. Walter was just talking their language.[1]

Barr took Walter to nearby Ironwood to train while Williamson engaged Hahn as his coach. Traveling back to Bessemer for the week, Barr then acted as Walter's betting agent, using the wad Walter had brought with him.

The day of the race, a stranger, attracted by Walter's independent spirit, offered a warning. A couple of toughs were waiting for him on the train platform, he said, who were going to pick a fight. The plan was to get him thrown in jail so he'd have to miss the race and lose his forfeit. It was good advice, Walter found, and sure enough he was immediately accosted by three "pug-uglies" stepping off the train in Bessemer. They tried to provoke him but, knowing their plan, Walter was able to talk his way into a position to get away.[2]

The racecourse was down the main street on packed dirt as hard as concrete. Williamson turned up with an axe to chop holes for starting blocks. He refused to let Walter borrow it, but when he set it down, Walter grabbed it and got a few of good chops in before a couple of Williamson's backers wrestled it away. It got Walter enough of a toe-hold started to make a difference.

It didn't really matter though, as the race was no contest; Walter won with little challenge, collected his winnings and got out of town.

Over the next month, Walter traveled around Lake Superior with Barr using many names like "Thompson" or "Renwick" or "Johnson". He was reckless and casual now that he was a true professional, and made little effort to hide the fact that he was not what he professed to be, using his racing outfit and spiked shoes. As one paper remarked, "He claimed he was no runner but it took him no time to find his much used track suit[3]".

His first stop was Ishpeming, a little farther west, where he won a 100-yard race, then went on to athletic meets in Milwaukee and Livingston, Wisconsin before finally getting another matched race, with none other than Archie Hahn. In some of these races he was working against himself, as witnessed by the race report in one paper, "He got such a lead in the first fifty or seventy-five feet that he looked back at the others and beckoned them on!"[4] It was very uncharacteristic behaviour for an experienced hustler trying to coax out matches.

Winning events so flagrantly in all these towns under different names started a guessing game for local running enthusiasts and newspaper reporters as to Walter's true identity. Walter made the mistake of being too obvious in his use of aliases, carelessly not taking his identity seriously. Newspapers ran headlines like, "Under What Name Will He Run Next?" Reporters, determined to identify him, calling him the "galloping unknown", circulated his photo, looking for information about him. This kind of attention is not what a hustler wants, but Walter seemed to be enjoying the whole charade.

Walter didn't help his case by posing a challenge in the newspaper to take on any Michigan athlete in any one of 12 events for $100 a side.[5] He was clearly a professional; the papers accused him of being a hustler and warned off anyone thinking of taking him up on his proposition. Reporters sent his photo to colleges all over the states, from New York to Oregon, looking for information. After one race the local paper reported,

> *"We are soon to know who this Johnson or Renwick is as several good pictures were taken of him and have been sent to several colleges in the States for information. We all admit he greatly outclassed Evejeth and won the race*

fair and square but it was a rotten trick. Someone must be hard up."[6]

The match race with Hahn should have been high profile. Archie was an acknowledged college champion, one of the fastest men in America. But it was a race for a mere $40 a side, nothing like you'd expect for a big race between the college and Olympic star against the renowned and mysterious "galloping ghost". Walter saved no newspaper article about the match, if there were any. The terms of the race gave Walter a 4 foot head start over a 65 yard course, a sign of Hahn's reputation. Then Walter won by 10 feet! Given Hahn's credentials and ability (he was a sub-10 second man in the 100 who had held the world record and won three Olympic gold medals) it seems unbelievable he could lose that badly. Walter hardly mentions this match in his book, making the whole affair hard to untangle. It was most likely a fixed race to cash in on an unsuspecting crowd. Walter needed a big fish to get the gamblers to open their wallets.[7]

This match had an interesting, and telling, epilogue. A month later, sportswriter Lou Marsh in Toronto published a short article about this race. His point was not who had won but that Hahn had raced a professional, Walter, and yet maintained his AAU amateur card. (He also reported Walter relieved a local sucker of a $500 wager on Hahn in that race).[8] This was a shot across the bow in the Athletic Wars. Marsh's Toronto paper was an organ of the CAAU and was trying to discredit the upstart AAFC and its ally, the American AAU, which Hahn represented.

Walter, then back in Toronto on his way north, wrote that he stormed into Marsh's office and demanded a retraction, asserting that he had never run a race against Hahn in Michigan as he had reported, and threatened that if no retraction followed, "he better be a good fighter or a good runner". The next week, Marsh duly published a short letter Walter had given him denying the race ever took place.[9] In his private notes, Walter followed up this anecdote saying, "I never ran any footrace in Michigan but did in Wisconsin"[10], describing the race again. Walter had been disingenuous and misleading, but technically truthful, and that was consistent with his code of ethics. This again smells of a fixed race with a successful hustle of a gambler's wad, followed by Walter's bullying defense of his friend's amateur status. One did what one had to on the professional circuit.

A further twist in the story came soon after when an American writer, Sullivan, likely James Sullivan, President of the AAU, wrote a long piece defending Hahn's honour, in direct contradiction to Walter's position.[11] Yes, the race was run, he said, but Hahn was already an openly and honourably professed professional at the time, having informed the AAU of his coaching job at Forest Grove University. Sullivan was only concerned with protecting Hahn's reputation, most likely after talking to him personally. Maybe this was Hahn's response. In any case, Walter came out looking bad from any angle: either a dirty hustler or a bullying liar. It took a lot of political savvy or abundant self-deception to maintain an upright moral code in the world of professional running, Walter knew, and sometimes one or the other would get exposed. Luckily the whole issue faded away after that and Walter moved on.

By this time, Archie's warning that matched races in Michigan were hard to come by was proving to be true.

From Wisconsin, Walter and Barr headed back to Hancock, Michigan and the big Irish games put on by the Ancient Order of Hibernians. Walter was hoping to set up a match with a local hotshot. "I was tempted to take the name of 'Casey' or 'Muldoon'", Walter said, "but that was carrying things too far".[12]

When the starter called the sprinters up to the line for the race, Walter crouched down right beside Dooley, the local hero. Without moving a muscle on his face, Dooley elbowed Walter, the mysterious hustler, in the ribs, almost knocking the wind out of him. Angered and bruised, Walter made sure he won the race and then confronted Dooley nose to nose. The end result was that Dooley wouldn't run another race with Walter under any circumstances. Another hustling opportunity lost in Michigan.

Next, Walter entered the games in Marquette, Michigan, (as "Johaneson" even trying to fake a Swedish accent to fit in to this immigrant community), winning several events and the few dollars that went along with them but striking out on matches yet again. Likewise, Walter's open offer again made there to take on anyone in any of 12 different events was ignored; his dominating performance in the games intimidated any takers. He wasn't being very smart as a hustler in Michigan.

Finally, in the next town, back in Ironwood, he was found out. The local movie house owner had figured him out after corresponding with a police detective friend in Toronto who knew all about Walter's exploits. Word spread; Walter was the Canadian All-Around champion. That was the end of the Galloping Ghost's Michigan sojourn.

By now it was mid-September, 1907. It hadn't been a very lucrative summer for Walter, and Jack would be waiting in Elk Lake for his cash for winter supplies before freeze-up. Looking for a fresh start, Walter headed back across the Canadian border to Port Arthur. As he said, "I was rather glad to be Walter Knox once more, my galaxy of names having become birdensome (sic) and it was hard to keep track of just who I was and when"[13]. Here he stepped right into a shot putting contest, with the kind of stakes that were more to his liking.

A 250 pound behemoth, Constable Hein, was challenging all comers in an 8, 12 or 16 pound shot put match for $250. Walter seemed to have found his head again here and was wary. When he heard Hein had never been extended, Walter only offered to put up $50 on the two lighter weights, hedging his bet. If he was really that good, it would be no problem getting down a big bet on the largest ball.

With a week to prepare, Walter was likely able to get some

significant bets down, here in a gambling town, a nice change from the slim pickings in the States. Throwing first with the 8 pounder, Walter tossed it out 52 feet 8 inches, a mark just eight feet short of the world record. He wasn't taking any chances. Hein's put was 9 feet shorter. With the 12 pounder, Walter was again a full 5 feet farther. That was that; Hein wanted nothing to do with the 16 pound shot against Walter.

Then two old "acquaintances" made their appearance. Walter had responded to a challenge in the paper for a matched sprint for up to $1000 a side, with his own public acceptance in the paper. The runner was Alf Cooper, whom Walter had raced here two years earlier on his way out west. In that race, Walter couldn't drum up any bets so let Cooper win. Cooper was confident of another win now and had good backing in the town, having beaten several good runners in the meantime. Soon the second "old friend" made his presence known. It was Fred Mitchell from Fernie! Walter had double crossed him in a big race in Nelson and outwitted him in the re-match to take his forfeit money in 1904. Mitchell was a dirty-dealer, a fixer of races who would stoop low to come out on top. He was handling Cooper now.

It didn't take Mitchell long to approach Walter with a deal. He wanted Walter to put up only $200 (instead of the $1000 stake) but agree to lose again. Money could be made from side bets they would share. Walter played for time. He found, through a friend, (he seemed to have one in every town), a wealthy, eccentric Englishman backer who would take all the bets Mitchell wanted to lay on Cooper if Walter could double cross him again. "Let's teach the bally rotter a lesson!" was his motive, needing only Walter's word that he could beat Cooper. With that arrangement in his back pocket, Walter found Mitchell and took the deal, passing over $200 to guarantee he wouldn't double cross him again.

This race caught the town's attention. Cooper was a real local hero who commanded a lot of faithful support there. Newspaper articles predicted the race would draw the largest crowd ever assembled in the district. The runners gave themselves a week to prepare and get their bets laid. Cooper, confident the fix was in, even had a large trophy made for the winner labeled with his self-proclaimed title of "Champion of Western Canada". The race was set for a Thursday in late October over 100 yards. Walter, dealing with the difficult and incessant Mitchell, had allowed himself to be talked into giving Cooper a two yard head start, making Cooper even more confident. They were to race down Court Street in Port Arthur, near Pearl Street.

Over 500 spectators gathered in the crisp fall air, lining both sides of the racecourse. The betting was brisk, but "perhaps not as much as the Port Arthur group (Cooper's people) looked for", the paper reported. The starter, calling the runners to their marks, kept having to halt the proceedings to push the crowd back off the racecourse. It was four o'clock in the afternoon before he could get everyone organized.

At the sound of the gun, Walter false started and was called back. He was penalized one yard, now positioned three yards behind Cooper. At the second gun, Walter exploded out of the blocks ("Knox is a wonderful starter" the paper noted) and had passed Cooper by the 50 yard mark. Mitchell's face must have dropped as he realized he was being double crossed again. Walter won by a full three yards. Mitchell got to keep the $200 Walter put up as a forfeit against their fix, but he lost many times that amount in side bets, mostly to Walter's English backer.

Walter, his friend and the eccentric Englishman met back at the hotel to divvy up their winnings. Strangely, the Englishman gave his share to Walter too.

"Take it, m'lad, and make no bother about it. I have plenty of money, enough to take a flyer if I wanted. What got me into this bally thing, you know, was for the satisfaction of being able to say to my fellow townsmen that they saw a truly run race and that it was my good fortune to be able to keep it straight."[14]

Walter met many characters on the frontier, shysters, thugs, enthusiasts, rubes, even honest men, but this was the most interesting turn of events he had ever faced. He took the money, likely clearing over $700, even after losing the forfeit.

Around November 1st, Walter decided to head home. His last race, humourously reported in the paper, was a losing venture. Waiting on the dock to catch the steamer, Walter chatted casually, saying his goodbyes, as the mooring ropes were thrown aboard. Cocky he could rely on his sprinting ability to catch the boat, he raced down the dock, planning to take a dramatic leap aboard, a fitting farewell gesture for the "Champion of Western Canada". However, the 50 foot gap he faced was more than even he could do and he was stranded forlornly on the end of the dock, watching the ship sail away.

Maybe his big trophy was weighing him down.

17

Inner Turmoil

Walter arrived home in Orillia in November 1907. For some reason he chose not to head to Elk Lake and help his brother prospect that winter. By now, Jack had built a snug little cabin on the shore of the lake and had staked a claim nearby that was turning up silver tracings. But he was still out searching for the mother lode, venturing far inland. With thousands of other prospectors camping in the region there was a race on to find the silver, but not necessarily to dig it up; most prospectors sold their claims to the conglomerates and never intended to mine them themselves. Walter and Jack had corresponded by mail throughout his Michigan adventures, so Walter knew the state of Jack's work up north. Perhaps Jack wasn't ready for him yet, or maybe he still needed to find the right claim before they set to work digging up their fortune. Possibly the two of them agreed it would be more useful for Walter to make money to support their mining venture than to actually get up there to dig. For whatever reason, Walter was on the hustling trail again by January.

Before he could get away, athletic developments in Canada drew him into some political maneuverings and raised his hopes of returning to the amateur ranks. Late in November, Walter received word from the Amateur Athletic Federation of Canada, the renegade association formed to lobby for a less stringent view of professional athletes, that they had an offer for him.

There was a truce in the Athletic Wars with regards to the 1908 Olympic team. Both the AAFC and the CAAU were going to put forward athletes to the Canadian Olympic Association. The two rival associations agreed, in the best interests of Canadian sport, not to challenge the other's nominated athletes regarding professionalism. It was assumed they would both only put forward scrutinized amateurs (the focus of their conflict was over the team sport professionals). The Canadian Olympic Association would accept the athletes put forward and take the team to London for the games after a common Olympic Trials meet that would decide the makeup of the team.

The Ottawa branch of the AAFC offered to reinstate Walter as an amateur and name him to the team for the all-around competition. They added the inducement of a good government job at an above average $700 per year and promised a $100 per year raise for five years![1] The CAAU wouldn't be able to stop him without breaking their contract with the AAFC. Walter was tempted. (He found out later that "stuttering" Dave Belland, the matched race sprinter Walter pursued in Peterborough in 1903, had taken an AAFC offer and gone to the London Olympics to come near dead last in the 100). Walter knew he had a strong chance of winning the Olympic gold medal and proving to the world he was the best all round athlete there was.

Then, just a week or so later, articles appeared in papers across central Canada with the sensational news that Walter Knox had applied for re-instatement with the CAAU! Walter never mentions this in his writings, even his notes, but it was big news in the papers. "Walter Knox wrote the CAAU last evening formally applying for re-instatement to the amateur ranks and this afternoon he will interview President Stark…" one paper wrote.[2]

Walter's letter to the CAAU was full of untruths. He said he spent the summer in Port Arthur "and had abstained most wholly from athletics for months past", when, of course, he had been hustling his way across Michigan and Wisconsin that whole summer. He further claimed that unless the re-instatement by the CAAU came through he "intends to retire permanently from athletics", thus losing Canada the greatest all around athlete it ever produced, the newspaper report added.[3] Showing penance, Walter said he had just turned down a $120 a year coaching job at the Bozeman Agriculture Institute, demonstrating how serious he was to return to the amateur ranks. He goes on, with a straight face, in an interview with "The News" in Toronto:

> *"We all make mistakes sometimes and I certainly made a very grave one, but there were extenuating circumstances. There is more behind the case than the public know and I think if the actual circumstances were known that I would not now be in athletic disgrace. However, I have tried to live down the mistake I made and I think I have done so to some extent.*
>
> *I ask another chance and one more only and I will prove to Canadians that I am amateur in spirit. I want to get back to hang up a few marks for Canada and I will guarantee to establish some records that will not be equaled for a long time…*
>
> *When I disqualified myself there was really nothing in the athletic line to keep a young man in Canada. A couple of weeks a year was about the best we could do, and there did not appear to be a revival in sight. Anxious to be up and doing I transgressed the amateur rule and am sorry, very sorry."* [4]

Walter enlisted athletic interests and "influential local gentlemen" from his home town of Orillia to support him. "He wants to be an amateur", one of them wrote, "and has already been severely punished for his misdeeds".[5] The paper said "similar expressions of opinion were heard wherever athletes congregated" and that the news of his re-instatement would be "hailed with delight" at the Central YMCA. The delight would likely be much less evident at the West End Y.

In some respects, Walter had a case to press. Officially, his only transgression was taking the coaching job at Bozeman for four months. There was some debate, even then, as to whether that was a big enough issue to get him banned for life. There would have been many people willing to overlook that mistake, especially when a gold medal for Canada was on the line. "Hadn't we better clean the slate — reinstate our pros, one and all — and start over?" one columnist said, regarding the 1908 Olympic team during the Knox debate[6]. Had anyone found out the shenanigans Walter had been up to for the last six months, though, they could never have defended him.

The News, showing its bias, went on to say, "He is a splendid type of athlete, of pleasing personality, quiet and unassuming, and wherever he goes he has friends who wish to see the CAAU re-instate him". In the draconian athletic climate of the day, there was more likely a majority who were happy to see the book thrown at him; he broke the amateur rules, end of story. Likewise, Bobby Kerr, Ed Archibald, Cal Bricker, Tim O'Rourke and many others most decidedly did not think Walter was of a "pleasing personality". This would be another instance of Walter turning on the charm for the newspaper interview.

To Walter's chagrin, the CAAU, in spite of his lobbying effort, did not re-instate him, even with the mounting pressure in Canada to put on a strong showing at the London Olympics that summer. Their rules were clear: any professionalized athlete must wait a minimum of two years before being considered for re-instatement.

Walter then turned his attention back to the offer from the rival AAFC. He was seriously considering taking it after traveling to Ottawa to get the grand tour by the club officials there. A Toronto paper even reported that Walter had taken up residence in Ottawa and was about to be reinstated.[7] "I might have turned my life into sweeping offices or Heavens knows what", he said, until suddenly a better offer came along.[8]

The better offer came in the form of a letter from Walter McClelland, the mill worker who first insisted Walter *had* to come to BC where he could make a killing on the hustling circuit back in 1904. McClelland was working in a mill in Montesena, Washington, his letter said, where there was a "natural" waiting to be plucked. The manager of the mill he worked in was the son of the owner. He had run the sprints for Harvard and held a high estimation of his abilities. McClelland said he could guarantee Walter a good job in the mill, at $5 a day (well over $1000 a year at that rate) plus board. He could make that money while they worked up a match with this over-inflated rich boy.

It didn't take Walter long to make up his mind. In January 1908, he caught a train to the coast, kissing his Olympic dreams goodbye. In the best workingman's tradition, Walter chose the money and fun over the prestige and politics.

The job turned out to be everything McClelland had promised. "I was well satisfied with the work and my pay" Walter said, but getting the matched race was another story. The suspicious mill manager steadfastly refused to take the bait whenever Walter tried to entice him into a race. Even after running the shingling machine there for a month, Walter still found the manager standing behind him for an hour at a time, watching him, trying to figure out if he was legit as a shingler or really a hustler just working him into a high stakes matched race. Three months passed. Then, in an effort to prove once and for all he was a real shingler, Walter decided to make a show of going for the one day production record.

In Washington there were actual competitions among mill workers for production on the job. The record for shingling was

39,000 shingles produced in a day. Walter got into the habit of laughing the record off, saying he could beat it if he wanted to. One day came the "put up or shut up" challenge, with the mill manager attentively watching. The timber was all set up for him the night before, and in the morning Walter set to it. Ten straight hours of feverish work produced a pile of 40,250 shingles![9] There was no question Walter was a real shingler now.

However, it became clear there was never going to be a matched race and Walter decided to move on. Arriving in Seattle, looking for opportunities, Walter read with interest a report of the "great revivification" of track and field sports in California. He had no contacts or friends there but decided to go where the action was, far from the CAAU, and where he could be completely anonymous.

Walter settled in to San Francisco in May 1908 where he found a flourishing athletics culture. Casually hobnobbing with athletes and coaches in the prominent athletic circles here and there, under the new alias WR Kennedy, he got noticed and word spread that a "champion" was training at the Golden Gate field. Walter truly desired to get back into the amateur ranks, but at the same time wanted (or had) to continue his lucrative matched racing career. He seemed to be torn. When the opportunity presented itself to get his amateur card back, he grabbed it with both hands; having lost his amateur status seemed to make him want it even more. All of a sudden, being shut out of the big legitimate competitions was a problem for him. He thought he could be happy as a touring professional but his experiences in Michigan appeared to have soured him. At 30 years of age, his need for legitimacy was getting stronger, especially here in California where the athletics world was flourishing and his anonymity made a return to the amateur ranks not only possible but probable. But still, he was under pressure to make as much money as he could because Jack was counting on him; pressure enough to turn down the chance to go to the London Olympics where, by all accounts and unlike past Olympics, the best in the world were going to congregate.

Playing it straight and lily-white, it took him only three months to re-establish himself. He spent a couple of months being paid under the table to coach a high school team , a position that covered his living expenses and allowed him plenty of time to train. Then, in quick succession, two coaches approached him about joining their teams. His performances on the training field were becoming well known. The first, Dean Cornell, "a top notch rubber and trainer", was just starting a club and couldn't offer him an amateur card yet. The second coach, representing the champion Olympic Athletic Club, could and would. Walter, after feeling out the Olympic coach and being offered his amateur status back, admitted he was a professional whose real name was Walter Knox. In his writings, Walter admitted he wanted to come clean and be respectable if the right situation presented itself. This was it.

"We assumed that a man of your abilities was a professional," the coach responded, "but people here would like to see new faces competing and they would like to see how good you are."[10]

The coach assured him that if he was with the Olympic Club, there wouldn't be any questions asked about his past and no one would dare to protest him, the club's reputation and position in the west coast athletic world was so strong. Walter, with Cornell's approval, made the move. The official registration for his amateur card listed him as a past member of the great New York Athletic Club, the nation's strongest.[11] No one second-guessed the Olympic Club officials or checked up on this glaring falsehood.

Sure enough, less than three months after Walter had arrived in California, his shiny new amateur card was signed! The OAC was the dominant club on the west coast and apparently would do what it had to in order to stay on top.

"I was lily-white once more," Walter wrote, "but best of all, I was also Walter Knox — Walter Knox that was through with dodging and squirming every time someone clapped me on the back and I did not know whether I might be addressed as Wilson, Renwick or Kennedy."[12] (Just a few weeks earlier he had been approached by someone who knew him as Renwick, but promised not to let on. "Renwick's" reputation in BC as a sprinter had spread all the way south to California.)

Within days of his card arriving, he was competing in his first amateur meet — but not before Walter had his first fling in San Francisco's hustling world. Cornell, the first coach who approached Walter, told him about Jack Johnson, the great black boxer in town for a heavyweight championship fight. It was one of his runners who had to back out of a matched race with Johnson. The very next afternoon Walter, his new amateur card not even smudged yet, was shooting pool at Johnson's training base looking to get a high stakes match race. This overt hustling episode demonstrated that, even while working his way back into the amateur ranks, Walter was still looking for matched race opportunities; he still wanted it both ways.

The cognitive dissonance in Walter's psychological make-up had to be excruciating. At his core, Walter highly valued integrity; he had learned the unwritten code of loyalty and pride and emotional strength as a teenager in the gangs of Orillia. He saw the world in terms of right and wrong, good and bad, us and them. This became clear in how he described his later, respectable athletic career. But he also grew up in the workingman's world of negotiation, speculation, rule bending and winner-take-all. As many other upright athletes did in the world of professional sport, Walter learned to adapt his core values to the goals of getting ahead in the abnormal world of professional sport. The negotiation, the deception, the dance around the truth became an acceptable practice because that was the way to achieve the goal: making money and getting ahead. It was insidious.

Somehow, Walter remained convinced he was morally upright, believing he was just playing by the accepted rules of the game like everyone else. This was the workingman's traditional culture; it was business, everything was business. Above all, as a justification for his corrupt behaviour, was the "buyer beware" mentality. Everyone, that mentality assumes, has an angle they're working, and the person who works his angle better wins. Figuring out the other man's motives and deceptions, whether it be in buying his cow or accepting his matched race challenge, was part of the game; if you're too naïve, too bad. That was understood. Walter held no ill feelings towards the suspicious mine manager in Montesena who refused to race; he was shrewd and he was right to be. Good for him. Likewise, the blowhard weight thrower Walter fleeced at the hotel in Blairmore, Alberta, who insisted on a contest then and there, even when he suspected Walter of being a hustler, only got what he deserved. Under the buyer beware attitude, Walter was not obliged to reveal his whole story; that was up to the other guy to figure out, and if he was smart he'd investigate before accepting a challenge (the way Walter had when he checked out Batson, the black sprinter in Corry, Pennsylvania). Somehow, actively deceiving or misleading by using aliases and fabricated backstories became acceptable too. As Walter saw it, that was a long-standing part of the matched racing culture, and that made it all right. Everyone knew it went on.

It is hard for us to understand how he could do some of the things he did. The inner conflict he must have experienced, feeling morally upright yet freely behaving immorally in his chosen world, must have caused him bouts of inner angst he had no choice but to repress.

Maybe it was partly because the hustling world was so much fun. He clearly found the adventure, the profits, the winning invigorating and addictive. This adventure surely, to his mind, was just a blip in his life, sewing wild oats in his youth; it could be overlooked in the grand scheme of things. In his writings, it is apparent he understood what he was doing was morally wrong, but it was fun in a smirking, mischievous sort of way; he enjoyed winning and putting blowhards in their places. He was such a superior and deceptively good athlete, it would have been hard to not use that to his advantage, whether to make money or to embarrass some over-inflated show-off. Walter was a man of action; the mundane world of making a living in the shingle mill held no appeal for him. His need for adventure must have fed his rationalization of the hustling world as a culture unto itself, governed by a different code of ethics that he could step into and out of as he wished.

Walter's deeper sense of integrity was apparent in how he reviled haughtiness, condescension or belligerence in others. It appeared as pride or vindictiveness, but was based in his underlying egocentric self-esteem. He was always affronted when deceived by others, even in the course of working up a matched race when this was almost expected, and was always determined to right a wrong he perceived carried out against him. Walter lived by a code and had no tolerance for anyone who ventured outside what he perceived as "fair play" in the matched racing world. Play whatever games you want in setting up a match, but don't start messing around after the deal has been negotiated. Remember how focused he was to get a match with stuttering Dave Belland when he learned Belland's reputation was based on a sub-10 second 100-yard race that was a fraud. Walter had a long memory and a sure, to his mind, sense of right and wrong. Later in his athletic career, and in his life, he was able to demonstrate his ethics and value-based attitudes. He just had to get away from the hustler's world. It was the debased world of professional athletics in Canada that corrupted him; if he could have made a living in sport honestly, there is every reason to expect he would have.

How much were the Amateur Athletic Associations responsible for Walter's slide into the morally reprehensible behaviors of the matched racing world? They created and enforced the utter dichotomy of pristine amateurs and vile professionals. They decreed money had no place in sport and severely punished any athlete who disagreed. They did everything they could to suppress the working-man's traditional sports and his participation in truly amateur sports.

Unwilling to comply, Walter did the obvious and retreated to the frontier towns the amateur associations couldn't reach.

Walter was one of the many rural athletes who chose to defy the AAAs instead of giving in to their stringent rules or just abstaining from sport entirely. He thumbed his nose at the AAAs and their codes of conduct, staying far from their reach on the frontiers of society where the traditional sports world still thrived. The AAAs forced him into that choice. Walter chose his pride, his independence, his pragmatism and his right to make a living over his integrity and moral conscience. One or the other had to be repressed. Of course, he also tried to callously exploit both worlds too, in the best workingman's tradition.

Now, in San Francisco, when he had a chance to return to the amateur world, he played the part of the impeccably honest, respected sportsman. He made up his mind to be a true "hot foot" here, only venturing into the professional hustling world when there was a big payoff against a well backed runner whose reputation could excite the betting crowd (like big, brash, black Jack Johnson). He wasn't going to shy away from the hustler's world, where he would still flagrantly employ all the anti-ethical tactics he knew so well, he was just going to keep those two worlds separate. In the amateur meets, it would be all sportsmanship and fair play, although, in his notes (but not in his book), he did talk about bets of a couple of hundred dollars in the amateur meets in California.[13] These he would have kept very discrete, handled far from the field. No west coaster ever questioned his amateur status in California.

It was Walter's deep down ethical code, too, that drew people to him. He was reserved by nature, not the life of the party, but he was stalwart and appreciative of other stalwart people, able to banter and needle and be personable in their company. The Quinn boys in the Soo were initially abrasive to Walter, but after spending more time with them, Walter came to appreciate their brash, sturdy ways. And here in San Francisco, stalwart men surrounded him, the athletes who congregated on the fields then in the saloons, men Walter respected, even when he was intent on bettering them in their chosen events. Walter seemed to enjoy his time among these athletes in the amateur circles of California.

At the same time, as Walter admitted in his writings, he was tiring of the hustling world ("I had sickened of sailing all those months under the name of Kennedy…"). He wanted to be able step in and out of it freely again, to relieve the inner tension and to make the money he needed, while at the same time establishing himself both as a champion athlete and an honest man. His near decade of hustling was wearing on him.

That summer, 1908, Walter was aware of what had happened at the North American All-Around Championships in Brookline, Massachusetts two years previously, as he cut the article out of the paper.[14] The world champion, 37 year old Tom Kiely of Ireland, won. The paper (probably Orillia's) compared Walter's marks against Kiely's. It would have been no contest as Walter was significantly better in six of the ten events. (Whether Walter knew of Martin Sheridan's more recent championship scores from 1907 is not known, but Walter was competitive with anyone in the world by then):

	Kiely	Knox
100 yds	11 2/5 sec	10 sec
16 lb. shot	37'10"	44'
high jump	5' 2 ¾"	5'6"
pole vault	10' 9 ½"	11' 4"
broad jump	19' 10"	22' 5"

Perhaps seeing this missed opportunity was the impetus for Walter to get back into the amateur world. He had an ego. He was a proud man who, at 30 years old, must have seen time passing him by without the recognition he felt he deserved. If not for his being called out as a professional in Toronto, he would have been the North American All-Around Champion. That made three missed opportunities, four if you count the upcoming Olympics in London. How many more would there be?

So now here in California, in the summer of 1908, Walter started back on the road to respectability. He was out of the jurisdiction of the CAAU. He had the powerful Olympic Athletic Club vouching for him if the American AAU came by investigating. This was likely his last chance for respectability and he was going to take it.

18

California Here I Come

San Francisco's Olympic Athletic Club was a powerhouse, "one of the greatest aggregations of track and field stars ever assembled," Walter remarked, with a little exaggeration.[1] Foremost was Ralph Rose. Rose was the world champion shot putter. In 1904, as a six foot six, 235 pound 19 year old, he won the Olympic gold medal in the 16 pound shot put with a new world record of 48' 7". Surpassed by two Europeans, he came back in 1907, at a massive 286 pounds, to be the first man to break the 50 foot barrier and then to push the record to 51' 0", a mark unsurpassed until 1928! In an unsanctioned meet, he put the shot a whopping 54' 4" in 1909, the longest put recorded in the next quarter century. Rose was also the American discus, hammer and javelin champion. Pete Gerhardt was a sprinter, American Championship silver medalist and a semi-finalist in both the 100 and 200 at the 1912 Olympics. He ran 10.0 for the hundred yard dash and 22.1 for the 220, top flight times. Middle distance man Andrew Glarner was the best in the west and, though absent in 1908, Charles Parsons was a sub 10 second 100 man. These, and the cadre of men just behind them, made for an unbeatable team on the west coast, if not the country. Walter was training with the best now, and fully expected to beat them all, Rose included.

The Olympic Club coach had Walter enter the meet held the

weekend his amateur card was signed, but as unattached, likely to protect the club if someone challenged Walter's eligibility. His first amateur race, November 1st, 1908, a year and a half after being professionalized in Toronto, was a success. No one questioned his eligibility and he won his race, a 220 yard handicap where he was the scratch runner (each runner would be assessed a handicap, or head start, based on past results and assessed ability, against the fastest runner, the "scratch").

Walter Knox (left) in the S.F. Olympic Club jersey, 1909, with "Big" Hamilton of Denver Colorado. Walter jotted on the back of this picture that Hamilton's backers refused to support him in a proposed matched race with Walter.
Courtesy Orillia Museum of Art and History

Two weeks later, November 14th, he represented the Olympic Club in Oakland for the first time. Walter won the pole vault, clearing 11 feet, and came third in the long jump. But on December 4th at the indoor auditorium in San Francisco, Walter threw down the gauntlet in front of a large, cheering crowd. In the 75 yard dash, he broke the world's record by a tenth of a second with a time of 7.5 seconds! "Knox of the Olympic club, a new man on the Pacific Coast, but probably the fastest sprinter in the world today…" the local paper crowed.[2] Everyone now understood there was a new force to be reckoned with in their midst, raising the standards for everyone.

That was it for the fall season; the competitions shut down for a long Christmas break. But in the spring, Walter picked up where he had left off. Back at the auditorium in San Francisco on February 5th, Walter, after winning the pole vault, entered the shot put event against the dominant Ralph Rose. Here was five foot eight, 149 pound Knox utterly dwarfed by six foot six and a half, 285 pound Rose, a mismatch if ever there was one. But these teammates knew each other and neither took the other lightly.

Walter Knox is dwarfed by champion shot putter Ralph Rose, 1909
Courtesy Orillia Museum of Art and History

Both these athletes used the shot putting technique common to that era. The difference was Walter's quickness and efficient recruitment of every muscle in his body to loft the ball against Rose's massive heft and strength. Both athletes would stand sideways at the back of the seven foot circle holding the ball in their right hand, beside their shoulder, with their left shoulder and arm forward. The left arm was held straight out front to counterbalance the body, which leaned as far back as possible. From a slight crouch, the left foot would be lifted into the air (Rose was famous for his exaggerated leg lift) before an explosive hop on the right foot, combined with a forceful twisting of the body to propel the ball hand forward, would set up the big push with the right arm to heave the ball. As Walter knew, the faster you could shift across the circle, the faster the ball would be moving before you threw it. Speed across the circle was integral to improving the distance of the put. In later years, athletes would start with their backs turned all the way around and from a full crouch before exploding with the hop and spin. From a crouch, the ball was already moving upward too, before the arm even entered into it. Even later, and popular today, shot putters will do a complete 360 degree spin, like in discus throwing. But in Walter's day there was minimal use of the body in the throw, just a hop and a half turn; it was all arm. Walter was one of the first athletes to understand how the back and abdominal muscles, and especially the legs, should be recruited to assist the arm. He had learned this as a thirteen-year-old in Coldwater from the great George Gray. That was how such a lightweight could compete with the super heavyweight Rose, a man literally twice his size. Rose was comparatively spindly-legged and knock-kneed; his power was in his arm.

    With the eight pound ball, Walter was up first. Exploding across the circle, Walter knew he had unleashed a good one, but was as shocked as everyone else to hear the announcer exclaim it was a new world record! He had heaved the iron shot put 63 feet 5 inches, a full four inches beyond the record held by WW Coe, the only man to best Walter's childhood friend and mentor, George Gray.[3] Then

Rose stepped up, heaved, but fell short of Walter's mark. So did his next attempt. This looked to be an unprecedented loss for Rose in the event he owned. On his last toss, he got off a good one too and the iron ball fell just inches past Walter's for the win. Walter had held the world record for about 15 minutes. Papers from coast to coast, Walter said, reported on the remarkable competition (though no easterner thought to complain that Walter Knox had regained an amateur card). Walter had to console himself "with the grim satisfaction that if I had not pushed him he never would have made it."[4]

Walter Knox demonstrating his shot putting style, San Francisco, 1909
Courtesy Orillia Museum of Art and History

At this point, around March 1st, 1909, Walter decided to put on his "hot foot" hat again. Through the sprinting grapevine, he had heard of a very fast man having a field day in Mexicali, Mexico. Walter decided to go on a little "scouting expedition". Mexicali was 700 miles to the south, right on the US border 100 miles from the Pacific coast. Squat and dusty, nestled in the arid valley near the Colorado River's outlet, the town was a collection of adobe hovels filled with natives in sombreros and serapes, brandishing guns strapped across their middles and long, keen knives on their sides. Ferni and Verner and Nanaimo were rough, tough towns, but Mexicali, so foreign and so beyond the reach of familiar law enforcement, was more intimidating, and a very unlikely place for a footrace.

This was Mexico on the verge of revolution. Porfirio Diaz had ruled for over 30 years with an iron fist, imposing a harsh program to modernize Mexico. His strong-arm tactics, suspension of basic human rights and overt favoritism of the wealthy land-owning class over the peasant workers led to simmering unrest, especially in the poor north. In the fall of 1908, just months before Walter visited Mexicali, Diaz had promised to finally step down, only to rig his seventh election in a row to retain power, to the outrage of the peasants. The Mexican revolution erupted in 1910 under several leaders including Pancho Villa in the north. Northern Mexico was angry, depressed and lawless when Walter came there looking to make a killing.

Walter made the long train journey down to El Centro, the American town just across the border from Mexicali. Poking unobtrusively around town under the name "Wilson", he found the whispers were true and the chances of getting a match race promising. A Canadian, from Hamilton, ran a poolroom there and Walter chose to take him into his confidence, quietly informing him of his intent to set up a match race. His new friend referred him to an insurance man, a former sprinter, who knew exactly how good the Mexican was.

"He's very fast… it would take a whirlwind to beat him," was his expert opinion. Just recently, he said, Walker, the Mexican, had handily beaten two accomplished runners of known reputation who had traveled there to race him. He advised Walter to turn around and go home.

"There is only one way of convincing you," Walter responded, "and that is by actually showing you what I can do. As an old sprinter yourself, I would be unable to fool you."

So out on a country road, Walter ran two 50 yard sprints that left the insurance man gaping at the stopwatch. Walter now had an eager backer.

The very next day, Walter's new backer headed off to Mexicali to play the role of matchmaker for the first time in his life. He came back promptly at the appointed time, grinning with excitement. He had Walker's signature on an agreement for a 75 yard race for $100 a side to be run in a week's time, March 21st. They both sensed a big payday was coming.

For the next four days, Walter followed the same routine, training in the morning, every day in a new out-of-the-way location to avoid uninvited observers, then hopping the train to Mexicali to place bets. No one there knew he was the other runner so he found he had no trouble laying 50 and 100 dollar bets on himself. After his last two races, Walker had a growing reputation, and at every place Walter wandered into, bets were easy to find. This match was a popular topic for discussion all over town. After four days, he had $800 wagered. The big money, Walter knew, would come closer to the race.

Meanwhile, while training in El Centro one day, Walter ran into a little problem that required some quick thinking. His poolroom owner friend, who had driven him out to the country, had noticed Walter's kit bag sitting open. Walter saw him staring at the monogram inside, "WRK".

"So you're not 'Wilson'," he challenged.

"You take that from the initials, I suppose. Can you keep something to yourself?" Walter responded.

With that, Walter handed him a calling card that read "WR Kennedy", a card he had made up when first arriving in California thinking about hustling again. His friend felt truly on "the inside" now and doubly interested in seeing this match through to its lucrative finish. More importantly, Walter had successfully diverted any chance of his real name, Knox, getting mixed up in this matched race and possibly jeopardizing his amateur status.

A few days before the race, a friend Walter had summoned arrived.

Walter needed someone to fish out the high rollers in Mexicali, to find the big money bets. This was a dangerous town, Walter had figured out, and the man he called, Bates, was a bare knuckle prize fighter who knew his way around the betting world. Over the last couple of days before the race, Bates managed to get $2200 bet on Walter. Mexicali had never seen betting like this! It was going to be a big payday, as long as Walter won.

Walter still had not seen his opponent, only heard the stories about him, that he ran like the wind and had easily defeated top opponents. There was always a nagging uncertainty when racing a mystery man. But this was a 75 yard race, a race that could be won with an explosive start (which Walter had). It took technique and refinement to get a fast start. And besides, Walter had just broken the world record for 75 yards; no hick was going to beat him!

Mexicali was living up to its reputation as a rough and tumble town. One afternoon, Walter wandered into a gambling hall and was standing near a poker table when a commotion suddenly erupted. A shot rang out and one of the players slumped onto the table, shot through the chest.

"'That's what you get for trying to get a card from the deck!" Walter heard.

Walter high-tailed it out of there, no need to get embroiled in that kind of trouble, but returned a few hours later to find the game continuing as if nothing had happened. Upon inquiring what had been done with the unfortunate card snatcher, he was told the man was likely under the manure pile out back. This was no town to get into trouble in.

The morning of the race, Walter was resting on his bed. A rap sounded at the door and Walter called out for whoever it was to come in, thinking it was one of his cohorts. In stalked "one of the ugliest looking Mexicans" Walter had ever seen. He had a massive horse pistol holstered on one hip and a knife, fully a foot long, strapped on the other. The worn handle of the knife showed it had seen lots of action.

The man closed the door behind him. "You man who run?" he said, clumping across the room to loom over Walter threateningly.

Walter bolted upright on the bed. "Yes."

"You win race?"

"That's what I'm here for."

"You win race, you win last race. I bet on other fellow. I kill you if you beat him." His broken english only accentuated the bluntness of his words his words.

"A lot of big talk…" Walter shot back, belligerence always his first instinct.

"A lot of big gun…" the Mexican slowly replied, pulling out his weapon for Walter to see.

"That's only one gun. I'll be going so fast you'll be sure to miss me."

"Then I'll get you with this…" and out came the knife.

By then, Walter sensed the man's attitude and intensity were not play acting. Maybe this was not a man to provoke or antagonize.

"Maybe you won't have to use the knife or the gun. This is a footrace, you know, the other man may be a better runner than me." Walter scrambled to defuse the situation.

"I make sure. I be at finish. You be ahead I shoot."[5]

With that he left, banging the door behind him. Walter's instincts told him he'd better take control of this situation. This was a big, dumb thug he had to out-maneuver. There was too much money on the line to lose it this way. He pulled on his shoes and ran out to the street. The crowds had already gathered for the big event. Walter knew the chief of police would be patrolling and found him in short order. After he'd explained the situation, the chief asked if he knew the thug's name.

"No, but I can point him out to you," Walter replied. So they walked down the street looking. Casually, Walter asked him if he was a betting man.

"Only on sure things, and when I say sure, I mean it."

"Then sink the ship on my chances!" Walter assured him. Farther along, they split up, Walter on the street, the chief surreptitiously behind the crowd on the sidewalk. Sure enough, there was the Mexican, right near the finish line where he'd said he would be. Walter pointed him out.

The chief mouthed "Him?" to be sure then sidled in behind the man, pulling a glove onto his right hand. Without warning, he smashed his fist into the greaser's face, knocking him down like a sack of meal. Then he went to work with his feet: smack, smack, smack, the prostrate man took it right in the groin. It was no problem then for the chief to haul the whimpering man off to the cooler.

Walter wandered over to a fence to sit down and unwind; this was some kind of town. The race would be called very soon. Two men, whom Walter had set wagers with the first day he came to town, strolled up to him at the fence and, seeing him in his running gear, realized they had laid their bets with the actual runner himself. Walter told them he liked them and was going to give them a break. He confessed he was the world record holder over the distance and that they still had time to get some bets down on him to cover what they'd be losing.

Their response was belligerent.

"This says that my bet stands as right", one of the men said, jingling some coins in his hand.

Having tried to help, Walter replied, "OK, but it will have to be a gentleman's bet; I haven't a cent on me".

"Agreed" the man said, opening his hand to reveal three $20 gold coins!

Just then the call came for runners to go their marks. For the first time, Walter got a look at his unbeatable opponent, Walker. He did not recognize him. The man was fit and strong, built like a sprinter. Walter sensed he could take no chances.

Walter's El Centro friend had picked the starter, a relief since

Walter was on the lookout for unfair tactics. This was tension time, muscles taut, mind alert, heart pumping. Walter had to evaluate all the particulars negotiated for the race quickly to be sure everything would be on the up and up. His matchmaker was hopelessly inexperienced at this sort of thing. With all the big money laid down on the race, the motivation to get an edge via subterfuge would be heightened. Like a fugitive on the street, Walter eyed the crowd for accomplices, scanned the racecourse for obstacles and scrutinized his opponent for hints as to his intentions. He expected the worst.

Walter had no intention of being caught flat-footed at the starting line. After chatting with the starter to ensure he knew what he was doing, Walter walked to his place beside Walker at the starting line.

The starter called out, "On your marks!" The runners stepped up.

"Get set." And the two runners tensed and coiled, ready to explode.

Then Walter, timing the starter's pistol perfectly, yelled "GO!" and leapt out of the blocks.

Walker, confused by Walter's tactic, stumbled out of the blocks. Walter didn't false start, he yelled right with the gun. But it was enough to startle Walker and cost him a fast start, and the race. It was only a momentary advantage, a yard or two at most, but it was all that was needed in such a short race. Walter was risking jumping the gun and being set back a yard for the next start, but it worked out perfectly for him. He won the race comfortably.[6]

Walker came back furious, calling Walter everything in the book. The judges ignored him.

After taking this abuse stoically for a while, Walter finally responded with, "Aw shut up! The race is run and the judges have decided. Go soak your head and wash out your mouth".

The Chief of Police came up beaming.

"How did you do?" Walter asked.

"That's for you to guess." He said, grinning from ear to ear. "Did you get your money from the stakeholders yet? Come along with me and we'll see that there's no funny work there or with any of the bets you've made."

He then escorted Walter around town to collect all the bets he had made that week. Most surprising was the pair of gamblers Walter had tried to help just before the race. They were waiting for Walter at his hotel as agreed, with their losing stake and the three gold coins they had bet at the last minute.

It had been a wild week, and a profitable one. Walter had cleared $3000, out of which he gave a share to Bates, his betting man, and the El Centro insurance man, his matchmaker, who had been fabulously successful in his first foray into high stakes foot racing.

That afternoon, Walter was back on the train for San Francisco, an honest amateur again, ready to hold the other amateurs up to the highest standards.

There was an epilogue to Walker's story. After the race, Walter had asked Walker about running in California where he could make some money. He was interested so Walter directed him to a field in Oakland where he was sure to be noticed. Sure enough, a club offered him a place on their team, as he was a "10 second man" or even better, by Walter's estimate. Clubs, hoping to challenge the mighty Olympic Club, were looking for sprinters to take on Walter, the new hotshot. Walter and Walker first met in a meet where Walter had to give him a two yard handicap and still won by two feet, in 10 seconds flat. Walker claimed he had a slow start and that he would win the next race. They met a couple more times, the last one where Walker was given a four yard head start, but to no avail, Walter kept beating him. The club dropped Walker after that.[7]

Walter said Walker came to California to make some money betting and implied that he himself was regularly betting on himself in these amateur meets. Walker was upset Walter kept beating him because it cost him money every time. As much as Walter wanted to be taken seriously as an amateur, as a man of integrity and a champion in multiple events, he couldn't resist the opportunities to wager on himself; he simply didn't see why it was so wrong, other than being against the amateur rules. If no one knew he was betting, did it really matter? When it came to the actual competition, he was impeccably honest and fair, a true sportsman, able to sincerely congratulate a man who bested him. That was the upright code he lived by. Betting had nothing to do with it — at least, not in the amateur competitions.

In April, Walter was back on the amateur circuit again. The summer season was in full swing. He would compete in 14 track meets in 18 weeks that summer, competing in four or five events each meet, all along the California coast. In five consecutive weekends in five different towns all around San Francisco Bay, Walter was undefeated in the sprints and the long jump, also winning some shot put, pole vault and hammer throw events. His marks were world class but not always at his top level, given the grueling schedule. He did a 9 4/5 second 100-yard dash in Santa Clara, broke the track record for the 176 yard run (18.5 seconds) in Oakland and had a 23' 2" long jump, followed up by a 24' 2" exhibition jump, in San Francisco.[8]

The day after the Oakland meet where he set his track record, he accepted a challenge to an amateur matched 50-yard dash against Forest Smithson. Smithson was the fastest hurdler in America. He was the AAU champion in the 120 yard hurdles in 1907, Olympic champion in 1908 and the world record holder. But more importantly to Walter, he had bested world record holder Dan Kelly in a 100-yard dash in 1906, tying the world record of 9 3/5 seconds. (Smithson must have wanted this race too. He was a theology student at Oregon State University and was averse to competing on the Sabbath. This matched race was on a Sunday.)

A tremendous crowd showed up at Shellmound Park in Oakland on May 30th, the day after the big track meet. Word had spread through the crowd of the match the next day and everyone wanted to see the west coast's unquestioned champion take on the world record holder. The papers "whooped it up", according to Walter. He felt confident he could win, he just wondered by how much.

It was no contest; Walter won the 50 by an impressive two yards in a time of 5 2/5 seconds. There was no question in his or anyone else's mind he was one of the top sprinters in the world.[9]

After a week off, the meets continued, nine more over 10 weeks. After a few uneventful meets around San Francisco Bay, Walter made a foray all the way to Coalinga, near Fresno, 200 miles away and up in the mountains. His friends from the Mexicali foray, looking to make themselves a little money, contacted him about entering a professional track meet there. Walter had decided he was going to stick to the "straight and narrow" of the amateur world, unless, and only unless, a chance at a big betting windfall came his way. This was a professional track meet, a publicized professional competition like a highland games. If anyone knew he was there that would be the end of his amateur days. Sporting enthusiasts and newspaper reporters would be watching, so it was a curious decision to go. High in the mountains, far from the amateur athletic scene, it must have seemed a safe risk to Walter. He entered as "Tom Davis".

The meet itself was uneventful — Walter won the 100 and the hop, step and jump. Hopefully the betting was brisk enough to make it worthwhile, because Walter was about to get the scare of his life.

Back in San Francisco the next day, the chief of police, a past acquaintance in that relatively small town, walked up to Walter in his hotel lobby.

After some small talk, he suddenly said, "Knox, I'll have to ask you to come along with me to the police station."

Is this where my amateur career ends? Walter wondered, the Coalinga episode fresh in his mind. But where did the criminal angle come in, why the police? It was the first time he had ever been arrested. Walter remarked in his writings, "If there was anything I abhorred more than anything else it was that of breaking the law."[10] There's his code of honour again. In the "real world" he thought himself a model upright citizen; it was only in the frontier world of professional sport, where there were different rules to play by, that he would devolve into a deceptive shyster.

The chief was tight-lipped as to the charges. At the station, he ushered Walter into an office and sat him down. First one man entered, looked him over and left, then another. Not a word was said. Walter waited, and sweated.

Eventually the chief came back in, the stress lines gone from his face, replaced by a smile. "That's all, you can go now Knox."

"Why so mysterious, chief?" Walter asked.

"Those fellows came from a small town up in the Sierras," he said. "They and the whole town were taken for a killing by a foot runner who sailed under the name of Knox. Someone connected your name with the scalawag and down they came, armed with a warrant, to take you back to stand trial. I had them come in and take a look at you, but from first to last they were positive that you in no way resembled the fellow."

Walter couldn't get out of the police station fast enough. It was a scare that only heightened his anxiety the next weekend when his next scare came.

July 14th was the Pacific Coast Track and Field Championships at Ascot Park in Los Angeles. There was tremendous fanfare surrounding the meet with a parade before and a big banquet afterward. The Olympic Club was there in force, ready to defend its title, and its members enthusiastically took part in all the events. Decked out in their athletic gear, the team was making the walk from their hotel to the nearby stadium when suddenly Walter heard from the crowd on the street, "Hi there Wilson. Oh Wilson, how's Mexicali?"

Walter's knees buckled and his spine stiffened. He stared fixedly ahead, pointedly ignoring that taunt. Los Angeles was only 150 miles from Mexicali. That someone at the matched race 10 weeks previously was there in LA was not too surprising. But Walter had been thoroughly enjoying the festivities at the meet and was caught completely off guard, in public, with his teammates, so soon after his stressful arrest in Frisco. He was shaken.

All that afternoon he was on pins and needles, waiting for the axe of professional accusations to be lowered. But it never was. Applying himself to the task at hand, competing, he was able to concentrate and do his part for the team.

The Olympic Club won 11 of the 14 events, with Walter taking the 100 in 10 1/5 seconds and the long jump with a 22' 4" leap and placing second to Rose in the 16 pound shot put.

At this point, Walter was feeling unbeatable in the sprints; he had beaten all comers all summer, often giving away big handicaps. Typical posturing and braggadocio among the Olympic Club athletes on the training field one day led to the question of how fast Walter really was. Pressed to give his honest opinion, Walter ventured he could beat Gerhardt by five yards. This was the Gerhardt who had twice been the second fastest man at the national championship, who was in his prime and would make the final eight in two events at the next Olympics. He was a world class sprinter.

"Why Walter, the thing isn't logical. You'd have to beat the world's record to do that!" Gerhardt exclaimed, mostly defending himself.

"I might just do that!" Walter responded, cocky and confident.

That was that, there had to be a race. Five men lined up on the track that July 25th, 1909, to settle once and for all who was really the fastest. Walter was the scratch. Gerhardt started 4 yards ahead of him after refusing to go 5. Two other club runners got 6 and 8 yards and a visiting runner from the New York Athletic Club, a top east coast man, got 5. About 50 club members and friends lined the track to witness the big race. Five official timers were on hand: Walter Christie, coach at Berkeley, Dan Moulton, coach at Stamford, and three certified AAU timers. Bragging rights were on the line.

Walter won as predicted, two yards ahead of the New Yorker who beat Gerhardt. But that wasn't really important; what was the time?

Moulton spoke up first: 9 3/5 seconds! Equaling the world record. Then two more showed the same time.

The other two timers were silent. Finally one turned his watch for all to see: 9 2/5! The last timer smiled and showed the same time, a fifth of a second under the world record![11]

Now Walter, and everyone else, knew what he was capable of, though deep down he had always known it.

There was one more meet left for Walter, a routine contest at Palo Alto on August 14th. He had a field day there, winning the 100, the 220, the pole vault, the 12 pound shot put and the long jump. It was to be his last amateur meet.

The next weekend, the Olympic Club was traveling to Seattle for a big contest at the Alaska-Yukon-Pacific Exposition. It was a bigger affair than the Pacific Coast Championships and top athletes from across the country were attending. Ralph Rose, Glarner and Walter, the top athletes from the Olympic Club, were photographed by the newspapers prior to their departure. The pictures were printed repeatedly with long commentaries about the athletes and their prospects in Seattle.

Soon Walter was informed AAU officials were nosing around in San Francisco. Among them was a New York man, James Sullivan, President of the AAU, who knew all about Walter and events in Toronto two years previously. Walter was called to appear before them. When Sullivan refused to even shake his hand, he knew the jig was up.

When confronted, Walter freely admitted to being professionalized in Toronto. But they already knew that and had decided his amateur card would be rescinded. How did you get another amateur card, they wanted to know. Walter refused to answer. They went to work on him, pressing for answers, getting hot under the collar.

Finally Walter told them all to go jump in the lake and walked out. He was not going to implicate his friends on the club who had been so good to him.[12]

He wasted no time getting out of San Francisco. No goodbyes, no embarrassment, no explanations. He clipped out the morning newspaper articles and boarded a train before noon the next day, leaving the amateur world and any hope of proving he was the best athlete in the world.

Did Walter leave an impression in California? Sixteen years later, in 1925, on his first visit back to the coast, Walter ran into Dean Cornell. Now a successful career track coach, Cornell was the first coach who had recruited him in San Francisco. Cornell didn't recognize him, but Walter got him chatting about his athletes. His shot putter was good, he said, but nothing like a little fellow who could put, run and jump in the old days, a fellow by the name of Knox.

"He was the greatest piece of athletic flesh that ever lived!" Cornell exclaimed, not realizing who was right in front of him. "He would show some of these fellows who think they are champions just how things should be done!"

When Walter finally identified himself, Cornell jumped up and hugged him.[13]

Late in the summer of 1909, though, the train took a dejected and bitter Walter home to Orillia then on to Elk Lake by September 1st. Walter was now a prospector; at 31, his athletic days appeared to be over.

19

Prospecting

For two years, Walter's brother Jack had been diligently prospecting around Elk Lake, with some success. The town of Elk Lake, founded only three years earlier, now had 5,000 residents, a booming business district and better communication and transportation to the outside world via a convoluted steamship route. It also had diminishing silver deposits. Jack Munroe, the big miner who had discovered the silver there, was getting ready to move on to the next rush, realizing early how shallow the silver deposits were. Jack Knox had a claim near the lake that revealed promising tracings of silver, and he had thrown up a small cabin there to see him through the winter. Like most prospectors, Jack didn't waste time digging. He traveled farther afield in the warm seasons looking for the mother lode before someone else found it. The silver in the ground could wait. Once he had dug enough to evaluate its worth he would probably sell the claim to a conglomerate anyway.

By the fall of 1909, when Walter arrived on the scene, Jack had further claims staked in Lawson Township, 18 miles due west, and the Davidson Lake region, a further 18 miles northwest of that. The Davidson Lake claim was five miles due north of Gowganda, where another strike had occurred and a town had sprung up. Jack had a rough shack up at the Lawson claim but the snug cabin on Elk Lake was his headquarters. After a brief reunion at Elk Lake, Jack whisked his little brother off to the Davidson Lake claim to finish the prospecting season before freeze-up in late November.

It must have been a rude awakening for Walter after the comfortable life of the elite athlete. He had lived in comfort in San Francisco, spending a few hours a day at the track and resting the remainder of the day. Sure he was fit, but he wasn't rugged or hardened. He had supple muscle not the gristly muscle that comes from hard grunt work for hours on end. These first few months tramping through the bush, chopping firewood and digging would have had him re-evaluating his durability. But he was no stranger to hard work and would have adapted quickly and stoically.

Nothing was easy in the bush. To eat meat you had to go hunting. To fight off the cold you had to haul deadwood out of the forest and chop it up. Survival was tough, and then you had to find the energy to go prospecting. Supplies were a long walk away, and they had to be carried home. Jack Munroe, the discoverer of the Elk Lake deposits, famously carried a cast iron wood stove on his back the 50 miles from Cobalt to Elk Lake that first winter! Yes, life was hard, but all the men really wanted to do was prospect, tramping around in the bush all day, chipping at rocks, digging holes. Surviving took up too much of their time and energy. This life was a long way from the hotel in Frisco.

Jack and Walter applied themselves to their work through the fall, catching up and planning their futures until freeze-up. The second pair of hands would have made Jack's life a lot easier. By December 1st, 1909, they were back in the Elk Lake cabin, warm and comfortable. But the winter was the digging season, broken up only by frequent patrols of their trap-line. There was silver in that claim near the lake and they had to find out where. As Walter described it, the winter was all about, "dig, sucker, dig". Even so, he also described it as just as exciting as his athletic adventures.[1]

May would bring "break-up", the opening of the rivers and

water routes back to civilization. After a long, hard, isolated winter, break-up meant a holiday down in Elk Lake proper. Jack and Walter headed to town by canoe at the first opportunity.

Walter had gone to extreme lengths to hide his identity in the past, but here in the back woods he had stumbled across the best finishing touch he'd found yet. Walter grew a beard over the winter, "thick, long and abundant", he recalled. In the frozen north, a beard helped protect against frostbite; it was practical. He grew "rather fond" of his new appearance and kept it on past the spring.

There were many forms of entertainment in Elk Lake now, saloons, gambling halls, restaurants, but Walter was attracted to the pool hall, a game he was adept at. It happened that Jack Munroe was in the pool hall too, and in no time they found each other. Munroe had gotten his boxing start at the Olympic Club in San Francisco, where Walter did track. Walter sent his brother all his clippings and Jack showed them to Munroe whenever they ran into each other.

"So you're Walter Knox. I've heard a lot about you", Munroe, the Mayor of Elk Lake greeted him when they were introduced. He had said if Walter ever came north he wanted to meet him. In September, when Walter had arrived in the north, Munroe was in the bush. By the time he came back to town, Walter and Jack were in Lawson Township working their claim. Now, eight months later, the two champion sportsmen finally met. The three men retired to Munroe's room and talked until four in the morning.

Walter and Munroe were kindred spirits. Both came from working men's backgrounds, the Cape Breton mines and the Ontario lumber mills; both competed in sport at the highest levels as Munroe had defeated top contenders for the world heavyweight boxing crown, like Jack Sharkey, before losing to Jim Jeffries; and both were entrepreneurs looking to get ahead, Munroe as a prospector and investor, Walter as a hustler and now prospector. The only big difference in their backgrounds was the culture they'd had to maneuver through to get ahead.

Boxing was overtly professional and Munroe had some big paydays and even sparred daily on vaudeville stages in New York, Boston and Philadelphia for good wages.[2] Now he was a legitimate millionaire businessman and prospector, held in high esteem by the mining communities he frequented. Walter, on the other hand, had been driven to frontier backwaters under assumed names and he'd had to associate with gamblers and thugs in order to make his money in the track and field world. While Munroe was legendary, Walter was relatively anonymous, unable to compete on the biggest stages. They would have had a lot to talk about. They became good friends and would meet up frequently after that.

After a week in Elk Lake, the Knox brothers made the 30 mile trek by foot to their Davidson Lake claim, and on April 20th paddled down the lake to Gowganda, the nearest community, for supplies. They only meant to stay a couple of hours but they ran into a heavy stone throwing competition on the main street. Walter had to sit down and watch.

Soon he was heckling, "Fair, but I could beat that."

Persistently, getting louder, ignoring the angry retorts of the throwers, Walter carried on, until finally he stood up and threw $10 on the ground.

"That says I can beat any man in town!"

An old friend from Orillia, Howe the barber, snatched up the money, offering to hold the stakes if anyone took Walter up on his challenge. Then he whispered, "I know you, Walter; I've shaved off too many whiskers to not know what's underneath."

A strapping, six foot two fellow stepped forward, waving a $10 note. They each took their throws and Walter tried to make it close. Although the awkward rock was tricky to control, it took a tape measure to show Walter had won by just two inches. Ten more dollars for the kitty.[3]

That contest started the commotion as to who this little fellow was: some suggested he was Knox the athlete, but others argued he was just a prospector. Other challenges were issued; one man, claiming to be the wrestling champion of Ville Marie, Quebec, just across the lake from Haileybury, wanted to know if Walter could wrestle. Walter belligerently responded that he would take the man down right here in the street, right now.

That's when Howe the barber stepped in and asked Walter to set up a wrestling match, but to hold it in a few days as an attraction to advertise the opening of a blind pig (an unregulated drinking establishment).

Walter could wrestle. His bodyguard friend in Spokane, McMillan, had taught him many standard moves a few years ago, although Walter had considered himself an accomplished wrestler before that. With his quickness, agility and strength he was hard for any man to handle. The bout was agreed upon, and the speakeasy owner charged seventy-five cents admission to watch. Wrestling was one of the most popular gambling sports on the frontier and would draw a big crowd, Howe knew. Walter didn't say what the stakes were but they would have been significant to get him into this curious match.

The floor of the blind pig was covered in blankets from the jail to make a mat and the booze joint was jammed for the big event. The "champion" turned out to be a rank novice and Walter had him on his back in just four minutes. It was questionable whether his shoulders actually were pinned to the floor, though, and Bellduger, the champ, came up loudly complaining about the decision. The referee, a policeman from the south, declared a return bout would be needed to settle the bets.

A week later, a real ring was jury-rigged inside a tent at the main intersection of town. Bellduger waltzed around town all week bragging and saying if Walter wanted to play rough he could accommodate him. But the big match went even worse for him this time. He had asked the referee to bar toe holds. The referee had refused and Walter now knew what he was afraid of. Sure enough, Walter went right for the toe hold, in combination with a half nelson. Bellduger squirmed to escape and Walter squeezed even tighter. Bellduger was wrestling in his socks and now one slowly slipped off his tortured foot. When it slid right off, Walter lost his grip and Bellduger leapt up, scooted out of the ring and didn't return. The crowd burst into laughter. Later, Walter heard he had dislocated the poor fellow's big toe. I guess Walter was now the champion wrestler of Ville Marie, Quebec, without breaking a sweat... and was a little richer too, no doubt.[4]

In early May, Walter ran across a challenge in the Cobalt Nugget from a wrestler by the name of George Cleverley, or EA Hartley, as one newspaper reported it, who claimed to be the 138 pound Champion of Northern Ontario. He wanted a match with anyone at 145 pounds. Walter, at 150 pounds now, contacted him to take the challenge, even betting he could throw him twice in half an hour. Cobalt had built the Mine Manager's Association Sports Palace in 1905, under the direction of Jack Munroe, and now had a flourishing sporting community. Cobalt was the clearinghouse for all sorts of challenges. Boxing, wrestling, feats of strength and more were regularly promoted events among the miners, with athletes and strongmen traveling great distances to take part. The betting, of course, was the big attraction for the miners scratching out a living in that frozen backwater.

The match was to be held in Cochrane in early May, 100 miles to the north, in the gold mining country of the Porcupine rush. Walter headed up there a week early and stayed with a friend. They made the tour of all the bars, pool rooms and barber shops, managing to accumulate $125 in wagers which was more than enough to make the adventure worthwhile, assuming he won.

Walter was wrestling under an alias since "Knox the athlete" was well known up north, so when someone approached him calling him Knox, he knew this was trouble. The stranger wanted "to do business".

He offered to make all Walter's bets good if he'd only let Cleverley last past the half hour. Realizing this man would spread the word about his real identity if he didn't agree to the fix, Walter said OK. It was still money in the bank, less the original stakes Cleverley would take.

The match went as planned. Cleverley won the bet, only getting pinned once. But, immediately after the match, he cockily challenged Walter to an even match, best two out of three falls. Two nights later, Walter pinned him twice in 29 minutes, the time carefully pointed out in Walter's notes,. Clearly he wanted to prove, if only to himself, that he could have won the first bet if he wanted to. Again, Walter took a good sized winner's prize and half the gate, not to mention side bets, a sum that made wrestling seem like a worthwhile endeavor.[5]

On May 24th, the town of Elk Lake, like every other town in Canada, had organized a day of festivities, including a program of sports contests. Walter took another break from his toils at Davidson Lake and walked the 30 miles to town a few days in advance of the event. There was some work to do at the cabin there so Walter decided this was as good a time as any to do it, and then get in on the races. Against the local miners, Walter took five firsts: the 100, pole vault, shot, and standing and running long jumps. He hadn't lost much after almost a year in the bush.

With that taste of competition, Walter set to training again that summer with an eye on another hustling tour. He was ready on August 1st and headed south to North Bay. Shut out of any amateur meets, he looked for holiday games and professional gatherings, bent on accruing another nest egg. Of course, he had to use an alias all summer; everyone knew the name Walter Knox in the Ontario sporting circles.

North Bay's civic holiday games on August 3rd were a bust after a man in the crowd kept yelling out, "That's Knox. I'll bet two to one on him. He beat Kerr."

Then it was on to Orillia on the 6th, Campbellford on the 11th and Toronto on the 20th of August. At Campbellford, Walter was surprised by an Englishman, Charles Cropley, a new emigrant to Canada, who beat Walter in the sprint and the 220 and 440 events. Walter was adamant about a false start by Cropley in the sprint. "He was five yards out", he claimed, and never forgot it. At Scarborough, Walter publicly challenged him in the local newspaper, even offering him 3 yards in the 100, for a re-match. Cropley duly showed up; he lost to Walter in the sprint, but still beat him in the longer runs. These loses to Cropley must have taken a bite out of Walter's betting profits. The two would meet again the following summer: Walter had a long memory for people he felt had embarrassed him.

After these warm-up events, Walter headed back to the proven betting grounds of New England, the Labour Day Caledonian Games in Boston being his target. These professional games were the big sporting event of the year in the area, attracting top athletes and a good betting crowd. To hide his reputation, Walter entered as Charles Newton of Westport, Connecticut. Sitting in the staging tent before the games, he was approached by a fellow Walter recognized as a backer of the retired Arthur Duffy, the fastest sprinter in the world a few years back. He didn't recognize Walter, but knew he wasn't from the region, so it didn't take this athletics insider long to figure out Walter was a traveling pro. Immediately, he offered to work the betting crowd for him. That was just what Walter needed, a Boston insider who knew where the money was. Together they ticked off the events Walter could win and agreed to split any betting proceeds fifty-fifty.

Another familiar face, John MacDonald, the big professional who had almost outed Walter six years earlier, was also entered in the competition.. He was the dominant athlete in the Boston area in multiple events.

Up first was the 100, which Walter didn't enter. It was a handicap affair, which meant the athletes' backgrounds would have to be assessed to set the handicaps. As Charles Newton, Walter had no background and would have been challenged as to his identity. When asked by an official if he was going to run, Walter claimed he had just gotten out of the hospital and would need at least a three yard handicap if he were going to enter. They gave it to him, no questions asked! However, he won his first two heats so easily they made him the scratch runner for the final. When he won that, they only awarded him second place honours.

"That's what you get for fooling us!" Walter was told when he protested.

Walter then proceeded to beat all comers in the pole vault, hop, step and jump and running broad jump, each time relegating MacDonald to second place. Even after being outperformed in every event, the fuming MacDonald didn't realized who Walter was, that they had chatted at length at two different events in 1904 or that he had been ready to challenge Walter's amateur status then. MacDonald's best event, the 16 pound shot put, was next and again little Walter, with a 42' 10" toss, knocked the towering Scotsman down to second place.

Even after the meet, when a lavish ceremony was staged to award the prize money, MacDonald, standing right next to Walter, didn't recognize him. As far as he knew, Walter was Charles Newton. This was all very amusing to Walter, of course. These two would meet again in a few years with more on the line, where MacDonald would finally catch on to who this Newton really was.

MacDonald's failure to recognize Walter is a testament to the physical changes rapidly overtaking Walter's appearance with age. In his youth, he had been a slender, agile man with a full crop of thick brown hair parted neatly down the middle like a farm boy. Now, at 32 years of age, his hairline was rapidly receding and his face was growing paunchy. The slender physique was now thick and muscular after a year in the bush doing grunt work. With bulging shoulder and neck muscles, he looked more like a bull than the gazelle he once was. Walter had also become more adept at playing nondescript than he was as a novice hustler in 1904. He'd learned to be unobtrusive, evasive, bland. Nothing was presented for the other guy to remember in the way of mannerisms or personality. It is believable that MacDonald didn't recognize Walter (especially since Walter probably still had his full beard), though one would think his performances would have rung a bell with him.

At the end of the meet, Walter gathered up his split of the side bets, $125, and headed home. Back in Orillia, Walter managed to set up a matched race with a railroad worker whose father had been a great sprinter. This Boyd was ready to bet $300 on a match race, until a local tipped him off as to the identity of the man he was running against. The final stakes were set at a mere $25 a side. But it was still worth it, more than he could get in a few week's work in the mill, and Walter wasn't going to turn away even this gift; cash was hard to come by in the bush.

By October 1st, 1910, Walter, cash in hand, was back in Elk Lake, digging and tramping and feeding his gold fever.

The Highland Games Years

20

A Working Professional

That winter, Walter turned 33 years old. He knew his competitive days were nearing an end and was reluctant to let them go. But the amateur world was no longer an option as he was red-flagged both in Canada and the States. As for the hustling world, Ontario (north and south), BC, the prairies, the west coast, Michigan and New England were all out; he would be recognized, if not known by his real name, in all of those places, limiting his prospects. His options had shrunk to the casual holiday games that had been abandoned by any serious athletes with the AAU of C's organized track meets' ascendance over these traditional events.

Holiday games were becoming just that, three-legged races, carrying eggs on spoons and the like, not serious competitive events in the tradition that Walter had grown up with. The years from 1910 to 1912 were pivotal in the transformation of track and field in Canada. With the Athletic Wars over, the AAU of C had a firm grip on sport and was intent on putting the final nail in the coffin of the workingman's sports. The obvious route for Walter was to retire — he was 33 after all — and become a full-time prospector.

During the long winter of 1910-11, isolated in their cabin on Elk Lake, the Knox brothers continued to work Jack's original claim. They had spent the fall scouring the Lawson Township and Davidson

Lake claims for silver tracings, making enough to survive but not much more. Walter commented he had spent a lot of time hunting, bagging a moose with a 57 inch span. There were many other miners in the Elk Lake region all doing the same thing and periodically Jack and Walter would find acquaintances dropping in for a visit or a rest. One day "a couple of Scotties" were shooting the breeze with them. As Walter described it, they "went into raptures over what they called the Highland gatherings and the games that were part and parcel of them" back in the old country. What piqued Walter's interest was that these were professional games, with cash prizes for serious, well-trained athletes making a living honestly from sport.

In the back of his mind was the annual letter Walter had received that fall from Jim Baxter. Remember, Baxter saw Walter run in Maple Creek, Alberta in 1905 and offered to pay his shilling entry fee for the Powderhall Sprint in Edinburgh, Scotland, the unofficial world professional sprint championship. Every year for the past five years, Walter had received a letter from Baxter informing him that his entry, complete with the shilling fee, had been sent, under the alias of WR Stearns (the hotel proprietor in Maple Creek).

Walter and Jack talked it over. Walter wasn't getting any younger. There were no more opportunities for him here as an athlete. The mine, he said, "had been paying us back", but ready cash was still hard to come by. Walter wanted to go and see what he could do in the professional world of Scottish athletics.

"Nothing ventured, nothing won," was Jack's opinion, and it was decided.

As soon as break-up came on May 1st, Walter was off to Orillia to investigate the travel costs and availability. He had been training hard; his fire was back now that the long sought chance to prove himself against the best was dangling in front of him. After two weeks intensive training on the track and jumping pits in Orillia, he decided to test himself at the May 24th Games in Beeton, a rural community halfway to Toronto, then at the June 14th Caledonian

Games in Cobourg, on the Lake Ontario shore. Between them he entered 13 events and took 13 firsts. Three days later he sailed from Montreal.

Athletics in Scotland had evolved along different lines than in North America. Like Canada, they had their professionals and their amateurs, their Amateur Athletic Associations and their hustlers. But they also had a thriving circuit of Highland Games, Scottish festivals of culture that included sports events for cash prizes. The North American Caledonian Games were of trifling influence compared to the original Scottish version. These games were the high prestige competitions in Scotland; this was where the best athletes competed. To the south, in England, the AAA's ruled the roost. The fiercely independent highland Scots held fast to their traditional games and saw no moral issue with awarding cash prizes, prizes significant enough to support a professional class of athletes. The Scottish AAAs were isolated in the urban areas, completely shut out of the rural regions, populated by the fiery highlanders who chafed at the English influence in their country. The highlanders were remarkably similar in temperament to Walter: independent, stalwart, courageous and insular. As soon as Walter stepped into this world, he felt at home.

The Highland Games season ran from May 1st to the end of August, with every small community hosting its own games. There were fifty or sixty different games held every summer, some just a few miles and a few days apart. The games were the highlight of the year in each community, a highland cultural festival and celebration of everything that made Scotland their homeland. Crowds of 30,000 spectators were expected at the bigger games, but even the smallest crossroads games could get 7,000.

Everything was a contest: piping, dancing, tug-'o-war, wrestling; the heavy events of tossing the caber, putting the heavy stone, the hammer throw, the 56 pound weight toss; and the light events, sprinting, jumping, pole vault, hurdling, etc. Tartan was everywhere, banners would fly, wine and beer would flow. It was a celebration of manhood, of independence, of Scotland.

The athletes, originally strong farmers and herders like in Canada's holiday games tradition, had evolved by the 1850s into highly trained specialists who traveled from games to games, earning their living solely from the proceeds of their athletic prowess. These athletes trained vigorously and studied their sports. The powerful heavy event men had massive bulk, obviously built by years of heavy lifting, some with thighs bigger than their wives' waists. The light men honed their techniques year round; even the wrestlers had physiques of washboard abdominals, thick, rounded shoulders and ox-like necks that would not be out of place with today's top athletes.

But though these were all professional athletes, none of them would ever go on to glory in Olympic Games or contest for world amateur championships. The glory of Scotland stayed in Scotland. Some of the top strongmen of the time did tour the world, earning a living doing performances and challenging other strongmen to feats of strength, but it was all professional and businesslike. Again, we can see the appeal this culture would have for a man like Walter. Walter *Knox*, whose until then unappreciated Scottish heritage made this trip feel like a homecoming.

Now Walter understood why Jim Baxter described the Powderhall Sprint as the unofficial world professional championship. The best professionals in the world were here in Scotland because of the culture that supported them. Scotland was a magnet for men like Walter.

The Highland Games season ended in August and the light event athletes moved right into the "Pedestrian Enclosure" season, the track and field meets held on cinder tracks in purpose-built stadiums. This pedestrian season culminated in the Powderhall Games on January 1st (yes, January, often in the snow; these were hardy Scots after all) with the unofficial sprinting, hurdling, and long distance running championship that drew entries from all over the world.

Walter landed in Scotland for the circuit of Highland Games when these traditional events were at their height. This was "the greatest time of all for Highland Games" said David Webster, the renowned Highland Games historian.[1] In her final years, Queen Victoria had shown a great interest in the games, giving them a considerable boost. This newfound respectability had a lasting effect after her death in 1901, inaugurating a "golden era" that lasted until the First World War.

Walter took to the Scottish culture with enthusiasm
Courtesy Orillia Museum of Art and History

Equally important in their upsurge, was the passing of the "Street Betting Act" of 1906. This law made it illegal, with fines and imprisonment at hard labour for up to six months, to loiter or frequent the streets or public places for the purposes of betting or bookmaking. So, after 1906, bookmakers flocked to the Highland Games and professional Pedestrian Enclosures to make their living, leaving the amateur events alone.[2] The AAAs policed their grandstands, forcing the bookmakers to the now illegal public spaces outside, leaving them no choice but to head to the Highland Games. The AAAs in Britain finally had a tool to use in wresting control of sport from the bookmakers. The hard, manly culture that evolved around the Highland Games naturally included speculation and wagering, just as it had in Canada's holiday games culture. In Walter's time, the gambling was just as prominent in Scotland as it had been in Canada and the States. This was one more reason for Walter to feel at home.

This upswing in the popularity of the Highland Games after the turn of the century made them more profitable for a successful athlete but also made them more competitive. This could be a pretty good way to make a living and more young men were trying their hand at it. While there were lots of cash prizes and the betting money flowed, it was getting much harder to be the man who won it.

This was the world Walter was walking into, potentially profitable but highly competitive. There would be no easy wins for Walter in Scotland.

Walter's uneventful trans-Atlantic trip ended at a hotel in Glasgow. From there his first move was to visit Jim Baxter's parents in West Calder, 25 miles to the east. Jim had given him letters to deliver, which they were overjoyed to receive. Walter became a favourite son to the Baxters and they became a valued source of information to him. They were "the salt of the earth", Walter proclaimed. He spent just two days there, acclimatizing before he was off for his first competition.

It was the end of June now; the Highland Games season was half over. Walter was anxious to get on with his plans even though he was suffering from a bad case of diarrhea. He had missed too many games waiting for the spring break-up at Elk Lake; there would be no more waiting, Walter's adrenaline was pumping already.

On Wednesday, June 28th, 1911, the village of Shotts, some 14 miles west of West Calder, hosted its annual Highland Games. It was Walter's introduction to the traditional pageantry and rites of the Scots. It was also the highland Scot's introduction to Walter Knox, Canadian champion in five different events. Walter won the pole vault with a jump of 10' 11", near to the Scottish Games record, came second in the triple jump but was badly out-classed in the shot put. "I couldn't put it more than 38 feet, the weight men laughed at me entering, they were all big fellows," he said. He'd have to wait until he regained his strength before he could shut them up.

The local paper took notice of him. "At the Shott's Games a new man came on the scene and to the surprise of everyone defeated JA Speedie and Corbett in this their prize event. The stranger, whose name is AR Stearn, lately arrived from America…"

Walter used an alias here, the first and last time he was to do so. Always guarded, he was studying the lay of the land and needed the flexibility to change his identity if need be. However, after the games, he started inquiring about the Powderhall Sprint. He discovered that it was required for entries to be made in your "own and recognized name". And the risks of getting caught using an alias, Walter asked?

"Be thrown in jail", came the reply. "A short while ago one got by us. We traced and trailed him for six months and finally caught up with him. In court they threw away the keys on him — six months!"

From then on it was "Walter Renwick Knox" on every entry form. He didn't need to hide his identity here anyway. The competition was stiff enough that bets could always be found in spite of his reputation. Besides, the prize money alone could provide a tidy profit after living expenses. Walter, for the first time in his life, could be an honest athlete. Contests for prize money were abundant in spite of his reputation. What a weight off his shoulders. What freedom to be forthright and unafraid of exposure. How easy to engage in all the competition he desired without having to scrounge matches. There would be no more dealing with thugs or watching over his shoulder. No more poisonings. Sport was a job here like any other, an honest, respectable job. The best job in the world.

Walter set off on the grand tour: 31 different Highland Games in 72 days, 37 by the end of September. He found himself in a different village every other day, competing in four or five or six events at each Games, all against top flight competition. He was "Walter Knox", proudly building a reputation. In this culture, being a "big man" was everything. Walter took the circuit by storm and became the "biggest" man on tour. That summer he garnered 63 first place finishes, 37 second place and 31 thirds; remarkably, he won almost half the events he entered!

In his classic and concise history of the Highland Games, Webster calls Walter, one of a handful of athletes he specifically commented on over the 150 year history of the Games, "famous" and "the Canadian champion who broke so many Highland Games records".[3] Most notable were Walter's exploits in the pole vault. He won this event in 22 different Games that summer, changing the culture in that event. As Webster noted, "In the early days many of the heavies won prizes with the pole and not until Knox of Canada invaded the games did we see a light events man shatter all their records."[4] The pole vault had been grouped in with the heavy man's events like the caber and stone putting; men manhandled themselves over the bar. Walter showed them what a strong light man could do with proper technique. With the Highland Games at its peak, Walter became a standout.

Mapping out his travels makes a spider's web of a map. Some events were only a few miles apart, many of them clustered in the 30 mile radius around Edinburgh, in south central Scotland. But he traveled to the English Midlands, over 100 miles to the south, and to Inverness, a good 150 miles to the north. Back and forth, up and down Scotland, competing almost every other day. During his busiest week, he competed in six Games in six different towns in six days! The last one was after a 75 mile train ride. Incredibly, after all the exertion and travel, he won six events there. His day off was spent on a 100 mile train ride followed by two more days of competition. It must have been exhausting.

For Walter, ever the student of the science of sport, this experience would have been invigorating, if only for the exposure to new techniques. For example, prior to Walter's appearance, the pole vault event had been dominated by the larger, meatier men. The poles in Scotland were heftier, thicker through the middle and needing to be whittled down at the top to afford a comfortable hand grip. Lighter men like Walter could use lighter poles, making the run-up easier, a significant technical advantage when speed was directly converted to height and the boxless planting area had to be hit very precisely with the pointed pole. Missing your plant by just inches could ruin an attempted vault. Walter introduced some finesse to the vault in Scotland. This was evident as vaulting records were beaten by three smaller men (Knox, Speedie and Scott) at Games all across Scotland later in the summer.

Walter was also introduced to the "climbing-the-pole" technique used in England. The Englishmen, at the height of their pole vault, would balance vertically, their feet straight up in the air, and climb hand over hand up the pole before arching over the bar. At one location, they attached a platform with struts at the base of their poles so they could remain vertical (if they were athletic enough) as they pushed themselves to the very end of the pole, which remained completely stationary. Needless to say, the "climbers" received nothing but scorn from the traditional Scots.

The newspapers regularly commented on Walter's technique; he was a novelty and extremely popular with the crowds. "Knox has a peculiar style of high jumping, which attracted some attention. He takes a short run and coming close to the sticks makes a close-feeted leap"[5] (Walter jumped and laid out flat on his side, keeping his feet close together as he cleared the bar in what would become known as the layout style). "Knox's style in the long jump was also peculiar. Taking a long race, he rises beautifully from the mark, and when in mid-air performs a sort of pedal movement, which is supposed to add to his momentum."⁶ And in reference to his pole vaulting style: "He resembles no Scottish vaulter as to method… in-and-out, pendulum swing, double hitch, over the height"⁷ and "with that swing which is peculiarly his own, and wherein lies the secret of his successful vaulting".⁸ Like modern vaulters, Walter used the physics of momentum to his advantage more than the Scots, who relied on brute strength.

As he became better known, the papers also began commenting on his physique and temperament. Walter was "of the dapper type" and "of finely moulded physique, is of abnormally strong deltoid and calf muscles, has grit and determination abundant, and brings a keen intelligence to bear on his athletics."⁹ With an insightful observation, one reporter remarked, "Knox has a penetrating eye and I am wondering if he has not 'looked' too keenly at the big 'uns, and upset their game."¹⁰ There was the typical hyperbole too, but it was often repeated in Walter's case: "he is the best man, considering his poundage, to ever perform in Scotland… the most scientific ballputter ever."¹¹

By the end of the summer, Walter had become a real draw at the Games, "the man from Canada" the spectators wanted to see. The promoters did too. These were profit driven affairs run on gate receipts. The entry fees for the spectators provided the cash prize money and what was left over after expenses went to the organizers (often local associations). It was in their best interests to attract popular competitors like Walter as he drew crowds. For this reason, the promoters would often award a bonus for breaking a record and would offer a champion up to two pounds for a successful exhibition attempt at a record mark. It didn't take Walter long to figure this out. He remarked in his book, "By topping the mark by an inch or so (in the pole vault), then by coming back the next season and bettering it, this adds to the earnings."¹²

At one of his last meets of the season, the promoters offered Walter half a pound to try an exhibition attempt in the pole vault. He had won at the low mark of nine feet. They raised the bar six inches and he cleared it, then another six inches for another half a pound and he cleared that. To the crowd's cheers, they raised it another six inches and over he went again. Finally, to great roaring celebration, he slipped over the bar at 11 feet for a two pound bonus! To the promoters, it was money well spent.

Walter Knox pole vaulting at the highland Games. Note the lack of landing pits and the pointed pole stuck into the grass.
Courtesy Claudia Courtney

The Highland Games events were run on grass fields; there were no running tracks or jumping pits, they were rustic affairs compared to AAA meets. Often the fields sloped or were sloppy after dancing, piping or wrestling events. In the long jump, officials would sprinkle sand over flat dirt landing areas so they could see where the athlete landed. The pole vault standards were set up on the field, generally right in front of the spectators, with no landing pits, not even sand. The crowd loved the vault because it was a "test of courage". Many sprained ankles and broken legs resulted from awkward 10 foot drops (as Walter would discover, at the most inopportune time). That was part of the culture: the toughness, the durability, the fearlessness. But that was the nature of the Games: be tough, don't whine, and win. That was right up Walter's alley. He was a sportsman, he played by the rules, but he also knew how to win and was willing to push the limits of what was acceptable. The crowds and the promoters loved it.

Walter had a hugely successful summer. He won every event he tried at least once, including the heavy events of shot put and the 56 pound weight throw. In all the jumping events, all the sprints, many of the throws, he was the winner more often than not. At one event, he won the 56 pound weight throw for height. A bar was set up and the athletes, with their backs to the bar, threw the weight over it. Lightweight Walter, close to 100 pounds lighter than some of the competitors, won with a height of 10' 2".

Walter beat every top shot putter at least once, including the legendary AA Cameron who had held court in that event for over 10 years. He had a great rivalry with Scottish champion JA Speedie in the pole vault, another diminutive athlete at 5' 5". Likewise, the perennial jumping champion Bryce Scott traded wins with Walter in the long jump, triple jump and high jump (though Walter won the majority). He cleared 11' 6" in the pole vault, long jumped 22' 5", tossed the 16 pound shot put 45 feet (over 46 once, with a slight foul), high jumped 5' 7", all done on poor grassy fields with no soft landings or firm footings.

Four of the meetings stand out over the summer. First, at Inverness, way at the northern tip of Scotland, Walter set a new record in the pole vault for all of Scotland with a leap of 11' 6". Speedie was there and also broke the record of 11' on a day that must have kept the crowd on its feet. "Absolutely the best ever done in the history of Scottish Games!" exclaimed the newspaper.

At Wick, also in the far north, the best in the country had assembled on August 30th. Under championship-like excitement, Walter had one of his best days, winning the 100, pole vault, 22 pound shot put (against all the heavy men) and coming second in the long jump to Scott.

Finally, there were the double events, starting with the Scottish Championship Games at Aboyne, 80 miles north of Edinburgh, on September 6th. This was a full dress affair, kilts to be worn in every event but the pole vault (for obvious reasons). It should be noted that kilts were not mandatory until after World War I. In Walter's day, the athletes wore long shorts or tights. After the war, when the highlands had been stripped of their youth and the Games were suffering noticeably, the kilt was brought in as a return to tradition, to rouse the spirit of the Highland Games and to re-invigorate the culture. At Aboyne, Walter competed in a kilt for the first time. The events were carried out with extravagant ceremony and "meticulous exactitude", as Walter put it. On this big day, Walter won two events, the pole vault and the 180 yard hurdles, and placed third in three more events.

The next day was Braemar, the gathering of the clans, always a big event in Scotland. This year was special. For the first time in seven years, the king and queen were attending. Dukes and earls, proud tartan-clad Scottish nobles from every corner of the country, made their presence known to great fanfare. Papers touted it as "The greatest show on earth!"

The athletes treated this as more of a demonstration event for the royals but, of course, everyone wanted to win in front of the king. Walter's last event, the pole vault, was delayed and delayed until he started off to get into his civvies and head home. Officials raced up to stop him, saying the king had been delayed but was keen on the match after the close event the day before in Aboyne. As Walter related it, he jumped well, clearing 11 feet, but McKenzie, another top vaulter "chose this for his best day and topped me by 2 inches". Being a Briton in front of the king must have given him the last impetus Walter was lacking that day. He did win the long jump and placed in the shot though.

All in all, Walter left quite an impression on Scotland that summer. The papers took note. "Knox's tour has been signally successful, and several of his performances, particularly in pole vaulting, are in excess of anything previously noted at the Highland gatherings in this country."[13] "Knox, I believe, is the best all around athlete in the world. That looks like a big order, but there is no professional of reputation on either side of the Atlantic that he has not already beaten, either under his own or another name."[14] Walter was unbeaten in the standing high jump, rarely beaten in the pole vault, where he set a national record, won every event he tried at least once, and won almost half of the events he entered, which was almost unheard of over the variety of events he attempted. In August he had issued a challenge in the newspapers to any athlete in Scotland for an All-Around championship over 10 events. There were no takers. Walter was undeniably one of the "big men" of the Highland Games.

Whether all that success translated into a substantial nest egg is a good question. Walter never commented on how well he did financially. Each win was generally worth a pound or two, less for second and third. Games records garnered another pound or so and of course exhibition bonuses offered more income. In those years, a pound was worth about five Canadian dollars. Maybe, in official winnings, he cleared up to 200 or even 250 pounds in those three months, under $1300 Canadian dollars, a good income but less than he could get from one good matched race on the Canadian frontier.

Then there were the side bets. Bookmakers abounded and the spectators amused themselves gambling, it was fundamental to the culture. Every town had its celebrated son and the top Scotsmen like Scott, Speedie and Cameron would always be favoured over the upstart newcomer, at least at first. Not once did Walter mention wagering, except when he issued challenges in the papers, fishing for high stakes matches. None ever materialized. Given his incredibly hectic schedule, there would have been very little time for him to seek out wagers and collect them later; there was always another train to catch. Once Walter had settled into the Highland Games life, the money seemed to become secondary in importance, if one can believe that.

His fellow athletes presented him with "a handsomely bound volume of Burns's works" on his departure for Canada on October 8th. In this proud and businesslike athletic world, Walter had found his niche. He was appreciated by his associates and valued as a cohort. They all had common cause, not just in making a living as athletes, but in the moral philosophy of sport, that a man has a right to use his talents to his own ends and isn't morally decrepit for doing so. Here was a whole country thumbing its nose at the Amateur Athletic Associations, in just the same way Walter had tried to back in Canada.

But what about the great Powderhall Sprint on January 1st? There were two more months of "pedestrian enclosure" competitions Walter could have entertained himself at until the big day. One paper reported he had already been awarded a seven yard handicap over the scratch runner for Powderhall (it also said Walter had been avoiding many of the sprints at the major Highland Games to depress his reputation as a sprinter to get this handicap).[15]

Walter never said why he set sail for Canada then. Likely he wanted to get back to Elk Lake before freeze-up. Maybe Jack was on to something in the mine and needed him as their prospecting was about to take a real upturn. Maybe he was satisfied with his experience at the Highland Games and didn't need to prove himself any more. Maybe he was just tired. What a summer he had just had! He had to be tired.

In any event, he boarded ship at Clyde on October 8th and headed home to Elk Lake via Orillia. Several papers reported the same interesting comment from Walter, "Knox is in business with his brother at the silver mines and considers his present venture a holiday trip."[16] He stuck to that line all summer, even when it was obvious he was there to make some money.

As Walter left Scotland, one inquiring reporter asked him if he had any advice for youngsters just starting out in sport. Walter replied,

> "...first of all get the proper form in any event you intend trying, and get it right before you intend trying to make any great mark. You should never train until you are tired. Always feel as if you would like to do a little more. Get plenty of sleep and lots of rest. Never use tobacco or liquor of any kind. Never be afraid to take advice, as one is never too old to learn." [17]

That's a lot if insightful advice. None of the typical "give it your all" and "be a good sportsman" you typically got from athletes of the day; that was focused advice, advice from a student of sport.

Finally, in the last comment in his unfinished and unpublished book, Walter gives his most candid and heart-felt statement of his philosophy of sport, as confirmed by his time in Scotland,

> "My reasoning may be prejudicial, but here I found the conditions suited to an athlete who seeks profit from ability above average. The stress is put upon the deeds of the professional — in other words it gives the amateur something to shoot at. It takes out of the hands of men who, presumably, profit from rules that govern amateurism and allows the professional the right to conduct his own course of contests. All in all, I think we can learn a lot from the Scotch system of meeting this situation." [18]

We can see here a mature statement, not the simple nose-thumbing we heard from him even just a few years prior. This is a thoughtful man, at peace after finding what he had been searching for in frustration for years. Here, in conjunction with the advice above, is evidence that Walter possessed the cognitive attributes of a coach. The next summer would test those attributes.

21

Olympic Coaching Controversy

In the fall of 1911, Walter arrived in Elk Lake for another winter of toils in the bush with Jack. This was a familiar life for him by now. He never talked about their success or setbacks in these years of mining, only that the mines were "paying us back". In July of 1912, Walter remarked as an aside during a newspaper interview that he had "several large claims of big value".[1] There were enough encouraging returns to keep them at it, anyway. Walter commented he had spent much of the fall hunting, bagging another moose. Prospecting, Walter commented in a letter to friends in Scotland, is "a free and open life that suits him admirably".[2]

That winter, Walter was still pursuing fun and games too. After defeating George Cleverley, the 138 pound wrestling champion of Northern Ontario, in 1911, Walter caught the attention of the Middleweight champion of silver country, Wes Church. Church, from nearby Gowganda, challenged Walter to a match near the end of the winter of 1912. It was late April when Walter finally faced off against Church in front of 100 spectators at the Haileybury rink. Church, 10 pounds heavier than Walter, came out aggressively, doing all the work. Walter was constantly on the defensive; this opponent was much more experienced than the other wrestlers he had faced. But after 11 minutes, Walter got a half nelson established and took

Church to the mat for the first fall. Church sprang back to the attack, throwing Walter just six minutes later to tie the match. At one-all, the next fall would win. It took only six more minutes. Walter got a grip on the tiring Church and gradually forced him down. The match and the crown of Champion of Silver Country was Walter's, in a division above his weight, no less. Now he had two wrestling titles to go with his track and field accomplishments!

On May 1st, Walter left the bush and headed to Orillia to train for a matched race on Hanlan's Point early in May. He wanted another crack at Charles Cropley, the English sprinter he felt had jumped the gun to beat him in Campbellford a year previously. They had set up a series of three races, 50, 75 and 100 yards, best two out of three for the stakes (he never said how much). Walter won the 50 and 75. In the 100, Cropley jumped the gun again and the starter yelled at Walter to "go after him". Reeling him in but not quite catching him was an unsatisfactory result to Walter, but he won the match to assuage his ego.[3]

While Walter was playing around at wrestling and running, he was also pursuing a more serious sporting venture. The Canadian Olympic Committee sent out a request for applications for the position of coach and trainer for the 1912 Canadian Olympic Team, which was heading to Stockholm, Sweden for the Games in July. How Walter heard we don't know, but he duly sent in an application in April.

The Olympic Committee had identified five men prior to the call for applications whom they considered the front-runners, men with the prerequisite abilities to fill the position. Walter was among them. This was a position unlike what we find on modern athletic teams. The coach was a one man show, coaching all the athletes, not just the runners, throwers, and jumpers, but also the swimmers, bicyclists, divers, rowers and shooters. He also was the trainer and a "rubber", giving some of the all-important rubdowns after practices and competitions. He had to manage the team, arranging the training sessions and massaging the egos of the athletes to get the best out of them. There was no big support staff for the coach the way there is today, maybe one or two rubbers at most, and a manager. The coach, one man, could make or break the whole Olympic venture.

The five men identified as the top candidates by the Committee, even after the applications were sorted through from club coaches across Canada, were: Dr Barton, the varsity (University of Toronto) coach who handled the "Coronation" team so well, and who as an MD had an advantage in the therapy and rubdown department and was the decided frontrunner in the newspaper's opinion; Professor Williams, "one of the best instructors in gymnastics, wrestling and boxing in Canada" and not only knew athletics too but had been in charge of overseas athletics teams before; Tom Flanagan, a well-known and respected track and field man from Toronto, who "has many qualifications" the newspaper said; Bobby Kerr, Canada's great sprinter who won Olympic gold in 1908 and who had "much experience training athletes in Hamilton"; and Walter Knox, "the well-known professional athlete who is one of the wisest athletes in the land when it comes to advising athletes on how to improve themselves", and who knows "every angle of the game".[4]

From this list they chose Walter, obviously going for the coaching expertise over international experience and management skills. Walter had often famously stated, with some cockiness, that he could improve a rival's performance in just a week with a few pointed refinements in style. Everyone in the athletics world was aware of that. His own acutely refined technique was admired by everyone, especially when he defeated larger, stronger athletes in all the various track and field sports. His only weakness in this vein was with the distance runners, but they took care of themselves anyway. The Committee was well aware of Walter's prickly side, how he was disliked by some of the other top athletes because of his win-at-all-costs attitude and intimidation on the track. They also knew he had a more charming side, seen at times such as when he was lobbying to get his amateur status re-instated. In the end, the Committee wanted an expert coach, someone who could refine the athlete's performances. The professionals were still seen as the athletes who honed their technique, who trained harder, who studied sport in a scientific way. Though they were the big losers in the Athletic Wars, the sports insiders knew that a professional would make the best coach, and that outweighed personality issues and international experience on teams. It would be another decade before the amateur world would have coaches who had credentials that would rival the reputation of someone like Walter.

Of course, Walter was pleased to find the position as Olympic Coach came with "a big fat salary" of $300 for two month's work.

A curious boost to Walter's reputation that may have worked greatly in his favour here, was a movie shown in the new movie houses in the spring of 1912. A Medicine Hat newspaper reported that a "moving picture artist" had shot films of the Braemar Games in Scotland where Walter performed in front of the King and Queen and over 70,000 spectators.[5] "Views of Knox's performances" were shown across Canada. Crowds and pageantry like that could only have enhanced Walter's reputation in the minds of the Canadian sports elite.

In 1912, due to the large number of athletes vying for a place on the Olympic Team, the Committee decided to have an Olympic Trials athletics meet to decide the entrants for Canada. In 1908, Canada had its first trials meet to sort out the athletes put forward by the two rival Athletic Associations during the Athletics Wars. The success of that event set the precedent for 1912. Athletes attending the Dominion Trials would first have to place in a Provincial Trials meet, designed to weed out the numbers of Olympic aspirants. The two provincial meets were, of course, in Toronto and Montreal. The Olympic Committee, in selecting the team, considered performances at any and all of those three meets. Winning the Dominion Trials didn't put you on the team automatically.

Walter was named Olympic Coach in the latter part of May, just a few weeks after he had left the bush. He was present as an observer in Toronto for the Provincial Trials, the "Eaton Meet", June 1st, then headed to Montreal for the Dominion Trials June 8th. The next day Walter took over the team.

This was a sudden sequence of events for Walter, being named Olympic Coach one day and at the Olympic Trials just two weeks later, preparing to take over the whole team! There was no time for scouting, no time to get to know the athletes, no time to plan any training regimen. Goodness, there was hardly any time to shake the culture of northern Ontario mining towns out of his head, let alone get focused on track and field. It was strictly flying by the seat of your pants and assessing athletes through instinct and spur of the moment analysis. But Walter was comfortable acclimatizing to new situations and settled right to work. He had a week with the athletes in Montreal, a week on the boat and two weeks in England and Stockholm to prepare the team for the Olympics. He had 36 athletes under his care: 18 in track and field, 10 rowers, 3 shooters, 2 cyclists, 2 divers and one young swimmer, who would become the star of the team. His only support were two Olympic Committee officials, Secretary Norton Crow and Chairman James Merrick, and perhaps one rubber, that hadn't been decided yet.

The controversy started right off the bat.

At the Provincial Trials in Toronto, two top American sprinters, Alvah Meyer and Bobby Cloughen, entered the 100 metre race and were expected to dominate. In the surprise of the day, they were upset by an unheralded, but strapping, six foot, 23 year old black man from Winnipeg, "Army" Howard. Walter saw the race and was impressed with Howard's ability, however raw. The papers said "the long coloured boy… lacks style and form but gets there just the same".[6] Here was someone Walter could work with, a talent, he thought — if he could get through the Dominion Trials the following week.

Walter, though, expected an aging and out of shape Bobby Kerr, third in the final in Toronto, to be able to pull off the win in the sprint in Montreal.

The next week in Montreal, Howard "entirely outclassed the field"[7], defeating all the best sprinters in the country to take one of the berths on the Olympic Team with a time of 11.4 seconds, even into a stiff headwind. Right after Howard had won his place on the team, Walter pulled him aside for a chat. He had talked to some Winnipeg insiders after the big Toronto race and had been warned that "no one in Winnipeg could handle" Howard. Walter set the tone for Howard before the big sprinter could even say a word. As Walter described their interaction in his notes, "I knew he was a bad one" so "I told him that I had word that he was hard to handle and told him that we would be able to get along as long as he obeyed orders and if he didn't do that we would have trouble."[8] Howard, of course, agreed to follow orders.

After a few days of training, Walter found him to be just as described: lazy, self-centred and obstinate. They had another chat. Walter recorded the interaction this way, "I asked him again if he was going to do as he was told, if not he could pack his bags and go back to Winnipeg." Walter said Howard refused to comply and "I put him off the team. He had all the other boys all upset and spoiled their training."[9] The next day Howard re-appeared on the track and Walter had to ask the grounds man to eject him. After that, Walter wired James Merrick, the chairman of the Olympic Committee, asking him to direct Howard to follow instructions or go home. The next day at the McGill residence where the team was lodged, Howard, upset, called Walter over to show him a telegram he had received from the Committee chairman. It said to either follow instructions from Knox or go home. "I asked him what he was going to do and he started to give an argument, and I walked away from him", Walter recorded.[10]

The papers at the time quoted Walter as saying Howard was a

"swelled head" and had a "lack of discipline — something Howard cannot just grasp."[11]

The team was set to sail for Europe the next evening. Just hours before the team left for the ship, the Howard situation was discussed at an Olympic Committee meeting. Walter gave his side of the story. An official from Winnipeg, who had asked to be present because he'd have to explain to supporters back home why Army had been left off the team, had a chance to defend Howard. Howard was brought in but, as Walter put it, proceeded "to blow his head off". Walter self-righteously commented that now the committee could see what he had to put up with. Then, trying his best to be a diplomat, Walter said Howard was a sure points-getter at the Olympics, and "if he would sign a paper that he would follow my instructions I would be willing to take him along".[12] (In the papers the day after the trials, Walter was quoted as saying the team had only two certainties, Goulding will take the walk and Howard should win the 200[13].) A little while later, after receiving a telegram from Winnipeg, obviously in response to an appeal by the Winnipeg official, Howard signed. Walter was given permission by the Committee to send Howard home at any time. Then the team grabbed their bags and headed for the port and their waiting ship.

Walter's only comment on what made Army so disgruntled was this, "Of the men here now, Howard is the only one who refuses to obey me. He declines to do as he is asked, and insists on doing as he likes."[14]

The newspapers commented in more detail, though, and so did Army Howard. Howard had "persistently refused to obey the orders of Coach Walter Knox", the papers said. "Howard argued, and he had many sympathizers, that the kind of training he had done in the past was quite suitable, and he would adopt no other system." The papers printed Walter's remarks about Howard's "slowness of starting" that could be "easily remedied"[15]. "Howard still is a slow starter — he was the last man to break away after the pistol in every race," one reporter said [16]. At one point, Walter, likely trying to emphasize a technical point, took to the track himself to race Howard, beating him. The main issue, starting technique, was a strength of Walter's. The lesson only alienated Howard all the more.

Two different reporters recorded Howard's words of defense differently. In one paper he was quoted at length,

> "*The only difference between myself and Knox amounts to this: Knox wants me to train morning and afternoon. I have been accustomed to only training in the afternoon and when I did not feel up to the mark, to skip a day occasionally. My performances in the West and here during the last two years have shown the efficacy of my system… if I submit to the Knox system I know that I will be stale and played out when I get to Stockholm… personally I have only one thing against Mr. Knox, and that is that he has tried to discourage me, and has tried to belittle my capabilities.*" [17]

The second reporter recorded his words in the vernacular, incidentally, the version Walter cut out and sent home for his scrapbook, printed this way:

> "*Ah done train mahself for three years back, Mr. Knox, and ah done never got beat in all that time. Ah guess if ah kaint handle mahself right by now, ah doan want to go to no Olympic games.*" [18]

Whichever was the right voice (probably something in between) this version was an insulting display of prejudice by the paper, something Howard was well used to.

John Armstrong "Army" Howard was born and raised in

Winnipeg, the son of a barber. At about 20 years of age, he was noticed and recruited by the North End Amateur Athletic Club (NEAAC) for their sprinting team. He often said he had never lost a race. But he had been difficult to coach, developing a reputation for being obstinate.

The Provincial Trials in Toronto had been his introduction to a top flight competition and he demonstrated his talent by winning. But it was not easy for him. The papers always patronized him, using the epithets "the coloured boy from Winnipeg", "Smoke" and the "dusky flash", as was typical at the time. It was never just "Howard" the way all the other athletes were treated.

When he met up with the NEAAC team in Toronto for the Provincial Trials (he came a day late so he could play a baseball game) their hotel on Yonge Street refused him a room because of his colour. To their credit, the whole NEAAC (five people) walked out and booked into the Grand Central Hotel where he was accepted. Later, with the Olympic Team, at times he had to stay in a separate hotel and eat in separate restaurants. When Howard complained about the segregation, "he was chastised by team officials as uppity."[19] This kind of treatment could make any athlete disgruntled, angry and obstinate.

Even more demeaning, Howard was "made white" to be accepted on his baseball team in 1913. He was a standout on the Winnipeg Creamery Crescent Baseball Club for his athletic play, but when the team photo was published, his face was doctored to appear white; no black man could lead the team![20]

Canada was decidedly racist in 1912. In Howard's home town of Winnipeg, a few newspapers predicted that the Dominion Government, after an influx of Negroes from Alabama to the prairies, would move to exclude Negro immigrants in 1911.[21] In 1907, there were race riots in Vancouver over the "Yellow Peril" of oriental immigrants. The Ku Klux Klan had 13,000 members in BC and was just as prominent in Manitoba in 1910.[22] Even the Canadian

Army at the start of WWI would not accept blacks into their ranks. Canada was less violent in its racism than the US, which was at its apex for lynchings at that time, but was no less cruel. Army Howard grew up in this prejudiced world and wasn't adapting well. He took a stand against societal mores in 1919, when he returned from the war in Europe (he'd been a stretcher-bearer, the typical non-combat role assigned to blacks) with a white, English wife, and started a family. After attempting to settle into a homestead just north of Winnipeg, they were chased from the area by stone-throwing whites; an interracial couple was no more welcome there than in Mississippi.[23] She soon left him and re-married, while he took to work as a porter on the railway for six years, then to ranching in the Riding Mountains in Manitoba after that. Howard somehow raised his children alone, dying suddenly in 1939 at the age of 49.

Howard had "always been a hard boy to handle and decidedly headstrong" said one paper.[24] In 1911, he had been suspended for an entire season by the Manitoba AAA for a breach of the amateur rules, a matched race, and in the spring of 1912 had been suspended briefly again for another breach of the rules.

Did his obstinate attitude arise from his treatment by society? We'll never know, but all that pressure sure didn't help. To complain about racist treatment only to be called "uppity" by team officials had to drive him into his shell. Was Walter the right man to help him deal with all this prejudice? Probably not. In his notes there is hardly a mention of a black man without the epithet of "coon" attached or implied. He used the "dusky smoke" name for Howard repeatedly himself. Walter would not have been sympathetic, but would have been highly focused when trying to coach Howard's technique. Walter could focus. Howard, apparently, could not.

Four days into the trip across the Atlantic, animosity flared up again. Many of the athletes were complaining of Walter's training intensity by then, but Army Howard was the flashpoint. Howard started breaking curfew and resisting instruction. "Sheer disobedience to orders", Walter said to reporters. Howard, for his part, said he was "completely played out" on the boat, and claimed, "Why Knox made me train as hard as ever even while I was seasick going over!"[25] When Walter asked him, he says in his notes, to live up to all the rules the other boys were following, Howard "tried to give me an argument". Finally, in an exasperated attempt to stop his boasting, Walter challenged him to a 40 yard match with the stakes being Howard's attention. If Walter won, Howard would agree to clean up his act. Walter didn't mention what he put on the line. Arrogantly, Howard accepted. When Walter won, embarrassing the great Canadian champion who was going to win at the Olympics, Howard turned sullen, and no less troublesome, oppressed by a white authority figure.[26]

At one point, a few of the other athletes came to Walter, complaining about Howard's behaviour. Walter directed one of the weight men on the team to "give him a damn good licking", and if you need any help "get two or three of the others". [27] Walter promised to back them up and "there won't be anything said about it". They didn't do it. As Walter said, "they were afraid to tackle him". Throughout the trip, Howard was "antagonized by both officials and men on the team until the poor fellow didn't know half the time what he was doing", remarked Elwood Hughes, an independent coach traveling with the team. "He was the point of every practical joke and the butt for everything".[28]

Three days after arriving in England, Walter and Howard got nose to nose on the track. The day before, Walter had found Howard in a pub with the team rubber eating hot dogs and drinking beer, a banned behaviour. Walter was totally fed up with "Mr. Smoke". Then, that day, Walter had arranged time trials for the men to choose the runners for the 4x400 relay team. Howard strutted and bragged to all the men about how fast he was going to go, upsetting everyone, according to Jack Tait, a middle distance man also vying for a spot on the team.²⁹ Walter confronted him, ordering him off the track and out of the relay. Howard refused to move and defiantly remained at the starting line for his time trial. Tait recorded Howard as saying "he was going to run, and that there was nobody on the field quite big enough to stop him". That's when Walter got nose to nose with him, seeing red. Walter had a different definition of "big enough" than Army Howard. Agitated and full of bluster, Howard started to raise a fist, crossing a line Walter was waiting for. With a sledgehammer left into his midsection and a right uppercut to his chin, Walter laid him out! This was the last straw; he was off the Olympic Team. The chairman of the Olympic Committee saw the whole thing from the stands and concurred that Howard had made the first move.³⁰ The whole afternoon's training was disrupted by this fracas, and with so little time to hone his team, Walter was upset.

After practice, Walter headed into the change room to find Howard still sitting dejectedly on one of the benches. Walter closed the door, took off his coat and started rolling up his sleeves.

"Get ready", Walter growled, "I'm going to show you one white man that a nigger can't lick. And just because Jack Johnson is champion don't think you can lick anyone".

Walking over to Howard, he ordered the muscular six foot three inch athlete onto his feet. "I never hit anyone when they are down."

As Walter reported the episode in his notes, Howard just "bunched up in a heap" with his hands over his face saying, "Ah don't want to, ah don't want to fight".³¹

After the fracas, another meeting with Merrick, the Chairman of the Olympic Committee, had to be called. Walter refused to attend, saying he had "had all he wanted, and they could do as they wished about him going any further with the team." Merrick, uncharacteristically as he was a hard-nosed, decisive man, put it to a vote by his teammates, evidence there were two sides to the story. There had been considerable complaining about Howard's disruptions, but in the end they voted to take him along to Stockholm. Howard, though annoying, was seen as the lesser of two evils on the team, especially to Frank Lukeman, the sprinter and all-around man, and his buddy Halpenny. Lukeman was a handful for the coach himself. He was the leader in a growing revolt on the team against Walter's hard-nosed, taxing training regimen. Another Winnipeg North Ender, Joe Keeper, was also on the team and would have to answer to supporters back home if he voted to send Army home. Keeper, the distance runner from Winnipeg, was a full Cree Indian who grew up in a residential Indian school and would have innately understood the racism Howard had to overcome. It's not likely he would have sided with the controlling dictates of the white coach. That the majority of the team elected to give Howard another chance, implies there is more to the story than Walter's claim that it was all about Howard's intransigence.

Jack Tait, in a newspaper report after the Olympics, described Howard after the confrontation as "a very crestfallen personage", stating that, "you never saw such a change in a man in your life".[32] At the team meeting, Howard very publicly admitted it was all his fault and apologized to the team profusely, likely seeing his chance at the Olympics slipping away after all the hardship he had been through already. The athletes were in a very difficult position but, as much as they were annoyed by Howard, they disliked the staff more.

This was the climax to a rebellion that had been brewing among the whole team by then. Arriving at the Olympics a few days later, Frank Lukeman had the signature of every athlete on a letter for the Olympic Committee, putting their complaints, in part, this way,

> "The individual members of the team, for the most part, were thoroughly disgusted with the way the trip had been managed and the training they had received... that the training required of them was not adapted to their individual needs. On this point Knox had apparently stood firm and treated all with similar severity."[33]

In talking to a reporter after the Games, Lukeman and Cal Bricker, two of the top men on the team, "gave it as their opinion that Trainer Knox had overtrained them leaving other members of the team to themselves."[34]

In any event, the Olympic team now carried on to the Olympic venue for its final preparations with a persona non grata practicing all on his own, not talking to the coach. The team photo was taken of the 18 track and field athletes in London, just before departing for the Olympics. Army Howard was not included. In fact, the hotheaded Howard refused to be in the picture.[35]

The situation only deteriorated from there. Crow, one of the Olympic Committee managers of the team, got married the day they arrived in London and disappeared for a two week honeymoon. Merrick, Walter's only other support staff, was absent most of the time, enjoying himself around London and away for days at a time. Walter was all alone with an unhappy team. His untenable situation was described by Elwood Hughes in a letter to the Olympic Committee in August. Hughes was hired by the Hamilton Spectator newspaper to accompany Jim Corkery, who qualified for the Olympic Team by winning the Hamilton Spectator marathon. Corkery and Hughes, while traveling with the team, were independent due to their financial support by the newspaper, and ostracized for it.

> *"If it had not been for the voluntary assistance rendered by Walter Trivett, Secretary of the Ontario AAU, Knox would have been completely up in the air. As it was he was badly upset having so much work crowded on him that he was irritable at all times and couldn't be addressed by some of the men without being uncivil to them... the task of looking after everything was more than he or anyone else could handle with the result that his efforts were practically fruitless."*[36]

Trivett, when interviewed after the Games, had this to say, "The whole trouble between Knox and the team in my opinion lay in the fact that Knox was not a good judge of human nature".[37]

Walter had started to lose control of the team in London. As Hughes, a valuable objective inside source, observed, "Not only were the men confronted with opportunities to break training (in the big city of London), but they took advantage of them, in spite of all that was done to stop them".[38] Merrick and Crow, the team managers, set a horrible example for the team by gallivanting around the country, completely ignoring their obligations. The men, frustrated with an overbearing coach, cannot be blamed for looking for some relief.

Walter responded to his frustrations by acting out. Angry with the rubber who was late showing up at the stadium one day, through no fault of his own, Walter "seemed to lose all sense and grabbed him by the throat, and would have throttled him if some of the others had not interfered", recalled Lukeman, who continued with another anecdote. "One day he (Knox) had an argument with Duffy (a marathoner) that if he did not shut up he would knock his head off. Duffy, however, squared right off and told him to start and he would give him all that was coming to him. That settled Knox".[39]

The team that left London for Stockholm on July 2nd, four days before the opening ceremonies, was not a happy one.

22

The Stockholm Olympic Games

The Olympic Games, held between July 6th and 27th, were a spectacular affair; the weather was warm and clear throughout. While the London Games of 1908 were known as the Belligerent Games, Stockholm in 1912 ran the Meticulous Games. Everything was organized down to the tiniest detail and was run like clockwork. These were the first Olympics to use electronic timing on the track, the photo finish and a public address system. For the first time, athletes from all five continents participated. In Stockholm, the Olympic movement really hit its stride.

Walter's participant medal from the Olympics in 1912.
Courtesy Claudia Courtney

This should have been a triumphant Games for the Canadians and their small 36-man team. In 1908 in London, Canada's 87 man team won 16 medals: 3 gold, 3 silver and 10 bronze. In 1912, with less than half the entrants, the Canadians still won 3 gold, 2 silver and 3 bronze, dropping from 5th to 10th place in the medal standings. After the Olympic Trials, Walter, hadn't expected even that good a showing. The rest of the world had not quite left Canada, and its commitment to part-time amateurism, behind.

The discontent continued in Stockholm, though now aimed at the managers, Merrick and Crow, more than Walter. The team was put up in a small hotel and told to get their meals in a tiny restaurant nearby. The restaurant was crowded and often the athletes had to wait for two hours to get in. Several times competitors had to leave for the stadium without eating. Lukeman and several of the other athletes began searching out other restaurants on their own, using their own money. Of course, only Army Howard was ever chastised for breaking the rules on where and what to eat. Merrick never solved this problem for the athletes.

Walter's team came into Stockholm with many of the athletes at the top of their games, ready to take on the world in spite of all the ruckus of the previous month. Maybe Walter's training regime *was* the right approach. But, distressingly for Walter, his two most troubling athletes had their events up first, setting the tone for the meet.

The 100 metre sprint, Army Howard's first event, took place during the first two days of competition. This event was wide open, no runner had dominated the field since 1909 and several had a good chance of winning, including Howard. The three Germans who co-held the world record of 10.5 seconds were all eliminated early in the heats, making it a free-for-all.

But, as was typical so far for Canada's Olympic Team, controversy erupted at the worst moment. The day before the 100, the eve of the opening ceremonies, the Swedish team protested Army Howard, who didn't need any more problems. Walter, after their confrontation in London, had thrown him off the team and apparently informed the Swedish officials of that. After the vote to keep him on the team, a second telegram re-entered him. The Swedes were now saying that entry was past the deadline, so Howard should not be allowed to compete. Informed of this the night before the race, Howard went out for a night on the town. Next morning he went to the track to watch the races and found that the Canadian officials, probably Walter in what would have been a very magnanimous move, or Elwood Hughes, had managed to get him reinstated (managers Merrick and Crow, who should have been the front men in this controversy, didn't get to Stockholm until the next day). Howard had to rush to get ready for his heat with little warm-up.[1]

Running on adrenalin, Howard won his first heat in 11.0, a respectable time. Frank Lukeman also advanced to the semi-final, but Beasley and McConnell were eliminated. In the six semi-finals, only the winners advanced to the final. Lukeman finished third to be eliminated. Howard, embarrassingly, came last in his heat of six men. He had been complaining of a "stomach ailment" all day and just couldn't perform; obviously his night on the town was catching up on him. There were no encouraging words from his coach, the man who had crawled out of a deathbed after being poisoned in Nanaimo to win a sprint while completely woozy. Walter despised a quitter, and that's exactly what he considered Howard after that race. Five of the six finalists were Americans, one of whom, Alvah Meyer (who would win the Olympic silver medal) Howard had defeated at the Provincial Trials in Toronto a month before.

The second day, July 7th, Lukeman also contested the pentathlon. Twenty-eight year old Frank Lukeman had also been a thorn in Walter's side, mostly due to his cavalier and opinionated attitude. He was one of the athletes Walter accused of going to Stockholm for a holiday. Lukeman had been a top sprinter and jumper for the Montreal AAA but had many run-ins with his coaches and had left the club for the crosstown rival St Pat's AAA. He did return, then jumped ship for an Ottawa club and their offer of a good paying job (in the same way they had tried to entice Walter). But he was a top flight natural athlete. In the field of pentathletes, he placed 6th in the long jump, 11th in the javelin, 5th in the 200, 3rd in the discus and 5th in the 1500. Placings were based on the sum total of ranks in each event. Lukeman finished tied for 3rd. As a tiebreaker, their scores were entered into the decathlon tables, which awarded points for raw times and distances. Lukeman ended up fourth overall, just out of the medals.

However, this was the Olympics of the great American Jim Thorpe. Thorpe won four of the five pentathlon events to take the gold medal. Six months later, the Olympic Committee disqualified him when it was discovered he had accepted money to play baseball (as was common with US collegians, only Thorpe didn't know enough to use an alias) and took back his two gold medals. So a year after the Games, Lukeman was awarded the bronze medal. Walter had his first medalist, but no one knew it at the time.

As much as Walter was annoyed with Lukeman, he did post a strong result to buoy the team after Howard's disappointing effort. It was a few days until the team's next medal hopeful stepped up, and stepped up in a big way.

On July 10th, three days after the Howard debacle, young George Hodgson, an 18 year old who had just finished his first year at McGill University, competed in the 1500m freestyle swimming event. He was spindly and small, hardly finished adolescence, but, as Walter could appreciate, had developed his own unique modified trudgen stroke (an amalgam of the sidestroke and the crawl). With his new technique, he was unbeaten in the last three years. On July 10th, he stood on the pier overlooking the 100 metre course, bounded by pontoon floats inside the ocean break wall. He had already won both his heat and his semi-final convincingly, breaking the world record by 25 seconds. Knowing the gold medal was in the bag, Hodgson planned an assault on the record book. After taking the lead right off the gun, he set a new world record for the 1000m then kept swimming for the 1500m gold medal. Hodgson then continued on to set a new world record for the mile swim. Three world records in one swim! That gave the Canadian team something to cheer about. The 1500 record of 22:00.0 would stand for 12 years. Unfortunately, with the other competitions going on at the stadium, none of the track and field competitors were there to witness Hodgson's heroics.

July 11th was a big day for Walter's track and field athletes. Two more medals were to be won, but they would have to wait until Army Howard took his turn in his best event, the 200. Having shaken his upset stomach, everyone expected him to be a medal contender. He ran in a heat of only two men, winning, barely, in a slow time of 25.0 seconds. The other Canadians, McConnell and Beasley, were again eliminated. In the semi-final, where again only the winners would advance, Howard got his act together, running just over 22 seconds, the fastest he had ever done, but he finished third in his heat to be eliminated. The eventual silver medalist won his heat in 21.8 seconds. Howard immediately blamed Walter and his overtraining, saying he lost "every race in the last few yards".[2]

Howard's dismal meet was almost over. The Canadian 4x100 relay had finished 4th on July 8th and the 4x400 relay (yes, Walter let him run on that relay team) would finish 5th on July 14th. Howard never overcame his reputation as having choked in the 1912 Olympics, even after he came back to win the 100 and 200 at the 1913 Canadian Championships. You can be sure there were no pats on the back and heart-to-heart talks with his Olympic coach either. In fact, he was the one spreading the slanders about Howard after the Olympics.

After Howard fell flat in the 200, two more Canadians collected medals for Canada on July 11th. Walter's "sure thing", George Goulding, came through as expected and won the gold medal in the 10 kilometer walk. Goulding had competed in the 1908 London Olympics, not finishing the 10 k walk and placing 22nd in the marathon. However, he improved rapidly over the next three years, setting world records at every walking distance between 2 and 10 miles. In Stockholm, Goulding defeated the 1911 world champion, Ernest Webb, by just 11 seconds in his heat, but shortly thereafter was devastated by the news that his mother had died. It took considerable courage on his part to step up to the starting line a few days later and beat Webb again in the final by 22 seconds, leading from start to finish. After the race, Goulding, still distraught, sent a workman-like, sad telegram home, saying simply, "Won — George".

Then came the pole vault, Walter's pet event. Thirty year old William Halpenny represented Canada. Halpenny was the athlete who'd shown up at the 1906 Canadian YMCA Championships in the rain in Hamilton with the candy-striped pole Walter so disdained. He had been a top Canadian vaulter since 1904, but just missed out on his chance to go to the 1908 Olympics after losing to Ed Archibald at the Trials. But he bounced back and was Canadian Champion between 1911 and 1913. Originally from PEI, he was lured to the Montreal AAA by his good friend Frank Lukeman, and followed him back and forth to the St. Pat's AAA one turbulent year. At the 1911 Canadian Championships, Halpenny won, leaping over 12 feet, and was offered an attempt at a new world record of 13' 3". Eyewitnesses say he cleared the bar, but the corner of the number card pinned to his chest pulled the bar down.

Americans had recently dominated the pole vault, and it was expected they would take at least five of the top six spots in Stockholm. The world record had climbed to just over 13 feet, in part due to a new innovation. As can be clearly seen in photos at the Games here, a heavy beam was now being embedded in the ground right below the bar, for jumpers to butt their poles up against. Until just recently, vaulters had to stick the pointy end of their pole in the ground, and could easily plant it too far under the bar or too far away to make a clearance possible. Imagine running full speed with a heavy, 14 foot pole outstretched in front of you and trying to stick it in a cup. Only top athletes could coordinate that task and then manage to swing themselves up with the pole. Being able to slide the blunted pole along the ground until it hit the beam changed everything; the skill focused on the leaping now, not the planting.

But the poles were still stiff, made of wood or (lighter) bamboo; the flexible poles that catapulted the vaulters into the air, invented by Walter's buddy Harry Gill, were still five years away. And there were no soft landing pits to cushion the fall. In Stockholm there was a sand pit but it doesn't look very soft in photos.

That afternoon of July 11th, Bill Halpenny cleared 12' 4 ½" to be in the last group of six vaulters, along with four Americans and a Swede. The bar was raised to 12' 6", and Halpenny was the first to attempt it, a personal best height for him. On his first attempt, he sailed over the bar, setting a new Olympic Record, only to confront disaster. He landed awkwardly "on his breast" shattering two ribs. That was the end of his Olympic hopes; he had to withdraw. Three other jumpers cleared his height and more, the American Babcock winning at 12' 11 ½".

Halpenny had finished up in fourth place, but in only the second time ever at the Olympics, the Olympic Committee decided to award special medals because of their delinquency. The 4th to 6th place finishers were awarded bronze medals because of the "inadequacy of the landing pit". (The only other time this had been done was in London when officials helped the exhausted Dorando Pietri across the finish line in the marathon, disqualifying him, and then presented him with a special trophy later.) Halpenny really earned his bronze medal the hard way!

Walter would have been excited by the pole vault competition. When he toured Scotland in 1911, he claimed in all the papers to have a personal best in the vault of 12' 6". This leap was done in training, a newspaper reported, with several witnesses[3], "which stood as a world's record for quite a time"[4]. One wonders if Walter took a few attempts at the pole vault here after the meet, to test out the new innovation. He was training hard for a return to Scotland after the

Games.

Another of Walter's medal hopefuls took to the field the next day, July 12th, for the long jump. Cal Bricker was the talented young Canadian Champion Walter had defeated on his big day at the Canadian Championships in Toronto in 1907. At the time, Walter commented Bricker could jump just as well as he could but always seemed to falter when challenged. Bricker had rounded into one of the best long jumpers in the world by 1912 and was the defending Olympic bronze medalist. However, the Olympic Committee felt he did not perform well enough at the Dominion Trials and left him off the team. Walter spoke up for him, saying he knew what his trouble was and could help him. He was added to the team on Walter's recommendation. Both Walter and Bricker, coincidentally, were born in the same small Ontario town of Listowel, six years apart.

Walter taking a try at the pole vault in London during the Olympic training camp in 1912. Note the lack of a beam to butt the pole up against, or a landing pit.
Courtesy Orillia Museum of Art and History

Walter had worked hard with Bricker on his technique in London, not letting him jump all out until he had perfected a new style. As Walter reported it, Bricker snuck back into the stadium one day after practice to test himself all out and pulled a muscle in his leg.[5] The rubber directed Walter to the change room where he found Bricker broken down. He had soared a personal best 24' 2", but injured himself. Walter commented he felt he had a 25' jump in him but lost it that day. Bricker now had a built-in excuse if he failed to perform. His fortitude was going to be tested, especially with the gold medal unexpectedly up for grabs.

In the long jump in Stockholm, the favourite and defending champion, Frank Irons, had a poor day and didn't make the final, opening the door for the gold medal. Bricker qualified for the final in second place with a strong leap of 23' 7 ¾", behind the American Gutterson at a remarkable 24' 11". Neither man improved in their final three jumps and the third place man fell short of Bricker by less than two inches. Bricker now had a silver medal ("on a bum leg" Walter later wrote. "He missed the chance of a lifetime."[6]) to go with his bronze from 1908, and a notch in his belt in overcoming his weak-willed reputation, though surely questions lingered in the back of his mind about what might have been.

Undoubtedly, Walter tried to mentor Bricker at the Olympics. If anyone knew how to perform under pressure and focus it was Walter Knox. Whether Bricker was listening to his coach is another story; Bricker was one of the loudest voices after the Games in criticizing the treatment of the athletes.

July 14th brought George Hodgson back to the pool for the 400m freestyle final. He had won his heat in a slow time but won his semi-final in world record time, just one second ahead of John Hatfield, the famous English swimmer. The final on the 14th was expected to be a close race. On the dock, waiting for the gun, Hodgson's frail stature was dramatically exposed. Next to him was Harold Hardwick, the eventual bronze medalist from Australia. Hardwick was massive next to Hodgson, with a thick neck and broad shoulders, and would go on to win the Australian heavyweight boxing championship in 1915. Hodgson, Hatfield and Hardwick raced along together most of the 400 metres, exciting the cheering crowds. Muscular Hardwick took the lead halfway but then began to fade, leaving the two smaller swimmers to battle for the gold over the four lengths of the pool. Coming down the last length, the Canadian started to pull away and Hatfield couldn't respond. Hodgson took a full four seconds off the world record with Hatfield just a second behind for his second silver medal. Hodgson's world record of 5:24.4 stood for 12 years, until broken by the great Johnny Weissmuller in 1924.

Back at the track, Walter's charges won another medal that same day. Cape Breton strongman, Duncan Gilles, contested the hammer throw. Walter had commented in the paper that Gilles lacks style but that some attention could make him a champion.[7] Four weeks of technical coaching by the Olympic coach paid off, just as Walter predicted. The event was dominated by the American Matt McGrath, whose margin of victory was an astounding 21 feet! But Gilles pulled out the silver medal, besting the American bronze medalist by a mere 9 inches.

There was to be only one more medal for the Canadian team, a bronze by the rower Everard Butler in the single sculls on July 17th. Butler, the Canadian Champion from the Toronto Argonaut Rowing Club, qualified as one of the final four rowers to face off in two paired matches, the winners to vie for the championship. He was paired with the eventual gold medalist and lost by just a boat length. That left him tied for third, both men receiving bronze medals.

The Argonauts of Toronto also sent over a coxed eight man sculling team who were favoured for a medal. However, in the same matched race format, they lost a very tight race to the eventual gold medalists from England in the first round and were eliminated.

The Canadian team returned to Montreal to a celebratory reception. Several hundred McGill students met the boat at the pier to cheer on George Hodgson. As the hometown hero of the team, Hodgson was presented with a diamond locket and a medal by the Mayor of Montreal.

Then the commentary started. Everyone involved wanted to have their say, except the coach, who didn't return with the team. Walter was in Scotland, probably trying to put the whole Olympic experience out of his mind. Every newspaper published summaries with lengthy quotes from team officials. Canadian Olympic Committee Chairman James Merrick set the tone,

> *"I am completely satisfied with the work of Coach Knox. The whole trouble was stirred up by a few of the men who went over to Sweden believing it was one big holiday… It was a mistake taking Howard on the team. We did it for fear of leading some people to believe that race prejudice influenced the choice."* [8]

Then Merrick announced that he was through with athletics, "matters have reached such a stage that an honourable man cannot afford to have his name drawn into controversies." Obviously the team did not live up to the high ideals of sportsmanship espoused by the elites running the AAU of Canada. Merrick was also likely stung by the pointed barbs aimed directly at him.

"Howard was the cause of the trouble that existed", concluded Merrick, "his sympathizers being those of the same mental capacity". First he said he didn't want to appear prejudicial then a few paragraphs later he came up with that astounding comment. There were class and racial undertones, however unconscious, in the administration of sport in Canada.

James Merrick is an interesting and pivotal character in the history of Canadian sport. He was a hardline defender of the amateur ideal, who had negotiated the end of the "athletic wars" in Canada, embedding the amateur code for the next generation. He was Chair of the AAU of C, oversaw the creation of the Canadian Olympic Committee and then sat as its chair too. There was no more dominant personage in sport in Canada. Even though an energetic administrator who sat on more than a dozen various athletic associations, he was still a lightning rod for controversy. His saying he was through with sport was disingenuous at best. He was a political operator and an abrasive, confrontational lawyer who, clearly, was not well liked by the athletes in Stockholm.[9]

The athletes saw all the controversy in a very different light than Merrick. They presented their viewpoint to him in Stockholm, as Chairman of the Olympic Committee, in a letter signed by all of them at the very start of the Games, after the fracas in London. Frank Lukeman shared its contents with reporters as soon as he arrived home in Montreal. The athletes complained of the overtaxing training regimen Walter put them through, two-a-day workouts right from the start in Montreal and continuing on the boat and in London. Just as vociferously, they attacked Merrick and the Olympic Committee organizers. The Olympic Committee had neglected to hire any rubbers to go with the team to Europe, essentially expecting Walter to be a one man show. At the last minute, in response to the athletes' and coach's complaints, "Fuss" Kerrison was hired, using money from the Ontario AAU. Kerrison was the one popular official traveling with the team, but completely over-worked, and he was not to continue with the team to Stockholm after training camp in London (he did, after all, take Howard out to that pub for a beer, enraging Walter). Merrick hired a Swedish rubber after the Games started who was completely unsatisfactory.[10]

Lukeman went on to say that when the disgruntled team left London for Sweden, the athletes complained that Merrick and Crow didn't accompany them to organize their accommodations or registrations. They showed up the day after the opening ceremonies, five days after the team, missing the whole fiasco with Army Howard's apparent disqualification and the restaurant frustrations. They weren't there to mediate the athletes' complaints with their coach either, the single biggest problem on the team.

WF Trivett, the Secretary of the Ontario AAU, spent some time in London with the team and out of necessity stepped in to assist the harried coach for a short time. He blamed Walter's poor management of the men as the biggest problem.

> "He treated all the men alike and did not vary his treatment according to the men's various dispositions. Where a rough word will be the right thing for one man on an occasion, it will make another man sullen and unwilling to work at all." [11]

One of the athletes, Jack Tait, in commenting during the Games, only complained about Howard.

> "'Mistah' James Army Howard continues to hog the spotlight... his only fault being that he thinks he is the only runner living, and the only member of the team entitled to consideration. He has his own ideas about training that change with the weather. Coach Knox has exercised great leniency..." [12]

Army Howard, on leaving the ship in Montreal, was "very quiet" and had nothing to say to reporters. He was on the train to Winnipeg by five o'clock in the afternoon that same day.

Walter Knox, the coach, didn't comment on the whole affair until he sent a letter to the Toronto Star at the end of August, a month after the Games ended, and then gave an interview in October when he returned from Scotland. He piled on the athletes, sticking to two lines: they were lazy and they were difficult.

> "Army Howard... was the ringleader of the rebellion,

> *being always in some sort of trouble or other. If I had ever thought he was the unruly sort of individual he proved to be I certainly would have drawn the line at him even before we left the country. No person could tell anything to Lukeman either. He knew it all and was always ready for a scrap. Some of the boys imagined it was all a pleasure jaunt and I had the greatest difficulty in forcing them to stick to work and training.*"[13]

Was this the AAU of C attitude of the part-time amateur butting up against Walter's professional sport-as-a-career attitude? The AAU of C promoted sport as a pastime to be done in one's spare time, while preparing for careers in the real world. These athletes, while not living up to Walter's hard work ethic, were not necessarily performing below their home club ethic. Lukeman and Howard had had numerous run-ins with their MAAA and NEAAC coaches; it could very likely have been over their laziness. But these athletes were certainly never coached to train as seriously as Walter would have expected them to, especially in the short time he had to work with them. Maybe they were lazy and out for a holiday. Or maybe they were training as hard as they were used to, which wasn't hard enough for Walter. Certainly they were difficult and opinionated.

Walter continued,

> "*Howard told me from the start of the trip that he was accustomed to 'punishing' his stomach and I did consequently allow him to have a little bit his own way in the matter of diet. I gave him steaks and other things which the other members of the team did not enjoy. One day I found him with a big dish of chicken, celery salad and other highly seasoned stuff in front of him. Apparently I could not please him.*"

That type of food would have been a dietary taboo to a professional like Walter. Later, in a personal letter to his sister, Walter said, "Howard, alias 'Big Smoke' was good enough to beat the sprinters in the 200m, but he is not 'game', and is very hard to get along with".[14]

Finally, in the letter written at the end of August to the Toronto Star from Scotland, Walter wrote,

> *"Howard, the Big Smoke, was a bad one. He could get out of condition faster than any man I ever saw. I gave up hopes of him winning after we left London and he proved to be a quitter in the races. He is a good runner but brainless… Lukeman is an in-and-outer, he is a very uncertain athlete…and not the athlete I thought he was."* [15]

In another paper, this quote included, "The proper way to handle him (Howard) is to take a club to him every morning, and nobody wants to handle a man that way".[16]

What Walter decidedly did not comment on was the difficulty placed on him by Merrick's inattention. Walter was a man who had the attitude that you got things done; you didn't whine, you worked hard and just did it. He hated excuses. Walter never publicly criticized his employers, the Olympic Committee in general and Merrick specifically. There should have been serious complaints from him over Merrick's dereliction of duty and the complications that caused for him in his preparation of the athletes.

Finally, on August 24th, almost a month after the Olympic Team arrived home in Montreal, the one independent voice associated with the team spoke out. Elwood Hughes, the independent coach of one of the marathoners, who had spent the whole month on the fringes of the Olympic Training camp, published a letter with biting detail and bitter criticism.

> *"Few followers of the sport have any idea of the extent of the discontent which raged among the athletes. From start to finish there was trouble... The entire trip was spoiled through lack of management... (When Merrick and Crowe abandoned Walter in London) this left both the executive details, the coaching and the training to Walter Knox, who certainly was not fitted to look after the executive part of the work, and who in addition did not have the time to do it... The dissatisfaction over the restaurant (in Stockholm) caused more trouble than any single thing and the members of the team were not at all backward in expressing themselves... Knox punched Howard while the team was in London while several of the athletes who had grievances decided to keep their troubles to themselves rather than air them and get no satisfaction, as was the case all the time... Howard was a bad actor and a hard man to handle... At every stage Knox found himself up against trouble. With Crowe enjoying his honeymoon and Merrick in London having a good time, the coach had no one to refer things to, with the result that the team practically ran leaderless. I don't blame Knox so much as Merrick and Crowe."* [17]

One can see why Merrick said he was through with sport. He was being self-righteously demonstrative in blaming the athletes. The newspaper reports all through August, when they weren't judging Howard and Knox for their feud, all pointed a finger at him. It was a week after this letter was published that Walter was contacted and sent a letter to the Toronto Star, his first public comment on the Games, where he set the blame squarely on the athletes and made no mention of his superiors.

While Walter proceeded to Scotland and another round of the Highland Games, Army Howard returned home to Winnipeg. At the Canadian Championships in 1913, he dominated the sprints, and remained the fastest man in Canada until 1915, when he was finally, as a black man, allowed to join the Canadian Army.

Howard left a legacy for Canada in his grandchildren, who grew up persecuted in an era almost as racist as his. Two of his grandchildren, Harry and Valerie Jerome, children of a railway porter like Army, competed for Canada in the 1960 Olympics as sprinters. Harry went on to compete in two more Olympics. Valerie had been Canadian Champion in the sprint as a 16 year old before representing Canada at the Rome Olympics. But Harry was the standout, one of the dominant sprinters in the world in the early 60's, setting seven world records. He tied the 100m world record at 10.2 then 10.1 and finally 10.0 seconds. He set the 100 yard record at 9.2 and 9.1. Like his grandfather, Harry was "vilified" for not bringing home Olympic gold. He won the bronze in 1964 behind the incredible Bob Hayes, but that wasn't good enough. He, like his grandfather, was labeled with "not having the right stuff". Harry ran in Tokyo with a leg injury, not unlike his grandfather and his stomach ailment, and didn't rise above it the way the media expected. However, no one could accuse him of being "brainless" like they had his grandfather; Harry earned his master's degree, and Valerie likewise completed university to work as a teacher. Both Harry Jerome and Army Howard died young, Harry at 42 of a brain aneurysm, Army at 49. Their lives were similar in many ways, two generations apart.

Walter was probably of mixed feelings about the 1912 Olympics. He reveled in athletics at the highest levels but was utterly frustrated with the slackers on his team. With his Olympic commitments done, he wasted no time escaping the team once the competitions ended, leaving right after the last track and field event on July 17th, a full week before the closing ceremonies. He left the athletes under the care of Merrick and Crow, probably thinking it was about time they did something. His contract was to coach the athletes; he had done it, and now he was getting out of there. Walter booked himself on a ship to Edinburgh that night. The Highland Games season only had a month to go until the big championship Aboyne Games, and he wanted to get his turns in. Two days later he was competing.

23

Scottish Tours and Disappointments

Walter's ship brought him into Edinburgh on the morning of July 19th, 1912. He hopped straight on the train to get to the Highland Games at Thornton Junction, a sixty mile trip around the Firth of Forth. After seven weeks of being in a bad mood, this trip was like coasting into paradise. He was on his own again, totally in control, doing what he loved best: competing, and competing in a world of stalwart, proud men, not like the lazy Canadians he had spent so much energy goading through their exercises. This was his world. However, arriving in Thornton snapped him right out of his bliss.

He understood he would be arriving late, if he made it at all, but had entered events he knew were to be run later in the afternoon. But the first thing he found out upon arriving at the grounds was that the shot put had already been run. The sports committee's explanation was only that all the other shot putters were there and they had asked for the event to be held earlier. So they moved up the start time, ignoring the fact that one important entrant was not there.

Walter, his blood pressure rising, accosted the organizers, "Did it ever occur to you that the rest of the shot putters knew I would cut in on the first or second place, and if it was pulled off before I got here some of them would get a prize that they wouldn't if I was here?" Walter had been looking forward to stretching out in a friendly competition, venting some of the hangover-like frustrations that still simmered beneath his amiable demeanor. "If this is the way you intend to run your Games I'll never be entering again!"[1] Arguing was second nature for him that summer.

This got the committee thinking and finally they asked Walter what they could do to make it right. "The Man from Canada", they knew, was a big draw all across Scotland (Walter always wore a large, red Canadian maple leaf on his chest).

"Allow me to make a put against the winner's mark. If I don't beat it, I'll get no prize. If I do, I get the same prize as him."

It was agreed. Everyone would win, Walter if he performed would get his prize, the other winners would keep their prize money, and the organizers would get an exhibition by "the Canadian", upon his much anticipated return to the Highland Games. The mighty AA Cameron, the Scottish legend, had the winning put, 44 feet even.

Given three attempts like all the others, Walter, on his second attempt, sailed the 16 pound iron ball 46' 5", the best throw he made in his entire career! He bettered the winner by over two feet. That put would have won him the Olympic bronze medal nine days earlier. At a mere 150 pounds, it was a remarkable performance in a heavyweight event. There must have been some pent up energy coiled in Walter's muscles after the Olympics. The second place Scot, at this out-of-the-way Games, in the middle of the season, heaved the shot put far enough to place fourth at the Olympics too, showing the quality of the competition isolated in Scotland at their Highland Games.

Walter went on to win the pole vault as well, at its appropriate time.

Walter had been in training along with his Olympic athletes all summer. Just before leaving for Stockholm, he recorded marks of 22 feet in the long jump, 11' 2" in the vault and 44' 10" in the 16 pound shot put, marks competitive with his Olympians.

Walter was fit, but looking drawn now. Compact and muscular, with a head that looked a little too large for his frame, his face now showed the creases and lines of age and his hairline had receded to the top of his head, leaving just a tuft above his forehead. But his shoulders were still brawny and his biceps were impressive, as were his legs, signs of a well-cared-for physique. He was 34 years old and looked like a man approaching middle age — from the neck up. Not particularly photogenic, he always seemed to have a frown when the cameras came out, accentuating his weathered appearance. If it weren't for his reputation from the previous summer, he could have parlayed his aging appearance into a side bet bonanza with the young, up-and-coming local golden boys.

Walter Knox heaving the 22 pound shot put at the Aboyne Games before WWI.
Courtesy Orillia Museum of Art and History

From Thornton Junction it was on to the tour again, starting the next day in Douglas, 70 miles to the south. Twenty-three different Highland Games in sixty-four days. Twice a week he appeared in competitions all across Scotland, top to bottom, side to side. Hundreds and hundreds of miles on the train, in the automobile and behind the horse. Total results? Forty-one first placings, 15 seconds and 17 thirds (and none lower). After letting everyone else have their way for the first 12 weeks of the season, Walter dominated the circuit again in 1912.

The highlight of his tour came in the final competition of the year, September 20th, where he set a new pole vault record for all of Scotland. At Inverness, way in the north, in front of a prestigious crowd that included the Grand Duke of Russia, he cleared 11' 8", using a stiff, pointed pole and having no beam to butt it up against the way they'd done it in Stockholm.

Walter clearing the bar at a typical Highland Games. Note the bar is set as high as the standards will allow. Walter's record-setting efforts ran into this problem all across Scotland. Also note the 10 foot drop to a hard landing.
Courtesy Claudia Courtney

Equally impressive, Walter again defeated AA Cameron, the legend who'd been practically unbeaten in 11 years and who held the world record for every shot put event over 18 pounds. The victory came in the 16 pound shot put event at Bridge of Allen, one of the top Highland Games on the circuit. Cameron, a thick, muscular giant, fully 100 pounds heavier than Walter, was defeated by a toss of 44 feet. The newspapers fawned over that result all across Scotland.

Even before he left Stockholm for Scotland, Walter had issued a challenge in the Scottish papers to Speedie, Corbett and Scott, the top Scottish leapers, to a series of contests in the pole vault, long jump and standing and running high jumps. At the same time he challenged Cramb, Scott and McKenzie to a pole vaulting match. No one accepted.

By August 1st, only a couple of weeks after arriving in Scotland, Walter issued a challenge in the papers to anyone in Britain for an all-around match of nine events: 100 yards, 120 hurdles, one mile run, 16 pound hammer throw, 16 pound shot put, 56 pound weight throw, pole vault, high jump and long jump. The summer before, he'd had no takers in a list of just light events, so this year he said, "I am making a concession to the big fellows in putting three heavy events into the piece."[2] Later he added the 880 yard walk. There were no takers. Even after leaving Scotland, he claimed he would return if anyone wanted to take up his challenge. One reporter, in printing his challenge, commented, "For his height and weight I consider WR Knox of Canada to be the most wonderful athlete in the world at present time." "Knox is a phenomenon," exclaimed another.

Regarding his challenges, another reporter commented, "Wrestling has come to be regarded as an integral part of an all-around athletic program in Scotland, and I quite sympathize with the Scottish athlete's desire to keep it in the list of events."[3] This was likely posturing on the Scotsmen's behalf to evade a match; I'm sure Walter would have felt confident in his wrestling abilities too. McKenzie, the Scottish all-around champion, specifically refused to contest Walter, the paper saying he could win only three events.

However, one interesting match almost developed that summer. An Australian, Weller, challenged anyone in the world to an all-around match of 15 events (including swimming) in newspapers across three continents. Upon seeing this, Walter immediately forwarded his acceptance of the challenge and the side bet of an astounding $2500. His acceptance stipulated the match would have to be held in England or Scotland. This apparently was disagreeable to Weller as the match never happened.[4]

Near the end of September, 1912, Walter sailed for home. Once again, he opted to pass up the Powderhall Sprint, never saying why. Just before boarding ship, he told reporters that he would be returning to Scotland for the Powderhall. But by early October, after a quick visit in Orillia, he was back at Elk Lake working with his brother. Bundled in their cozy cabin with no way of training for a sprint, a mid-winter trip back to Scotland was out of the question.

In April, 1913, Walter, enjoying an unusually warm winter in Elk Lake, received an interesting letter from E W Johnson, who had won the All-Around Championship of America many years back, the same title Harry Gill had won in 1900. He was from Simcoe County, Orillia's county. Wouldn't it be great, he said, if another Simcoe county athlete, the third, could win the title? On April 4th, through the newspapers[5], Walter had issued a challenge to anyone in the world for an all-around match and Johnson was bringing news of a response. He proposed setting up a match for Walter.

The North American All-Around Championship had a long history but had only peaked in popularity in the last 10 years, since about 1900, the time Harry Gill won it. It evolved from the Caledonian Games in New England where single athletes sometimes won most or all of the athletic events at a Games. Challenges sprang up between the dominant athletes at different Games. As a result, the all-around was generally a matched affair in the workingman's (gambling) tradition. By the 1890s, the events were relatively standardized but, of course, the negotiated match could make whatever substitutions were agreed upon. Generally, in the course of one day, 10 events were contested: 100-yard dash, 16 pound shot put, high jump, 16 pound hammer throw, pole vault, 120 yard hurdles, 56 pound weight throw, long jump and one mile run. It was a grueling contest. You can see by the inclusion of the three heavy events, shot put, hammer and 56 pound weight, that the all-around evolved out of the Scottish games, where strength was a virtue.

A similar independent development of the all-around competition in both Scotland and Scandinavia occurred at the same time, though not so much in central Europe. As historian Robert Musil commented on the Austro-Hungarian Empire, "One went for sport, but not in the madly Anglo-Saxon fashion"[6]. By the early 1900s, matched contests for the World All-Around Title were being staged. The first great world champion was Tom Kiely of Ireland, who was at the end of his career at the time. The American Martin Sheridan, who dominated the all-around until 1910 or so, succeeded him. By 1912, Jim Thorpe had taken the American crown (in an AAU event), shattering all previous records before moving on to pro baseball and football that year. The vacant crown was then claimed by John A MacDonald of Boston in 1913. "Where he won his championship, no one knows, but he claims it and is willing to defend his honor", reported Lou Marsh in the Toronto Star[7].

The all-around's days were numbered by then. By 1904, the International AAUs had started dabbling with a new competition for all around athletes, the decathlon, though it was not regularly added to the list of events until 1911. Jim Thorpe's decathlon victory in the 1912 Stockholm Olympics really established the event as a mainstream Olympic and AAU event. This was a two day event with raw scores converted into points on tables based on the Olympic records from 1908 (the all-around was scored on a win-lose basis in each event, man on man, most wins took the match, all on one day, of course). The decathlon also eliminated the two heavy events and added the javelin and discus, leaving the shot put as the only strongman's event. After the 1912 Olympics, the traditional all-around competition began to go the way of the Caledonian Games, marginalized and forgotten. By the early 1920s it was essentially done, completely usurped in prestige by the decathlon.

But in 1913, the North American All-Around Championship was still a high profile event. That title established the winner as a top tier athlete, though a professional. Johnson was offering to contact John MacDonald, now the athletic director at Tufts College in Boston, to match Walter up against him for the title. Walter's challenge in the papers to all comers in an all-around match, aimed at Thorpe, and perhaps the Australian Weller, attracted MacDonald who, as the Toronto Star put it, "demanded a chance at Knox".[8] Walter jumped at the chance; he had been denied opportunities to win this type of championship several times in the past. MacDonald too, was eager, though his friends told him to beware of the stiff competition in Canada.

Walter had competed against John MacDonald in 1904 and 1910. He had been the dominant professional athlete in New England since then, a wonderful leaper and no slouch in the strength events. In 1910, Walter, using the alias Charles Newton, had humbled MacDonald in all seven events they contested at the Caledonian Games in Boston. It was obvious MacDonald didn't know the man he was challenging was *that* Charles Newton, otherwise he never would have made the match. Walter, likely with a smirk, knew the win was in the bag; he had only improved since then. Lou Marsh in the Toronto Star saw this as a closer match than Walter did. He printed the best past performances[9] for both Walter and MacDonald, and included Jim Thorpe for comparison too, complete with the points these would translate into on the decathlon tables:

	Knox	MacDonald	Thorpe
100-yd dash	9.8 (1000)	10.4 (874)	10.6 (832)
120 hurdles	16.8 (820)	16.8 (820)	16.6 (880)
one mile run	5:30 (639)	5:40 (589)	5:26 (659)
880 yard walk	3:50 (762)	4:00 (712)	3:48 (772)
high jump	5'6" (672)	6'1" (896)	6'2" (928)
broad jump	23'8 ½" (1000)	21'0" (756)	23'3" (972)
pole vault	11'9" (1000)	10'7" (776)	11'6" (952)
shot put	44'11" (900)	42'0" (760)	44'3" (868)
hammer throw	110' (579)	148' (1000)	122' (723)
56 pound weight	25'2" (488)	27'0" (576)	26'2" (536)
	7860	7931	7946

Where Marsh found these best performances is not referenced, but they are different than what other modern references now state (see below). In any event, there was considerable excitement in Toronto brewing for this match, egged on by the local newspapers.

On May 1st, Walter came down out of the bush to Orillia to commence his training for his 1913 tour of the Highland Games in Scotland. It wasn't until mid-June that Johnson confirmed the match was set for June 25th at Hanlan's Point in Toronto. That gave Walter only two weeks to get competition-ready, and necessitated changing his ticket on the ship to a week later.

Arriving in Toronto a few days before the event, MacDonald heard Walter was training at the university stadium and dropped in to pay his respects. When Walter saw him, he quickly retreated to the far end of the field, forcing MacDonald to stroll down there where they'd be alone. When MacDonald called out to him, Walter turned around and was recognized instantly.

"Oh! Had I known *you* were Knox I wouldn't be here! You weren't Knox the last time I saw you, and I understand now why my friends told me to stay away from Canada in an all-around match."[10]

Walter didn't want anyone else to witness this dramatic realization; it would totally ruin any betting prospects. MacDonald was committed, he had paid his forfeit money, so the only thing for him to do was carry on and hope for the best.

On Wednesday afternoon, June 25, 1913, these two athletes met to contest the Professional All-Around Championship of North America. MacDonald, at 6'1" and 190-odd pounds, towered over little Walter, 5'8" and 150 pounds. The newspapers described the match as attracting "a great outpouring of old-time athletes", including Walter's old friend from Orillia, and now prominent coach at the University of Illinois, Harry Gill, who acted as a timer in the match.[11] Tom Flanagan, the Toronto track and field promoter, recorded the match in detail.[12] Neither man was in great form, he said, but each did himself credit. The first two events went to MacDonald, the running high jump 5' 6" to 5' 4 ½" and the 56 pound weight throw 26' 7" to 22' 4'. Then Walter proceeded to win 7 of the 8 remaining events and "utterly outclassed his man in all of them," reported Flanagan. He won the shot put by 2' 3", the pole vault by almost two feet with a leap of 11' 3" and the long jump by over 3 feet. The sprints were easy wins, by 3/5 of a second in the 100 and over 5 seconds in the 120 yard hurdles (and MacDonald was "credited as being a good hurdler" said Flanagan). MacDonald coasted through the hurdles and Walter did too over the last half, putting in a slow time. Even the two events substituted at MacDonald's request went Walter's way: the discus, a win by 9 feet and the "three standing jumps" which Walter won by a combined 1' 8 ½" (replacing the mile and the walk). MacDonald's only other win was in the hammer throw.

The results were scored on the decathlon tables, which gave Walter the match 6,498 to 5,339, a trouncing (the scores were relatively poor because both men let up in the sprints when the outcome was apparent mid-race). "MacDonald is a good, even man but Knox is a phenomenal athlete!" Flanagan remarked. "Knox is able to do far better than that."

Twelve years after Walter deferred to Harry Gill in the North American All-Around contest in Buffalo, he finally got his title. It's hard to believe, given his ability, competitiveness and longevity that he never vied for a title like this before. It was always money, wanting to be remunerated for his efforts, that distanced him from these title events. Holding this title would have given him a reputation he didn't need on the hustling circuit. Pursuing his living from sport had necessitated anonymity in North America.

No comment was made in Walter's notes or in the papers about what the stakes were for this match, but eleven years later, looking back on his career with a reporter, Walter said he "received a medal and a cash prize of $1600."[13]

Seeing the end of his career approaching, Walter appeared even more intent on setting up matched contests with top flight athletes. It was as though, after years of toiling in anonymity for profit, he wanted to leave a legacy. As far back as 1911, after his first tour of Scotland, Walter had started issuing challenges to Jim Thorpe for an all-around match. As was the common practice at the time, these challenges were issued through newspaper reporters who were only too happy to print them. Walter never directly contacted Thorpe with a formal challenge, as far as we can tell.

The challenge went out again that spring, even before he left for Scotland. In the few days between the All-Around match and his boat for Scotland, he issued another challenge to Thorpe for a contest in the fall. Walter now had claim to the North American title and thought that would force Thorpe to respond, especially now that Thorpe had been professionalized and no longer had the excuse of protecting his amateur status. Reporters in all three Toronto newspapers remarked that Thorpe was the best amateur all-arounder, but in the professional ranks he could meet his match. They all proposed, as hometown papers do, Walter as his Waterloo.[14] The city of Vancouver immediately offered to host the match, or even one of a series of matches all across Canada.¹⁵ There was a little speculation by other Canadian sports reporters, stirring the pot, but no word from Thorpe.

Jim Thorpe was born to a white father and Indian mother in Indian Territory in 1887, nine years after Walter was born. After a difficult childhood in boarding schools, he was sent to Carlisle Indian School in 1907 where he excelled at track and football, being named a first team football All-American from 1910-1912. He competed in track only sporadically, and resolutely avoided training; the "lazy" moniker dogged him his entire life. But he didn't need to train. He easily qualified for the American Olympic team and at the Stockholm Olympics won the gold medal in both the pentathlon and decathlon (as well as fourth in the long jump and seventh in the high jump). Walter would have had a close-up look at him there, likely even chatted with him. After returning home, Thorpe entered into the AAU's all-around championship in September of 1912, winning handily. But he was professionalized early in 1913 for playing a little semi-pro baseball to put himself through school, a common practice for college athletes the universities conveniently ignored. As a result, in the spring of 1913 he joined the New York Giants baseball team to start his professional career. He never did serious track again.

Being the Olympic champion made him a target. Anyone who wanted to prove his worth looked at him as the yardstick, the greatest athlete in the world. Walter, after winning the North American All-Around title, set his eyes on him too, and anyone else he could coax a match out of. After the Olympics, one newspaper reporter commented that Walter was "the one man that would have given the famous Indian Thorpe, all around Olympic champion, his biggest argument".[16] Walter was working the newspapers to corner Thorpe[17], but Thorpe, in his lackadaisical, live-for-the-moment way, ignored him. He may very well not have known who Walter was; Thorpe wasn't all that interested in track, and during the few years he did do track, Walter was invisible in Scotland or Elk Lake. He was a baseball player now, traveling across the country all summer with his team. Not only was he in no position to take Walter on, he likely didn't care to. In October of 1913, when Walter wanted to set the match, Thorpe's Giants were in the World Series and then immediately embarked on a world tour (a remarkable six months, leaving in November of 1913 and literally circling the globe playing exhibition games[18]). This window of opportunity for Walter to test himself against the unquestioned best in the world just never opened.

Looking at their career best marks makes one think it could have been a competitive match, though Thorpe was decidedly better. It is worth noting that Thorpe was 6'1", five inches taller than Walter, and at a lean 190 pounds, fully 40 pounds heavier.

	Thorpe	Knox
100-yard dash	10.0	9.6
long jump	23'6"	24'2"
shot put	47'9"	46'5"
high jump	6'5"	5'7"
440 yard run	51.8	60.0
120 yard hurdles	15.6	15.8
discus	136'	128'
pole vault	11'0"	12'6"
javelin	163'	-----
one mile run	5:26	5:30

But that, of course, is all speculation. Walter knew he would have been in tough, he had seen Thorpe compete. What he also knew was that a match like that could breed some serious betting. And in a do-or-die contest, with big stakes on the line, Walter understood he could use all his wiles, the psychological tactics and intimidations learned over years on the hustling circuit, to his advantage. As well, he expected to be more durable for the grueling one day match after his summer in Scotland and Thorpe's notorious lack of training. In a close match anything could happen. But it was not to be. In the only comment published as to this match, Thorpe was said to not be able "to find the time".[19]

Sometime after New Years of 1913, Walter, for the first time, took on an agent. It became young Jack Johnstone's responsibility to get Walter some championship matches. How this relationship developed, Walter never said. Walter was still in Elk Lake when they got together, but Johnstone was very active on Walter's behalf that spring. Johnstone contacted newspapermen at all the Toronto papers and several in Scotland, and most likely in New York where Thorpe would notice. This relationship paid off for Walter.

Walter (seated) with his new agent Jack Johnstone.
After being repeatedly ignored by his biggest rivals, Walter was determined to set up some championship matches in 1913.
Courtesy Orillia Museum of Art and History

On Saturday, June 29, 1913, Walter set sail for Scotland and his third tour of the Highland Games, apparently leaving Johnstone behind. He had an added incentive this year, thanks to his new agent. Bryce Scott, the Scottish champion leaper, had agreed to a match. Walter had Johnstone issue all-around and all-jumping challenges in the Scottish papers in April, pointedly calling out specific athletes, and Scott was the first taker.[20] In a letter dated May 21st, he agreed to a contest of seven jumps: both running and standing long, high and triple jumps as well as the pole vault. Details, he said, could be worked out after Walter arrived in July. In fact, it took until a week before the match on August 16th to settle the terms. In a letter to the paper, Walter said, "He is the man I am anxious to meet, particularly as he won the all-around at Bridge-of-Allen last year, but if John Speedie wishes to challenge the winner, and I should be so fortunate as to beat Scott, I shall be pleased to give the Falkirk champion a match." In 1912, Walter had set the stakes at five pounds; no mention of the stakes was reported in 1913.[21] Obviously money wasn't the motivation, unless it was all in side bets.

Walter had also challenged Findlay Cramb, the British all-around champion, to a match, through the papers as usual. He set the event list to entice Cramb. In addition to the standard 100-yard dash, hurdles, mile, long jump, high jump, shot put and pole vault, Walter included tossing the caber, the 56 pound weight for height and the hammer. This was a strong man's contest he proposed. The Powderhall grounds were suggested as the venue for the October 11th match. Cramb immediately replied, also through the papers, "I am prepared to meet him over the events he states for any side stakes he cares to mention."[22] After two years of prodding, Walter finally had his match set with the British champion.

Another top British all-arounder, Sutherland, declined the challenge, only to be aggressively attacked in a Scottish newspaper by Johnstone.[23] The article describes Walter's "plan" to first meet MacDonald for the North American title, then Sutherland for the Scottish and finally Thorpe for the World crown in October. Judging by this letter, Walter had a bit of a pit bull working for him to arrange this plan. Undoubtedly, Thorpe heard from him that summer too. As late as mid-August, Walter was still "waiting for word from Canada with regard to the proposed Thorpe match".[24]

Johnstone was also the point man for Walter in the negotiations with "Mr. Firth" in Scotland. Firth had issued an open all-around challenge in the papers that Johnstone accepted on Walter's behalf[25], proposing the standard track and field events. Firth then responded, in the papers as usual, fodder for the reporters, that he was only interested in a real all-around event including swimming, fencing, dancing, rope-climbing, shooting, cricket ball bowling, "physique development", skating, club swinging, wrestling, cycling, boxing, weightlifting, as well as the jumping and throwing events. This sounded like a non-starter for Walter, but Johnstone pursued it anyway.

In the meantime, Walter started another tour of the Highland Games on July 9th, four days after his ship docked. It was another active summer, 26 Games in 13 weeks, two a week, with similar dominance as the last two years: 38 first placings, 10 seconds and 12 thirds. All the more remarkable, Walter bypassed the smaller Games in the first half of the season, focusing on the major Games in the second half. Once again, he pushed the Scottish pole vault record up, this year to 11' 9". After disembarking from the boat in July, he told a reporter, "I will attempt to break all the pole vault records when I get a special prize for doing so."[26] He was unbeaten in the pole vault that summer (as well as the last) and set the vaulting record at 23 different Highland Games, garnering himself a nice bit of extra cash.

At his second competition, Jedburgh, on July 12th, Walter had the chance to test himself in a series of jumps against Bryce Scott, whom he was set to meet for the jumping championship of Scotland on August 16th. They jumped six events against each other and each won three. Not only that, the margin of difference was often only an inch or two; they were evenly matched. The deciding seventh event, the standing long jump, they "both ducked" the paper said. The results can be seen on the table below.

On August 4th in Manchester, they met again, this time over five jumping events. This time Walter won three out of the five, boosting his confidence heading into the big match in two weeks. A local newspaper sponsored this contest and Walter probably took home a tidy winner's stake. Again, the results are below.

By now, word of the Jumping Championship was spreading, thanks to the sports reporters. Two of the best jumping athletes Scotland had seen in many years were about to face off for the championship. The organizers at Crieff, where the contest would be held, heavily promoted the match, boosting attendance at their Games. They also minted a special gold medal for the winner in order to make the title of All-around Jumping Champion of Scotland official. Several times in the various papers a reported prize of "$200"[27] was quoted as the side bet between the two jumpers, only adding to the excitement.

Walter only scheduled two Games between the 4th and the championship on the 16th, Dundee on the 9th and Kincardine on the 15th, allowing himself time to sharpen up the day before the match. He was going to be rested and at his best.

At the meet the day before the jumping championship he had spent two years arranging, Walter badly sprained his ankle landing in the pole vault. He had to travel the 25 miles to Crieff that afternoon to discuss postponing the jumping championship with the officials there. It couldn't be changed, the officials said; they had heavily advertised it and a very large crowd was already assembling in town for the big event in the morning. "Go through with it for our sake", they asked Walter. The highland Scots were a tough people; a mere sprained ankle was something to be overcome. So Walter went to Scott and explained his situation. Walter said he'd compete if Scott would agree to meet again later that summer for another championship contest. He did so, and Walter told the officials he would go through with the match in the morning.[28]

Thirteen thousand people, a record, crowded the field for the Crieff Highland Games in the morning. In addition to the prize money for each event, the organizers posted a hefty (for them) 10 pound prize for the winner of the jumping championship, plus the gold medal worth three pounds. Given how close their previous two encounters had been, the betting in the crowd would have been brisk, "the Canadian" against the Scottish Champion.

Newspaper photo of Walter (right) and Scott (left) before their All-around Jumping Championship of Britain, August 16, 1913
Courtesy Orillia Museum of Art and History

Walter made his way painfully out onto the field, hiding his limp. Like all athletes in Scotland, Walter generally competed in bare feet squeezed into thin, low cut leather shoes. But not on this day; a photo of the jumpers clearly shows Walter in socks up to his mid-calf, hiding the swollen, black ankle. Nothing else covered his ankle except the long trench coats the athletes wore to fend off the chill air off the moors. But the crowd was far away, and the papers never mentioned Walter's injury, only that he "seemed well below form".[29] He was the stoic Scot that day.

Bryce Scott and Walter Knox were both smaller men, Scott an inch taller but Walter about 10 pounds heavier. Scott was a lithe, more wiry athlete, Walter agile but much more powerful, with thicker arms and legs and a much more squat, solid midsection. From a distance, they were easily identifiable by their physiques. Walter, of course, also had that great big red maple leaf on his chest.

As expected, Scott took four of the first six events and tied the fifth. Walter only managed to take the standing long jump. Nursing his sprained ankle, he no-heighted in the high jump and passed on the triple jump. The final event, after the affair had been decided, was the pole vault, and the jumpers put on a thrilling display. Both cleared 11', the highest mark on the uprights. There was a delay while officials fashioned extensions so the bar could be raised. Scott eventually cleared 11' 4" but Walter continued over 11' 7", just an inch below his Scottish record.[30] But it was too little too late; Bryce Scott took the gold medal and the title.

	Jedburgh July 12		Manchester Aug 4		Crieff Aug 16	
	Knox	Scott	Knox	Scott	Knox	Scott
Long Jump	**21'3"**	20'10"	-----	-----	20'11"	**21'5"**
Standing Long Jump	-----	-----	-----	-----	**9'11"**	9'9.5"
High Jump	No Ht	**5'7"**	5'3"	**5'8"**	No Ht	**5'6"**
Standing High Jump	**4'11"**	4'10"	**4'9"**	4'8"	4'9"	4'9"
Triple Jump	42'4"	**43'10"**	40'6"	**44'10"**	pass	**42'6"**
Standing Triple Jump	39'0"	**39'2"**	**33'0"**	30'9"	30'0"	**31'1"**
Pole Vault	**11'2"**	10'7"	**11'0"**	10'9"	**11'7"**	11'4"

As can be seen in the results above, all the contests were close. Walter put up a fight, even with his throbbing ankle. He opted to skip the triple jump, knowing Scott generally bested him there, so as to rest his ankle.

Looking over all the jumps in their three meetings that summer, the best performances in each event would give the title to Scott four events to three, though they were all very close. Scott had an honest claim to the title, in spite of their agreement to re-do the match later.

It turned out that Scott, grasping the championship medal, had no intention of letting Walter take it from him. Walter, writing in 1950 at the age of 72, said, "And I am still waiting for another match"! His opinion of Scott, one of his best friends on the tour, was ruined.

> *"I had considered him one of the finest sportsmen that I had met in all the games I had taken part in during my years of competition, but again you meet some people who cannot stand defeat and don't consider their word worth very much if it is going to take away some glory that they think they have won. I lost faith in a Scotchman's word after that, and made up my mind that I wouldn't be caught by any of the rest of them."* [31]

Attempting to establish his legacy, and after waiting two years for Scott to make this match, Walter was stung by the double cross. The bitterness lasted his whole life.

But there was still the British All-Around Championship match with Cramb in six weeks to look forward to. The Scottish newspapers began promoting it while the negotiations were still ongoing. As late as mid-August, the details were still not set; haggling over which events to include continued, and even Vancouver was reported as a possible site for their match[32].

Walter continued on his tour of the Games, giving his sore ankle only four days' rest, but he did avoid sprinting for a few weeks. Then it was off for competitions on August 20th, 21st, 23rd, 26th, 29th and 30th in six different villages, covering fully 500 miles of travel from the top of Scotland to the south, to the far west and to the east. He couldn't have made a more difficult schedule if he had tried. He was now being paid five pounds appearance money to come to some of the Games, he was that big a draw.

After that, Walter slowed down, competing in only four more meets in the next month. He had twisted the ankle again on September 10th and it was not healing well. The All-around Championship with Cramb was set for early October and Walter realized he needed to rest.

After his last competition, at Wigtown on October 4th, Walter contacted Cramb and called the match off. He must have been terribly disappointed — and very wobbly. Likely he was giving up some forfeit money too although the stakes were never published. The newspapers quoted him as saying, "his ankle will not stand the training he has to do to get into proper trim, and he feels in consequence he could not do himself justice".[33] Likely he didn't want to lose because of his injury the way he did with Scott, and not be able to get a re-match. Like he said, he wasn't going to trust the Scots any more. Cramb seemed willing and confident to take him on, so Walter was going to keep him on the hook for the following season.

After all his work getting matches set up that summer, it must have been hard to see those two slip away. Time was not on his side.

There was one more opportunity to salvage this season, legacy-wise: the Powderhall Sprint. After the Wigtown Games, Walter went away for a "keep", which he described as "your expenses are paid (likely by gamblers) and you go away some place to train".[34] He had two months to get his ankle strengthened before the Sprint on January 1st. Finally, after three seasons in Scotland, he decided to take a shot at the big sprint, the whole reason he had come to Scotland in the first place. Elk Lake would have to wait.

Walter found two backers (likely the ones who supported his 'keep') who were keen to work the gambling crowd; that, after all, was the raison d'etre of the Powderhall Sprint. They machinated to manipulate the odds on Walter and get a good handicap. Somehow Walter was assigned a mark 7 ½ yards in front of the scratch runner, a head start that made winning the Powderhall crown very possible, if not likely. His reputation in Scotland was as a pole vaulter not a sprinter, and he hadn't run a sprint in a Games since early August, driving down his reputation and driving up his handicap. Up until a week before the race, the odds set for him to win were 20 to 1. Walter's backers were to put 100 pounds on him to win at those odds. Coming out on top would net him 2000 pounds. But his backers were slow in getting the bet down. A week before the race, Walter did his last speed trials, at a private dog track outside Edinburgh. Word got out about his fast times there and his odds immediately dropped to 5 to 3. As Walter said, "there was no use betting after that".[35]

The Powderhall Sprint was the unofficial world professional championship. However, it was not just a race to see who was the fastest. Every runner was assessed a handicap, a head start, based on his ability as judged by the officials; this was an event for the gamblers, the men who thought they knew who was dogging it and who was over-matched. Often a slower runner with a big handicap was the Powderhall champion. Runners went to great lengths to get bigger handicaps; some lost on purpose there "for 10 years", Walter said, until their handicap grew to a mark from which they thought they could win. Over 120 runners entered the 1914 race. Heats of five or six runners at a time would be run, each runner starting at a line a certain number of yards ahead of the "scratch" runner's mark. The scratch runner would cover the full 130 yards, all the others somewhat less. Walter's 7 ½ yard handicap made the race very winnable for him.

He won his heat easily, running just fast enough that his handicap wouldn't drop (they were re-assessed after each round). Only the winners moved on. In his second heat, Walter discovered there was another runner who had lain off just as he had in the first round. He was going to have to go all out to beat him and move on. Perplexingly, Walter dropped out of the competition, not even running the second race. Why? "I was not going to tip off my speed for nothing", Walter said in his notes.[36] If his backers had gotten his bet down at 20 to 1, he likely would have done whatever it took to win. But with only prestige on the line, well, there were more important things. It was back to being all about the money again.

Instead, Walter went up to Aberdeen the next day and won 15 pounds in a sprint there. At least that would have covered his expenses.

Walter now found himself in England in the dead of winter. For the first time since his foray into California in 1909, Walter decided to forgo prospecting with Jack and spend the winter in England. Something came up there that was far more interesting.

24

Finally, Respect and a Legacy

After the 1912 Olympics in Stockholm, there was great consternation in Britain. At the London Games in 1908 Britain had dominated, placing first in the medal standings with more than triple the number the second place Americans won. But in Stockholm Britain had slipped to third place behind the US and Sweden. By 1914 it looked like Germany had passed them too and even little Finland was a worry. This would not do. "Our athletic ability has dwindled to the lowest possible ebb," commented one reporter.[1]

The British Amateur Athletic Association debated the problem for over a year before deciding to act. What was perceived with casual arrogance in 1908 as England's inevitable dominance by their deep pool of talented athletes had now been proven to be willful blindness and mismanagement on the part of the AAA. "The team, the manner of its selection and its management were all criticized and generally denounced," reported one paper at the time.[2] The athletic officials in Britain concluded their athletes could no longer be left to their own devices in their preparations and selected to the team in a slipshod way. The AAA had decided it had to take steps to re-gain their rightful position among the top athletic countries in the world by actively modernizing their approach to developing an Olympic Team. This was an era of keen competition between European countries, in trade, in their militaries, in colonial development, in patriotism. Sport was a natural extension of this culture, and the British were determined to be pre-eminent again.

One of the biggest problems was the stubborn British adherence to the philosophy of the all-around athlete. It was concluded in the AAA meetings that the specialization by athletes in only their best event had thrust the Americans ahead of the world.[3] Total focus on every technical advance in just a single event was working for them. As well, England's system of isolated athletes working with whatever coaching they could find had clearly left their athletes at a technical disadvantage. Many athletes were actually getting bad coaching, direction in technique that was counter to the latest advances.

First, it was decided, they needed a "national training fund" to support a new program. The "British Olympic Financial Committee" was created and subscriptions totaling 10,000 pounds were quickly collected "to support the athletes".[4] This was a very controversial move in this age of amateurism. Many purists argued this was supporting professionalism and many commentators in the press even called for Britain to skip the 1916 Olympics if this fund was created. The powers that be, though, forged ahead in spite of this backlash.

Their next step, with this fund in hand, was to hire a National Head Coach who was adept at identifying and developing the best talent, someone who would be given enough time to implement a system and have it come to fruition in time for the 1916 Olympics in Berlin. A National Coach, technically sound in all track and field events and up to date on the latest developments, a person who could coach the coaches and identify the talents, someone adept in "scientific coaching",[5] was the objective. The debate raged as to who that man was. In early January 1914, just a week after the Powderhall Sprint, the AAA committee contacted Walter.

Walter was identified as "a man of education and supreme knowledge in athletics, and an absolute master in theory and practice... practical, painstaking, enthusiastic... yet quiet, unassuming and undemonstrative".[6] He was, as everyone knew, the famous all-around champion of America and Scotland. "The wide range of events on which he can give theoretical advice as well as actual demonstration make him invaluable".[7] This reporter went on to describe him as "a superb trainer, a man of unfailing resource, and gifted with a dogged determination... but he is by no means a talker". Papers all over England listed his career accomplishments, his big day at the Canadian Championships in 1907, the All-Around title, his dominance at the Highland Games; he seemed the perfect man for the job. To top off the argument, he already had experience as an Olympic coach.

But he was a hard sell to some. "There was much opposition," one reporter commented, "when this Scottish-Canadian athlete was appointed".[8] This would be "the first time that an outside trainer has been appointed to fill such an important position... For Britain, which from her capricious store has tumbled trainers of eminence all over the world, to call in the aid of an outsider indicated a truly remarkable condition".[9] But the decision stood; Walter was their man.

He was offered a three year contract (one year pre-paid in advance, an impressive 400 pounds), starting immediately, "to assess, then develop England's athletic talent", giving him the power to appoint a team of assistants "under his immediate supervision and direction."[10] After his last Olympic experience, you can be sure Walter was going to get this position set up right. He would need time, he would need control and he would need support from the committee, three things that were decidedly lacking during his Canadian experience. Walter gave this advice to the committee, as related through a reporter later that summer,

> "We require a national training ground so that men can come to be trained by the *official coach and his assistants*. One of the troubles that we are up against is that much

of the training is being done by different coaches in a way which is considered inadvisable, and not in accordance with proper standards."[11]

This concept of a permanent national training camp was revolutionary. Unfortunately, it was also expensive as it required supporting the facility and paying the travel and accommodation of the athletes among other costs. But this comment shows Walter's forward thinking and serious consideration of the problem.

"Here they regard the main end of sport as recreative", Walter commented with some lament.[12] He had a vision to change that attitude.

He spent February and March identifying and hiring 22 assistant coaches, spread across England, Scotland and Ireland. Walter knew time was not on his side and, with his typical focused determination, set to work. By the spring, he had started to identify the talent and was traveling the country giving training instruction, educating the coaches as to his methods. One reporter described Walter's approach, "to practice what he preaches is to be his policy of the future, for he intends by demonstrations, particularly in the field events, to create enthusiasm for the sport."[13] By May, Walter had formed "centers for coaching" all across the United Kingdom.[14]

All track meets in 1914 were required to add every Olympic event to their agendas (including the "abnormal" field events of discus and javelin). Even more controversial, measurements were to be recorded in the metric system, just like the Olympics.[15] In stuffy old England, home of the Imperial System of feet and inches, imagine the kerfuffle raised by replacing the 100-yard dash with the 100-metre event. Everyone could see there was change in the air, and the focus was clearly on the 1916 Olympics.

Once the summer season started in May, Walter was back on the road, traveling to athletic fields all across England, Scotland and Ireland, giving demonstrations, explaining the science of athletic movement, instructing coaches and athletes on the intricacies of conditioning and jotting down the names of athletes to watch. In some respects, he was bringing the Highland Scots culture to the Lowlanders: the professional work ethic, the attention to detail, the practice-until-it's-perfect mentality. He ran clinics with "hundreds" of eager athletes, "all afternoon and evening… working like a nigger," one official said. "My word, Knox is doing a great work, and if he does not revolutionize our boys athletically by the Olympics in 1916, I'm a Dutchman."[16]

Periodically, a newspaper article, written in Walter's name or at least corrected grammatically (his extensive notes demonstrate he did not have the literary capacity to write them himself), would appear, focusing on the modern techniques of one specific event in acute detail. For example, the Sporting Chronicle on August 20th, 1914, published a 1200 word article attributed to Walter on the subject of the pole vault. He started with a little gossip about the Americans to catch the reader's interest, followed by a description of the history of the development of pole vaulting technique. Then it was a technical explanation on how to pole vault, the different styles and the modern approach, complete with pictures of him flying over the bar. "Always start the jump as the pole touches the ground… grip the pole so your thumbs are towards the top of the pole… he goes over the bar facing it, and he starts his turn as soon as he leaves the ground… pole vaulting requires speed up to the jump as well as spring, and the athlete should practice sprinting." The Knox approach to athletics was making waves all across Britain.

How different this was to his Canadian experience. Walter had time to work with athletes and coaches in a relaxed atmosphere. The athletes, by all accounts, were honoured by his attention and enthusiastic whenever and wherever he appeared. He was developing a program. There are no reports as to how well the local coaches took to his style or, perhaps, interference. Walter was "courteous but insistent", as one reporter put it.[17] But, if any difficulties arose, Walter had the support of the AAA who would back him up.

By all accounts, Walter was enjoying his summer. He was keeping fit and trim putting on demonstrations almost daily. But, in all of 1914, he only competed in two Highland Games, both in September. He had a new focus now. In August, he commented in his notes, he had things running in good shape.

Earlier in the summer, around June 1st, while Walter was touring the country administering his Olympic program, he was approached by a man from the Sporting Chronicle newspaper. The paper was sponsoring an All-Around Championship for the British Isles and they wanted Walter to enter. Obviously Walter wanted to, but his contract with the AAA stipulated he would withdraw from all professional sports events while in their employ. Urged to ask for an exemption, Walter requested permission to compete in this important event. The AAA committee refused.

But Walter wasn't a man to give up easily. He approached them again saying, "The general public doesn't know very much about me, and if I could win the championship, which I'm pretty sure I can, it will show the public what kind of man you selected to coach the British athletes."[18] After a few days consideration, they agreed to allow him to compete in this one event and no other. Perhaps there was still some controversy over hiring a foreigner to coach the Brits. Walter didn't care why they changed their mind; he was just relieved he wasn't missing out on another opportunity to win a championship.

The Chronicle had rounded up about seven entrants, including Findlay Cramb, the man Walter had challenged the year before, the reigning British All-Around champion. By the time the match came off, though, only two entrants were left, Walter and Cramb, by far the two best athletes. The paper promoted it as the World's Championship and put up a prize of 50 pounds. Walter had two months to prepare for the August 1st event, and spending every day at one track or another gave him plenty of opportunity to get in shape.

The match came off at Manchester on August 1st and 3rd (as the papers reported it). Eight events were to be contested in a win-lose method of scoring.

Walter knew Cramb as they had met numerous times on the Scottish tour. He considered him a "fair all-rounder". They were of similar physiques, Cramb a little taller and Walter a little thicker, though both were agile men. The big difference between the two was their age. Cramb was the "student-athlete" still in his early 20s. Walter was 36 years old, as ancient then as he would be in today's sports world.

Findlay Cramb, the British All-around Champion, preparing to throw the hammer.
Courtesy Orillia Museum of Art and History

Walter, after visiting athletic fields every day for months, was fit and strong on the day of the World All-around Championship match with Cramb.
Courtesy Orillia Museum of Art and History

On the day, Walter proved the superior athlete. The sprints were easy wins for Walter, both the 100, in a slow 11.5 seconds, and the 120 yard hurdles. Then he won the shot put with an impressive 45' 7", the pole vault at 11' 6", the broad jump with a leap of 21' 6" and the discus with a toss of 114' 10", a superior throw for Walter. Cramb took the high jump at 5'6" and the hammer with a 110' heave. Six events to two; Walter was now the World All-Around Champion. Really the only serious challenger left, as far as Walter knew, was Jim Thorpe, and he didn't care to respond to Walter's challenges.

They squeaked this championship in just in time. On July 28th, 1914, the whole world began to fall apart. Austria-Hungary declared war on Serbia that day to start the cascade of war declarations that would set the world on fire: World War I had started. Britain entered the fray on August 4th, the day after Walter won the title. Within months, it became clear that this was not going to be a short war and the International Olympic Committee cancelled the 1916 Berlin Olympics.

Sometime in September, the British AAA informed Walter his services were no longer required. Every man was expected to defend his country and the government was not going to encourage its best athletes to avoid their duty. The whole Olympic program was cancelled for the duration.

Early in October, 1914, as the British Expeditionary Force dug in for the bloodbath of the battle of Ypres in Belgium, and the Canadian soldiers marched out for their first action, Walter caught a ship for Canada and was back in Elk Lake before freeze-up.

The Prospecting Years

25

New Directions

November 1914 found Walter happily ensconced in his brother's cabin at Davidson Lake in Northern Ontario. Before leaving Scotland he had put out challenges in the papers again to anyone who wished to contest his World All-Around title. Not surprisingly, given the war, there were no takers. At the same time, Walter told reporters that the 1915 season would be his last in competition. By the time he reached Davidson Lake, he probably realized he had already run his last race; the war had put an end to most organized athletic competitions outside the military. By Christmas, he had ballooned to 170 pounds.

An interesting article on the front page of the Scottish paper "Health and Strength" in January updated the Scottish sports enthusiasts on what "the Canadian" was doing. The photo shows Walter and his brother Jack (almost a carbon copy of him, short, thick and balding) with their dog team in front of their log cabin at Davidson Lake. Walter, obviously in a letter, said,

> "While hunting the water froze up, and then we had to walk. Usually we lived and slept in a tent, but on two nights we stopped out in the bush without blankets. We lay down on the brush, with a big fire in front of us. It

was not over comfortable, and I don't think I shall try it again. One night it was 13 degrees below zero."[1]

The hunting trip was worthwhile, though. The photo shows the big moose they bagged.

Walter (right) and Jack (left) with one of the several moose they bagged during their prospecting years.
Courtesy Orillia Museum of Art and History

The silver claims Jack held in the Gowganda region, while supporting them, were turning out to be sparse, not the mother lode. In the past nine years there had been at least four big rushes in the region and Jack had just missed out on staking the big claims. That winter he decided to head out prospecting again to stake some new claims. There were more gold and silver deposits to be found. He was going to head west to a likely looking region just 30 miles south of the Porcupine, where the big mines developed from the gold rush in 1909 were still turning out prodigious amounts of gold. The undeveloped West Shining Tree Lake District was his goal.

Walter didn't go with him. Early in December 1914 he was back home in Orillia looking for opportunities. What caught his eye, of all things, was coaching hockey. Ontario had a thriving amateur hockey league. Every town of any size had a team that played a season from January to March. The Senior league champion would vie for the Allen Cup with the champions from Quebec and the West. But the Ontario Hockey League also had an Intermediate division, a league for senior teams from smaller towns, with some 40 teams spread across the province playing for their own championship. The Intermediate team from Galt, in southwestern Ontario, was looking for a coach for their team made up of soldiers from the local 122nd Battalion. In checking out this opportunity, Walter ran into Lou Marsh, the sports reporter for the Toronto Star newspaper, who told him he should look into the Picton team too. In mid-December, Walter, the famous Olympic coach, had two teams vying for his coaching services. Just after Christmas he signed on with Picton, a town of 3,500 people on the Bay of Quinte at Lake Ontario's eastern end.

Walter had played hockey as a youth in Orillia and was familiar with the game. He was not a team sportsman himself but he was adept at analyzing and strategizing, and certainly could coach individual athletes. But most importantly, he brought a work ethic and hard-nosed attitude to the game. His new team was young, smaller than some of the competition, but in this era of no substitutions, youthful vigor and endurance could be an advantage. The seven players (three forwards, two defence, a goalie and a rover) played the whole game, two 30 minute halves. Their first game was January 8th, giving Walter only 10 days to whip them into shape.

The OHL Intermediate league was divided into 13 divisions; each division winner played four rounds of playoffs to declare the provincial champion. Picton played in the largest division that included six teams between Oshawa and Belleville.

Walter's Picton team tied for first in the division with a 9-1 record. A two game total point division championship was held and the Picton boys came out on top 9-8 over Peterborough. Over 800 fans, a quarter of the town, showed up to support the team. In the playoffs, the boys ran out of steam, losing the two game series to Brampton 10-5. The eventual Ontario champion was, ironically, Walter's home town of Orillia, a championship (coupled with the Junior championships they'd won the previous two seasons) celebrated for many years.

By March, Walter was back home in Orillia. He never clearly stated that he went back to coaching in Picton, but he certainly was the coach there in the 1919 season and it is likely he spent January and February in Picton every year as a sporting hiatus from the challenging events to come in the Shining Tree District with Jack. Walter was to be a coach in some form almost every year for the next 20 years, mostly as a full time job. Soon he wouldn't need to coach to earn a living but chose to anyway; sport was his life.

Back in Orillia he had to find a way to make a living. Obviously he wasn't inspired by the hardships Jack was enduring year after year. Heading off to rough it in the bush, starting over from scratch once again, was not where Walter wanted to be. He was also clearly not interested in the military and the war. He was still well under the age limit to enlist, 45, and there was considerable social pressure to do so. By the spring of 1915, it had become clear this was not going to be the short, glorious war everyone had expected. Recruiting ramped up and voluntarily enlisting to do one's duty for the Empire became the honourable thing to do, swelling the Canadian military. But Walter did not share this view. He never showed any interest in the war at all, likely thinking it was none of his business. Walter always looked out for number one first.

In April, 1915, Walter bought a pool hall in Orillia, attached to the Daly House, a large hotel and not-too-secret drinking establishment in the dry town, and settled down to the life of a businessman.[2] One wonders about the social implications this had for Walter. People knew of his hustling shenanigans through the rumour mill and local scuttlebutt and were aware that he was a bit of a con artist;

now he was avoiding military duty. Orillia was a conservative and highly patriotic town, loyal to the crown. There was a very high enlistment rate there; the whole Orillia Intermediate hockey team, for example, enlisted into the Sportsmen's Battalion. But Walter Knox, the greatest athlete in the world, in this time of crisis for the Empire, was more inclined to run a pool hall. There had to be social fallout. It was one thing to stay home to work in the many industries in Orillia supporting the war effort, or even to head north to the mines digging up the valuable raw materials to support those industries, but a pool hall? There was no way of spinning that as patriotic. There would have been cold shoulders.

Walter Knox, world champion, with his awards.
Courtesy Orillia Museum of Art and History

As with most things requiring coordination, Walter was a hotshot pool player. At Jack Munro's pool hall in Elk Lake, Walter had once put a couple of hustlers to shame, running a table several times in a row to win a tidy bet. With this move, it is clear he had retired from the athletic life and was settling down. Or, more likely, the war had killed any opportunity to pursue his athletic life and had retired him. In fact, on April 28th, Walter officially announced his retirement from athletics in the Orillia newspaper.

The reporter commented, "From general appearances it would certainly appear as though his decision to permanently retire is genuine".[3] It is hard to picture Walter sitting on a stool all day, collecting quarters from greasers whiling away their days. His gritty, determined, focused work ethic must have grated at the laziness of the pool hall life. But there he sat.

An interesting note in the local paper on May 3rd showed Walter had lost none of his spring. A delivery wagon raced past his shop one day, pulled by a runaway horse, certain to topple and crash. Walter raced out the door and was able to leap into the careening wagon. "It was swaying and I expected to see him pitched headlong out of it," eyewitness Tom Phillips reported, "but he reached forward down around the shafts and finally got the reins. Then he brought the horse to a halt."[4]

About this time, another interesting episode in Walter's life was coming to a head. A man with Walter's remarkable history was sure to have old ghosts reappear from time to time, and in this case it was George Turner, a wrestler Walter had defeated two falls to one a few years back in Haileybury. Walter never mentioned this match in his notes or clippings at the time but, according to Turner, it was during the two year period, 1911-1912, when Walter defeated George Cleverley and Wes Church for their titles in the Silver Country (it's likely Turner was actually Church wrestling under another name now).

Since their match, Turner had been undefeated. He had hooked up with wrestling promoter WB Naylor who had taken him on a two-year barnstorming tour of the Midwest as part of a group of wrestlers taking on all comers. He had trained with world champions Frank Gotch and Farmer Burns, the two most dominant wrestlers in the world for over 15 years. In 1913, he moved to England where he won the lightweight championship of England and wrestled the world lightweight champion, Joe Stecher, to a dramatic 3½ hour draw. He ran into Walter at a track meet in Manchester, and publicly challenged him to a match for 25 pounds. Walter politely declined; he was in his term as British Olympic coach and was not allowed to partake in any professional sporting activities.

Turner was determined to avenge the only loss of his career. In the fall, after Walter's coaching tenure had ended, another challenge came in the papers. By then Walter was on his way to Davidson Lake and ignored it. By Christmas, Turner had the promoter Naylor hounding him. A challenge published in Walter's hometown paper, the Orillia Newsletter, again formally challenged him to a match, winner take all of any stakes he pleased, including all the gate receipts. Furthermore, Turner would come to Orillia to wrestle in Walter's home town. On February 16, 1915, Walter finally accepted the challenge, with a short note published in the Orillia Newsletter calling for stakes of $50 a side plus the gate, with the match to be fought on the stage at the Orillia Opera House. Naylor immediately covered the $25 forfeit and set the match for Monday, March 15.[5]

Walter had a month to get in shape. Just before leaving the North at the start of December, he had badly sprained his wrist, likely the reason he postponed accepting the match until February. He had put on 15 pounds and had been relatively inactive for three months coaching the hockey team. And he was 37 years old.

As with any match, the details were precisely negotiated. The match would follow "The Police Gazette" rules in "catch-as-can style". These rules, popular in the US, allowed submission holds that forced an opponent to give up or face injury. Like the mixed martial arts competitions today, as long as both wrestlers wanted to continue, the referee was not to stop the fight. In the negotiations, only the "strangle hold" was barred.

This was the era of professional wrestling before the staged farces had come about. The first of the fake wrestling traditions, entertainment with masks and costumes, not sport, began in the 1920s. This was serious, dangerous sport in the rural matched contest tradition. The only sport more popular in the US at the time was baseball.

Over 200 spectators turned up to witness the big event in Orillia's stately Opera House. Walter was a local icon, the World All-around Athletic Champion. The locals had followed his career for 15 years as all his achievements (with the exception of his hustling exploits) were duly reported at length in the papers, even those carried out across the pond in Scotland. Orillia was a sporting town, the "Town of Champions" as it was known then, and not unfamiliar with betting on matched events. No doubt Turner found more than enough interest to cover any bets he wanted to make on himself.

Referee Charlie Gaudaur, brother to Orillia's world champion sculler Jake Gaudaur, called the wrestlers into the ring at eight p.m., in front of a raucous, partisan crowd. The match was over in short order. Walter pinned Turner for the first fall in less than five minutes. The second fall was tougher to get, but 12 minutes "of strenuous work" later, Walter had him on his back again to win the match.[6]

Turner was up immediately, aggressively demanding a re-match. Walter, in response, had the referee announce an offer to pin him three times in an hour for $100 a side. The crowd would have hooted their approval. Soon the date of May 3rd, six weeks later, was announced, again at the Opera House. Turner wisely left town to lick his wounds and re-tool his attack, now that he knew what he was up against. He was a seasoned veteran wrestler. He was going to have to change his style if he wanted to beat this athletic pit bull.

The six week break between bouts brought significant changes to

Walter's life. First, he bought the pool hall and became a sedentary businessman. This match would have been a good promotion for him. But more importantly, news from Jack was trickling in. The Shining Tree claims he had staked in March and April looked better than expected. Walter would have been put on notice by his brother to get ready to join him soon. Then, likely unbeknownst to Turner, his manager, Naylor, had quietly offered Walter a place in his troupe of touring wrestlers. Having just decided to retire from athletics, probably the last thing Walter wanted to do was go back on the hustling circuit as a wrestler, an even more grueling profession. Walter said no thanks.

The terms of the re-match included a five minute rest interval after every fall, with the clock still running towards the one hour time limit for Walter to pin Turner three times. Gaudaur was to return as referee, being "perfectly satisfactory the last time", according to Turner.

The Opera House filled up again on May 3rd, one of the last big events there before fire gutted the building. The betting was just as brisk as at the first bout. On this night, the paper reported "a splendid exhibition" was put on by the wrestlers, and "the match was fairly even".[7] Walter got the first fall at 15 minutes. But then Turner threw him eight minutes later. With the two five minute breaks after the falls, 33 minutes had passed, more than half the allotted time. Eight minutes later, Walter threw Turner again for his second fall. Only fourteen minutes remained for Walter to get the third and winning fall. Then Turner got behind Walter, caught him in a bear hug and lifted him off the ground for what would be his second throw, almost certainly leaving no time for Walter to win the bet. But Turner leaned back too far and lost his balance as Walter struggled to free himself. Turner fell, landing hard on his back with Walter right on top of him, and knocked himself out cold. In fact, Turner hit his head so hard, he could not be revived for three hours. Because Turner did not wrestle for the full hour, the match was awarded to Walter. What an event![8]

The next morning, Walter was back sitting on his stool in the pool hall. He probably made more that night than he would in a year of business.

Walter, undoubtedly uncertain about his future, had to make up his mind. He could stick with the pool hall, pursue coaching positions, go back into the athletics game, join Jack as a miner or even, if desperate enough, join the army, as any loyal man had to consider in those patriotic days. His mind would be made up soon.

By the fall of 1915, Jack Knox knew he was onto something big. He had staked a number of claims near West Shining Tree Lake and not only found gold, but he found free gold nuggets on the ground! He had located several large veins of high quality gold. With the discovery came the race to locate the best claims as fast as possible without anyone seeing him hustling around. The most critical decision was when to stop looking and make the trek into town to register the claims and get the gold assayed, letting the world in on his find and opening the floodgates. After that, Jack would have to defend his claim from the freebooters who inevitably came trying to grab the loose surface gold from under his nose. After 10 long, hard years in the bush, imagine the excitement. Jack would have sent word to Walter at the first opportunity.

Walter never said when he left for the north or what he did with the pool hall, only that he spent the next five years in the bush. During that time, he is also reported to have taken several short term coaching jobs, like the one in Picton, suggesting he was never a full-time miner. By 1920, he was describing himself as a "mine manager" and later a "mine broker". Whatever he was doing up there, he kept at it the rest of his working life. He also kept at his coaching the rest of his life. It is apparent over the next four years, the war years, that he spent most of his time at the mines but took extended hiatuses to coach in Southern Ontario. He was coach of the University of

Toronto track team in 1918. He was still involved with the Picton hockey team in 1919. In 1920, one paper stated that Walter "has had several offers to coach college track and field teams in Canada". He even ventured out to Regina that same year to coach their hockey team briefly.[9] Also in 1920, he took on two high profile coaching positions that left him a permanent part-time miner. Mining was never in his blood the way it was with Jack. Whether hard-luck mining or strike-it-rich mining, Walter never stuck with it. He was always drawn to the sporting life.

Jack threw up this rough cabin on his new claim in the Shining Tree District quickly so he could get out prospecting. Walter, cradling a bunny, stands in front of several more hanging rabbits they likely had trapped. Note the long toboggan for hauling supplies.
Courtesy Orillia Museum of Art and History

The trip to their claim could be made from Toronto in 24 hours. The CNR railway stop at Kashbaw, north of Sudbury, linked to a motor launch which boated supplies to West Shining Tree Lake. From there it was a short paddle, about five kilometers northwest of the present day town of Shining Tree on that lake, to Wasapika Lake and the Knox camp. In the winter, a government ice road had trucks driving all the way to within a half mile of the camp, which is how the heaviest equipment got in. Jack had staked claims totaling 1700 acres, later to be known as the "Knox block".[10] Only a small portion of it had surface gold, but the property would prove valuable in the future as the underground gold was followed. They were 30 miles due south of the Porcupine and Timmins and 110 miles due north of the boomtown of Sudbury. Shining Tree was far more accessible than Elk Lake or Gowganda had been.

Jack's claims were part of a major gold field. Eight prospectors struck it rich when their claims were developed into major mining operations. Of course, individual prospectors couldn't do all the tunneling themselves. The common course was to investigate enough to know what was likely in the ground then approach the moneyed mining companies to negotiate a deal for them to develop the operation. The gold veins ran from the surface underground into the Precambrian rock, requiring dynamite and heavy machinery to follow the veins.

In 1916, the Knox brothers employed 15 men at their mine. A number of surface veins were being trenched and a shaft 25 feet deep had been dug. The shaft followed a vein that was three inches across on the surface and widened to an eye-popping 14 inches at the bottom. The paper remarked that Walter was seen in Toronto that spring, 1916, with ore assayed "very high to the ton".[11] They had found tracings 200-500 feet away and were planning to sink another shaft.

The Knox brothers had struck it rich!

By 1916, five of the originals had sold out to the major interests who had the wherewithal to exploit the finds. The Cobalt Mining Company had sunk a shaft just four miles north of the Knox's. But Walter and Jack, ever the independent men, took on the daunting, and risky, task of developing their mine themselves. Even by 1920, Walter still described himself as a miner, "using his pick and shovel on his claims". He managed his mine the same way he coached his athletes, by example. His men would have been expected to put in a solid day's work, just to keep up with the boss.

Much of their profits would have been sunk back into the mine in wages, supplies, transport and equipment. Without capital, mine development was a slow process. But the gold was there, it was just going to come out of the ground more slowly that way. Walter and Jack, determined, independent and tough, were set on exploiting the claim the hard way. The money would trickle in slowly but hopefully, in the end, there would be more.

Jack Knox in his happy years after striking it rich
Courtesy Orillia Museum of Art and History

Walter Knox, successful mine manager, in a studio portrait from this period
Courtesy Orillia Museum of Art and History

The Coaching Years

26

Another Tour of Olympic Duty

In 1920, Walter was now a miner, or "mine manager" as he put it. The gold mine had two shallow shafts and two crews of men working them. It was expensive to operate the mine but a steady stream of gold was coming out of the ground, providing Jack and Walter a level of comfort and security they had never known.

But Walter was still drawn to the sporting life. Now 42 years old, his prime competitive days were long past. His weight had ballooned to 189 pounds, making him look portly. With his thick middle, sagging face and bald head covered by a "comb-over", he looked every inch the part of someone's middle-aged uncle with his pants hiked too high. However, under the layer of fat was a dense layer of muscle honed with a pickaxe and shovel. Walter was still fit, just padded now. Facing reality, Walter increasingly turned to coaching to feed his competitive urges.

In January of 1920, the Canadian Olympic Committee unexpectedly contacted Walter inquiring about his interest in coaching the Olympic Team again. To their surprise, Walter put them off. He had resigned his position as Olympic Coach for the British Olympic Committee in 1914 with the promise he would be at their service after the war if they wanted him. Essentially he didn't resign, but took a forced leave of absence. Before he could pursue the Canadian job, he felt he owed it to the Brits to give them first crack at his services. A letter to London gave him his answer: There were enough competent coaches at home, they responded brusquely; his services were no longer required.[1]

As requested, Walter submitted an application to the COC to be Canada's Olympic Coach. Early in February he was given the appointment. Obviously no serious search was made for other applicants; Walter was their man and they didn't hesitate to get his signature on a contract.

Not everyone was happy with the choice. The Central branch of the Great War Veterans Association formally posted a "strong protest" to Walter's selection. They recommended Bobby Kerr, who was still active in athletics in Hamilton, as their choice.[2] But overall there was little objection and the COC had their way.

This turn of events requires us to look at the politics of Canadian sport again, because the man in charge of the Canadian Olympic Committee, who likely, through his dominance of the committee, pressed for Walter to be named coach, was none other than James Merrick. Merrick was the COC chair for the 1912 Olympics who traveled to Stockholm with the team as manager and was a big part of the problems there. After the Games, he said to reporters he was through with athletics as "an honourable man cannot afford to have his name drawn into controversies". But apparently he wasn't through with athletics, and that surprised no one. The COC had gone inactive for the duration of the war and had only met again in the spring of 1919, after the war ended. Soon after, the International Olympic Committee stated its intention to hold the 1920 Olympics on schedule in Antwerp, Belgium. Merrick was still chair.

James Merrick was an industrial lawyer from Toronto. As head of the Toronto faction in the "athletic wars" between 1907 and 1909, he negotiated the truce and union of the two associations, creating the new AAU of C as the governing body of all amateur athletics in Canada. As the President of the new union its first three years, Merrick was instrumental in making the amateur rules as stringent as possible, later even going so far as to suggest criminal prosecution of professional athletes who managed to compete in the Olympics.[3] He was a hardline proponent of the amateur ideals. An extremely energetic administrator, Merrick was better known as an "abrasive, confrontational and obstinate", hard-nosed negotiator.[4]

Merrick and Walter knew each other well after the 1912 Games. Both were no-nonsense men-of-action who saw the world in black-and-white terms. More importantly, after Merrick was accused of dereliction of duty in Stockholm, causing the team no end of trouble, Walter refused to assign him any blame, the only person to stand up for him. Walter had his back. Now it was payback time, or so it seemed.

This was a political move on Merrick's part. He couldn't go wrong with Walter as coach; his credentials were top-notch and he had proven he could coach (and he was still active in athletics as coach for the University of Toronto in 1918). This gave Merrick the opportunity to organize the 1920 team meticulously, thereby proving the 1912 controversies must have been the fault of the athletes. That would explain why, in spite of the 1912 debacle, he had himself named manager of the team again. Not only that, he even took COC Secretary Norton Crow (who treated the 1912 Olympics as his honeymoon, on the COC's ticket) along again too. If these Games ran smoothly, and he was going to make sure they did, it would change the perceptions of the problems in 1912.

Merrick dove into his work in December of 1919, displaying his flair for administration. That month, while other countries were still assembling their Olympic Committees, he booked hotel rooms for the team in both London, for training camp, and Antwerp, and organized food services. At the Games, many other national teams were in an uproar over accommodations, quite a few sleeping in schools.[5] Merrick was way ahead of the game and it showed.

That December, he approached the government for funding. World War I had only ended on November 11th, 1918 and Canada, heavily in debt due to war loans, went into a short, but severe depression in 1919. The government was cash-strapped. Merrick wasn't going to let that stop him though. The Minister of Finance, the Hon. Mr. White, had been a classmate of his back in the 1890's, and Merrick made a personal call to him to discuss the Olympic funding. It was by no means a necessary thing for the government to put up any money, not with the myriad of pressing needs in all financial sectors across the country. But Merrick secured a commitment of $15,000, not a lot but enough to get started.[6] He then approached all the provincial sports governing bodies for financial support and got $5000 from Ontario and a commitment for another $5000 from Quebec (though that grant never materialized).

In 1912, it cost $328 to send each athlete to the Olympics. Merrick estimated that cost had risen to between $500 - $800 by 1920.[7] It was going to be a smaller team unless private funding could be found. Merrick informed the sports with gate receipts (hockey, boxing and wrestling) that their associations would have to fund their own athletes.[8] Private sponsors for other athletes like the marathoners could be sought out later. The COC even made an "appeal to patriotic citizens and sportsmen" to help raise the further $20,000 they felt was needed to fund the team.[9] By the end of January, the Olympic financing was already taking shape, fully six months before the Games, and the federal government could probably be counted on for a little more once the Olympics got closer. Merrick would work on that.[10]

By January 1st, 1920, Merrick had rapidly advanced the Olympic plans. As Merrick said, "No other country will look better after their athletes than Canada."[11]

Meanwhile, Walter started his planning immediately after he was hired on February 9th. He had experienced both the fiasco of 1912 and the successful program he implemented for the British Olympic Association in 1914. At his hiring, Walter insisted he would need the money to support a program similar to his British scouting and development program if he were going to take the job. He got it. While Walter was named "Head Coach" for the Olympic Team, he was given the right to appoint "Honourary Coaches" anywhere across Canada, and was told "Honourary Managers", who would pay their own way, would accompany the rowers, hockey team and boxers to Antwerp as well.

Walter spent the next two months planning a scouting and development trip across Canada to find the talent. As he told the papers then, "He is closing up his business affairs now in order to be free to devote his entire time to the business of rounding up a Canadian team."[12]

By the time he left for the West on April 9th, Walter had gotten his weight back down below 170 pounds. "Although about 15 pounds overweight, (Knox) is a perfect specimen of an athlete. In build he resembles Georges Carpentier the famous French boxer," remarked one reporter.[13] He had to be in shape, his coaching style depended on demonstration and vigorous interaction with the athletes. He wasn't going west just to see what the athletes could do, he wanted to coach them, show them how to improve. He was going to get his hands dirty and had to be fit.

Over the next seven weeks, Walter made stops in 13 cities and towns, no more than three days each on average, and logged thousands of miles on the train. In each town, Walter had set up and advertised an athletic "meet" in advance where any athlete with Olympic aspirations could come out and vie for the attention of the Head Coach of the Canadian Olympic Team. Walter emphasized he was not only interested in the established stars but also anyone who thought they had some ability, however raw, "to chiefly uncover any new material, that it may be developed," as Walter put it.[14] He wanted to assess not only the track and field athletes but also the wrestlers, boxers, cyclists and even swimmers. Between clinics, Walter was the guest speaker at luncheons, honourary starter or judge for races or wrestling matches and generally a high profile celebrity. The organization must have strained his capabilities.

The trip out West included visits to Fort William, Winnipeg, Brandon, Regina, Moose Jaw, Medicine Hat, Calgary, Vancouver and finally Victoria. On May 8th he turned around and visited Calgary, Edmonton, Saskatoon and Regina before catching the train to Toronto around June 1st, with brief stops in Winnipeg and Fort William.

He left quite an impression on the West. The Fox film company showed up on the Vancouver field one day to film what Walter was doing with the local athletes.[15] Movie theatres across the country ran the newsreel promoting Walter and the Olympic Team. The university in Vancouver even offered him their head coaching job if he wanted it, but he declined because of his "considerable business interests in the East".[16]

On his tour, Walter saw hundreds of athletes. Everyone got at least a few moments of personal instruction, "helpful criticisms" and practice pointers. Walter never allowed anyone to "go all out", as per his philosophy of perfecting technique before pushing it, often calling to runners "that's enough" before discussing what they were doing right and wrong.[17]

Walter met some of the established athletes like Beasley, the sprinter from the 1912 team (whom Walter thought little of), and John Cameron the weight thrower and Canadian amateur all-around champion. He also made some great discoveries. In Winnipeg, a strapping young man, 6'3" and 220 pounds, stepped up in his street clothes and put the 16 pound shot over 41 feet on his first try! That put him in the first tier of shot putters not only in Canada but in the world. Walter left officials "camping on his tail" to groom the young man for the Olympic trials. He didn't show up.[18]

Up in Brandon, Walter discovered Tommy Town, a five mile

runner. Walter was so impressed with his ability, he predicted he could place at the Olympics. He did make the team.

Also in Winnipeg, Walter convinced a runner by the name of Armstrong to give up the mile for the sprints. It was too late for 1920, but Armstrong did develop into a top flight sprinter the following year. Also in Winnipeg, Walter met Cecil Coaffee who impressed him in the sprints. Coaffee made the team, but only through Walter's intervention.

The trip out West reminded Walter of his reputation there. It had been 15 years since his hustling days. Several times, he recalled, a stranger came up to him saying he thought his name was "Renwick" or "Wilson" and having a good chuckle with him over one of his matched racing exploits years back. He even ran into Charley Walmsley, his great backer for two years in Nelson, BC, who was also surprised to find Walter was not "Renwick".

If nothing else, Walter's tour drummed up a lot of interest in the Olympics in particular and track and field in general. Arriving home in Ontario, though, Walter made some biting comments to an Ottawa reporter:

> "*We have started away too late on Olympic matters. Here we are six weeks from sailing time and the material has not even been culled over, let alone developed. If Canada does not make a good showing at the Olympic Games it is not for lack of athletic material! ... The principle reason Canada has not had more track and field champions at the present time is lack of coaching... Of all the places I visited I did not see one athletic field that was equipped for athletics... I could name several athletes in the city of Toronto who if they had been coached properly would have been world's champions today.*" [19]

He was being a little demanding of a country that had just

climbed out of the decimation of World War I, but he made his point: Canada had to create a better sports ethic if it was ever going to be competitive again. He had just seen what Canada had to offer and was not impressed; he knew there were few medals to be had in Antwerp now. These had to be biting remarks to James Merrick who, more than anyone else, was responsible for the culture of sport in Canada. Merrick promoted the amateur code of part-time athletes, the antithesis of Walter's professional philosophy.

But on his western tour, Walter was careful to spout the party line. One reporter commented, "He is well acquainted with the most intricate points of amateurism, physical condition and sportsmanship generally".[20] Another said, "He thought that it would be inadvisable for the association to mix with professional sport".[21] Never again would Walter say anything publicly promoting mixing money with sport. He had made a good living as a runner, had been contemptuous of the amateur rules and had tried to play both sides of the game for 20 years, but now, after his career as an athlete was over and he was on the COC's payroll, he toed the party line. We'll never know what he really believed then regarding payment to athletes (30 years later, he was still enamoured with the Scottish Highland Games model of paid performances), but on this Western tour he touted the importance of pure amateur athleticism.

His rant in the Ottawa paper was an appeal to the sports officials and athletes to work harder. Canada was falling behind the rest of the world, but not for want of talent, just for want of work. Athletes had to train more and officials had to provide more support.

Walter continued his talent-assessing tour in June, holding clinics in Toronto, Ottawa and Montreal. This was the sporting hotbed of Canada and Walter got to meet all the top athletes. He gave few a chance at the Olympics, though he did discover a javelin thrower, A Stewart, who tossed it 120'. With a little instruction, he threw it 152', breaking the Canadian record. Stewart improved again at the Trials but at 164' he was not good enough to make the team as the

Swedes were throwing over 200'.

There was one significant athlete Walter didn't get to meet that spring, Earl "Tommy" Thomson, the world record holder in the 110m high hurdles. Thomson, a Canadian who had lived in Long Beach, California, since he was eight years old, was the NCAA and AAU champion in the States, representing Dartmouth College. The COC had contacted him regarding the Olympic Team, but had received no response. Thomson, apparently, was investigating his options for the US Olympic Team and deflected the Canadian overtures until he heard in June that his Canadian citizenship made him ineligible for the US team.[22] Frustrated, the COC instructed Walter to put the pressure on him to declare for the Canadian team. Walter duly sent him a strongly worded letter.

Walter was as adept at the javelin as any other event.
Courtesy Orillia Museum of Art and History

Finally, on June 23rd, just two weeks before the Olympic Trials, Thomson responded, declaring his intent to compete for Canada. There was no fanfare in the paper but likely a sense of relief in the minds of the Canadian Olympic officials.

Thomson would turn out to be a bit of an enigma for Walter. Supremely talented, he was almost a shoo-in for the gold in the hurdles, but he was also a potential medalist in the 400 hurdles, the pentathlon, the long jump and the high jump. Even though he was described as good-natured with an ever-ready smile, he and Walter grated on each other. Thomson had not trained since mid-April and was lackadaisical when he showed up in Canada for the Dominion Trials.[23] Someone like Walter, with his all-business work ethic, just couldn't understand Thomson. But he was really Canada's only hope for gold in track and field. He was important and it was up to Walter to get him to perform.

To select the team, the COC set up two stages to the Olympic Trials. On July 10th, Provincial Trials were held in Ontario, Quebec (with the Maritimes) and the West (in Winnipeg). The top athletes at each would be eligible to attend the Dominion Trials at the MAAA field in Montreal a week later. The COC estimated they had the funds to send about 70 athletes to Antwerp for the Olympics, if a further $20,000 could be raised from "patriotic citizens and sportsmen". It couldn't be and only 52 ultimately went, including an entire 8 man hockey team, the Winnipeg Falcons, for the first ever Olympic hockey tournament. There was only room for about 10 track and field athletes. It was clear the COC was only going to send over athletes who "had a chance", that is, were competitive with the best in the world. Winning the Trials didn't ensure a spot on the team. Selection was to be made by the committee with the Head Coach's input.

Walter attended the Ontario Olympic Trials at the Exhibition field in Toronto on July 10th. The trials were held on a slow cinder track and a reporter commented, "There wasn't a single performance all afternoon that would warrant sending any of the competitors to the Olympic meet in Antwerp".[24] The 100-yard dash was won by Alex Ponton in a slow 10 2/5 seconds. Likewise, the 220 was run in an unimpressive 22 4/5. But Ponton had no fears; he had a private backer, Hamilton Wills, who was paying his expenses to go to the Olympics.[25] He just had to be good enough to be selected by the COC. This race, at least, proved he was the fastest in Ontario.

Stewart, Walter's protégé in the javelin, shattered the Canadian record of 135 feet with his 158 foot heave, but didn't impress Walter; he was still 40 feet behind the Europeans.

To make matters worse, Walter heard that week that Tommy Thomson had decided not to go to Antwerp. It had been only two weeks since he sheepishly and belatedly stated his intent to represent Canada instead of the US. "It is hoped that enough pressure can be brought to bear on Tommy Thomson, the world's record holder in the hurdles, to have him run for Canada," Walter remarked to a reporter at the Provincial Trials, igniting that public pressure.[26] You can just feel Walter's blood pressure rising. Whatever happened to men of character, men who stood by their word?

The Trials were a dismal experience for Walter. He had hoped at least a few of the athletes would rise to the occasion. None did. "It would be much better," Walter told a reporter, "to pay out the money that would be wasted in financing the winners to Antwerp in sending a competent man or men through Canada looking for and developing promising athletes." Furthermore, Walter pointed out, taking a direct dig at the Canadian sports ethic as espoused by the AAU of C, "We have no stall-feeding clubs, and most of our lads have to work for a living and spend their spare time in athletics".[27]

After the meet, Walter held daily training sessions for the top athletes who were intending to make the trip to Montreal for the Dominion Trials in a week. There was work to be done and little time to do it, and Walter expected them all to be at the field.

One athlete, special to Walter, was Charlie Boyle. In 1909, Boyle, as a 16 year old, was the fastest runner in Walter's hometown of Orillia. Walter had worked with him periodically, teaching him the finer points of sprinting, when he passed through town over the next few years. As an 18 year old, he ran 100 yards in a remarkable 10 seconds flat! At the 1912 Olympic Trials, Boyle was expected to be a challenge to Army Howard in the 100, only to suffer an attack of appendicitis the week of the meet. Boyle had distinguished himself in the war and was trying to make a last-gasp comeback for the 1920 Olympics. Unfortunately, at 27 years of age, he didn't have it any more, but Walter worked with him all week in preparation for the Finals in Montreal.[28]

A week later, on July 17th, Walter was at the MAAA athletic field in Montreal for the Dominion Trials, the last chance for the athletes to put up marks worthy of selection to the Olympic Team. Unfortunately, the day dawned cool and damp with a strong wind, poor conditions for the athletes. Only a disappointing 1500 spectators showed up, the empty seats obvious.

But Tommy Thomson showed up. He entered three events and won them all handily, the 110m hurdles in 15.2, half a second over his best, the high jump in 5' 10", below average for him and the long jump in a mediocre 22' 7". None of his marks were outstanding but that didn't matter; the world record holder was there and everyone expected him to rise to the occasion in Antwerp. He had exactly one month to get into better shape.

The newspaper report quoted these words from Thomson: he was busy "clearing up the misunderstanding caused by various conflicting statements attributed to him… Those stories got me into a lot of trouble because Walter Knox wrote and gave me the deuce… Wouldn't a fellow be an awful ass to miss the chance of competing in an Olympiad?"[29]

Alex Ponton won the 200m race in a slow 23.2 seconds, over a second and a half off the Olympic record. Then he fell all the way to third place in the 100 behind the winner Coaffee, who ran a mediocre 11.2 seconds. Coaffee, a youngster from Winnipeg, had a "withered" and paralysed right arm and ran in a lunging style, though with a "grand stride". He had speed but could he be coached in that condition? Would Ponton's 200 be enough for him to be named to the team?

Stewart improved his javelin throw to 164' but would not be selected.

Likewise, the discus and shot put champions were left off the team because their marks were not competitive enough. The big youngster out west had beaten them all with his one heave of the shot put in his street clothes. I bet Walter was disappointed he didn't show up.

The pole vaulter was a full three feet below the Olympic record.

There were some highlights though. A great duel developed in the 5000m run. Leitch led the whole way before being out-kicked in the final 150 metres by Tommy Town. Both men ran times competitive with the world's best but the COC only selected Town for the team. In what had to be a huge slap in the face for Leitch, the third place man, Edward Lawrence, winner of the 1500 race, was named to the team as well as he could run the 10,000 too.

Smyllie ran a strong 400m race of 51.4 seconds but was ultimately left off the team.

EC Freeman showed himself to be a contender on the world stage in the 3000m walk by posting a time just 43 seconds off the world record. He made the team. Hector Phillips won the 800 metre race in a Canadian record time of 1:57.2. Though he was a full six seconds off the Olympic record, he made the team.

Then there were the heavy men. John Cameron, Canada's all-around champion, was named to the team for his win in the hammer throw, and would be entered in the pentathlon and decathlon too. Archie MacDermid, Cameron's fellow Vancouverite, won the 56 pound weight throw and made the team, also getting to contest the hammer in Antwerp. Finally, John McEachern came second in the 56 pound weight and shot put contests with strong heaves, just behind the winners. He was on the bubble waiting with Smyllie, Leitch, Ponton, Lawrence, Coaffee and high jumper Kennedy for word from the COC of their decisions.

There was one dark horse too. George Goulding, winner of the 10k walk at the 1912 Olympics, was still competing and still at the top of his game. But he had been declared a professional during the war because "he was engaged in YMCA athletic coaching". A lobbying effort was under way to have him reinstated as an amateur, just as the Americans had recently done with a few of their top athletes. He was expected to be on the team.[30] However, the ideological AAU of C refused, and Goulding was out.

After the Trials, Walter met with the five man Canadian Olympic Committee to select the team. They had money for about nine men. Thomson, Town, Cameron, Freeman and MacDermid were givens. Phillips in the 800 was good. The committee then decided to add heavy man McEachern and distance man Lawrence, two somewhat controversial choices likely based on Walter's assertion that he could work with them. Finally, they took Ponton. He won the 200 but lost badly in the 100 to up-and-comer Coaffee. But he had a backer who would pay his way. That put Ponton on the team.[31] The nine men were selected.

Next morning, the criticism started. The "bubble" men and their coaches complained. Why only nine athletes? The Manitoba contingent objected strenuously to Ponton's selection over Coaffee.[32] The Quebec AAA, who placed no athletes on the team (and coincidentally never paid their promised $5000 to support the Olympic Team) strongly condemned the committee. They clamored for the selection of McGill's high jumper Bill Kennedy, the top Quebec athlete, but to no avail.[33]

Walter had been a big part of the selection process, offering opinions on the athletes he thought had potential to improve with his coaching and who were as good as he was going to get. That's how McEachern, the heavy man, fully 6'4" and over 250 pounds, made the team. Walter said he could get more out of him.

The attacks turned towards Merrick, the COC chair. Why were two managers, Merrick and Crow, accompanying the team? Couldn't one be left home to make room for another athlete? Merrick's response to the reporter relaying this question was condescending. "My experience of former similar trips has shown me that they (the athletes) become so obsessed with the purpose of their trip that they have to be looked after like children."[34] Both Merrick and Crow made the trip again.

Walter (left) with the 10 men selected to the 1920 Olympic Team right after the Trials. Back row, Tommy Thompson, Hec Phillip, Cecil Coaffee, John Cameron, Alex Ponton, Archie MacDermid, John McEacheran. Front row, EC Freemen, Edward Lawrence and Tommy Town.
Courtesy Orillia Museum of Art and History

But the team roster was not finalized. The Manitoba contingent continued to pester Walter about Coaffee the next day. Walter liked Coaffee and his potential as a sprinter but the decision was made, all the money was spent, all the spots were taken. The day after the Trials, when the team was catching a train to their new quarters, Walter, at Coaffee's request[35], wired the Winnipeg District Committee from the train station to say that, "if they could supply the necessary funds I would guarantee that Coaffee would be allowed to join the team".³⁶ Immediately, a reply came back that the money was forthcoming. Walter turned and ran down the platform yelling to the conductor, "Wait, wait!" as he searched for the small group of unsuccessful athletes there, waving farewell to their friends on the team. Walter grabbed Coaffee (by the good arm) and told him to get on the train — he was on the team. How dramatic! With the money coming, Walter had no problem clearing his decision with the COC.

Coaffee's selection completed the 10 man Olympic athletics team. (Big John McEachern's entry was apparently withdrawn after reaching Antwerp; he's not listed in any results, even as a no show, and an entry for Bill Kennedy was made at some point, though he did not compete or make the trip to Antwerp).

The Antwerp Olympics were scheduled from April to September 1920. In April, the ice hockey teams assembled for the first ever Olympic hockey tournament. The Canadian Allen Cup champions, the Winnipeg Falcons, represented Canada, paying their own way, and brought home the gold medal, outscoring the competition 29 to 1, though squeaking out a 2-0 semi-final victory over the US. Interestingly, 7 of the 8 skaters were of Icelandic origin and their nickname, the "Falcons", was chosen because it was a symbol of Iceland. The "Canadian" team was really made up of patriotic Icelanders!

The rest of the competitions would start in July.

27

The Antwerp Olympic Games

Walter's participant medal from the 1920 Olympics
Courtesy of Claudia Courtney

Antwerp was an interesting choice for the Games. Belgium had been devastated by WWI. The Germans had rolled through the small country without warning, in the execution of their "Schlieffen Plan" to rapidly encircle Paris and knock France out of the war. Belgium's economy was in tatters as was its farmland and infrastructure after four years of battles and occupation by the enemy. As a show of support to that small country the other major powers had sworn to protect, the IOC awarded it the Olympics in 1920. After the "Meticulous Games" in Stockholm, these were disorganized and frustrating for the athletes, not to mention austere. There weren't enough practice fields or hotel rooms. The judges made arbitrary and inconsistent decisions and changed the timing of events without notice, causing delays and fights as athletes raced to the venues unprepared. But given their short notice, barely a year, it is impressive they pulled the Games off as well as they did.

A record 2600 athletes participated, and it could have been more since the defeated countries, Germany, Hungary, Bulgaria, Turkey and Austria, were not invited. The Olympic flag with the five interlocking rings was introduced in Antwerp, as was the Olympic Athlete's Oath. The Olympic movement was developing even if the Games were austere.

Canada's team shipped to Europe in stages, according to the competition schedule, again demonstrating Merrick's organizational talents. The hockey team went first in April. The trap shooters went on July 11th. Walter, as Head Coach, went with the main body of athletes on July 24th. This group included the 10 track and field competitors, the nine boxers, three marathoners and two cyclists. Walter was responsible for the management of these athletes. On August 7th, four swimmers, one diver and one wrestler departed. Then finally, on August 13th, the 5 rowers got underway.

Again, Merrick proved his worth as an organizer. With soldiers still de-mobilizing from Europe and many ships having been de-commissioned after the strain of war work, shipping was hard to find. The American team actually had to have an act of Congress passed to secure passage for their Olympians.[1] But everything ran smoothly for the Canadians.

Walter's contingent spent two weeks training in London . There were no showdowns this year the way there had been with Army Howard and Frank Lukeman in 1912, but it was not all smooth sailing either. The pranks and practical joking started up immediately as the men got to know each other. When the athletes began to get out of hand, waking people up in the middle of the night, breaking curfew and throwing food, Walter stepped in, this time with Merrick right beside him. The "track and field men", Walter told a Toronto Star reporter, "yielded to advice when called to account for horseplay and practical joking which annoyed their comrades and which caused complaints to me".[2] Or, as Merrick put it, "The discipline of the Canadian team was good after one little showdown when some kickers signed an agreement to be good and play the game."[3] But some of the boxers did not "yield to advice".

The boxing team was disgruntled from the very start of the Olympic selection process. The process of each province putting forward a representative in each weight class for a selection tournament was not well organized or communicated. The contending boxers were "confused" about what they had to do to be considered.[4] All they absolutely knew was that they had to have an amateur card. So, by the time they climbed aboard the ship for London, they were already unruly because of their treatment.

It didn't help that the general opinion of the reporters was "that the boxers will not score any points to help the Dominion total".[5]

The boxers, well, three of them anyway, did not heed Walter's words and they butted heads throughout the whole Olympic program. As Walter said after the Games, "The majority of them were gentlemen and acted as such, and were amenable to discipline at all times... Not so with these three boxers".[6] Once again, Walter displayed little tact in dealing with strong-headed men.

In coaching the track and field men, Walter had learned his lesson in 1912. There was only one practice a day, from 2 to 5:30 each afternoon. That was more than these athletes were used to anyway. Forcing more on them, Walter had learned, just got their backs up.

The only real issues that flared up during these Olympics were the result of the Belgian Olympic organizers. Walter told reporters, "Four days after we arrived in Antwerp we were ordered off the stadium and they had no place we could train".[7] He and Merrick found an old, unkempt football field where the athletes were forced to make their final preparations in the week before the Games. This took a toll on the men. Cameron sprained his ankle so badly he couldn't take part in the Olympics. Tommy Town got a "stone bruise" on his foot and still had his foot up the night before his race. He ran poorly. And Art Smoke, a new and talented marathoner, the class of the three Canadians, instead of contending for a medal, "never should have started". Forced to train on a cycling path, he was hit and knocked over by a bike, suffering numerous skins and bruises. After bravely starting the marathon, he did not finish.[8]

The final indignity for the team happened in the opening ceremony, and this was the only misstep by Merrick. He forgot to bring a Canadian flag for the athletes to march behind. When he produced a tiny flag the size of a "women's handkerchief", there was an uproar by the team and they marched without one.[9]

The 1920 Canadian Olympic Team. Walter is third from the right.
Tommy Thompson, the star of the team, but a frustration
to Walter, is sixth from the left.
Courtesy Orillia Museum of Art and History

The track and field meet got started on August 15th with the heats of the 100m. Canada's two entries, Ponton and Coaffee, were 22 and 23 years old respectively. Coaffee placed third in his heat (running in about 11.3 seconds) and was eliminated. Ponton came second in his heat with a time of 11.1 and advanced to the quarter-final. His time of 11.4 in that race put him last and he was eliminated. The gold medalist, American Charlie Paddock, ran it in 10.8 seconds.

Next up, Hec Phillips ran the 800m. He went slower than he did on the cold windy day in Montreal, and was eliminated.

The 400m hurdles and the high jump were also held that day. Tommy Thomson, though potentially a medalist in both, competed in neither of them. His big race, the 110 hurdles, was up in two days and he opted to rest. He wasn't even entered in another event.

The 5000m event was run the next day, Monday the 16th. This was the big race for Tommy Town. Before the athletes left Canada, the sports reporters were of the opinion that there were only two contenders for a medal on the Canadian athletics team, Thomson in the hurdles and Town in the 5000.[10] Town lined up for the start with his badly bruised foot but did not finish the race. What a disappointment for the team. And what bad luck to have three of their top men sidelined by injury. Town did manage to finish the 1500m and the cross country races later but was not a factor in either of them.

The pentathlon was also held that Monday. Cameron was out with his badly sprained ankle. Thomson, a medal threat, opted to skip that event too in order to prepare for the hurdles the next day. Looking at his scores in the pentathlon events, it is clear he would have won a medal with a reasonable performance and would have had quite a duel with the gold medalist, the championship likely coming down to the faster man in the 1500m run. Seeing Thomson pass on that event would have been irksome to Walter, a man who routinely competed in six events in an afternoon, three or four times a week in Scotland. Here was a chance for Olympic glory, a chance to score points for the team. Maybe the pentathlon would have been tiring the day before the hurdles, but why not the 400 hurdles or high jump two days before? Walter knew all about missed opportunities and it would have been gnawingly frustrating to see as fine an athlete as Thomson pass these events by. They would have had trouble discussing all this though - Thomson was almost completely deaf.

The heats of the 110m high hurdles were carried out on August 17th, the third day of the meet. Thomson, the world record holder at 14.8 seconds, was finally jumping into action. Tall, 6'1", and 190 pounds with a strong athletic physique, Thomson was built for the high hurdles. The barriers were three and a half feet high, almost chest high to puny Walter, but Thomson could smoothly glide over them with his long legs. The runner had to be sure to clear them too; they didn't fall over easily like modern hurdles. Made of heavy wood for durability, they were supported by braces extending a good foot out each side of the hurdle. If you clipped one with your knee it would hurt, and likely send you flat on your face.

Thomson was confident of a win here. Though he had beaten them in the past, he knew the Americans, Barron and Murray, were no slouches. In his first heat, he ran an easy 15.4 seconds to place 2nd and qualify for the semi-final. Thomson and Barron then both won their respective semis in 15.0 seconds to tie the Olympic record. The big showdown would be the next day in the final.

Thomson did not compete in the long jump that day either, another strong event for him. The 110 hurdles would be the only event he contested, even though he was a medal threat in five events. The schedule did not work in his favour.

Next day, Thomson came to the track confident. At the gun, three men exploded ahead of the field, tied at the 50m mark. Then Thomson pulled away, winning by several yards in the world record tying time of 14.8 seconds. Barron came in second in 15.1. Canada had its first, and only, track and field medal. At the medal ceremony, Merrick still hadn't located a Canadian flag so Thomson received his gold medal under a British flag.

Walter would have been happy to see that gold medal performance but obviously was ticked off by Thomson's attitude. There were more medals to be won; was the man really so soft he could only do one race? Walter—hustler, miner, Highlands Scot—came from a tough world where you sucked it up and got the job done. Toughness, that was character, not this good-natured, delicate I-can-only-run-one-race attitude. What was wrong with these modern athletes?

Adding to Walter's frustrations was the fact that Thomson was a "night man".[11] He and Coaffee and several others habitually broke curfew, out for a good time on the town. And now that his meet was over, only four days into the competition, things only got worse. Walter commented in a letter to the Toronto Star after the Olympics, "Coaffee did not show very much… it is hoped if he ever gets another chance to go to the Olympics he will pay a little more attention to the training rules and may do better".[12] Walter commented that he thought Thomson was going to lose the hurdles due to his lack of work ethic and that he could have won the pentathlon "but didn't have time for athletics after his win". In his notes, Walter said, "while he (Thomson) won he was lucky after the way he carried on during the time getting ready for the games".[13] Thomson was on holiday after the gold medal race and showed no regrets about missing events he could have won a medal in. There was no understanding and no love lost between Thomson and Walter. (Coaffee, by the way, went on to a very successful career, tying the world record of 9.6 seconds in the 100-yard dash, going to the Paris Olympics as team captain and defeating the great Canadian sprinter Percy Williams twice just before Williams' Olympic victory in 1928).

The rest of the meet was uneventful for Walter's Canadian team. Archie MacDermid missed out on a medal in the 56 pound weight throw by less than two centimeters, and placed 9th in the hammer. Coaffee and Ponton repeated their mediocre performances in the 200. The marathoners came 13th and 15th. In the walk, Freeman "did the very opposite of what he was told to do" and was eliminated in the heats.[14]

However, over at the boxing arena it was a different story. The tournament ran from August 21st to 25th, just after the track meet, in eight weight classes. On the final day, after all the elimination bouts, five of the nine Canadian boxers had landed in medal matches. They had left Canada with reporters saying they had no chance. Just like in the recent war, the Canadian fighting spirit caught everyone by surprise. Twenty-two year old Bert Schneider won the gold medal in the welterweight class. Middleweight Art Prud'homme and bantamweight Cliff Graham won silvers. Lightweight Chris Newton and Middleweight Moe Herscovitch won bronze.

The Canadian boxers were cocky, free-spirited underdogs. They liked to play pranks, they liked to stay out late, they didn't like to listen to their coach. But they won medals.

The track and field men had 10 days off while the boxing tournament was going on and they made the best of them by taking tours of the battlefields and exploring the nightlife of Antwerp. In his notes, Walter expressed how moving it was to see all the flattened towns. He would have had no regrets about avoiding the senseless destruction.

A couple of weeks after the track meet, the swimmers started their competition. Big, strong George Vernot won Canada's final two medals, a silver in the 1500 and a bronze in the 400. The rowers had their boat damaged in the ocean crossing and were not a factor in their races.

The final medal count for Canada was nine, three of each colour. Canada was most obviously slipping behind the rest of the world athletically. Nothing showed that better than the high profile track and field contests. Outside of Tommy Thomson, who trained in the US, Canada was not a factor. Walter Knox, at age 42, would soon show he could have won some events at the Canadian Olympic Trials. The athletes, and even more the Canadian sports officials, should have been embarrassed that their glorious athletes could be beaten by their dumpy coach.

One controversy happened on the boat back across the English Channel to their waiting trans-Atlantic ship. Walter got into another scrap with the athletes. The affair is murky as the team tried to keep it quiet in the end. But Walter claimed he was punched by gold medal boxer Bert Schneider. Schneider denied it.[15] Flyweight Harry Turner, captain of the boxing team, backed Schneider up, saying he was the "most good natured" of the boxers and not one to quarrel. Turner said, "Some of the boys, while having fun, were noisy, and Knox told them to stop. There was trouble then and some blows were stuck, but while I do not know who struck Knox, I do know positively it was not Schneider, he was not even concerned in the row, nor was I."[16]

Schneider famously never lost a bout in his whole career. If it was him, Walter would have been lucky it ended after a few punches.

Upon arriving back in Canada, the boxers, in a letter given to a Toronto Star reporter, charged that Merrick, Crow and Knox "regarded the trip as a joy ride" and neglected their charges.[17] They accused Knox of "calling the boxers roughnecks, and treating them in anything but a gentlemanly manner."

Walter did not travel home with the team and was not there to give his side of the story. Merrick defended him as best he could but was not present at the scuffle. Walter had hopped a train to Scotland and didn't return to Canada for another month.

He was contacted though, and an article appeared in the papers titled, "Knox Replies to the Boxers Charges". He went on the attack, the only strategy he knew.

> "I absolutely deny that I at any time called boxers or any other athletes either individually or collectively roughnecks or no-accounts. But if they want to start a little trouble I will call certain of the boxers, particularly two Toronto boys and one Montreal man, roughnecks and prove it if they want a showdown... They created trouble in the dining rooms by throwing food and water about and continually annoyed players by practical jokes during training and sleeping hours. They were on the carpet several times and that did not stop them, until we threatened to send them home."[18]

That was the end of the whole affair. There was no response from the boxers and it was all quickly forgotten. But once again we see Walter ultimately resorting to physical confrontation in handling a conflict. Whether this had any bearing on his never being selected as Olympic Coach again is debatable, but Walter did actively pursue the position unsuccessfully up to and including the 1936 Olympics.[19]

More likely his association with Merrick red-flagged him with the COC. In 1922, Merrick was appointed to the International Olympic Committee, only the second Canadian to achieve that honour. He was a curious choice since Olympic founder Baron de Coubertin's criteria for IOC members included being "an aristocrat" and not being part of national sporting associations, that is, a power broker in sport. Merrick, a commoner, was the epitome of a sports power broker. Likely his strong stance in favour of pure amateurism swung the idealistic IOC his way. Merrick, in the two years leading up to the 1924 Olympics, developed "high tensions" with the Canadian Olympic Committee, to the point where the COC tried to have him dismissed from the IOC. After three years of backroom brawling by letter, the IOC affirmed his position with them. However, Merrick did not attend a single IOC meeting between 1927 and 1932.[20] If Walter was identified as "Merrick's man" there was no way he'd ever be named Olympic Coach again.

Right after the cross-channel ferry landed in England, and following the fistfight, Walter immediately left the team in Merrick's hands and headed to Scotland to try his hand at a couple of Highland Games. Way back in March, when he was training in order to drop 20 pounds, he was planning this excursion. Merrick was fully informed in advance and it was even reported in the newspapers as early as June. At age 42, for the fun of it, Walter was attempting a comeback.

He traveled to Edinburgh and spent 10 days training at the Powderhall grounds, intending to only enter shot put contests. But Fred Lumley, the owner of the grounds, persuaded Walter to do some pole vaulting, even going to his sporting goods store to fetch him a pole. Walter easily cleared 9'6" and "right there" decided to train for the vault again.

Ready to test his luck, Walter entered the Aboyne Games in the 16 and 22 pound shot puts and the vault. Against the best Scotland had to offer, Walter won both shot put events, heaving the 16 pounder a remarkable 45 feet (good for about 5th place in Antwerp). At the Canadian Olympic Trials in Montreal, the top two marks were just over 40 feet. Walter, overweight and sagging, could easily have made the team! His efforts made a dramatic impact. As an "old timer" he was the last of the 12 contestants to take his turn. Little flags scattered across the field marked each throw. When the "old timer" got up and put the ball a full foot and a half beyond the farthest flag, the crowd erupted. "The Canadian", with the big red maple leaf on his chest, was back. Walter was very proud to have thrown his age, over 42 feet at 42 years of age. After that, he went out and won the pole vault at 10' 8", only five inches short of the winner at the Canadian Olympic Trials.

The next day was the Braemar Games, the games of pageantry the king and queen attended. Walter won the 16 pound shot put at 42' 6" and the pole vault at 10' 7".

At both these Games, Walter duly collected his prize money, even winning a bonus for having three victories at Aboyne. After six months of promoting "pure amateurism" for the Olympic Committee, he was now happily collecting money for his athletic efforts. One wonders what his friend James Merrick, a staunch idealist when it came to amateurism, thought of his friend and handpicked Olympic coach casually disregarding everything he had spent his life promoting.

Though Walter, in his Olympic experiences and in his next foray into the coaching world, publicly and, by all reports, enthusiastically, espoused the amateur ideal, it is obvious here that in his heart he still saw nothing wrong with accepting fairly won prize money. When it came to sporting ideals, Walter was a sincere proponent of fair play, hard work and character, and in these ways he truly supported Merrick in his program to promote pure sport. But when it came to sharing the proceeds of an event with the athletes and the "part time" ethic for amateurs in Canada, Walter surely had issues with him.

28

Putting Ontario on the Right Track

The 1920 Olympics were a wake-up call for the sports administrators in Canada. It was apparent Canada was no longer competitive for Olympic medals in track and field. Right after the Olympics, in the fall of 1920, the Montreal AAA hosted a conference to discuss "ways and means of starting a concerted movement to secure a proper representation of Canada at the next Olympic Games".[1] They concluded a series of Provincial Championships and an annual Dominion Championship was the answer.

Walter disagreed. In a long interview in the paper that September, he strongly asserted his opinion that "Canada... will always be behind unless they go into the schools and develop the schoolboys".[2] He had started that type of program in his six months as British Olympic coach in 1914. His grassroots program of identifying and developing athletes and training coaches had just started showing results when the war broke out and put a stop to it. He knew it would work. He had seen how athletes had been floundering on their own, lacking competent instruction. That's what Canada needed, Walter argued. In a column in the Toronto Star under the byline of Canada's Olympic Coach, Walter later wrote, "I believe the salvation of athletics in the province of Ontario depends upon organization, competition and proper coaching... and it behooves those in authority to see to it that the boy in school has the proper instruction in those things that will give him a strong, healthy body as well as a mental education".[3]

He found some support for his suggestion with sports leaders. That fall, at a meeting in Toronto of the AAU of C, the "reconstruction committee" (part of Canada's post-WWI transition planning), which included James Merrick and Norton Crow, recommended that "the rapid spread of supervised sports could immediately inject strength, resourcefulness and social discipline into the war-weary population. Sports would counter the 'negative recreation' of idleness and delinquency among boys and veterans".[4] However, the cash-strapped federal government had no money for their suggested program.

There was the political will in Ontario though. Inside the new populist and moralistic Ontario government, a movement coalesced, driven by an influx of returning veterans and the enduring anti-professional legacy of the AAU of C, which would shape Walter's future.

The new farmer-labourer provincial government of EC Drury (who, incidentally, was born a few days before Walter and grew up in the same community of Coldwater, suggesting they must have known each other as youngsters) picked up on the cries of "degenerate professionalism" and proposed regulation of boxing and wrestling to combat these "licentious" sports.[5] Even as late as 1920, the professionals were still described as "sport prostitutes" and official policy was to eradicate the pay-for-play athletes in the sports deemed amateur. Pro hockey, baseball, boxing and football were launching into a golden age of popularity and were beyond reach for the conservative sports administrators. But that made them all the more intent on keeping the amateur, and especially the Olympic, sports pristine. Drury's new Ontario government decided to impose controls on the worst of the pro sports, boxing and wrestling, the sports most associated with corruption and gambling. It was a populist move that would play well to his moralistic political power base.

It also played well with the returning veterans of the First World War. These men had been indoctrinated with boxing and wrestling as a part of their training and enjoyed congregating at matches. Boxing gyms were a social meeting place for the vets; big bouts were a natural draw for them. But many of the veterans were repelled by the ingrained corruption and the seedy gambling culture. Cleaning up the sport could only attract votes for Drury.

Drury's Ontario Athletic Commission Act of 1920 imposed government supervision on professional boxing and wrestling, a 5% tax on gate receipts and a system of licensing on all athletes, trainers and promoters in those industries. In effect, they were regulating the sports, driving the shabby promoters and bookies out of the gyms. The upshot of this Act was a financial windfall for the province, a windfall that they were going to use to shore up the amateur sports. It was a tax-the-pros-to-pay-for-the-amateurs policy.

Five commissioners were appointed to oversee the program and to use the accumulated funds to promote amateur sport. Once the OAC commissioners had established their regulatory control over boxing and wrestling, they began putting their emphasis on the amateur sports side of their mandate. Patrick Mulqueen, the honourary coach of the oarsmen at the 1920 Olympics and the soon-to-be chair of the Canadian Olympic Committee, headed up the amateur sports side of the Commission, the spending side, which answered to the Ministry of Health but in reality had a free hand. The evolving plan became just what Walter had been urging. Walter and Mulqueen had been in communication that fall and there is no question Walter had some influence in the direction the plan took. In a talk Walter gave in 1928, he commented that he, in discussing the problems with athletics in Canada and the formation of the OAC with Mulqueen in the fall of 1920, had specifically suggested that any income the government received from a tax on professional sport should be "spent in schools, in coaching, lectures and educational movies".[6]

In 1920, physical education in schools, if there was any,

concentrated on calisthenics and drills, a program developed in the 1890s; any extracurricular sport was organized by the boys and girls themselves. Few teachers became involved in organizing sports and those few were characterized more by enthusiasm than by expertise or knowledge of rules.[7] As an example, in Walter's home town of Orillia, the official history of the high school states, in reference to the 1920s, that "There was little organized sport at the school, the serious basketball was at the Y!"[8] The OAC, with their stable financing, sought to change this state of affairs.

The money raised by taxing the professional sports was going to be used to train teachers in physical education, provide direct expert coaching to schoolboys (not girls, who were still excluded from the majority of Olympic competition) and stimulate competition. Ten thousand copies of a booklet containing the rules to all the standard sports were printed and distributed as a start to the program.

But most importantly to Walter, the OAC set up a program, in association with the Department of Education, to send a prominent coach throughout the province to conduct clinics in public, private and industrial schools and community clubs. The OAC was also going to develop a system of regional athletic meets and a provincial schoolboy championship. That was the exact program Walter had been lobbying for all fall: identify the talent, instruct it, train teachers to carry on the coaching and then provide competitive opportunities.

In February of 1921, Walter Knox was hired to be that traveling coach for the Province of Ontario.

Walter was still, in 1920, heavily involved in the mining endeavours at Shining Tree Lake. By then though, he was gradually giving up the pick and shovel work and spending his time managing the work crews along with his brother Jack. The mine was steadily producing gold and their bank account was growing. Walter didn't need to go work for the OAC, he was financially set for life. But he was a sportsman. His comeback in Scotland at age 42 that summer, while rewarding, had shown him the decline in his abilities was underway. It took longer to recover from a training session and he was more prone to injury. For a man who had taken such meticulous care of his health and who never entered a competition he was not thoroughly prepared for, it was clear his competitive days were over. Coaching positions were now his access to the sporting world, a world he still clung to.

Walter never commented on his arrangements with Jack regarding the mine, whether they split the profits 50-50 or not, or the work. Jack had done all the backbreaking labour in the early years, enduring all the hardships of the prospector's life. Early on, Walter had only popped into his life every so often, staying several months at a time to help, and then leaving again. Walter's main contribution appeared to be the money to invest in their venture. In the last five years though, Walter had spent the majority of his time at the mines. They must have had an amicable business relationship; it endured for over 30 years. But whatever their arrangement, Jack let Walter go off on extended hiatuses from the mine, even after they struck it rich, to coach hockey, various track teams and the Olympics. Coaching with the OAC was just another one of those jobs. Sport was a central part of Walter's make-up and Jack had undoubtedly figured this out by now. The OAC job being a new program, it probably looked like a tentative venture in 1920, another short-term hiatus from the mine, a couple of months each spring and fall. It would turn out to be a 15 year obsession.

In the fall of 1920, when the OAC hired Walter, he was a fit 42 year old, but bald on top and thick through the middle. He had trained hard for his Olympic and then Highland Games excursions, getting his weight back down under 180 pounds. Once he started coaching for the OAC he had to keep that fitness level up. In fact, he always used himself as an example and inspiration to the groups he addressed. An Orillia newspaper in 1923 said, "Walter is still 'some boy' as an athlete, and looks to be good for anything yet.

His magnificent development is certainly a wonderful proof of the value of athletics in building up the strength and agility necessary to perfect physique."[9]

Being the traveling coach for the OAC brought a lot of responsibilities. Walter had free reign to set up a program to achieve the goals set out by the Commission, but was monitored by some enthusiastic and passionate men with idealistic expectations. Walter consistently communicated the goals of the OAC this way:

1. To see boys and girls built up physically as well as mentally
2. To get children interested in play and out of mischief
3. To develop provincial and national champions

This was a program under the auspices of the Ministry of Health. The physical, mental and social well-being of children, and hence future society, were the chief goals of the program. The sports leaders of the day, including Walter, quietly put a lot of emphasis on the third goal, essentially winning Olympic medals. All three goals could be, and were, fulfilled concurrently, although by 1930 the emphasis would became weighted to producing champions and the program suffered for it in support. But in 1921, when Walter was preparing to get it off the ground, the school boards were brought on side with the health and well-being rhetoric.

The biggest sales point for the boards of education was the fact that this program cost them nothing. The OAC, through its tax on professional sports, paid the coach, supplied all the equipment and materials and did the organizing. All the principal at a school had to do was book off the time for a clinic. It really was a win-win-win situation for the students, schools and sports organizations. Even the boxing industry benefited through the promotion of their sport, Walter carefully talked positively about boxing at every clinic, saying things like "Boxing is the best thing to make a boy control his temper, for by losing it he finds his punishment is worse".[10]

There was a massive amount of work for Walter to get started on for the OAC and only a few months to do it. As was typical with Walter, he was willing to work extremely hard when committed. And he was committed; he had spent his life in the pursuit of physical fitness and sporting excellence and saw this program as a vehicle to instill his philosophy in all the schoolchildren in Ontario. He was passionate and determined to be ready to go into the schools in the spring, just three or four months away.

To prepare, he first had to settle on his program, what to teach and how. Then he had to approach all the school boards in Ontario to offer his services and explain the OAC program. He had to get materials printed and buy equipment. He likely had to buy a car as several of his tours of the province were by "motor car". One of the first orders of business, an idea ahead of its time, was to produce motion pictures of exemplary athletes performing in many different sports as a demonstration tool. Even more revolutionary, Walter wanted to be able to run them in slow motion. These were just the first steps in his job and they all had to be done right away to be ready for the warm spring weather before the schools got out in 1921. Fortunately the OAC provided whatever funds he needed.

On March 16, 1921, Walter assembled some of Canada's most famous athletes to shoot his demonstration movies.[11] He had contracted with the Pathe Company to do the filming, some with special slow motion film. Bobby Kerr, the 1908 Olympic gold medalist, now 40 years old, and Alex Ponton of the 1920 Olympic team demonstrated sprints. Olympian George Goulding showed speed walking styles and Jack Tait of Walter's 1912 Olympic team did the middle distance running. Carruthers, the U of T varsity star, ran the hurdles and Vincent, from Hamilton, demonstrated the pole vault. The rest of the field events were covered by Walter himself. All these men gathered for Walter and the OAC on the University of Toronto stadium track to make the films on what must have been an unusually warm March day. In the end, Walter had three 2000 foot films covering all the track and field events. Later, other sports were added including swimming, skating, gymnastics and throwing a "curve ball" in baseball.[12]

By then, Walter had made his contacts with the school boards and had set up the first clinics. That first year he called it his "model school"[13] and ran it with the help of PJ Mulqueen and sometimes assisted by George Goulding, the 1912 Olympic gold medalist in the 10k walk.[14] Mulqueen, of the OAC, a top notch rower in his younger days, was "deeply interested" in this branch of the Commission's work and accompanied Walter the first few times (imagine having your over-enthusiastic boss looking over your shoulder). Walter gave a lecture on the goals of the OAC and healthy living, demonstrated a few track and field events and then let the boys up to give it a try under his watchful eye. As Walter commented to a reporter, he hoped some "male teachers" would take up his instruction and qualify to teach.

At the end of the spring school term, Walter ran a clinic for the teachers to train them in the basics of coaching, hoping to inspire them to integrate a physical education program in their schools. But the teachers were tough to win over. In April of 1922, Walter commented to a reporter, "Apparently public and secondary school teachers are not as keen as they might be on the matter of athletics… possibly because these lessons are given for free they are not sufficiently appreciated."[15] But over the course of the next decade, with the school boards promoting the OAC program vigorously, more and more individual teachers hopped on board.

During the summer of 1921, Walter made a tour of the "northern districts", from Orillia to North Bay to the Soo, organizing the schools and bringing them on side.[16] In the spring of 1922, he had everything in place to really get some work done with schoolboys all across Ontario.

In 1922, Walter spent 105 days offering clinics for the

Commission, being paid $10 a day plus expenses, a very healthy wage.[17] The typical clinic started with a talk about the OAC and the benefits of sport. Then he'd run one of his films, pointing out the basic technical aspects as the film ran. After that, the kids were taken out to the track for a personal demonstration by Walter, followed by some practice and races. A session would take about two hours and Walter would often do more than one in a day. Generally, he coordinated a time with the principals, both public and high school, often together, in advance, to combine kids from several schools for one big presentation. It was not uncommon for him to have 500 students listening at one time. The papers almost always commented on how he kept their rapt attention with his movies.

As an example of his content, Walter always included a presentation on "starting in the sprint", explaining what had become known as "the Knox Method".[18] First he pointed out the importance of digging holes for a foot grip "crossways" so the back of the hole would be firm, then discussed the all-important placement of the holes. At the time, it was popular to crouch down with the hands and forward foot right on the starting line, the idea being to have that first step as close to the finish line as possible. The Australians, he would then explain, now proposed extending the back leg so the knee was not bent.

Walter disagreed with both ideas and proceeded to demonstrate why, using both himself and volunteers. If the front foot was on the line, he explained, the rest of the body was slow to push past it as the weight of the body was behind the foot. Walter proposed putting the front foot eight inches behind the line for a faster start. A straight back leg such as the Australians suggested had no power, Walter said, and then clearly demonstrated that using volunteers; move the hole forward so the knee was bent. In effect, Walter was teaching them to dig their holes closer together than contemporary convention dictated. The boys now felt they had a "step up" on anyone else, some inside information. This type of mechanical analysis was completely new to the novices, both students and teachers. The demonstration where

Walter made an obvious improvement in a runner's "jump" was not soon forgotten. That sort of approach was carried out with regards to every aspect of all the athletic events.

Three YMCA athletes demonstrating the popular starting technique in the 1920's: front toe right on the starting line.
Courtesy Orillia YMCA

OAC coach Walter Knox demonstrating the "Australian Start" with the straight back leg.
Courtesy Orillia Museum of Art and History

Walter demonstrating the "Knox Start": toe 8 inches behind line and back knee bent.
Courtesy Orillia Museum of Art and History

The 1922 spring sessions were hugely successful. In Midland, for example, Walter spent two full days giving instruction to over 700 students. Then he rented the local movie house to show his demonstration films to over 300 of them.[19] The second year of the program saw the school boards enthusiastically promote the OAC clinics.

The message Walter delivered on behalf of the OAC centred on "the benefits of sport". "Games are fine," Walter would say, "and essential, but the right kind of living is necessary along with it. Everyone should indulge in some kind of sport".[20] Sport is important, Walter said, because "by developing healthy, strong bodies their capacity for study is increased."[21] He insisted that "An active brain is not much use unless you have a healthy body, and the most successful businessman is the one who takes an active part in sport!"[22]

Walter always used himself as an example of "sturdy manhood"[23]: fit, healthy, non-smoker and non-drinker, successful businessman, expert coach, world all-around champion at age 36 – the kind of person the kids should aspire to be. The 1920s was the era of sports heroism with such immortalized champions as Babe Ruth, Jack Dempsey and Johnny Weismuller idolized by boys everywhere. Walter, while wanting to encourage interest in sport this way, also wanted to focus the kids on amateur sports and the aspiration to become an athlete. He wanted to be inspirational. In a talk to the Picton Kiwanis Club in 1928, a reporter described Walter pointing out that his

> "*companions in boyhood looked like old men now and couldn't run across the street, whereas he, as his audience could testify, was a perfect specimen of good health and physical fitness. Mr. Knox told of how he worked from six in the morning until six at night and then would put on his track suit. People would laugh at him, but now the tables were turned.*"[24]

Of course, Walter also included in every talk and most interviews his standard line, "Every boy should learn to box and run. If they didn't want to fight they could run. If they didn't care to run, they could fight".[25] This often got a good laugh from his audience, but Walter was serious, a sturdy man could take care of himself.

And Walter could be cutting in delivering his message. During a presentation in Port Arthur, Walter singled out a cigarette smoker. "You can tell them," he said, pointing a finger at the small boy, "cut out the tobacco and form a habit that is worthwhile and you will get somewhere!"[26] Equally pointed barbs could be directed at overeating and alcohol just as easily too.

After the widely successful 1922 spring sessions, in towns all across the province, Walter began planning the next stages of his OAC program. Two big additions to his program were introduced that fall.

The first innovation was to include girls for the 1922 fall sessions. Women and girls were largely excluded from sport before the First World War for their own good, females being delicate and their reproductive organs susceptible to injury, or so the medical and sports leaders generally thought. Inroads were being made for women by 1920 though. For example, at the 1912 and 1920 Olympics there were some women's swimming and diving events. The OAC's original mandate was for boys in the best "muscular Christianity" way, but Walter added girls in just the second year. In fact, Walter was already working with female athletes in 1922. On June 2 that year, he held a tryout at Dufferin Park in Toronto for a team of girls to attend a track meet in Philadelphia. At the meet in the States, Jessie Glover broke the world record for the high jump, future world record holder Rosa Grosse won the 100-yard dash, Dorothy O'Neil won the high jump and their relay team won.[27] There was a rising women's sports movement in Canada, and it is clear that, in 1922, Walter was a promoter of girls' participation in sport before it was widely accepted. In September, all the girls were allowed to miss class to attend his OAC clinics too.

Second, and more importantly, in the fall of 1922, Walter organized the first athletic competitions for schoolchildren under the OAC's auspices. This was a massive undertaking. The province was divided into eight "sections": Western, Central (Toronto, Hamilton, Niagara), Georgian Bay (Lindsay to Midland), Peterborough, Kingston, Ottawa, Northern Ontario and Fort William/Port Arthur. Each school or town was to run its own trials and the best performers would be eligible for the Sectional meet. The winners of each event in each age group at the Sectional meet received an all-expenses paid trip to the Provincial Finals in October. Second place finishers were eligible to attend too, but at the school board's expense.[28]

This program had to evolve over a few years, given the size of the undertaking, but by 1925 the Provincial Schoolboy and Girl Finals were hugely successful. The final list of events that year was:

Public School
    12/13 year olds: 100, 220, high jump, long jump, pole vault, 440 relay
    14/15 year olds: as above

High School
    Junior (15 years and under 115 pounds): as above
    Intermediate (17 and 135 pounds): as above, plus 440, 880, shot put, 120 hurdles
    Senior (20 and no weight limit): as above, plus one mile run

The OAC had the money to support that kind of program, subsidizing boys and girls from all over Ontario to attend the championship meet. In fact, there was enough money for the OAC to build the most modern indoor athletic facility in Canada. The Civic Arena at the Canadian National Exhibition grounds was secured by the OAC in 1922 and converted into a running track and jumping pits for the sole use of "schoolboys".²⁹ Walter had been harping for years about the lack of athletic facilities across Canada. Once again, the OAC used its wherewithal to act on something Walter was advocating for.

Walter's job included extensive administration of meet entries and results. Undoubtedly school officials did most of it but Walter was the ultimate overseer. This was Walter's original vision come to fruition: to provide every school boy and girl with a chance to try athletics so top prospects could be identified, coached and given the opportunity to compete. Now all that was needed to complete the feeder system for Olympic champions was focused attention on the top athletes.

While it was the OAC program that opened the door to a program like this, it was Walter who effectively created it. In 1922, Walter was promoted to "Chief Coach" of the OAC and the Cornell University coach, Nick Bawlf, was added to the Commission's team with the responsibility to implement the program in the Ottawa area. As the 1920's rolled out, other coaches toured for the OAC, teaching swimming and various sports, but Walter was the "Head Coach".

Right from the beginning, the rural areas latched onto the program more enthusiastically than the big cities. Likely this was due to the limited opportunities in the outlying areas. In 1923, Walter spent only 11 of his 97 clinic days in Toronto.³⁰ He would make a tour of a district, always giving equal importance to the small rural schools and the bigger urban schools. The OAC got their money's worth out of him; at one point that year he visited 16 different Niagara region schools in a week!³¹ On a trip north from Orillia in September of 1923, he visited 14 towns in two weeks on his way to the Soo. A remarkable 3,500 kids attended his clinics on that trip alone.³²

Some of the schools, especially the rural ones, began to respond the way Walter had envisioned. By the mid-1920s, inter-collegiate competitions were developing in a range of sports, including track and field. More importantly, teachers were becoming involved, helping the students organize and train. For example, the first Orillia

Collegiate Institute yearbook in 1925 described six school teams, four for boys and two for girls. JC Smith, a young teacher in his mid-20s, coached both the boys and girls hockey teams and boys track team, while Miss Mitchell coached the girls basketball team (they practiced and played in the YMCA gym down the hill, the school didn't build a suitable gym until 1949). The boys rugby and basketball teams were on their own.[33] Walter ran his clinic in Orillia every year, and after three years, the high school had two teachers coaching and inter-collegiate games against schools from Barrie, Midland, Lindsay and Penetang. This was probably not a coincidence.

By 1923, Walter had his patter down. His focus was healthy living and the importance of sport as a part of that. That year he gave a talk in Toronto to over 1000 boys at an event sponsored by the Evening Telegram newspaper in promotion of their new "Boy's Own Evening Tely" edition. Walter was in fine form and the paper reported many of his axioms in a talk entitled "How each and every red-blooded boy present might become a champion!":

> *"You must be fair, a good sport, and play the game"*
>
> *"A boy who can hold his temper will get to where he wants to be"*
>
> *"Don't stay up late at night or eat too much"*
>
> *"It is up to you younger boys to carry on the work of Canada"*
>
> *"Every boy can be a grand winner, but not every boy can be a good loser, and a good loser will not always lose"*
>
> *"Never accept a nickel, the time may come when you want to enter a competition and will be disqualified"*[34]

Walter's message was blunt, not pithy; workmanlike, not flowery; practical, not idealistic. It was an amateur message of civil, duty-bound, moralistic living delivered in a professional's focused, practical, ego-centric manner. Though Walter walked the walk of amateurism now, his underlying worldview was still that of a professional: work hard, be smart, don't take anything for granted and watch out for number one.[35]

By 1924, Walter had the OAC program well in hand. He was touring five months a year (spring and fall) running clinics in every corner of the province. He had his message honed to a smooth delivery. His schoolboy championships program was running better every year and some "good material" was being identified. More and more teachers were taking Walter's training program and incorporating physical fitness into their curriculum. It should be only a matter of time before great Olympians began to emerge from Ontario.

The 1924 Olympics served to re-emphasize the need for a program like this. Once again, Walter let it be known he was interested in being the Olympic coach. Even as late as April, 1923, one newspaper remarked, "Walter is likely to be named as coach of Canada's Olympic Team next year".[36] However, by 1924 new IOC member James Merrick was in open confrontation with the Canadian Olympic Committee, and Walter, as "Merrick's man" was never in the running to be the coach, even though Canadian Olympic Committee Chairman Patrick Mulqueen was Walter's boss as director of the OAC's amateur sport program.

JR "Cap" Cornelius, the prominent coach at Hamilton's Central High School and the Hamilton Olympic Club, a hotbed of track and field, was selected to coach the team. He was a no-nonsense Scotchman of military bearing ("Cap" stood for Captain), a real zealot in the world of track and field who ascribed to the "no-pain-no-gain" school of athletics.

It was just as well Walter was sidelined though; the 1924 Olympics were a fiasco for Canada. The track athletes were disgruntled over the style of coach Cornelius, had a conflict with manager Mulqueen over which rubbers were hired, were ignored when they presented the managers with their "worn out running shoes" and seven of them were actually left behind in London and had to spend the night in the police station.[37] On top of all that, the Canadian team became the laughing stock of the whole Olympics when they actually protested two of their own athletes! The Canadian Olympic Committee took four swimmers to Paris but, just before the Olympics started, the Canadian Swimming Association protested the two strongest swimmers, who were both from Winnipeg. The CSA said they should be disqualified because they didn't take part in the trials meet in Montreal (the host Montreal AAA dominated the CSA). The IOC upheld the protest, the Winnipeg boys were disqualified and the two remaining Montreal swimmers fared poorly in the races.[38]

In track and field at the Paris Olympics, Canada's disappearance from the top ranks of nations was glaring. The 27 member track and field team won no medals and managed only three placings: 4th in the 400m run, a fifth in the pole vault and an eighth in the hammer throw. Beyond that, the Canadians were not a factor in any of the contests. Overall, the 65 member Canadian team picked up four medals, two silvers in rowing, a silver in shooting and a lone bronze in boxing. Canada dropped to 18th place overall behind lowly Australia, war ravaged Austria and the tiny new country of Estonia. It was an embarrassment.

Now more than ever, it was apparent a program like the OAC was needed if Canada was ever going to be competitive again. It was too early in 1924 for Walter's program to have developed an Olympic gold medalist, but in four years' time his program would get its ultimate judgment by how well Canada fared at the 1928 Amsterdam Olympics.

The year 1924 was pivotal for Walter in another way too. He

got married. Up to this point there had been no mention of women in Walter's life. In his unpublished book and notes he makes no mention of the fairer sex. Being itinerant, constantly on the move and never in one location for more than six months at a time, it is not surprising he was unable to develop a relationship with a woman. He never mentions anything about "a girl in every town" or frequenting a red light district; if he did so, he did not record it, or even mention having a girlfriend as a youth. So when a wedding announcement appeared in the newspapers in June of 1924 it must have been surprising to some of his friends and acquaintances.

Mary Boyce was "a rabid hockey fan" in Picton, Ontario, though she was a resident of nearby Wellington. Walter first met her in 1919 while he was coaching the local hockey team. They ran into each other in the Bristol Store one day and developed a friendship. That the Picton hockey team was "unbeatable" that year could only have endeared him to her. Their relationship was strong enough to endure his 1920 Olympic travels, his return to the Shining Tree mines then his four years wandering all around Ontario as the OAC coach. And how much potential did Walter have as a husband? His life was on the road or at the mine, not very enticing for a wife. But he was, at 46 years old, very healthy and vigorous, financially set for life and his reputation as an athlete and coach was second to none. Mary was into middle age too (we don't know if she was widowed or never married) and, apparently, was adventurous. They must have made a good match; their 20 year marriage survived in spite of Walter's constant traveling. Walter, though, in spite of having the wherewithal for exotic travel, was obviously not an experienced ladies' man: he took Mary on a honeymoon to romantic Detroit.

Within months of his marriage, in another wild divergence in Walter's colourful life, he bought, of all things, a ranch in California. He and Mary traveled down there in the fall of 1924. The "Robla Lomas" ranch was described as "one of the largest and most promising ranches in California",[39] situated in the foothills of the Sierra

Nevadas near Fresno, halfway between Los Angeles and San Francisco. The nearest community was Woodlake, a small town nestled in the San Jaoquin valley just 20 miles from the mountains. Walter had visited that area in 1909 for a professional track meet in Coalinga, some 80 miles away. Whether his connections to the San Francisco area in 1909 or connections Mary had to California led to this unlikely purchase we don't know, but Walter had visited the area briefly 15 years earlier.

Robla Lomas was a cattle ranch. But Walter bought it at the height of a foot and mouth disease outbreak. Roadblocks had been set up all summer, on the major roads up and down the valley where animals had to walk through a pool of disinfectant and people had to wipe their feet in treated sawdust in an effort to contain the outbreak. The cattle industry was devastated. Likely Walter picked up the ranch at a fire sale price. He never intended to go into the ranching business but he did know the San Jaoquin valley was a productive agricultural area, mainly for citrus groves. It was also a booming region. A light railway connecting Wood Lake to Fresno had just been built in 1919 and the quiet village was flourishing. This must have looked like a promising investment.

A newspaper report said Walter and Mary intended to spend the next few winters there, developing the property.[40] The ranch supported a large stand of oak as well as rangeland suitable for conversion to orchards. How Walter intended to manage a project of this magnitude at his age, while still keeping his hand in at the mines with Jack and traveling all over Ontario five months a year for the OAC is puzzling.

The local Woodlake newspaper seemed taken with this new pair of prominent landowners. They were newsworthy enough to have their whole itinerary printed for their drive back to Ontario along the Santa Fe Trail in May of 1925 (gravel roads all the way). Mary must have been game; this was not a trip for the faint of heart. Walter became well known in the area after giving a talk to the local school association, widely reported in the papers, on his work promoting physical education in Ontario schools.[41] After his first two winters there, he never mentions the ranch again, but it is notable that Mary, when she died in 1944, was in California.

In a life that was full of odd and interesting turns, this California episode had to be one of the strangest. It may well be that the California ranch was a driving factor in the next big move in Walter's life. In 1926, he and Jack sold the mine.

It took a lot of capital to run a mining operation. As long as the ore was near the surface, a crew of men with pick axes could make an operation efficient. But once you had to start tunneling, heavy equipment was required, and that cost money, capital investment. There was good money to be made by milling your ore on site and avoiding the expensive transport of raw ore to offsite locations. But building a mill was beyond Walter and Jack's means.

The Knox brothers started digging their first shaft in 1916. By the early 20's it is apparent they had two shafts at least 25 feet deep. To go much deeper by hand would have been very difficult. The mine was profitable but it was becoming clear the rich seams deeper in the rock were going to require a significant investment to mine. They had tapped the easy ore.

Late in 1925, they began looking for investors. They found interested financiers in New York City and sold the controlling interest in their mine, the 1700 acres comprising the "Knox Block", to them in early March of 1926. Besides "cash payment the Messrs. Knox retain 38% interest in the property"[42] the Orillia newspaper reported. The Knox boys had held out longer than most of the original prospectors who struck it rich in Shining Tree. Through their independence and hard work, they had achieved financial security and a respected reputation in the district. With the sale of the mine, they were wealthy men. Walter never commented on how much money he put in the bank after the sale but it was enough for him to call himself "financially independent".

This was the ultimate rural workingman's success story. Walter took the money he won from years of hustling matched races — from the big Negro Batson in Corry, Pennsylvania, from Walker in the frightful visit to Mexicali, Mexico, from his squalid performances across the upper Michigan peninsula — and invested it into himself and his family and their own sweat and determination. Shrewd management of that investment, smart prospecting, multiplied their worth many, many times over. The workingman's tradition was to take risks, and there couldn't be any riskier investment than greenhorn prospecting. While most workingmen live out their years in the modest life they had always known, Walter was one of the lucky ones who found that pot of gold at the end of the rainbow. Was it hard work, was it wily risk taking or was it just luck? In Walter's case it was all three.

Even after the sale, Walter never left the mining business; he still had considerable shares in the new mining operation and eventually the position of "President of the Churchill Mining and Milling Company". So while he was spending months touring Ontario putting on clinics for the OAC and trying to figure out what to do with the ranch in California (not to mention his new wife) he was still fulfilling administrative obligations for the mining company. Often, while he was on a trip north putting on OAC clinics, he'd do some mine tours and oversight, killing two birds with one stone while he was north.

The headquarters for the Churchill Mining Company were in Cadillac Township, Quebec, and after 1927, he had to spend part of each year there. Likewise, he had oversight responsibilities at the Shining Tree mine that required his attention and presence on an ongoing basis. For example, in 1927, just after the sale of the mine, Walter was in charge of the test pitting right next to one of the existing shafts that started to turn up more "free gold". He had to hire more men and buy more equipment to start another shaft to exploit this find.[43] That would be a full time job for most men. Walter was heavily involved with the OAC in the spring and the fall that year and had started doing some private coaching in the summer to help develop women's athletics in Canada in preparation for the 1928 Olympics. Undoubtedly the company had competent managers on site to run the day-to-day operations at the mine, but Walter, as the man in charge, had to be there or in constant, regular communication. Selling the mine should have reduced his workload to free him up to coach, but the mine expansion continued to demand his time.

By 1934, the next time Walter recorded anything about the mines, he was being sent by the company on exploration and development projects to locations from Quebec to Sault Ste. Marie. For example, in 1934 the Soo newspaper reported that Walter was in town looking to hire "15 or 16 men" and purchase "considerable equipment" to open up the new "Algold Mine" in nearby Goudreau.[44] He had just come from Toronto where he had been looking for an engineer for the "Shining Tree mill". It is a testament to his work ethic that he continued to toil for the mines and work for the OAC, pushing himself as hard as ever, right into his 60s, even though he had a bank account that could afford him a comfortable retirement anywhere he chose. He never commented where Mary lived, though at some point they bought a home in Toronto. She certainly didn't follow him around constantly, but she did travel on at least one OAC tour of the north with him in 1925.

He continued the mine work until 1944, when he was 66 years old, long after he had retired from the sporting world.

29

Developing Olympic Champions

In 1925 the OAC Schoolboy Provincial Championship program really took off. It had taken a few years to get the schools onside, to get more and more schools participating. Even though the OAC paid their expenses and sent Walter right to their schools to drum up enthusiasm and help set up a local track meet, the schools still had to have a teacher or two willing to do the leg work of setting up a local meet. The teachers, it seemed, were not too interested. Up until that year, Walter said the schools "lacked the unanimity necessary to hold one big Provincial Championship meet — public, separate and high".[1] But by 1925, the Sectional meets in all eight regions of Ontario were well attended by the athletes who had won at their local meets. In 1925, the first Provincial Schoolboy Championship was held, with strong participation from all eight Sections in the province. Walter, after four years of touring the province, finally had his infrastructure in place and had created the excitement he had hoped for among the boys and girls.

This was the first program of its kind in Canada. The AAU of C had been holding Provincial and National Championships since 1884 and Walter had won titles in both, but they were adult or senior events. The OAC program was specifically for school age boys and girls, from as young as 10 years old to high school seniors. This was to be a feeder program for the senior championships; Walter was quite up front about that, he wanted to develop Olympic champions. As one newspaperman put it in 1926, "Today Knox is engaged in the greatest athletic enterprise ever attempted in this country".[2]

The school boards were onside with the OAC program because it promoted healthy living and combated idleness. But Walter and the OAC members began to put more emphasis on the identification of future champions, goal number three in the OAC mandate. In Sault Ste. Marie in late August of 1925, Walter, in a presentation to the school board there, said, "Canada has been falling behind in the quality of its representatives at the Olympic Games and we hope that some promising material will be found in the course of the proposed activities".[3] As the Provincial Schoolboy Championships continued to grow through the second half of the 1920s, the top athletes began to receive more attention. In 1926, Walter attended the Sectional meet in the Soo. The local paper excitedly pointed out that the winners were to receive special coaching sessions from Coach Knox[4]. This special attention made the school boards uneasy, but as long as every child had the benefit of hearing Walter's presentations and were able to participate in the coaching sessions and local meets, they appeared willing to live with the growing emphasis on the better athletes.

The OAC program was making headway with the top athletes by 1926 too. At the 1926 Championships alone, 27 new schoolboy records were set. In the past season, 90 per cent of the provincial records had been broken! The sprints had been bettered by up to 2/5 of a second, a one mile record was beaten by over a full minute. A long jump record was beaten by over two feet and a high jump record by 14 inches; a new pole vault record was set, two and a half feet higher than the old record and a shot put record was bettered by 10 feet.[5] There were remarkable and dramatic improvements in just about every event in every age group. Mass participation and improved coaching and organization were working, just as Walter had predicted.

That mass participation was the key to the program's success, at least in developing champions. Schoolboys and girls with athletic talents, who otherwise would never have had the opportunity to even try track and field, were identified and encouraged. In 1928, over 5000 athletes attended the eight Sectional Championship meets.[6] These were the kids who qualified a decidedly larger pool of students who had the chance to try organized athletics at all the local school meets. That year, 218 students, the cream of the crop, attended the Provincial Schoolboy Championships with all expenses paid by the OAC.

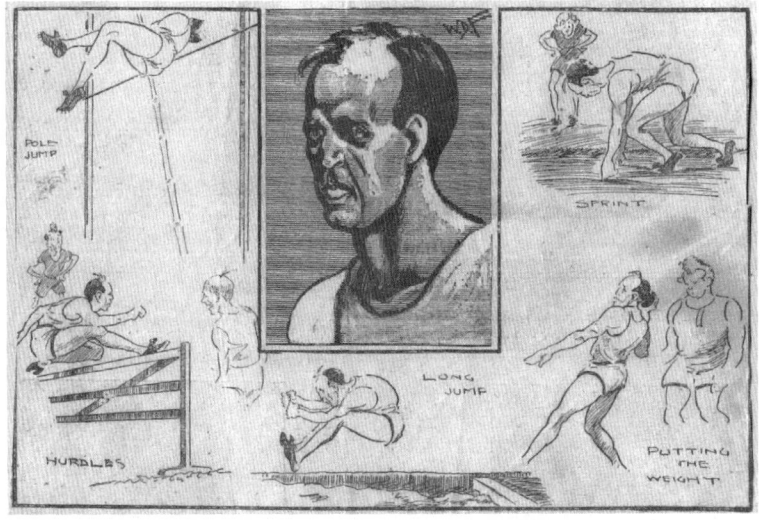

This was a typical item newspapers ran, promoting the OAC program when Walter was coming to town. Many local papers published long articles describing the OAC program and it's famous coach, drumming up interest in athletics in the town.
Courtesy Orillia Museum of Art and History

Mass participation was the big reason the records dropped so dramatically. To encourage that participation, Walter and Nick Bawlf provided over 200 clinics in 73 towns and cities that year.[7] Talent identification was Walter's most significant contribution to the Canadian athletics program, getting talented kids interested in track and directing them to the local AAU of C club (if there was one). Walter's energy, passion and the sweat of his brow made the program a success. His high quality coaching was important too, but without the high number of schoolchildren participating, he would have had a smaller pool of talent to coach.

Walter noted two of his success stories in a 1926 newspaper article. High schooler Harry Shancy of Midland had been doing 5' 8" in the high jump and 19 feet in the long jump, two outstanding marks. After spending time with Walter, he cleared the bar at 6' 3/4" in the high jump and leaped 22' 3" in the long jump, scores competitive with the best in Canada. Jack Broderick, also of Midland, improved in the 12 pound shot put from 36 feet to 47 feet after training under Walter.[8] With those marks, both athletes would have qualified for the 1928 Olympic Trials, but being from a small rural town that lacked an AAU of C club put them at a distinct disadvantage. Neither made the Olympic Team. Walter's biggest problem with Canadian sport was the lack of competent coaches, as demonstrated by these two boys.

The OAC, in support of Walter's high performance program, gave him permission to take up to seven boys to Montreal in 1926 for the new Dominion Interscholastic Championships, all expenses paid. The four boys Walter selected won six firsts and three seconds, breaking five records.[9]

The OAC program was working, at least with regards to its third goal of identifying talent and producing champions. Whether Walter was having an impact on the boys and girls in terms of being healthier and into less "mischief" is hard to measure. But he was developing better athletes at the top end.

Major changes came to the OAC program in 1927. After the positive reports from the Departments of Education and Health about the OAC program, the new Conservative government decided to widen the "sin tax" on professional sport to expand support for amateur sport. The five percent gate tax was lowered to just two percent, but was now applied to the gross gate receipts in all the major professional sports, including hockey, football and baseball. However, only the boxers and wrestlers (where corruption was still suspected) had to pay licensing fees and fines for non-compliance (in some years these additional fees brought in more than the gate tax). This widened sin tax resulted in a significant increase in the revenue of the OAC; in fact the OAC budget more than doubled.[10] By the late 1930s, 12 different sports were paying the OAC gate tax.

This increase in revenue allowed the OAC to start directly assisting the sport governing bodies. Up to 20% of the OAC revenue began to be donated to amateur sport associations by the 1930s.[11] Furthermore, the increase in gate tax revenue enabled the OAC to realize a long-standing dream, the creation of a provincial training center for top schoolboys and girls.

That was the tipping point that turned the schools away from the OAC program. By the early 30's, Walter's clinic and competitive program was being viewed as weighted too heavily towards the top athletes and school participation flagged. By 1933, Walter commented that he was spending only a fraction of his time visiting schools; as he said, he was "a part time coach". In fact, the traveling coach program was cancelled by the OAC in 1931 due to lack of funds as their revenue dropped with the Great Depression. Walter was only being sent out to the schools sporadically now. The schoolboy championships and the summer training camps continued as the main emphasis of the OAC program.

Planning for the provincial training center got underway in 1928, but before its construction, Walter turned his attention towards a new project. The 1928 Olympics in Amsterdam were quickly approaching and for the first time there were going to be track and field events for women.

Prior to World War I, sport for women and girls in Canada was limited to holiday fairs, church picnics and the odd school field day. The AAU of C had no interest in providing competitions for girls, deeming them too delicate. Fears of exhaustion, infertility, and a loss of grace were routinely trotted out as justification. The consensus among coaches and medical experts supported this view.

A concerted international effort to change this state of affairs began right after the war ended. When the international sports governing bodies haughtily refused to accommodate women athletes, the women, in October 1921, formed the Federation Sportive Feminine Internationale (FSFI) to organize competitive opportunities for themselves, in direct competition with the International Amateur Athletic Federation (IAAF), the governing body for men's track and field, which would not allow women into their meets. The first international athletic meet for women was held in 1921 and the first world championship under the FSFI was staged in Paris in 1922. That was the same year Walter Knox invited girls to take part in the OAC program, only six months after the founding of the FSFI. He was a supporter of women's sport right from the beginning. Canada did not join the FSFI until 1924, but, Walter had already taken a team of women down to Philadelphia where they dominated a track meet in 1922. By then, Canada's first women's athletics club, the Toronto Ladies Athletics Club, was formed. Momentum was gathering, thanks in no small part to Walter Knox and the OAC who had been drumming up interest via its grass roots school program.

Women's athletics in Ontario really took off in 1923 when the annual track meet at the Canadian National Exhibition grounds in Toronto added a list of women's events. With enthusiastic support from the sports journalists who editorialized heavily in favour of the initiative, the meet was a great success. In very short order, athletic clubs for women began to pop up and women and girls gravitated to them. Many of the girls enrolling had had their first taste of competition with Walter Knox's OAC program in their schools.

Hesitantly, the AAU of C and IAAF began accommodating women in 1924. At the Ontario Championships that year there were two events for women: the 100-yard dash and the 4x100 relay. Rosa Grosse, one of the athletes Walter had taken to Philadelphia, broke the women's world record in the 100 there by over a second!

Athletic feats by women were seen as a symbol of a changing gender order, commented sports historian Ann Hall, and were widely supported by society in the 1920s;[12] in all aspects of society in the 1920s, women were stepping out from behind the shadows of men. The major sports organizations were belatedly conceding that fact and reluctantly opening up their competitions to women.

In 1925, the AAU of C was invited by Great Britain to send a women's team to London for an international competition. Hastily, they held a selection meet in Toronto and paid the expenses for 10 women and two coaches to make the trip to London, England. Walter was selected as coach, demonstrating the respect he had engendered by the women's sporting movement. However, the AAU of C insisted that only female coaches would be allowed and Walter stepped aside.[13] A Female Ontario Track and Field Championship was held that same year with a full roster of events. Bobbie Rosenfeld, the outstanding athlete from Barrie, Ontario, won four events and set world records in the 100 and 220 yard dashes. After these successes, the WAAF (Women's Amateur Athletics Federation) was formed in Canada to organize and promote women's sport.

By 1926, the athletic programs for women and girls in Canada and internationally were developing quickly. The International Olympic Committee, historically a staunch opponent to women's participation in sport, began to see the light. For the 1928 Amsterdam Olympics a limited program of women's events was organized under the auspices of the IAAF, prompting some countries (like Britain) that supported the FSFI to keep their women home. Canada, one of the early participants in women's sport, was in a position to make a strong showing. Walter Knox, one of the earliest high profile promoters of girls in sport, was going to be a part of it too.

Canada sent six women to the Amsterdam Olympics in 1928 — the "Matchless Six" as they became known — who dominated the meet. Walter was the coach for two of those women: sprinter Florence (Jane) Bell and high jumper Ethel Catherwood. Three of the others, Bobbie Rosenfeld, Jean Thompson and Myrtle Cook, Walter had spent some time with as a consulting coach.[14] He was a significant player in the success of the group.

Catherwood was a prodigy. Encouraged to jump in her back yard by her father, she was discovered by a local coach who entered her in the first Saskatoon City Athletic Championships for women in 1926 where, as a 19 year old, she broke the Canadian record. Later that summer, at the Canadian Championships, she broke ("wrecked" the paper said) the world record with a jump of 5'3".

In January of 1928, she moved to Toronto to pursue athletics. Teddy Oke, a multi-millionaire mining magnate and sports enthusiast, offered Ethel and her sister jobs in his brokerage house, free enrollment in Business College and a place on his Parkdale Ladies Athletic Club (PLAC), all in the name of promoting Canadian sport. When she got to the brokerage house, she found it stocked with many aspiring amateur athletes taking advantage of Oke's philanthropy. As an enticement to attract her, Oke hired Walter, the great Olympic and OAC coach, to work with her at the PLAC.[15]

Catherwood did not join Oke's Parkdale club immediately; there was a power struggle going on between the two largest women's athletic clubs in Toronto (hence Oke's recruiting of top athletes) and she was leery of getting caught up in the politics and losing any chance of making the Olympic Team.[16] But, as she told reporters, she came here, "to complete her commercial education and to obtain the benefit of the coaching of Walter Knox whom we recognize as the best coach of track and field athletes in Canada".[17] When she competed at the Canadian Olympic Trials, she was wearing the Parkdale colours.

Here was another project in Walter's busy life, but one he was passionate about. Women's athletics seemed to capture his enthusiasm in the early 1920's and he stayed involved with that sport until the end of his coaching career. Walter worked with Catherwood throughout the spring (when he wasn't touring schools for the OAC or keeping track of his mining interests) and also coached her Parkdale teammate, Jane Bell, on a regular basis. After chatting with Walter that spring, a reporter said, "Of the other girls Mr. Knox coached, Florence Bell, Bobbie Rosenfeld, Jean Thompson and Myrtle Cook, he has the greatest admiration for them, each one in her different way, and he talked very entertainingly about them all."[18] It is obvious Walter was enthusiastic about women's athletics.

In the lead-up to the Olympics, a reporter asked Walter about sports being harmful to women. Walter replied that "some people claim that such strenuous athletics unfit a girl for married life and motherhood. That is not borne out by facts".[19] He pointed out the example of Rosa Grosse, who'd had a long career as a sprinter, breaking a world record, and then had a child. "I do not see why she cannot be a mother and still keep up her athletic training", Walter commented. In fact, Grosse would make a comeback in 1930. As was his tendency, Walter was being blunt and opinionated, refusing to be swayed by conventional thought that was not justified by common experience. He was an independent, practical thinker, a trait common to the professional mind-set.

Coaching Ethel Catherwood that spring, Walter tried to change her whole style of jumping from the common and basic "scissor kick" to the newer "lay-out" technique.[20] A jumper at that time had to have a foot go over the bar first. In the scissors, the jumper remained upright with the leg nearer the bar thrown over first, followed quickly by the other leg as the body stayed perfectly upright. In the layout, the athlete jumped outside foot first, tucking the inside leg up and over as the jumper laid out flat across the bar (Walter had introduced this novel technique to Scotland 15 years earlier to quizzical interest). It was a radical change. The biggest difference was the layout jumper landed jarringly on her side instead of gracefully on her feet. Catherwood tried the new technique but in the end insisted on returning to the scissors. Walter, the paper said, showing his pragmatism, agreed it was the right move.

Walter's "layout" technique. This photo is of a standing jump.
From a run he would be able to lay out flat on his side.
Courtesy Orillia Museum of Art and History

Two stars emerged at the Olympic Trials in Halifax. Bobbie Rosenfeld, the aggressive all-arounder who could sprint, jump and throw with the best in the world, scored the most points, placing in the sprints, the 800, the long jump and the javelin. But not far behind, in both points and popularity, was Ethel Catherwood, the world record holding high jumper who came second to Rosenfeld in the javelin, only a few feet behind. Five women were obvious picks for the Olympic Team, all being gold medal prospects. The sixth and final selection to the Olympic Team that day was Jane Bell, the hurdler and sprinter Walter had developed at Parkdale. She had been on the bubble, nervously waiting for the announcement. Undoubtedly, Walter's tutelage that spring had improved her performance, helping her over the Olympic threshold.

Immediately, Teddy Oke started lobbying for Walter to be sent to the Olympics as a coach for the ladies' team. Walter coached two of the six and had consulted with three of the others. They all knew and respected him. Oke raised $1000 and sent a letter to the Canadian Olympic Association, offering the money to cover Walter's expenses in Amsterdam.[21] But the call never came and Walter was left in Canada reading the papers for the daily results of the Olympic competitions like everyone else.

In the five events offered the women in the Olympics, the Canadians won two gold, a silver and a bronze medal (and set two new world records in the high jump and the 4x100m relay) and should have won more. The 100 metre world record holder, Myrtle Cook, was disqualified for false starting and Jean Thompson, the world record holder in the 800, was fighting an injury and finished fourth.

Catherwood was the star for the Canadians. In winning the gold medal in the high jump, she used tactics Walter would have understood and condoned. As the bar moved up through the heights, the other competitors became annoyed that Catherwood kept jumping, and easily clearing the bar, with her warm-up suit still on. In effect, she was sending the message that these heights were routine, she didn't even have to break a sweat, even as other jumpers were falling by the wayside. It was a professional psych-out job Walter would have appreciated. When she finally took the track pants off, she was the only jumper to clear the height.

The 1928 Olympics really established women's sport in Canada. The newspapers fawned over the Matchless Six; the public cheered. More and more girls began showing up at the ladies' athletic clubs. Walter, in his role as Chief Coach of the OAC and as a consulting coach to many athletes all across Ontario, was a big part of this development.

It is significant to note that five of the Matchless Six were Ontario girls, four from Toronto and one from Penetang (Ethel Catherwood was from Saskatchewan). Three of those were teenagers during the mid-1920s, the years Walter's OAC program took off. Two of them, Jean Thompson and Jane Bell, had likely been involved in the OAC program. Ethel Smith dropped out of school in grade eight but might have been there for the first couple of OAC years. There is no question Walter had an influence on the development of the Matchless Six.

But more importantly, what Walter did for the girls was create a culture of female athleticism in Ontario that fostered their competitive opportunities. After he opened up the OAC program to the girls in 1922, they had the chance, for the first time, to train and compete in organized track meets through their schools and soon the AAU of C. He kept enthusiastically recruiting and developing girls and women in athletics his whole career, mentoring several more champions in the coming years.

But what of the boys and men? Walter had been promoting athletics in the Ontario schools for seven years now and had set up the Provincial Schoolboy Championships where the record book was re-written year after year. He had promoted athletic programs in schools all across the province and trained teachers in the rudiments of coaching. He had taken many of the star talents under his wing, giving them special attention and personal coaching. Surely some of the graduates of this program were now ready to contend for medals at the Olympics.

In 1920, when Canada's Olympic fortunes were in serious decline, Walter said the answer was to "develop the schoolboys": identify the good athletes, provide competent coaching and set up official competitions for them. Now, seven years later, those boys should have grown up to be contenders. Was he right?

Apparently, yes. After fading from 12th to 13th to 17th place in the last three Olympics, Canada rebounded to 10th place in the medal count in 1928. The four gold medals won in 1928 were all in track and field. In the previous two Olympics combined, Canada had won exactly one medal in track and field, Tommy Thomson's win in the 110 metre hurdles in 1920. The Canadian team was nowhere to be seen in 1924. But in Amsterdam, Canada's track and field men won two gold, a silver and a bronze, led by Percy William's stunning victories in the premier events, the 100 and 200 metre dashes. In 1932, Canada's men would increase their medal count to six with one gold, a silver and four bronze. In 1928, Canada's track and field team was once again a force to be reckoned with on the world stage.

Of course, Canada's women's track and field team was about the best in the world that year too, adding to the resurging prestige of Canada's athletic programs.

It is hard to judge how big an effect the Ontario Athletic Commission program of developing the schoolboys and girls had on this resurgence. After the Olympics in 1928, the OAC proudly stated that over 90 percent of the Ontario athletes had received assistance from its coaches.[22]

The 1928 Olympic track team was made up of 26 men, 13 of them from Ontario, a pretty typical share, historically, in Canada. However, none of the medal winners, including the four members of the 4x400 relay team, were from Ontario. The best placings by Ontario athletes were a 4th by Vic Pickard in the pole vault and a 5th by Johnny Fitzpatrick in the 200. However, circumstances negated some other top showings. In 1928, high jumper Alex Munroe had already cleared the height in other competitions that won the Olympic gold medal. In Amsterdam, he failed to clear the bar in all three attempts at his low opening height and finished last. The 4x100 relay team, with three Ontario boys, was a medal contender until they dropped the baton and were disqualified

In spite of not winning any medals, it was clear the Ontario men had still made a big improvement on the 1924 showings, demonstrating the point that Canada was again competitive across a number of events. What the schoolboy program had done was to develop a grassroots consciousness and enthusiasm for athletics. The athletics culture and coaching expertise to support it was growing. Better talent, identified in the OAC program, was gravitating to the athletic clubs run through the AAU of C.

The star of the Canadian Olympic team, even more famous than the Matchless Six, was Percy Williams, a schoolboy from Vancouver. His is a remarkable story. Upon entering high school in 1924, this skinny waif of a boy was mandated to take part in a physical education class like all the other students. The next year, though still a somewhat reluctant athlete, he was matched in a running race across the football field with the city schoolboy champion. Percy won.

A local coach took him under his wing and, with some unorthodox training techniques, developed him into the Provincial Champion sprinter while still in high school. Though he had run fast, he was not taken seriously as a threat at the Canadian Olympic Trials in Hamilton because he was barely 5'6" tall and 125 pounds. He was also somewhat frail after a bout of rheumatic fever. Cyril Coaffee, a two-time Olympian and former world record holder in the 100, was the favourite. He didn't even make the team as Percy won (tying the world record) and two Hamilton boys who had graduated from the OAC program came second and third. Still not considered a genuine threat at the Olympics, Percy won the 100, and a few days later won the 200. Percy then finally enjoyed the respect he deserved.

Percy Williams, though not from Ontario, did benefit from the new culture of athletic opportunity and health promotion for boys. Had BC not had a policy of mandatory participation in an athletic class, this shy, frail boy may never have been discovered. In Ontario, Walter's OAC program was far more advanced and organized and it showed at the Olympic Trials.

Of the 16 Ontario athletes to make the Olympic Team, only

one was too old to have taken part in the OAC program. The vast majority of the other Ontario boys likely had met Walter at least once in their school years and heard his stories, learned his scientific approach to athletics and had their strong and weak points assessed by Canada's great Olympic coach personally. They would have had the opportunity to showcase their natural talents and puff up their egos at the Provincial Schoolboy Championships. Most importantly, they had been identified as talents through the OAC program and would have caught the eyes of the local AAU of C clubs, like Cap Cornelius's Hamilton Olympic Club that placed eight athletes on the men's track and field team in Amsterdam.

The success of the OAC program generally, and the Olympic Team specifically, was the impetus for the next big stage in Walter's development of schoolboy and girl champions. In 1928, Walter initiated his plan for a provincial schoolboy training camp.

Walter spent July 1928 reading the papers and following the results of the Olympics, especially of the women he coached. But he was also busy organizing a first attempt at an OAC Provincial Training Camp. In August of 1928, a month after the excitement of the Olympics in Amsterdam, Walter took his hand-picked group of twelve top high school boy athletes to a camp he set up in Indian Village, Goderich, for two weeks of total focus on track and field, all expenses paid by the OAC.[23] The success of this camp led to the development of a permanent OCA camp.

Early in 1929, the OAC purchased 17 acres of land on Lake Couchiching, across the water from Orillia, Walter's home town. With a $50,000 budget, the farmland was cleared and leveled and a top-notch 440 yard cinder running track was built, along with all the jumping pits and throwing circles an athletic coach could want.[24] The furnished sleeping cabins, dining hall and other necessary buildings constructed could accommodate 66 athletes plus staff; a swimming dock and tennis courts were also built.[25] This was no half-hearted effort; the OAC "provided every modern convenience" including running water and electricity, luxuries many households were still doing without.[26] Every boy received a full medical examination by the camp doctor upon arrival (for some, likely their first exposure to a doctor) and the doctor remained at camp for the duration.

As the construction workers were leaving (a week late) the first group of 20 boys was arriving (postponed one week) for a three week training camp, starting the second week of August. As usual, Walter pushed the agenda.

Walter was in charge of the programming. His stated philosophy for the camp was "care will be taken that these boys build up rather than burn out in their training".[27]

The OAC built this state of the art cinder track right on the shore of beautiful Lake Couchiching in 1929, across the lake from Walter's home town of Orillia.
Courtesy Orillia Public Library

The boys selected were the outstanding athletes from high schools across the districts, boys "who show above average keenness in their studies".[28] Walter ran two, three-week sessions every summer thereafter with a select few boys from every district who were fully subsidized by the OAC, along with 20 or 30 others who paid a $10 per week fee.[29] Historian Bruce Kidd pointedly remarked that track and field and swimming were the focus of the camp. "Hockey and wrestling, whose professional activities gave the Commission the bulk of its revenues, were not offered at all".[30]

This stretch of shoreline, north of the Rama Indian Reserve and the National YMCA Training Centre at Geneva Park, was already the home of another camp, the Orillia YMCA's Camp Summerland, and two more camps would be built nearby in the 1950s. It was a wilderness area with a wonderful shoreline. The neighbouring Orillia Y camp, maintaining its wilderness setting, lacked both the running water, electricity and even the sleeping cabins the OAC campers enjoyed. Those two camps, the OAC and Orillia Y camps, were on opposite sides of a small bay; the boys could almost wave and yell to each other. No doubt the OAC boys, with their fancy camp and status as specially selected top athletes, felt a little superior.

The camp was the beginning of the end for the OAC traveling coach program into which Walter had invested so much of his time and energy. Seeing such a large proportion of the OAC revenue directed into this camp for the elite athletes, the principals began to pull their schools out of the program they thought was about promoting healthy lifestyles. The full-time traveling coach program was cancelled in 1931, after which time Walter visited schools only sporadically, as money was available. The Depression curtailed attendance at pro sports events, shrinking the sin tax revenue the OAC received. With a large, fixed proportion of that revenue earmarked for the camp and travel expenses to send top Ontario athletes to provincial and national competitions, it was the traveling coach program that suffered for the revenue shortfall.

In 1934, in order to placate the Department of Education, the OAC made the camp available to the Department for the upgrading of their physical education teachers.[31] The camp was also offered to the amateur sports governing bodies to host their own training camps. That was likely a financial decision. Renting out the camp was a revenue generator.

Interestingly, the OAC camp was limited to boys only. Though the Women's Amateur Athletic Federation lobbied for girls to be included, they were never accommodated. The Orillia YMCA camp across the bay likewise denied girls a summer camp opportunity. They said camp life was "too rugged" for them. Starting in 1937 though, the OAC did allow the WAAF to rent the camp for a girl's leadership development program similar to the OAC's, but at their own expense.[32] Walter never commented on this state of affairs, but undoubtedly would have been a promoter of including the girls.

The OAC camp flourished through the 1930s; Walter ran it until 1935. Being selected to go by the OAC was a great honour and an opportunity not to be missed. It was the final piece in the vision Walter had promoted in 1920 to put Canada back on the international track and field map. He was justly proud of his accomplishments in the Canadian sports world and Canada was more competitive because of his work.

The correlation of Walter's work developing schoolboys and girls to help make Canada competitive on the world stage and Canada's actual success on that world stage is remarkable. In the two Olympics prior to the OAC athletes' graduation to Canada's Olympic track and field team (1920 and '24), Canada won a single medal in athletics. In the next three Olympics, after the OAC had been steadily identifying and encouraging boys and girls to take up track and field long enough for them to rise to the top, Canada won 21 medals in athletics, five of them gold! After World War II and the closing of the OAC summer camp program in 1942, which essentially shut down the entire OAC program for promoting track and field, Canada disappeared from the Olympics again, especially in track and field. Between the 1948 Games and Greg Joy's iconic high jump silver medal in 1976, almost 30 years and seven Olympics, Canada won three track and field medals, a silver and two bronze. In 1952, '56, '60, '68 and '72 Canada was shut out of the medals in track. Walter's OAC program was obviously a part of Canada winning 21 medals in three Olympics. When it stopped, so did the medal haul.

The OAC athletics program was replaced by the rise of high school athletics programs, the very thing Walter had encouraged, getting the schools to add athletics to the curriculum. However, Walter also promoted just as strongly, the training of teachers as coaches, something that fell by the wayside. After the war, teachers who often had limited expertise in coaching attempted to run the school athletics programs and participation dropped to a fraction of what it had been during Walter's touring coach days. The mass participation and athlete identification withered. Our feeble Olympic results underscored that fact.

Walter was acutely aware of the wasting of all his work with the OAC as he witnessed his feeder program for the amateur clubs, the traveling coach program and the Provincial Schoolboy Championships, being handed over to inexperienced high school coaches. After World War II, when Walter fully realized how far the state of track and field had fallen, he was fully retired and too old to do anything about it. But it is clear in his scattered comments it ate at him.

Retirement

30

Some Final Flings Before Retirement

By 1930, Walter should have been slowing down. His weight had well exceeded 200 pounds (he called himself a "light heavyweight" now) and his face sagged noticeably; permanent dark bags hung below his eyes. The close-cropped hair in a ring above his ears was graying, and there was nothing left on top. He was 53 years old. But, reminiscent of his heyday, his sturdy neck, erect posture and the intent glare of his blue eyes reminded everyone he was not to be trifled with. When he shook your hand, you knew it had been shaken. He could still run, jump and throw but now his top athletes could outdo him. In the past, he had always staked his credibility as a coach on the fact that he could outperform his charges, even on the Olympic teams, as he did when he raced Army Howard. Now, though, he had to rely on his moral authority as an Olympic Coach and Chief Coach of the OAC, a more difficult approach for someone like Walter who grew up in the rural workingman's culture of "put up or shut up". His years of pushing himself physically and the constant travel were beginning to show.

Often he couldn't help himself. Walking by the U of T Varsity Stadium track one day in the fall of 1929, Walter saw some of the university boys pole vaulting, and making some obvious errors. Wandering over, he asked if they had a coach, and they replied that they did not. He then proceeded to give them a few pointers and even demonstrated, hoisting the pole while still in his street clothes, complete with hat. After nipping the bar down on two attempts at six feet, Walter decided he better get serious. He took off his hat. With the boys snickering at his bald pate, he sailed a few feet over the bar, silencing them. They had no idea who their self-appointed tutor was.[1]

Many of his star OAC grads all over Ontario still requested that he stop in on his travels to assess their training, demands on his time and energy he couldn't turn down. He also began taking on new coaching positions in the early 30's and continued to casually lobby to be Canada's Olympic Coach again. On top of that, he spent several months a year managing his mining interests, something that could and should have been a full time job (he had an office in the Royal Bank building in downtown Toronto now).[2] There was no question he was getting older; he just wouldn't admit it.

In 1929, Walter took a position as one of a group of seven specialist coaches at the Toronto Central YMCA, his old stomping grounds. Walter was to be the javelin and discus coach, likely on a strictly consulting basis.[3] He was still heavily involved with the schoolboy program and in the spring of 1929 took a Canadian team of prep school boys to Milwaukee for the Marquette University Relays.[4] Of course, there were still the Ontario Schoolboy Championships to run and the National Championships to attend as well. That summer, Walter also took on the position as coach of the Toronto Police Association Athletics team (a major club then). He ran practices for the team every Thursday in preparation for competitions in Baltimore, Montreal and Hamilton that summer.[5] On top of all that, Walter and Nick Bawlf spent a week in each of the eight OAC Districts coaching the top athletes that spring.[6]

In 1930, Walter began a four year stint as the track and field coach of Queen's University in Kingston, Ontario. That required him to be in Kingston for three weeks each fall to prepare his athletes for the Provincial Championships in the middle of October. He was only able to take this commitment on after the OAC fall program as traveling coach had ended, freeing up his time. In his second year at the university, the Queen's team jumped up in the standings, capturing two gold, a silver and a bronze medal.[7]

Also in 1930, the Ontario Track and Field Championships were held in Orillia. The athletic field at the Oval was in sorry shape nine years after it had last hosted the Provincial Championships (evidence of the decline of rural communities in the 1920s). Walter was brought home by the town to help redevelop the facilities and organize the meet that spring.[8]

Then there were the women. After the 1928 Olympics, Walter continued to scout for female talent, undiscovered material that some focused coaching could develop. In 1929, he started working with Jean Godson at Hampton Park in Toronto.[9] She was an up and coming thrower who was nearing the Olympic standard and who was already a Canadian champion.

Walter (right) with the Toronto Women's relay team in 1928.
From the left are Captain Hughes and the runners Grace Conacher, Bobbie Rosenfeld, Myrtle Cook and Rosa Grosse.
Courtesy Canadian Sports Hall of Fame

Still a coach at the Parkdale Ladies Athletic Club, he had started working with Dallas Creamer, the fastest sprinter in Canada. In Walter's words, Dallas was, "the only one close to Stella Walsh's speed", Walsh being the new world champion. Creamer had skipped the 1928 Olympic Trials but came into her own in 1929, winning the Canadian championship in the 220. In January 1930, Walter took Creamer to Philadelphia where she came second to Walsh indoors. In February, they traveled together to New York for the big Milrose Games to take on Walsh in the 220 again.[10] Creamer beat every other top American but Walsh.

But in 1930, Walter made his biggest sporting discovery in, of all places, his home town of Orillia. That spring, while visiting home, Walter had casually mentioned to a friend, butcher John McInnes, to keep an eye open for "good material", as he did with friends all across Ontario. One day a customer came into the shop and mentioned a big farm girl who "tossed a grain bag as though it were a powder puff". After visiting her himself, McInnes called Walter, who promptly made a special trip to the farm seven miles north of town to meet 17 year old Mamie Shrum. The big, strong "milkmaid" told Walter she would "be very glad to participate in sports".[11]

Walter had a chance to work with her in six training sessions over six weeks that spring, teaching her how to put the shot. By the end of that time, she was consistently bettering the Ontario Championship throw from the previous year. With that rudimentary instruction, he entered her in the Ontario Championships at Varsity Stadium in Toronto. The favourite at the meet was another of Walter's star protégé's, Jean Godson, the Canadian shot put champion. On that Saturday in mid-August, literally from out of nowhere, Mamie put the eight pound shot 34' 8" to win the title, probably shocking poor Jean Godson. Bobbie Rosenfeld's Canadian record was only 36' 3", not too far off for someone who had only had six practices.

Three days later, Mamie was entered in the first British Empire Games in Hamilton, which doubled as the Canadian Championships.

She won again with a toss of 33' 10". This "incredibly strong" farm girl went from not knowing what a shot put was to Canadian champion in six weeks. Remarkable.

Mamie's success was reminiscent of another local Orillia athlete who had done much the same thing 40 years earlier. George Gray, whom Walter had retrieved shot puts for as a youth, had shown up at the Canadian Championships only to be questioned by the officials who called his entry "irregular". It was the American champion, Flannigan, who pleaded to let the poor boy have a throw. One throw was all he needed to win the event. He went on to be undefeated and world champion for 17 years. Many old time Orillia sports buffs experienced deja vu with Mamie Shrum.[12]

The big reception for her in Orillia was delayed three weeks (at her request) so Walter could attend. That September day, bunting was strung up and the town band paraded her up onto a stage in the park where her coach and the local dignitaries honoured her with glowing speeches. They presented her with a gold wristwatch and a club bag as a sign of the town's admiration. Walter's comment, as reported in the local paper was, "Never in his lifelong experience as an athletic coach had he seen so phenomenal a performance by an athlete so inexperienced... She has the greatest future of any woman athlete in Canada".[13] This shy, bulky girl must have been overwhelmed by the attention.

Mamie, in her few comments, declared her intention to take up the discus and javelin, under Walter's tutelage, for the next summer's season.

She didn't re-appear again until the summer of 1932 as a 183 pound, muscular 19 year old. In the time in between her appearances, Walter became her "ex-coach" and then her "coach" again.[14] No explanation was given in the papers.

At the first meet on May 24th, she broke the Canadian record by eight inches with a throw of 36' 11". Then, at the Ontario Championships in Hamilton, Mamie heaved the shot an astounding

39' 9", bettering Rosenfeld's old Canadian record by over three feet. However, with his experience, Walter knew the shot had to be accurately weighed to validate the record. It turned out the ball was five ounces light and the record was nullified. She would just have to do it again at the next meet.

Mamie Shrum, Canadian shot put champion, 1930
Courtesy Orillia Public Library

The next meet was the 1932 Olympic Trials in Hamilton. Mamie, in her "cool, methodical" way, rose to the challenge, winning the shot put with a mark of 37' 3". She followed that up with an unexpected win in the discus, an event she had tried for the first time in competition only that spring.

To everyone's surprise, Mamie Shrum, the "phenomenal talent", was not selected for the Olympic Team. There was no women's shot put event at the Los Angeles Olympics and the officials felt her 103' discus throw was too far off the Olympic qualifying standard of 120 feet to include her. Walter put in a forceful appeal on her behalf, arguing she had put up a mark "near" this standard but had stepped a few inches over the line, fouling the throw. Walter assured them she could beat the 120' mark. The officials disagreed and left her home.

The next summer, Mamie married a man from the neighbouring farm, ending her athletic career (though she did appear at the 1934 Ontario Championships to win the shot put). Upon her announced retirement at the grand old age of 20, the newspaper reporter remarked, "She never did appear overly interested".[15]

Such was Walter's life in the 1930's. Constantly on the go, visiting every part of Ontario, obligated to coach in so many places he must have been in danger of forgetting which field he was supposed to head to. He had bought a house in Toronto, partly so Mary could live near her aging mother. He had to check in at his office downtown regularly to monitor the progress of the mines too.

A busy life, but just the way he liked it. From the age of 21, when Walter first struck out from home for the mill in Verner, he had never stayed in the same place for more than about six months (even during his five year stint at the mine after he and Jack struck it rich he would leave for a few months each winter or spring to coach in Picton and Toronto). Thirty years of constant motion. Always looking for that next opportunity. He was still doing that in the athletics world, only now it was the search for the "good material" in athletics, the prodigy who needed guidance.

Suddenly, in 1933, just after his most recent prodigy, Mamie Shrum, got married and retired, a whole new project opened up for him.

Out of nowhere, the AAU of C announced a softening of the amateur rules in the fall of 1933. The world of AAU of C athletics at the end of the 1920's was still as anti-professional as it had ever been. The amateur rules instituted at the end of the athletic wars in 1909 were still in force. Under those rules, Walter had been professionalized for coaching a college team for four months and given a lifetime ban, end of story. He was still officially listed as a professional.

The AAU of C announced, to Walter's complete surprise, that professionals could now apply for re-instatement after only three years of banishment. On hearing the news, Walter exclaimed to a reporter, "I'm feeling like a two year old!" and immediately applied for re-instatement at the age of 55.[16]

In January of 1934, Walter was in the first group of 22 professional athletes to get their amateur cards back. The group included 14 hockey players, four baseball players, two boxers, a swimmer and Walter. He was the only one past his mid-20's.[17]

"You bet I'll be back in active competition," Walter trumpeted when asked. "I'll be back into shot putting and discus throwing, although I may not do any more running… I'm not going to try to get into shape in a month like the younger fellows, and when I compete I'm going to win so they won't be able to laugh too hard at me".[18]

It is one of those interesting coincidences that the President of the AAU of C in 1934 was J Howard Crocker, the coach at the Central Y in 1907 who urged Walter to get in there and show them what he had the night before he was going to be outed as a professional at the Canadian Championships. He broke the news to Walter that he was going to be professionalized, and 27 years later was responsible for getting him his amateur card back.

Several clubs immediately expressed interest in Walter as a member. In February, Walter not only joined the new Beaches Olympic Club but he took on the head coaching duties along with Hec Phillips, the middle distance runner Walter had coached at the 1920 Olympics.[19] The Beaches Club was in a big membership drive, hoping to attract 1000 members in order to make the construction of a new clubhouse possible. Walter and Phillips were big name draws. With the summer outdoor season opening in April, Walter had three months to get his weight down and his technique sharpened.

Of course, Walter's overseers at the Churchill Mining Company chose this time to open a new gold mine north of Sault Ste. Marie,

Some Final Flings Before Retirement — 413

and directed Walter to take over the project. Thankfully, Walter liked his car, because all that spring he drove back and forth between Toronto, where his office and the athletic fields were, and the Soo, where he was organizing men and material for the 30 mile expedition into the bush to the Algold mine site. Several of his many interviews regarding his athletic comeback were given to Soo reporters.

Walter Knox, President of the Churchill Mining Company (third from left) and a work crew at a mine site in Northern Ontario in the 1930s.
Courtesy Claudia Courtney

Given all these responsibilities, not to mention how hard he had to work to get back into competition shape, Walter waited until the end August to enter a track meet. He was a little philosophical when questioned about it.

"If I want to get in shorts and show the boys how I think things should be done it is not because I want to win medals. I think I've got something young athletes could use to advantage".[20]

Even more telling, Walter continued, "As an amateur I can sit on amateur boards or club committees and perhaps do some good."

Lou Marsh, the legendary Toronto Star sports reporter who had seen Walter in his prime, commented that Walter could still "throw the discus farther than any man in the country".[21] His reappearance at an athletics meet was an interesting sideshow for the reporters.

The meet he chose was in Orillia, their big "Week of Sports". Top athletes from all along the Montreal-Toronto corridor attended; this wasn't just a local affair. It was a gigantic event for the town, competitions in every sport were staged and celebrations of the town's remarkable sporting history took place all week. Harry Gill, Walter's boyhood friend who was now the top US college coach, came home to referee the track meet. The official program, a good-sized book, devoted several pages to Walter alone, and his rise from local boy running and jumping on Gill Street to his world all-around championship.[22] Walter was a celebrity in Orillia, and the fact that he was making his amateur return there was fitting.

On August 18, 1934, Walter entered the special "shot put for men over age 45" event and won with a put of 35' 7", but as the only entry. The meet organizers implored him to enter the open competition too. The locals didn't just want to see him compete, they wanted to see him win, and against worthy competition. After some persuasion, he relented. As always, Walter hesitated to enter into any competition he didn't know he could win, even at this advanced age.

Walter improved his effort to 37' 11", good for second place against the youngsters. The winner, Alex Munro of Toronto, was in a tough spot against the hometown hero making his big return to the amateur ranks, and made it even worse by beating him by a mere three inches. Encouraged, Walter then entered the discus competition where he finished in third place behind two Toronto throwers, one from his own Beaches Olympic Club, with a throw just short of 100'.

Walter's return to the amateur ranks was a rousing success. He not only avoided embarrassing himself, he almost won, feeding the heroic, myth-like status he held in his hometown. You can just picture the short, squat man with the ring of graying hair edging his otherwise bald head, hefting the shot put over his rotund abdomen, a comical sight next to the fit athletes who surrounded him. But then, as the iron ball soared past all the previous marks, the hometown crowd would have absolutely erupted in applause. That's a story with staying power. Banquets and parades were staged all week long and Walter was one of the centres of attention. As a professional, he'd had to shy away from this kind of notoriety. As a newly minted amateur, he could afford to bask in the attention.

It was the last track meet he would enter. "I'm not going to go too hard and ruin my health at this stage of the game", he said, although in 1947 Walter noted that his last official performance was in a 100-yard dash in 1937, which he won against a field half his age.[23] His return to amateur competition completed one record Walter was highly proud of (the grammar is typical of him):

> *"I won my first prize when I was seven years old at Aurora I won second in 100 yds and first in the standing broad jump, I won last prize in Orillia when I was 57 years old making just 50 years between the first and last prize won by me (sic)."*[24]

In fact, less than a year later, in 1935, Walter decided to retire from the athletic world altogether, at least from the myriad of obligations he had now. He planned to step in as a consultant here and there when he wanted. No more traveling to the ends of the earth for scouting or coaching or competitions. It was more fun to just drop into a practice field and see what was going on.

He was 57 years old, independently wealthy and had all the work he wanted with the mining company. It was time to let younger bodies take care of the athletes in Ontario.

He had to consider Mary too. She was getting on in years and needed him home more. He had been a part-time husband for over 10 years, always traveling, always pre-occupied with this athlete, those misguided officials, that mine issue. She must have been a very patient woman who now deserved a real husband.

Walter stated his mindset very clearly in a 1939 letter to the Orillia YMCA, on the event of the Y's 50th anniversary, "I feel that it is much better to be enjoying health than to be seeking it at my age, and attribute this to the early days of my life in building up my body".[25]

He had strong opinions about the state of things that reporters let him voice when they interviewed him as he was considering retirement.

Regarding the Ontario Athletic Commission program he was such a big part of, Walter said in the fall of 1934, "The results obtained from the work of the commission had not come up to the hopes we held out at first, but good progress has been made and still better progress was likely to be made from this time".[26] He didn't realize the OAC athletics program was on the downside of its effectiveness and that its whole amateur athletics program would be shut down in 1942. To be fair, Walter had reason to expect more from the OAC camp. He last ran it in 1934 and his successor as coach there was his old friend Harry Gill, the just-retired and legendary coach of the University of Illinois. The camp couldn't have been left in better hands.[27]

He continued in the same interview with his opinion of track and field in Canada, "The trouble with Canadian track and field athletics today was not that there weren't enough good athletes, but that there was a decided lack of good, organized coaching," a theme he had harped on for over 20 years.

As for the athletes, "The trouble with the present day athletes is that 80% of them are racing to train instead of training to race. That's it in a nutshell".[28]

And, "The modern athlete doesn't show as much interest and enthusiasm as those of yesterday. The difference in conditions has brought about that change. Fellows and girls have 20 places to go whereas years ago they only had a few".[29]

Some Final Flings Before Retirement — 417

Finally, Walter commented on the Olympics, "Watch Germany... (They) were following a system of developing, training and coaching that was certain to show results. Their young men were being given every encouragement".[30]

Walter lightened up in retirement too. He enjoyed telling this anecdote that occurred in the mid-1930s:

> *"Walter Knox... pulled a good one on Playfair Brown, the podgy matchmaker at the Shamrock Athletic Club the other day up at Varsity Track. Brown, despite his corpulency (sic), is quite active and fancies himself as a foot runner. Knox, knowing this, wagered Brown a deuce that he could spot him twenty yards in fifty and give him a beating. Brown grabbed, so they measured out fifty yards, stepped off Brown's handicap of twenty and placed the pair on their marks. Both crouched. When the gun fired Knox shot by Brown in the first ten yards and won as he pleased. He (Brown) could not figure out what had happened.*
>
> *While he had crouched for the start Knox had sneaked up behind him and when the gun went off was only a yard away."* [31]

Somehow he had found the time to take up golf in the mid-1920's, and now devoted more time to that in retirement. He had his standard jokes there too. A Scotch pro in Detroit, he would say, told me the secret to prevent topping the ball. I'll tell you fellows but don't spread it around. As they leaned in for the whispered words of wisdom, Walter would say in a hushed voice, "turn the ball upside down".[32] And he described playing "motor golf": a long drive and a couple of putt-putts.

Years later, Walter was chatting with Paul A Davis, the sports reporter for one of the St. Petersburg, Florida newspapers, and he related a remarkable offer he had received in 1936. As he told it, the Government of Japan contacted him to come and coach their national track and field team. How they came to approach Walter he never said. The Japanese, after 30 years of steady economic development, had become a world power and apparently wanted to hire a coach who could make their athletes a force in the athletic world. Japan was to host the 1940 Olympics and was determined to make a strong showing. The offer was for a three year contract for the whopping sum of $10,000.[33] Walter said he had his bags packed and was ready to go when the deal fell through.

That episode was odd in that Walter had retired and certainly didn't need the money; adventure and respect must have been the attractions. Fortunately the offer didn't come any sooner or Walter would have been caught in the maelstrom of war. While he was preparing to go, likely with Mary too, the military took over the government and cancelled the offer. Within the year, Japanese soldiers were marching into China, instigating a brutal eight year conflict that only ended with the dropping of the atomic bombs on Hiroshima and Nagasaki.

In 1936, Walter finally took Mary on a long-delayed holiday. They spent a month attending the Olympic Games in Berlin. That's not necessarily the way Walter wanted to go though, he thought he'd had a place on the Canadian team as an assistant Olympic Coach sewn up. Walter had been chatting with some members of the Canadian Olympic Association and "made it known" he would like to be an assistant coach for the Olympic Team in Berlin. He didn't get a definite response either way. The local Orillia paper had already been lobbying for his appointment that year.[34] However, a few days later a sports reporter misquoted him in the Toronto Star, claiming that Walter felt the Canadian Olympic Team had no chance to gain any points. Soon after, Walter received a letter from the COA asking him to resign. With a bit of ironic chuckling, Walter claimed "the unique distinction of being asked to resign from a position to which he was never appointed".[35]

In the end, he and Mary traveled to Europe on the same ship as the Olympic Team. Walter would have had time to visit with some of his OAC grads and the other athletes he knew aboard ship. "That made the voyage more interesting," he said.[36] He and Mary were even invited along on an Olympic Team sightseeing trip and dinner in Paris. The Olympic Committee had provided Walter with a pair of prime front row seats for every day of the track and field competitions; they sat just "eighty feet" from Adolph Hitler.[37] Walter, in a long letter to the Orillia Newsletter, called the Berlin Games "the best ever held by any country in every respect". He added that, "I never saw so many policemen and soldiers in my life in a country that is not in trouble. It was all done for an effect and was very impressive."

However, Walter was not so impressed with the Canadian team.

> *"It was announced that Canada had the largest and best team that ever went to the Olympic Games. This was not what I thought, also several others that were familiar with the condition of the team (sic). I don't think Canada or any other country can hope to compete with other nations that prepare for four years instead of a few weeks such as Canada did this year. There is a reason for it and that reason is a lack of funds".* [38]

Commenting on Canada's silver and three bronze medals, Walter wrote, "Had they been prepared I think they would have won some events".

After the Games, Walter and Mary toured the Low Countries and then the British Isles, their first extended holiday together since they drove home from California in 1925. Walter was 58 years old.

Coming home to Toronto, Walter focused on his work for the mining company. He and Jack, who was rarely mentioned in any newspaper clipping but was still involved with the mining operation in a similar capacity as Walter, were being sent on scouting trips across the north from Quebec to Thunder Bay.[39] Together they were developing a promising property in Long Lac, due north of Lake Superior, around that time.

Walter continued his work for the mining company until 1944 when he was 66 years old. During those World War II years, mining became an essential industry, making it important for experienced men like Walter to remain at work. But in 1944, Mary died. Walter went into full retirement. After the war, he bought a property in a "tourist court" in Plant City, near St. Petersburg, Florida and began spending his winters there. His time was spent "golfing and fishing and resting up", he said. An avid golfer, he could still shoot in the mid-80s up to the time of his death. He was a familiar sight around Orillia in the summers during those years, still a going concern, though he spent the warm months mostly at the cottage he and Mary had shared in Wellington, near Picton. In August, 1950, at the age of 71, he even re-married down in St Pete's, to another Mary, Mary Bush.

Walter Knox c. 1940
Courtesy Orillia Museum of Art and History

Walter never commented about any involvement in athletics after the war; he was getting pretty old for all that by then. The state of track and field in Ontario had deteriorated during the war. In his last years, Walter "lamented the lack of interest in track and field".[40] The OAC and their traveling coaches and provincial camp had ended as a program, replaced by high school programs. Most high schools had a track team of some sort, run by teachers of varying ability. The Provincial Schoolboy Championships had been replaced by the OFSAA (Ontario Federation of School Athletic Associations) track and field championships, again run by volunteer teachers.

Had Walter dropped in at a local high school track he would have found a program still in rudimentary development after the sports hiatus during the war. In Orillia, OCI, the Orillia Collegiate Institute, had athletics programs run by just one (though remarkable) man, Russ Jerome. He coached all the sports teams, football, track, basketball and more by himself. The school didn't even have a real indoor gym until 1949. There was no track club in town, the high school was all there was. Even the YMCA had gotten out of the competitive athletics business.[41] Had Walter shown up at the field, he likely would have been disappointed after all the work he had done to get Ontario on the right track. A feeder system, his main goal in developing the OAC traveling coach program, had failed to develop in Orillia (and most other places).

Walter died in St. Petersburg on March 3rd, 1951, of complications after a stroke. He was 73. He had traveled up to Shining Tree to his favourite fishing hole that fall and then taken a driving tour of New York State on his way back to the cottage at Wellington. He was as vigorous as ever, "the picture of health", a reporter said. Then the stroke hit. He was laid up for some time before succumbing in March. Jack had died in 1937 and his other brother, Will, in 1936. Walter had committed his whole life to building up his health, holding himself up as an example every boy should strive to emulate. In the end, he outlived his two brothers by 15 years. It paid off for him. His older sister, Mary, had died too, in 1945, leaving only his younger sister, Belle, in Edmonton, to mourn him. He had no children.

31

Epilogue

Months before his death, Walter was asked by a sports reporter what the highlight of his athletic career had been.

"I guess that was the time in Scotland," he replied, recalling his return to the Highland Games in 1912 after leaving the Olympic Team and all the turmoil in Stockholm behind. He arrived to find the shot put event had been moved up and that Cameron, the dominant strongman at the time, had won it with a put of 44 feet.

"I remember I was boiling angry… and I wanted to show them up. I threw the shot 46' 5", the best I ever made."[1]

That was Walter's persona in a nutshell. He didn't reminisce about his world championship or all the high stakes matches he had won. He remembered putting the scurrilous officials and the massive Scottish legend, Cameron, in their places. Righting the injustice perpetrated on him was all-important. And, of course, as this anecdote shows, when it really mattered, Walter performed.

Walter was a proud man. Right up to the year of his death, if a reporter asked him about his marks, he could recount his personal bests in 15 different events (see appendix 1) and tell them the details of when and where and who it was against and more for every one of them. These details were reported again and again with amazing consistency over the years. The first page of his unpublished autobiography lists them, the very first page. That is, and always was, the starting point for his life's story. That's how good I was, in every event, now let's talk.

Walter never outgrew his workingman's roots. Though he spent his coaching career preaching honesty, fair play and character, the amateur ethic decreed all-important by the AAU of C, it is clear that, deep down, Walter valued justice, winning and the self-centred, taking-care-of-business attitude he learned at the local rural fairs and on the hustling circuit. After all, that's the attitude that rewarded him. He retired wealthy by looking out for number one and reinvesting in himself. All his self-sacrificing work coaching and running clinics in schools came to naught. By 1950, as he neared the end of his life, Canada's track and field team was in as sorry a shape as it had ever been.

One reporter, who had coached with him at Queen's in the 30's, called him "cocky" and a "bull terrier", then followed that up by saying that anyone who could run a hundred in 9.6 had a right to be.[2] Walter would have agreed.

Just before he died, the Canadian Sportswriters voted on the best track and field athletes of the last half century. Walter was voted into third place.

When informed of this great honour, Walter expressed "disappointment".

"I guess they've forgotten me", he said.[3]

In his own mind, he was never anything but the best. The top vote-getting athlete was Percy Williams, the remarkable double gold medalist at the 1928 Olympics. One wonders how those two would have done racing each other in their primes. I'm sure Walter didn't wonder; he always felt he could beat anybody, one way or another. There's more to matched racing than just running fast.

Second place in the voting was Bob McFarlane, a middle distance runner from the 1948 Olympics, the top runner in Canada at the time of the voting, who held "a flock" of Canadian records. You can

Epilogue — 425

just read the back of Walter's mind though: But where was he at the Olympics? He didn't even make the final in his best event. When the pressure's on, you're supposed to win.

Walter could admire other athletes, but he couldn't lose to them. If it was a contest, Walter was in it to win, even an arbitrary ranking like this. It was all business for him. He would have been happy he was voted ahead of Bobby Kerr and Frank Lukeman, two of his peers who had run up against his business end. He would have been thoroughly insulted if Tommy Thomson, Canada's world record setting hurdler in 1920, had been ranked ahead of him, a slacker if ever Walter had seen one.

In 1955, Walter was voted into the new Canadian Sports Hall of Fame with the charter group of 54 inductees. Their write-up on him included his list of personal bests as an amateur and his professional Highland Games bests (exactly the same list Walter always rhymed off). They also acknowledged the reality of his professional hustling tours and the high stakes betting he was involved with, a rather magnanimous admission, given the sports world was still lily-white amateur. His contributions with the OAC as a coach developing Ontario's schoolboys and girls, 15 years of diligent toil, are mentioned in one brief line, almost as an afterthought. Walter would have been proud to be acknowledged in that way, though he would have wished his work identifying and developing future track stars had taken a little more prominent place in his story. He was proud of that.

In 1960, he was inducted into the Canadian Olympic Hall of Fame, this time as a builder, acknowledging his work with the 1912 and 1920 Olympic teams. Again, his work developing the Ontario schoolboys and girls, his most important contribution as a builder as it had a significant impact on Canada's Olympic successes in 1928, 1932 and 1936, went unnoted.

In 1966, he was one of the first inductees into the new Orillia Hall of Fame.

Clearly he was not forgotten, even though he felt forgotten. All of this recognition happened after his death.

Walter Knox was a success story in the rural workingman's tradition. He knew his talents and pragmatically applied them to further his condition. In the athletics world, that meant he had to ignore the AAA's and their rules and brazenly follow the money into the world of professional hustling. In that tradition, he re-invested his profits back into himself in further speculation. In his case, that included supporting Jack's prospecting and the lure of the big windfall. He developed the traditional work ethic, rarely stopping to enjoy his hard-earned wealth until he was ready for retirement (as Mary surely found out in the 1920's). But in the end he was a success; he had parlayed his talent into a fortune that afforded a comfortable retirement. He was one of the lucky ones. Most workingmen lived out a life of modest means.

One of the legacies of that success was having his name left on the map. The "Knox Block", the 1700 acre claim Jack had staked in the Shining Tree district, was later turned into "Knox Township" in the Cochrane District. There is now a "Knox Lake" where their mine was located too. Not many workingmen received that privilege.

Walter Knox was a difficult man to get a handle on. He was not one to reveal much about himself. Rarely, he said, did he run a whole 100 yards hard, just hard enough to win. Why show what you've got — who knows who else is watching and what future matches may come out of a race? Always look just good enough. Look beatable. On the pro circuit of Highland Games in Scotland where Knox ended his career, he would often take the prize money for winning then turn around and out-do that mark two or three times in shot put or pole vault to earn bonus money from the organizers.

His colourful life, fed by his daring pursuit of competition as a livelihood, was contrasted by a personal world with high walls around it. He made many friends and kept amiable relationships with his old hometown compatriots, but few people knew him on more than a superficial basis, many only knew him as someone else. Like any good poker player, he held his cards very tight to his chest during his hustling years, never revealing more than he had to so no one would be able to see how he played them. He even kept men who were trying to help him, who were on his side, at arm's length, giving them only the information about him they needed to know.

That was the safe life of a professional athlete then, and he was exceptionally good at it.

It is serendipitous that Walter, with his prodigious physical talents coupled with a sturdy personality, came along at that precise time in the history of Canadian sport. The draconian amateur rules of the day made his choice to go on the hustling circuit his only real choice. If he had been a part-time amateur athlete, as the Amateur Associations encouraged, trying to perform after a 60 hour week of hard labour in the shingling mill, he never would have developed into the magnificent performer he became. The rules that marginalized athletes who wanted to make a living out of their abilities sent Walter down the only road available to talented men of modest means. As a professional, he trained harder, competed more and studied the science of athletics more intently than he ever would have as an amateur. Luckily, he had the temperament to not only survive but to thrive in that world. In the end, those draconian rules made him into a better athlete.

And then those rules forced him overseas, to Scotland and the Highland Games, where he found his niche. Here were honest, stalwart men, and a culture that appreciated them. To his last day, Walter promoted the Highland Scots as having got sport right. He was there right in their heyday too, at the peak of the culture. Serendipitous.

Coming out of the bush in 1920, Walter landed in Ontario during its years of sporting angst as everyone wondered what was happening to Canada at the Olympics. He found the opportunity to institute his precise vision for correcting Canada's sporting ineptitude with the Ontario Athletic Commission. He was the right man in the right place at the right time. How often does an opinionated know-it-all actually get to carry out his "solution" on a grand scale? Walter was not one to miss out on an opportunity, or the chance to create an opportunity. The OAC was another fitting niche for him. Proud, authoritative and independent, a vagabond like Walter fit perfectly into the traveling coach program. It was a tailor-made venue for Walter to re-build his reputation as an upright pillar of health and fitness, the self-made man who should be emulated.

And what adventures he had! It is difficult to read through the recollections of his life and accept everything at face value. There were so many remarkable events: the big matched race wins, the poisoning, besting giants AA Cameron and Ralph Rose in the shot put, taunting Jack Johnson, setting world records in three diverse events, the baseball triple play, his improbable wrestling successes against George Turner in Orillia, his dominating wins in the all-around championships, Olympic coach, striking it rich in gold country, the enviable coaching record, especially with the women, president of a mining company. Could they all be true? Other than some of the details surrounding the matched race exploits that no one else could have known, the contemporary newspapers confirm them all. Even his recollections years later were still consistent with the contemporary newspaper reports. Of course, he was guilty of leaving out some of the less glorious episodes, like his blatant lying to the AAU of C to try to get his amateur status back in time for the 1908 Olympics and his shabby matched race with Archie Hahn. Who knows what other unflattering events he conveniently omitted, things only he would know about. In the preface of his autobiography he clearly states, "it has been my thought to tell the bad along with the good", but assuredly, he left some uncomplimentary episodes out. He did have a remarkable memory and was a bit of a stickler for detail in his writings. His life was an audacious adventure and he remembered every inch of it.

But that doesn't mean it was as happy a life as one would expect with all that success. He had to live out his years with a thick skin even long after he gave up his aliases.

The sporting community's attitude toward Walter after World War I was split: he remained part hometown hero and part disgraced con man. In 1907, right after Walter defeated five amateur champions in their own events at the Canadian Championships, when he should have earned respect for his remarkable abilities, the chair of the tribunal banishing him as a professional could not contain his contempt. Walter's four months of coaching at a college was, apparently, unspeakably vile to him. Rumours of his hustling exploits and running under assumed names that circulated along the grapevine only fed this attitude of revulsion the amateurs had towards him. Two years later, when having his amateur status revoked again in San Francisco, the President of the AAU refused to even shake his hand. Walter had to just shrug it off but it is clear it hurt deep down to be denigrated like that. Walter may have been pragmatic, but he was still proud.

Twenty-five years later, after winning the World Professional All-around title, coaching two Olympic Teams and putting his heart and soul into the OAC program to help develop boys and girls for Canada's Olympic Team, he was widely respected for his expertise and work ethic. But that undercurrent of professionalism still haunted him. When offered a chance to re-gain his amateur standing in 1934, at the age of 56, he was first in line. He thought being re-instated would redeem his reputation. That professional branding, though, never could be washed away.

In 1939, my father, Fred Town, was selected as one of the two District athletes to go to the OAC camp, a great honour. Three years later, Fred broke Walter's 12 pound shot put record at the Orillia Y, a record that had stood for over 25 years. Walter sent him a very encouraging letter when he heard of this feat and included one of his many medals. Fred was suitably impressed and kept the letter his whole life. However, years later when I, as a boy, asked him who Walter Knox was, I was given a decidedly mixed answer. Walter was a great athlete, he said, but… he was a hustler, he cheated people out of their money. This was in the 1960's, long after Walter was gone. No one knew the specifics of Walter's hustling career but rumours persisted a half-century later, in spite of all the positive things Walter had accomplished. In the 1920's and 30's, when Walter was working to redeem his reputation, the rumours would have been even stronger.

Walter couldn't escape his past. Boys who were so impressed by the great Olympic coach who visited their school, that paragon of health and character, would go home to vague slanders against him by their fathers and uncles who had been around long enough to hear them. Fred Town was one of those boys.

Walter lived out his life with an asterix beside his name. He was great, but… No one knew any specifics, just the rumours, because Walter had been so careful to keep his shady exploits to himself. But that asterix, those rumours, followed him to his death and beyond.

Appendix 1:
Walter Knox's Personal Best Performances

Walter, over the 36 years after he retired from competition, scrupulously reported his best performances consistently to reporters time after time. Below is the list of marks he claimed as his best[1], I've added the details where possible.

50 yards	5 2/5 seconds	1909, May 30 matched race with Forest Smithson at Shellbourne Park, Oakland
75 yards	7 ½ seconds	1908, Dec 4 indoor amateur world record
100 yards	9 3/5 seconds	1909, July 25 ties world record in scrutinized time trial, San Francisco
176 yards	18 1/5 seconds	1909, May 29 Shellbourne Park, Oakland, one lap of the track, track record
220 yards	22 4/5 seconds	

440 yards	60 seconds	
880 yards	2 minutes, 5 seconds	
standing broad jump	10' 7 ½"	
standing three jumps	33' 7"	
standing high jump	5' 0"	1913 Jedburg, Scotland
standing hop, skip, jump	31' 7"	
hop, skip and jump	47'	
broad jump	24' 2"	1909 in competition, San Francisco
high jump	5' 7"	1911 at a Highland Games in Scotland
8 lb. shot put	63' 5"	1909, Feb 5 broke world indoor record only to be bested by Ralph Rose by 2 inches, San Francisco Auditorium
12 lb. shot put	55' 4"	
16 lb. shot put	46' 5"	1912, July 19 Highland Games, Thornton Junction, Scotland
22 lb. shot put	37' 8"	
16 lb. hammer throw	125'	
56 lb. weight throw	25' 4"	
discus	125'	
pole vault	12' 6"	1909 in practice, San Francisco, equaled world record

Appendix 2:
More Walter Knox Quotes on Athletics

"Few days (as a teenager), however, were too short to get in my licks at practicing. And when I say that I mean the hard, grueling grind with perfection so far out in front that it seems you can never catch up with it." — Hot Foot, autobiography, p23.

"I developed from nothing to a champion in one year of sprinting." Regarding his four months at college in Beloit under Harry Gill's tutelage. — Notes for autobiography, 1903 p1.

"The tougher they came the better I liked it." — Hot Foot, autobiography, p14.

"Track and field sports of those days were so limited in the scope that a top notcher could obtain meager returns on the abilities that the good lord gave him. If I chose to accept hazards to that mercurial quality known as "reputation" it was my choice, and thereon I must stand or fall." — Hot Foot, autobiography, preface.

"To me it was a laugh to see how many of those getting ready went at it as though these (training) *periods were the contests themselves."* — Hot Foot, autobiography, p3.

"Ferguson is a good man (but) *does not know how to use his body to the best purpose in running.* (I) *can take Ferguson and make him four yards faster in his time in the 100-yard sprints inside of two weeks"* — Vancouver paper, June 8, 1906, in Knox Scrapbook p29.

"They've had the gun on me more than once but they have four-flushed so often about getting me that I am more afraid of some disappointed bettor potting me without saying a word than I am about these chaps who show guns and knives and tell you what they are going to do." — Toronto Star 1911, from Knox Scrapbook, p91.

"One thing that was drilled in to me both by Gill and Head Coach Hollister (at college in Beloit) *was that the word of the coach is law. When I was given instruction these were to be carried out to the letter."* — Hot Foot, autobiography, p43.

"Here was a Negro out in front of me and it just wasn't in the cards for a white fellow to take a coloured man's dust." — on racing Poage in college — Hot Foot, autobiography, p47.

"If you are an amateur, be a true one; but if you are a professional go out and take the money. But whatever you are, whether amateur or professional, play the game squarely and fairly." — clipping in Orillia Museum of Art and History, Knox file.

From a reporter regarding betting in amateur meets, *"A remark about "amateurism" paying better in the States* (than Scotland) *brought a lot of interesting reminiscences from Knox who agreed that it would be better not to publish them."* — Knox Scrapbook, p182, 1913.

"Learn to do things correctly all the time. Practise, practise, practise at a lower height (in the pole vault), *and don't go higher until you can do it correctly, and so on until you reach your limit."* — Health and Strength, May 9, 1914.

"Americans, leaders in specialization, particularly have shown what can be done in athletics by absorbing all our knowledge, and then wisely adding to it. Whether this specialization is entirely for the good of amateur sport is a debatable matter." — Sport and Play and Wheel Life, May 9, 1914.

"I attribute my success to keeping in good condition at all times. I never use liquor or tobacco, and always do exercising of some kind. I know dozens of athletes who were at their best ten years ago when I was in good form myself, but they could not make a credible showing in any event now." — Toronto Globe, Oct 8, 1920.

" I am satisfied that if I had some of the men I met (scouting the West in 1920) *in my care for two months they would be capable of winning in Belgium* (at the Olympics)." — Toronto Star, June 1920, in Knox Scrapbook, p201.

"The building of a sound body is on par with building a sound and active mind, and the two should be developed simultaneously." — California newspaper, 1926, in Knox Scrapbook, p220.

"The road to the top is gained only by adopting the correct methods, hard work and the determination to arrive." — Orillia Newsletter, April 29, 1931.

"The success of my number of years in competition is due to the fact that I never would compete in any events unless I was physically fit and in first class condition." — Orillia Newsletter, Sept 2, 1936.

Regarding the 1936 Canadian Olympic coach, "*The coach they had was the poorest excuse for one that I have ever seen on any team.*" — Aug 7, 1936, letter to sister from Berlin — Orillia Public Library, Harold Hale collection.

"*When we used to go prospecting, John would put away his pipe and at the beginning of the journey would tire easily. But after a few weeks of not smoking he could keep pace with me. That's the best proof I could offer.*" — clipping in Orillia Museum of Art and History, Knox file. Feb 14, 1949 St. Petersburg newspaper.

"*If you take up boxing and find you are not going to be very good at it, you had better practice running.*" — clipping in Orillia Museum of Art and History, Knox file.

"*Games are fine and essential but the right kind of living is necessary along with it. (I do) not favour smoking, knowing as all do, that it hurts the wind, etc.*" — clipping at Orillia Museum of Art and History, Knox file.

"*Another thing that the athlete should avoid is overeating. Few people today die of starvation, but there are people dying of over-eating.*" — clipping in Orillia Museum of Art and History, Knox file.

"*Sometimes someone would point out many champions who smoke and drink. I used to say they would be better if they didn't.*" — Orillia Newsletter, Sept 20, 1950.

From an "old Scot's wife" in Lanarkshire, Scotland regarding Walter, "*Man, ye hae a rare pair o shoulders and shanks on ye!*" — Knox Scrapbook p147, 1912.

Appendix 3:
Walter Knox Life Timeline

Growing Up

1878 - born January 27 in Listowel, Ontario, though the family settles in Toronto by year's end.

1893 - May 24th, Walter's first entry into an adult competition ends badly.
- Knox family moves from Coldwater to Orillia.

1899 - Walter strikes out on his own taking shingling job in Verner.
- Sept 22, wins silver medal in pole vault at the Canadian Championships.

1900 - July 12, first use of an alias, Midland.
- July 14, wins pole vault at Ontario Championships.
- Sept, wins pole vault at Canadian Championships over American IK Baxter.

1901 - June 16, wins gold and silver medals at Pan American Exhibition Games in Buffalo.
- works briefly in Newfoundland as shingler, decides to retire from athletics to pursue this career in Verner, Parry Sound and, briefly, Orillia.

1903 - Jan, enrolls in **Beloit College**, Wisconsin to train under Harry Gill.
- breaks indoor **pole vault world record** at 11' 2" but the record is not ratified as bar fell down during re-measurement.
- first sprint victory over established opponent, George Poage, the conference champion.
- Conference Championships, places 2nd to Archie Hahn in 100 on sprained ankle.
- July 8, first use of an alias for overt hustling, wins 11 events in Sault Ste. Marie.
- learns hustling ropes the hard way in disastrous attempted con of Dave Belland in Peterborough.

The Hustling Years

1904 - Jan, assists detective to solve a case in Southbridge, Massachusetts.
- first meeting with professional John MacDonald on tour of New England meets.
- August, relocates to Slocan, BC, then Nelson to start **professional hustling career** using name "Walter Renwick".
- wins high stakes races against Douglas, Mitchell, Wilkinson and Hummel but is cheated out of $500 in race with "Big" Smith by corrupt judge.

1905 - Apr, enrolls at **University of Illinois,** helping to establish Harry Gill as top athletics coach.
- Aug 4, defeats Tom Morris, a top tier sprinter, in Spokane, Washington.

- Aug-Sept, tours small towns of **Alberta and BC** winning many sprinting and throwing contests as "Wilson" or "Renwick".
- Oct-Nov, won three high stakes races in BC and Saskatchewan with a fourth that fell through when he was recognized.

1906
- Jan, given an amateur card by the **Central** YMCA in Toronto.
- Feb, defeats top Canadian pole vaulter, Ed Archibald.
- March, sets new YMCA **world indoor shot put record** in Toronto.
- May, Nanaimo, BC, defeats Ferguson in high stakes matched race after being poisoned, then is beaten up.
- Aug 9, YMCA Penman Games in Orillia, wins 3 events and high point shield.
- Sept 15, wins high stakes match race with Henry Batson in Erie, Pennsylvania.
- Oct 5, Hamilton, won 4 events at Canadian YMCA Championships.
- Jack Knox starts prospecting in Northern Ontario, Walter bankrolls him.

1907
- Jan, Walter takes job as coach at **Montana Agricultural College in Bozeman**.
- June 8, **Walter's "Big Day"**, winning five events at the CAAU Championships in Toronto, defeating champions Kerr, Archibald and Bricker. However, is outed as a professional, ending his amateur career in Canada.
- July-Sept, tours **Michigan and Wisconsin** looking for matches with little success.
- Defeats Archie Hahn in what was probably a fixed race.
- Sept and Oct, wins two high stakes contests in Port Arthur, shot putting and sprinting.

1908 - Jan, starts work as shingler in Montesena, Washington, maneuvering for a high stakes race that never happened.
- May, moves to **San Francisco** and re-gains an amateur card in the fall.

1909 - Feb 5, breaks **world record in 8 lb. shot put** only to lose contest to Ralph Rose.
- March, wins tense high stakes match race with Walker in Mexicali, Mexico.
- Apr-Aug, in 14 athletics meets in 18 weeks, Walter posted lifetime best scores in the pole vault (12' 6"), long jump (24' 2") and 100 and 50-yd. dashes (9.6 and 5.4)
- May 30, defeats top sprinter Forest Smithson in an amateur 50 yd. matched race.
- July 25, **equals world record in 100-yard dash** in a well scrutinized match race in San Francisco.
- August 19, Walter **declared a professional** by the American AAU.
- spends winter prospecting with Jack in Elk Lake region.

1910 - May, wins two wrestling matches in Northern Ontario over Belldruger and Cleverley.
- Aug, after several meets in Ontario, Walter enters the Boston Caledonian Games and defeats local champion MacDonald in every event they contest.
- Oct, returns to Elk Lake and prospecting.

The Highland Games Years

1911 - June 17, sails from Montreal for Scotland to tour the **Scottish Highland Games**.

| | - June-Sept, competes in 37 Highland Games winning a remarkable 63 firsts, 37 seconds and 31 third placings, becoming famous as "the man from Canada".
| | - Oct, returns to Elk Lake and prospecting.
| 1912 | - March, wins wrestling title "Champion of Silver Country" from Church.
| | - May, hired as **Head Coach of Canada's Olympic team**.
| | - After weeks of roiling controversy throughout training camp that culminated in Walter's fistfight with Army Howard, the Olympic track team performs reasonably well, winning 5 medals.
| | - July 17, Walter leaves the Olympics as soon as the track meet ends for another tour of the Scottish Highland Games, leaving the managers to escort the disgruntled team home.
| | - July-Sept, competes in 23 Highland Games winning 41 first placings, 15 seconds and 17 thirds (and none lower), setting a new Scottish pole vault record.
| | - Sept, sails home and returns to prospecting in Elk Lake.
| 1913 | - June 25, wins **North American All-around title** from John MacDonald at Hanlan's Point in Toronto. Challenges Jim Thorpe for World title through an agent he hired to book high profile title matches. Thorpe disinterested.
| | - June, returns to Scotland for a third tour of Highland Games. In 26 Games, Walter wins 38 firsts, 10 seconds and 12 thirds, and again breaks his own pole vault record.
| | - Aug 16, loses match with Bryce Scott for the Jumping Championship of Scotland due to a badly sprained ankle.

	- Oct 4, has to withdraw from long-sought match with Findlay Cramb for the All-around Championship of Great Britain due to poorly healing ankle.
1914	- Jan 1, enters the Powderhall Sprint for the professional world championship but withdraws after his first race due to poor wagering odds.
	- Jan, hired by the British AAA as **Head Coach of the British Olympic Team** on a three year contract. Spends six months touring the Isles setting up training centres and developing coaches and athletes.
	- Aug 1-3, wins **World All-around title** in match with Cramb.
	- Sept, with the start of WWI British Olympic program suspended, Walter released from his contract.
	- Oct, Walter heads home to Elk Lake and prospecting.
1915	- Jan-Feb, coaches Picton hockey team.
	- March 15, defeats George Turner, English wrestling champion, in match at Orillia Opera House.
	- Apr, buys pool hall in Orillia.
	- Apr 28, **officially retires** from track and field competition at age 37.
	- May 3, wins closely contested wrestling re-match with Turner in Orillia.
	- summer, leaves pool hall to join Jack in **Shining Tree** where Jack has struck it rich in gold on his new claims.

The Prospecting Years

1916	- Walter and Jack decide to develop their **gold mine** themselves and not sell out to a conglomerate. They begin 10 years of pickaxe work and hire two crews of 15 men to work their claim.

1916- 1920	-	Walter alternates periods of mining with hiatuses coaching hockey and track and field teams from Picton to Regina.

The Coaching Years

1920	-	Feb, Walter hired to be **Head Coach of Canada's Olympic Team** again.
	-	Apr 9-June, Walter tours the West and then Ontario and Montreal scouting for talent for the Olympic team.
	-	July, the Canadian track and field team disappoints at the Olympics with only a solitary gold medal performance.
	-	Aug, in a return to the **Scottish Highland Games** at age 42, Walter wins a remarkable 4 events in two Games, throwing his age in the shot put, 45 feet at age 42.
1921	-	Feb, Walter hired by the new **Ontario Athletic Commission** as the traveling coach to implement a healthy living and athletic identification program in Ontario schools. Walter will work for the OAC in this capacity for 14 years.
	-	spring, Walter conducts his first OAC clinics in schools, his "model school".
1922	-	June 2, Walter begins his interest in girls athletics, holding a "try-out meet" and then taking a team of girls to a meet in Philadelphia where they dominated.
	-	Sept, Walter includes girls in his OAC athletics program.
	-	Oct, Walter stages the first schoolboy track and field meets under OAC auspices.

1923 - Walter continued juggling his gold mine work with Jack, the development of the OAC program and the development of women's athletics.

1924 - Walter applies but is rejected as Olympic coach. The Olympics are a huge disappointment for Canada, especially in track and field.
- **Walter marries** Mary Boyce.
- fall, Walter buys the Roblas Lomas ranch in California and takes an extended holiday there with Mary.

1925 - Walter stages the first **Ontario Schoolboy Championship** meet with strong representation from all 8 distracts, establishing the forerunner of the OFSAA provincial high school championships.

1926 - March, Jack and Walter sell a 62% stake in their gold mine to New York interests. Walter becomes **"President of the Churchill Mining and Milling Company"**.

1927 - in addition to his mining and OCA obligations, by this year Walter has become one of the most high profile coaches of female athletes in Ontario.

1928 - Jan, hired by the **Parkdale Ladies Athletic Club** to coach their athletes including Ethel Catherwood and Jane Bell, two women who would go to the 1928 Olympics.
- passed over again as Olympic coach, even for the inaugural women's team, Walter reveled in the successes of both the "Matchless Six" women's team, as he had coached five out of six members, as well as the men's track team, which reasserted itself with four medals. Graduates of his OAC development program had a significant impact on the team.
- Aug, Walter hosts first OAC schoolboy summer training camp in Goderich, Ontario.

1929 - Aug, the OAC builds the **Provincial Training Camp** near Orillia for the top schoolboy athletes identified by Walter's OAC program.
- Walter takes on coaching positions with the Central YMCA and the Toronto Police Association in addition to the casual consulting he does with athletes all over Ontario
- Walter is working with top women Dallas Creamer and Jean Godson now.

1930 - Walter starts a four year commitment to coach the Queen's University track team each fall.
- Walter discovers Mamie Shrum in Orillia and coaches her to a Canadian Championship in the shot put in 6 weeks.

1931 - OAC traveling coach program cancelled. Walter visits schools only sporadically over the next few years but continues to run the Provincial Championship meet and the summer training camp.

1932 - Mamie Shrum wins Canadian championships in both shot put and discus, shattering the Canadian shot put record.

1934 - Jan, Walter gets his **amateur card back**, announces his return to competition.
- Walter takes on Head Coach position with the new Beaches Athletic Club in Toronto.
- Aug, at age 56, Walter wins a second and third place at a track meet in Orillia.

Retirement Years

1935 - **Walter retires** from both competition and coaching, turning the OAC camp over to Harry Gill.

1936	- after actively pursuing an Olympic coaching position, Walter is rebuffed again, but travels with the team to watch the Olympics and holiday.
1944	- Mary dies.
	- Walter retires from the mining company at age 66.
1946	- Walter purchases a house in St Petersburg, Florida where he spends his winters "resting up". Still fit and active, summers are spent between Shining Tree, Orillia, Toronto and his cottage in Wellington.
1950	- Walter places third in the voting for greatest Canadian track and field athlete of the half century. He is "disappointed".
1951	- March 3, Walter Knox dies of a stroke in St Petersburg.
1955	- Walter elected as a charter inductee into the new Canadian Sports Hall of Fame.
1960	- Walter inducted into the Canadian Olympic Hall of Fame as a builder.
1966	- Walter inducted into the Orillia Hall of Fame, his home town.

Citations and Notes

Three main sources were used as the starting point for this book, all three created by Walter Knox himself. First is the scrapbook of newspaper clippings Walter meticulously clipped out of the paper throughout his travels and sent home, where his family dutifully pasted them into a book. There are well over 1000 clippings, cramming 278 pages of the large scrapbook, all directly describing Walter's exploits. In 1949, Walter either decided to or, more likely, was asked to write down the story of his hustling years. He had typed up a summary of his life in sports in the late 1930s and expanded this recollection in 1949. This resulted in the two other primary sources: 40 typewritten pages of notes (though a few were handwritten), obviously written and updated by Walter, and the almost finished autobiography covering his life from birth to 1912. Again, the autobiography was obviously ghostwritten by someone, only cryptically identified by his initials on the corner of a note asking Walter for a clarification (he and Walter acknowledged each other several times in answering questions and fleshing out information through Walter's notes).

Walter's notes display his rudimentary education: a total lack of grammar, terrible punctuation leading to run-on sentences of several hundred words and no composition skills. Walter never made it to high school and his public school attendance, as he freely admitted, was spotty. His autobiography is clearly written, though chatty and awkwardly organized, definitely by a different hand than the author of the notes who was blunt and opinionated.

Direct quotes of conversation throughout this book are taken verbatim from Walter's autobiography or notes. Sometimes the language or grammar is awkward but the words are precisely reprinted as Walter remembered them. Nothing is fictionalized or enhanced in this book.

Chapter 1 – Who Is This Guy?

1 – Knox, W.R. (1939) Scrapbook of collection of personal newspaper clippings 1898-1939. Held in Orillia Museum of Art and History, Orillia, Ontario. p91. The description of this encounter with Jack Johnson is an amalgam of several different recollections Walter published over the years, the above reference being where this particular quote came from. This is a story he trotted out to reporters regularly, a story that, typically for Walter, remained essentially the same over 40 years of re-telling.

2 – Knox, W (c1949) Notes for preparation of autobiography. Orillia Public Library, *Harold Hale Papers Collection*. Johnson, Hahn and Walker Stories, p1. This is the main reference for this story, though the first citation above and another newspaper clipping in the scrapbook on page 89 cover the encounter in detail too.

3 – Knox, W (c1949) Notes for preparation of autobiography. Orillia Public Library, *Harold Hale Papers Collection*. Johnson, Hahn and Walker Stories, p1

4 – A white sense of superiority fostered during the slavery period still festered in North American society, legitimized in the American "Jim Crow" laws that severely restricted the blacks' voting rights and established segregation as official policy. Black men were commonly seen as inferior brutes who needed to "know their place". Repeatedly in his writings, Walter made statements that demonstrated he adhered to this deep-rooted cultural assumption.

Chapter 2 – Learning the Ropes
1 – Knox, W (1951) *Hot Foot*. Unfinished and unpublished autobiography. Complete copy in Orillia Museum of Art and History, Orillia, Ont. p15.

2 – Ibid. p17

3 – Canadian Sports Hall of Fame website. *Walter Knox*. Retrieved from http://sportshall.ca

4 – Richmond, R. (1996) *The Orillia Spirit*. Toronto: Dundurn Press. p40. Orillia's temperance bylaw was not rescinded until 1961.

5 – Ibid. p9. As Richmond points out, Orillia was a remarkable town in those years, "the town of champions", first town in North America to build long distance electrical lines from its own power dam, first town in Canada with a successful socialized medical plan, "the principle industrial center between Toronto and North Bay", home to the "finest small town YMCA in North America". This was no ordinary town in those years and "the Orillia Spirit" moniker was justly earned.

6 – Knox, W (c1949) Notes for preparation of autobiography. Orillia Public Library, *Harold Hale Papers Collection*. Early Years. p1.

7 – Ibid. Early Years. p1.

8 – Knox, W (1951) *Hot Foot*. Unfinished and unpublished autobiography. Complete copy in Orillia Museum of Art and History, Orillia, Ont. p22.

9 – Ibid. p20.

Chapter 3 – A Big Time Amateur
1 – Knox, W (1951) *Hot Foot*. Unfinished and unpublished autobiography. Complete copy in Orillia Museum of Art and History, Orillia, Ont. p5.

2 – Ibid. p9.

3 – Ibid. p9.

4 – Ibid. p34.

5 – Ibid. p34.

6 – Ibid. p36. Walter and Harry almost met with disaster on the way to this meet. In their hotel room in Hamilton the night before there was a gas leak from the lamps used to light the whole building. Walter woke up suddenly in the middle of the night and had the wherewithal not to light a match to look around. It would have been the end of both of them!

7 – Ibid. p 38. As a competitive rural youth, Walter had much experience in wrestling and fighting, especially in his wild summer on the streets of Orillia with his gang. As will be seen in wrestling matches in Walter's future, he was a pit bull, compact, very strong and remarkably agile — a handful for even very accomplished fighters.

8 – Knox, W (c1949) Notes for preparation of autobiography. Orillia Public Library, *Harold Hale Papers Collection*. Handwritten addendum in first version only, 50 Years in Sports, No 3, p28.

9 – Knox, W (1951) *Hot Foot*. Unfinished and unpublished autobiography. Complete copy in Orillia Museum of Art and History, Orillia, Ont. p40.

Chapter 4 – The Workingman's Sporting Tradition

1 – Marks, L. (1996) *Revivals and Roller Rinks: Religion, Leisure and Identity in Late Nineteenth Century Small-town Ontario*. Toronto: U of T Press. p90.

2 – Zarnowski, F. (2005) *All Around Men: Heroes of a Forgotten Sport*. Scarecrow Press. p8.

3 – Walmsley, K.B. (1999) The Public Importance of Men and the Importance of Public

Men: Sport and Masculinities in Nineteenth Century Canada. In White, P. and Young, K., eds, *Sport and Gender in Canada*, pp. 24-39. Don Mills. Oxford University Press. p28.

4 – Bouchier, N. (2003) *For the Love of the Game: Amateur Sport in Small Town Ontario, 1838-1893*. Montreal: Mcgill/Queens University Press. p4.

5 – Zarnowski, F. (2005) *All Around Men: Heroes of a Forgotten Sport*. Scarecrow Press. p10.

6 – Ibid. p9.

7 – Howell, C.D. (2001) *Blood, Sweat and Cheers: Sport and the Making of Canada*.

Toronto: University of Toronto Press. p60.

8 – Metcalf, A. (1988) Leisure, Sport and Working: Some Insights from Montreal and the Northeast Coalfields of England. In *Leisure, Sport and Working Class Cultures*. pp. 65-76. Toronto: Garamond Press. pp. 68-69.

9 – Marks, L. (1996) *Revivals and Roller Rinks: Religion, Leisure and Identity in Late Nineteenth Century Small-town Ontario*. Toronto: U of T Press. p83.

10 – Cosentino, F. (1973) *A History of the Concept of Professionalism in Canadian Sport*. Doctoral Dissertation: University of Alberta. CJHSPE 6, no.2 (Dec 1975) pp. 75-81. p48.

11 – Bouchier, N. (2003) *For the Love of the Game: Amateur Sport in Small Town Ontario, 1838-1893.* Montreal: McGill/Queen's University Press. p11.

12 – Ibid. p11.

13 – Zarnowski, F. (2005) *All Around Men: Heroes of a Forgotten Sport.* Scarecrow Press. p12.

14 – Walmsley, K.B. (1999) The Public Importance of Men and the Importance of Public Men: Sport and Masculinities in Nineteenth Century Canada. In White, P. and Young, K., eds, *Sport and Gender in Canada*, pp. 24-39. Don Mills. Oxford University Press. p29.

15 – Metcalf, A. (1970) Physical Education in Ontario During the Nineteenth Century. *Canadian Association For Health, Physical Education and Recreation.* 37(1), pp. 29-33. p30.

16 – Ibid. p29.

17 – Ibid. p31.

18 – Hall, A. (1999) Creators of the Lost and Perfect Game? Gender, History and Canadian Sport. In White, P. and Young, K., eds, *Sport and Gender in Canada,* pp. 5-23. Don Mills: Oxford University Press. p12.

Chapter 5 – The Elites Take Over

1 – Walmsley, K.B. (1999) The Public Importance of Men and the Importance of Public Men: Sport and Masculinities in Nineteenth Century Canada. In White, P. and Young, K., eds, *Sport and Gender in Canada*, pp. 24-39. Don Mills. Oxford University Press. p32.

2 – Bouchier, N. (2003) *For the Love of the Game: Amateur Sport in Small Town Ontario, 1838-1893*. Montreal: McGill/Queen's University Press. p74.

3 – Ibid. p79.

4 – Willis, J. and Wettan, R. (1976) Social Stratification in New York City Athletic Clubs, 1865-1915. *Journal of Sport History*, 3(1), pp. 45-63. p47.

5 – Kidd, B. (1996*) The Struggle For Canadian Sport*. Toronto: U of T Press. p18.

6 – Metcalf, A. (1987) *Canada Learns to Play: The Emergence of Organized Sport, 1807-1914*. Toronto: McClelland Stewart. p161.

7 – Hyde, F. (Sept 11, 1936). Professional Sport a Half Century Ago. *The Woodstock Daily Sentinal-Review*, pp2-3. p3. This extended interview with Alby Robinson, a professional runner in the "good old days" starting in 1879, is a remarkable account of the workingman's sporting tradition and how it had degenerated into a betting free-for-all. His recollections and experiences are quite similar to many that Walter Knox had a generation later. There are precious few other firsthand accounts of the day-to-day life of a professional athlete prior to WWI. Professionals competed under aliases, kept a low profile and flitted across the province or country avoiding the press. At the time the existence of professional athletes was well known but a sporting gathering may not know one was in their midst until it was too late and he would be gone before anything could be done about it.

8 – Ibid. p2.

9 – Bouchier, N. (2003) *For the Love of the Game: Amateur Sport in Small Town Ontario, 1838-1893*. Montreal: McGill/Queen's University Press. p80.

10 – Morrow, D. (2005) *Sport in Canada: A History*. Don Mills: Oxford University Press. p74.

11 – Bouchier, N. (2003) *For the Love of the Game: Amateur Sport in Small Town Ontario, 1838-1893*. Montreal: McGill/Queen's University Press. p58.

12 – Howell, C.D. (2001) *Blood, Sweat and Cheers: Sport and the Making of Canada*. Toronto: University of Toronto Press. p31.

13 – Cosentino, F. (1973) *A History of the Concept of Professionalism in Canadian Sport*. Doctoral Dissertation: University of Alberta. CJHSPE 6, no.2 (Dec 1975) pp. 75-81.

14 – Ibid. p52.

15 – Ibid. Abstract.

16 – Metcalf, A. (1987) *Canada Learns to Play: The Emergence of Organized Sport, 1807-1914*. Toronto: McClelland Stewart. p121.

17 – Ibid. p121.

18 – Cosentino, F. (1973) *A History of the Concept of Professionalism in Canadian Sport*. Doctoral Dissertation: University of Alberta. CJHSPE 6, no.2 (Dec 1975) pp. 75-81.

19 – Bouchier, N. (2003) *For the Love of the Game: Amateur Sport in Small Town Ontario, 1838-1893*. Montreal: McGill/Queen's University Press. p64.

20 – Howell, C.D. (2001) *Blood, Sweat and Cheers: Sport and the Making of Canada*. Toronto: University of Toronto Press. p42.

21 – Kidd, B. (1996*) The Struggle For Canadian Sport.* Toronto: U of T Press. p31.

22 – Howell, C.D. (2001) *Blood, Sweat and Cheers: Sport and the Making of Canada.* Toronto: University of Toronto Press. p52.

23 – Metcalf, A. (1988) Leisure, Sport and Working: Some Insights from Montreal and the Northeast Coalfields of England. In *Leisure, Sport and Working Class Cultures.* pp. 65-76. Toronto: Garamond Press. p69.

24 – Ibid. p54.

25 – Ibid. p54.

26 – Walmsley, K.B. (1999) The Public Importance of Men and the Importance of Public Men: Sport and Masculinities in Nineteenth Century Canada. In White, P. and Young, K., eds, *Sport and Gender in Canada*, pp. 24-39. Don Mills. Oxford University Press. p32.

Chapter 6 – The Late Blooming Freshman

1 – Knox, W (1951) *Hot Foot.* Unfinished and unpublished autobiography. Complete copy in Orillia Museum of Art and History, Orillia, Ont. p 42.

2 – Ibid. p45.

3 – University of Wisconsin Badgers website. Celebrating UW's African-American Olympians: *George Poage*. Retrieved from http://uwbadgers.com.

4 – Knox, W (c1949) Notes for preparation of autobiography. Orillia Public Library, *Harold Hale Papers Collection*. 1903, p1. This was a typical comment for Walter. He only recorded competing against black athletes a few times but he always included a derogatory comment like this in every account. As much as it is distasteful today, it was typical of the times. Though Walter

was prejudiced against blacks, he does not seem to be any more prejudiced than the culture itself was. He certainly did show an appreciation of a fine athlete, white or black, he just couldn't *lose* to any of them.

5 – Knox, W (1951) *Hot Foot*. Unfinished and unpublished autobiography. Complete copy in Orillia Museum of Art and History, Orillia, Ont. p 48.

6 – Ibid. p48-49.

Chapter 7 – The Adventure Begins

1 – Knox scrapbook of newspaper clippings. Archived at Orillia Museum of Art and History, Orillia, Ontario. p202.

2- Knox, W (1951) *Hot Foot*. Unfinished and unpublished autobiography. Complete copy in Orillia Museum of Art and History, Orillia, Ont. Ch8 p11.

3 – Ibid. p 63. This was a not uncommon scam. Alby Robinson in a newspaper interview in 1936 described using this exact same ploy in the early 1880s.

4 – Knox, W (c1949) Notes for preparation of autobiography. Orillia Public Library, *Harold Hale Papers Collection*. 1903, p2.

5 – Ibid. 1903, p2.

6 – Knox, W (1951) *Hot Foot*. Unfinished and unpublished autobiography. Complete copy in Orillia Museum of Art and History, Orillia, Ont. p69.

7 – Ibid. p73.

Chapter 8 – A New England Adventure

1 – Knox, W (1951) *Hot Foot*. Unfinished and unpublished autobiography. Complete copy in Orillia Museum of Art and History, Orillia, Ont. pp. 73-74.

2 – Ibid. pp. 76-77.

3 – Ibid. pp. 82-83.

Chapter 9 – The Wild and Wooly West

1 – Knox, W (1951) *Hot Foot*. Unfinished and unpublished autobiography. Complete copy in Orillia Museum of Art and History, Orillia, Ont. Ch8, pp. 2-3.

2 – Ibid. Ch8, p11. The mechanics of setting up wagers on matched races was well established after 50 years of professional athletes touring holiday fairs for profit. As Walter found out in BC, having partners who did the actual betting, the negotiations in the saloons, pool halls and barber shops, as well as the collections after the race, made the whole endeavour more lucrative. More bets could be laid, more capital was at hand to do the betting and more muscle could be brought to bear on reluctant losers of those bets. As well, Walter could focus on the task at hand, winning the race.

3 – Ibid. Ch8, p7.

4 – Knox, W (c1949) Notes for preparation of autobiography. Orillia Public Library, *Harold Hale Papers Collection*. 1904, p3.

5 – Knox, W (1951) *Hot Foot*. Unfinished and unpublished autobiography. Complete copy in Orillia Museum of Art and History, Orillia, Ont. Ch8, p7.

6 – Ibid. Ch8, p8.

7 – Knox scrapbook of newspaper clippings. Archived at Orillia Museum of Art and History, Orillia, Ontario. p21. *The Nelson Tribune,* date unknown. The local papers loved to print stories of extravagant betting, which only fanned the flames of the betting crowd. Matched racers always tried to set the date of a match at least a week away to allow the reporters time to whip up interest, both to sell more papers and to boost the profits for the winner. The matched racers and the reporters were symbiotic. This page in Walter's scrapbook has 6 or 7 pre- and post-race reports, all from the local papers.

8 – Ibid. p21. *The Nelson Tribune,* date unknown.

9 – Knox, W (1951) *Hot Foot.* Unfinished and unpublished autobiography. Complete copy in Orillia Museum of Art and History, Orillia, Ont. Ch8, p10. As Walter states it several times in his notes and autobiography, it was not uncommon for shifty supporters of a runner who was likely to lose or who had lost already to accost the stakes holder and steal the money. Being the stakes holder was a dangerous job and Walter reports a few instances in his career when the stakes holder backed out at the last minute, obviously intimidated and fearing for his safety.

10 – Ibid. Ch8, p11.

Chapter 10 – Once More for Harry

1 – Knox, W (1951) *Hot Foot.* Unfinished and unpublished autobiography. Complete copy in Orillia Museum of Art and History, Orillia, Ont. Ch9, p2.

2 – Ibid. Ch9, p4.

3 – Ibid. Ch9, p3.

4 – Knox, W (c1949) Notes for preparation of autobiography. Orillia Public Library, *Harold Hale Papers Collection.* 1905, p1. Cooper had a long and

successful matched racing career, beating several sprinters of reputation. In 1983, he was inducted into the Northwest Ontario Sports Hall of Fame partly on his reputation as having beaten the great Walter Knox. You can read about him on their website: http://www.nwosportshalloffame.com

5 – Knox, W (1951) *Hot Foot*. Unfinished and unpublished autobiography. Complete copy in Orillia Museum of Art and History, Orillia, Ont. Ch9, p8.

Chapter 11 – Barnstorming

1 – Knox, W (1951) *Hot Foot*. Unfinished and unpublished autobiography. Complete copy in Orillia Museum of Art and History, Orillia, Ont. Ch10, p1.

2 – Ibid. Ch10, p1.

3 – Ibid. Ch13, p7.

4 – Ibid. Ch10, p3. It is interesting that in his notes and autobiography, Walter often records his quoted utterings as belligerent and arrogant. In trying to coax out a matched race, this was sometimes obviously an act he put on, trying to create a confrontation. But in a situation such as this with his sponsor, Frank, there was no reason to behave so arrogantly. This is the voice Walter chose to be remembered in, brash, condescending and belligerent, and he used it consistently in all his recollections. Maybe it was pride, or maybe he really was a bit of an SOB.

5 – Ibid. Ch10, p5.

6 – Knox, W (c1949) Notes for preparation of autobiography. Orillia Public Library, *Harold Hale Papers Collection*. 1905, p3.

7 – Knox, W (1951) *Hot Foot*. Unfinished and unpublished autobiography. Complete copy in Orillia Museum of Art and History, Orillia, Ont. Ch 10, p5.

8 – Ibid. Ch10, p7.

9 – Ibid. Ch10 p8-9. Walter often said there was a lot more to winning a matched race than running fast. This is probably the best example of that philosophy.

10 – Ibid. Ch10, p12. Matched racing was a buyer beware world where every detail was negotiated and scrupulously refereed. Here we see how cagey the professional runner had to be to avoid being cheated. Sometimes even the referee was untrustworthy.

11 – Ibid. Ch10, p13. Remember, this race was run in December on the prairies; it was cold and the ground was frozen, making the time all the more remarkable. Baxter, the timer, was a running aficionado with experience handling a stopwatch, but we don't know where he was standing to get an accurate view of the finish. Given that Walter truly ran "all out" in this race to overcome his 9 yard setback, it is possible, though hard to believe, he ran at world record speed, half a second faster than he had ever done in a meet. Whether his time was that fast or not, the fact remains he came back from a 9 yard handicap to beat a strong runner, leaving an enduring impression on Baxter, a man who knew the running world.

Chapter 12 – The Athletic Wars: 1907-1909

1 – Morrow, D. (1986) A Case-Study in Amateur Conflict: The Athletic War in Canada, 1906-08. *British Journal of Sports History*, 3(2), pp. 173-190. p178.

2 – Metcalf, A. (1987) *Canada Learns to Play: The Emergence of Organized Sport, 1807-1914*. Toronto: McClelland Stewart. p103.

3 – Cosentino, F. (1973) *A History of the Concept of Professionalism in Canadian Sport*. Doctoral Dissertation: University of Alberta. CJHSPE 6, no.2 (Dec 1975). p134.

4 – Metcalf, A. (1987) *Canada Learns to Play: The Emergence of Organized Sport, 1807-1914*. Toronto: McClelland Stewart. p118.

5 – Ibid. p118.

6 – Smith, R.A. (1993) History of Amateurism in Men's Intercollegiate Athletics: The Continuance of a 19th-Century Anachronism in America. QUEST, National

Association for Kinesiology and Physical Education in Higher Education journal, 45, pp. 430-447. p433.

7 – Metcalf, A. (1987) *Canada Learns to Play: The Emergence of Organized Sport, 1807-1914*. Toronto: McClelland Stewart. p119.

8 – Ibid.

9 – Cosentino, F. (1998) *Afros, Aboriginals and Amateur Sport in Pre-World War One Canada*. Canadian Historical Society Booklet, Roberto Perin, ed. Ottawa.

10 – Smith, R.A. (1993) History of Amateurism in Men's Intercollegiate Athletics: The Continuance of a 19th-Century Anachronism in America. QUEST, National

Association for Kinesiology and Physical Education in Higher Education journal, 45, pp. 430-447. p435.

11 – Ibid. p435.

12 – Ibid. p435.

13 – Morrow, D. (1986) A Case-Study in Amateur Conflict: The Athletic War in Canada, 1906-08. *British Journal of Sports History*, 3(2), pp. 173-190. p176.

14 – Kidd, B. (1996) *The Struggle For Canadian Sport*. Toronto: U of T Press. p31.

15 – Ibid. p31.

16 – Ibid. p31.

17 – Morrow, D. (1986) A Case-Study in Amateur Conflict: The Athletic War in Canada, 1906-08. *British Journal of Sports History*, 3(2), pp. 173-190. p178.

18 – Ibid. p179.

19 – Ibid. p182.

20 – Howell, C.D. (2001) *Blood, Sweat and Cheers: Sport and the Making of Canada*. Toronto: University of Toronto Press. p64.

21 – Kidd, B. (1996) *The Struggle For Canadian Sport*. Toronto: U of T Press. p59.

Chapter 13 – Amateur Records, Dirty Dealings and Duping the "Coon"

1 – Knox, W (1951) *Hot Foot*. Unfinished and unpublished autobiography. Complete copy in Orillia Museum of Art and History, Orillia, Ont. Ch14, p1.

2 – Knox, W (c1949) Notes for preparation of autobiography. Orillia Public Library, *Harold Hale Papers Collection*. 1906, p1.

3 – Ibid. 1906, p1. Walter was constantly torn between winning a prestigious amateur prize like the Olympics and making money hustling. When push came to shove, he generally chose the money-making venture over the reputation-building venture. It was clear as his career drew to a close that he yearned for the respect the reputation-building events could have given him.

4 – Knox, W (1951) *Hot Foot*. Unfinished and unpublished autobiography. Complete copy in Orillia Museum of Art and History, Orillia, Ont. Ch11, p4.

5 – Knox scrapbook of newspaper clippings. Archived at Orillia Museum of Art and History, Orillia, Ontario. p91.

6 – Ibid. p91. A Nanaimo Paper, June 1906.

7 – Ibid. p91. A Vancouver paper, June 8, 1906.

8 – Town, D. (2008*) Building Character: Stories From Orillia's Remarkable YMCA, 1872-1955*. Self-published by the YMCA of Simcoe-Muskoka, Orillia, Ont. p 32.

9 – Knox, W (c1949) Notes for preparation of autobiography. Orillia Public Library, *Harold Hale Papers Collection*. 1906, p3. This is a very controversial anecdote. A star amateur, an Olympic gold medalist for Canada, was blatantly fixing an amateur race and proposing betting on his races. Both were flagrantly against the amateur rules and ethics, and would result in a lifetime ban if discovered. Bobby Kerr, one of Canada's most respected athletes, was never found out and went on to a successful career as a top

coach in Canada. Walter recorded this episode in three different places in his notes and autobiography, obviously insistent that it happened.

10 – Bouchier, N. (2003) *For the Love of the Game: Amateur Sport in Small Town Ontario, 1838-1893*. Montreal: McGill/Queen's University Press. p64.

11 – Knox, W (c1949) Notes for preparation of autobiography. Orillia Public Library, *Harold Hale Papers Collection*. 1906, p3.

12 – Ibid. 1906, p4

13 – Knox, W (1951) *Hot Foot*. Unfinished and unpublished autobiography. Complete copy in Orillia Museum of Art and History, Orillia, Ont. Ch12, p2.

14 – Ibid. Ch12, p5.

15 – Ibid. Ch12, p7.

16 – Ross, M.G. (1951) *The YMCA in Canada*. Toronto: Ryerson Press. p190.

17 – Knox scrapbook of newspaper clippings. Archived at Orillia Museum of Art and History, Orillia, Ontario. p43 and 45.

18 – Ibid. p41. *Toronto Globe and Mail*, Oct, 1906.

Chapter 14 – Getting In on the Ground Floor

1 – Farmiloe, D. (1994) *The Legend of Jack Munroe*. Windsor: Black Moss Press. p92.

2 – Leacock, S. (1912). *Sunshine Sketches of a Little Town*. McClelland and Stewart. p44.

3 – Farmiloe, D. (1994) *The Legend of Jack Munroe*. Windsor: Black Moss Press. p29.

4 – Ibid. p99.

Chapter 15 – A Magnificent Day... Except for "The Photo"

1 – Knox scrapbook of newspaper clippings. Archived at Orillia Museum of Art and History, Orillia, Ontario. p51.

2 – Ibid. p51.

3 – Ibid. p53.

4 – Knox, W (1951) *Hot Foot*. Unfinished and unpublished autobiography. Complete copy in Orillia Museum of Art and History, Orillia, Ont. Ch14, p6.

5 – Zarnowski, F. (2005) *All Around Men: Heroes of a Forgotten Sport*. Scarecrow Press. p130.

6 – Knox, W (1951) *Hot Foot*. Unfinished and unpublished autobiography. Complete copy in Orillia Museum of Art and History, Orillia, Ont. Ch14, p7.

7 – Ibid. Ch14, p8.

8 – Knox scrapbook of newspaper clippings. Archived at Orillia Museum of Art and History, Orillia, Ontario. p91.

9 – Ibid. p57.

10 – Ibid. p59.

Chapter 16 – A Tour of Michigan

1 – Knox, W (1951) *Hot Foot*. Unfinished and unpublished autobiography. Complete copy in Orillia Museum of Art and History, Orillia, Ont. Ch13, p6-7.

2 – Knox, W (1949). "I Got a Run For My Money". Canadian Sports Hall of Fame Museum, Toronto, Ontario. Paper, 4 pages. Walter, near the end of his life, chose to record this hustling episode in a separate paper, as an example of the risks involved in the hustling world. He makes a point of saying the shopkeeper who tipped him off about the thugs waiting for him at the train station commented, "I've watched you around town and you mind your own business and bet your own money. Most professional footrunners are always trying to get someone else to back them and then throw the race. You're different and I want to help you". In this version, Walter also says just before the start of the 50-yard match race (after the hole digging fracas) that he asked Williamson if he'd "like a little advice about starting? I wouldn't want to take an unfair advantage". He then proceeded to demonstrate his explosive start "with such drive that sparks flew from the rocks as my spikes hit hard." His humbled opponent then confessed "I know you can beat me". The race was over before it started.

3 – Knox scrapbook of newspaper clippings. Archived at Orillia Museum of Art and History, Orillia, Ontario. p63.

4 – Ibid. p63.

5 – Knox scrapbook of newspaper clippings. Archived at Orillia Museum of Art and History, Orillia, Ontario. p65.

6 – Ibid. p63. There are a series of spiteful newspaper articles like this from different towns in his scrapbook, all directing pointed barbs at him. Week after week, it must have been hard on his self-esteem, but Walter trooped on, determined to find a high stakes match race.

7 – Knox, W (c1949) Notes for preparation of autobiography. Orillia Public Library, *Harold Hale Papers Collection*. Johnson, Hahn and Walker Stories, p1. Walter mentions this episode in his autobiography in one line as an aside, after cynically acknowledging it in his notes in one embarrassed sentence. In his scrapbook, he pasted three brief newspaper articles about it (p69). It was controversial, it sullied his friend Hahn's reputation and he did all he could to bury the whole story. Even in his notes it is an afterthought, omitted from the main chronological text and added in an addendum very briefly along with two other stories.

8 – Knox scrapbook of newspaper clippings. Archived at Orillia Museum of Art and History, Orillia, Ontario. p69.

9 – Ibid. p69. Marsh published Walter's letter but included his threat.

10 – Knox, W (c1949) Notes for preparation of autobiography. Orillia Public Library, *Harold Hale Papers Collection*. Johnson, Hahn and Walker Stories, p1.

11 – Knox scrapbook of newspaper clippings. Archived at Orillia Museum of Art and History, Orillia, Ontario. p71.

12 – Knox, W (1951) *Hot Foot*. Unfinished and unpublished autobiography. Complete copy in Orillia Museum of Art and History, Orillia, Ont. Ch13, p7.

13 – Ibid. Ch13, p9.

14 – Ibid. Ch13, p12.

Chapter 17 – Inner Turmoil

1 – Knox, W (1951) *Hot Foot*. Unfinished and unpublished autobiography. Complete copy in Orillia Museum of Art and History, Orillia, Ont. Ch15, p153. "They took me to the high mountain to show me the valley of good fortune that swept in all directions…" Walter wrote. He also commented the AAFC was "a motley organization".

2 – Knox scrapbook of newspaper clippings. Archived at Orillia Museum of Art and History, Orillia, Ontario. p61. Likely the *Toronto Star*.

3 – Ibid. p61.

4 – Ibid. p63.

5 – Ibid. p61.

6 – Ibid. p61.

7 – Ibid. p73.

8 – Knox, W (1951) *Hot Foot*. Unfinished and unpublished autobiography. Complete copy in Orillia Museum of Art and History, Orillia, Ont. Ch15, p153.

9 – Ibid. Ch15, p156.

10 – Ibid. Ch15, p161.

11 – Knox scrapbook of newspaper clippings. Archived at Orillia Museum of Art and History, Orillia, Ontario. p79.

12 – Knox, W (1951) *Hot Foot*. Unfinished and unpublished autobiography. Complete copy in Orillia Museum of Art and History, Orillia, Ont. Ch15, p161.

13 – Knox, W (c1949) Notes for preparation of autobiography. Orillia Public Library, *Harold Hale Papers Collection*. "Johnson, Hahn and Walker Stories", 2 pages. p2.

14 – Knox scrapbook of newspaper clippings. Archived at Orillia Museum of Art and History, Orillia, Ontario. p73.

Chapter 18 – California Here I Come

1 – Knox, W (1951) *Hot Foot*. Unfinished and unpublished autobiography. Complete copy in Orillia Museum of Art and History, Orillia, Ont. p171.

2 – Knox scrapbook of newspaper clippings. Archived at Orillia Museum of Art and History, Orillia, Ontario. p73.

3 – Ibid. p17. It was as outlandish then as it would be today for one athlete to set world records in both the sprint and the shot put. The physique and the skill sets are completely different in those two events. Walter had broken a pole vault world record too, another completely different endeavour. There have been few, if any, athletes as versatile and accomplished as Walter Knox.

4 – Knox, W (1951) *Hot Foot*. Unfinished and unpublished autobiography. Complete copy in Orillia Museum of Art and History, Orillia, Ont. p171.

5 – Ibid. p167.

6 – Ibid. p170.

7 – Knox, W (c1949) Notes for preparation of autobiography. Orillia Public Library, *Harold Hale Papers Collection*. "Johnson, Hahn and Walker Stories", 2 pages. p2.

8 – Knox, W (1951) *Hot Foot*. Unfinished and unpublished autobiography. Complete copy in Orillia Museum of Art and History, Orillia, Ont. p171.

9 – Ibid. p172.

10 – Ibid. p173.

11 – Ibid. p175.

12 – Ibid. p176.

13 – Knox, W (c1949) Notes for preparation of autobiography. Orillia Public Library, *Harold Hale Papers Collection*. 1909, p3.

Chapter 19 - Prospecting

1 – Knox, W (1951) *Hot Foot*. Unfinished and unpublished autobiography. Complete copy in Orillia Museum of Art and History, Orillia, Ont. p177. As Walter often said, they both had a bad case of "gold fever"; the excitement of striking it rich could come with each shovel full of dirt or chipped rock. Men were getting rich all around them, it seemed like only a matter of time before they would strike the mother lode.

2 – Farmiloe, D. (1994) *The Legend of Jack Munroe*. Windsor: Black Moss Press. p42. Munroe even starred in a movie called *The Road To Ruin* to cash in on his celebrity.

3 – Knox, W (1951) *Hot Foot*. Unfinished and unpublished autobiography. Complete copy in Orillia Museum of Art and History, Orillia, Ont. p179.

4 – Ibid. p182.

5 – Knox, W (c1949) Notes for preparation of autobiography. Orillia Public Library, *Harold Hale Papers Collection*. 1910, p4.

Chapter 20 – A Working Professional

1 – Webster, D. (1973) *Scottish Highland Games*. Edinburgh, Scotland: MacDonald Printers. p22.

2 – Ibid. p109.

3 – Ibid. p18.

4 – Ibid. p118.

5 – Knox scrapbook of newspaper clippings. Archived at Orillia Museum of Art and History, Orillia, Ontario. p107.

6 – Ibid. p107.

7 – Ibid. p99.

8 – Ibid. p135.

9 – Ibid. p103.

10 – Ibid. p99.

11 – Ibid. p111.

12 – Knox, W (1951) *Hot Foot*. Unfinished and unpublished autobiography. Complete copy in Orillia Museum of Art and History, Orillia, Ont. p194.

13 – Knox scrapbook of newspaper clippings. Archived at Orillia Museum of Art and History, Orillia, Ontario. p116.

14 – Ibid. p117.

15 – Ibid. p111.

16 – Ibid. p103.

17 – Ibid. p116.

18 – Knox, W (1951) *Hot Foot*. Unfinished and unpublished autobiography. Complete copy in Orillia Museum of Art and History, Orillia, Ont. p197.

Chapter 21 – Olympic Coaching Controversy

1 – Knox scrapbook of newspaper clippings. Archived at Orillia Museum of Art and History, Orillia, Ontario. p120.

2 – Ibid. p166.

3 – Knox, W (c1949) Notes for preparation of autobiography. Orillia Public Library, *Harold Hale Papers Collection*. 1912, p1.

4 – Knox scrapbook of newspaper clippings. Archived at Orillia Museum of Art and History, Orillia, Ontario. p120.

5 – Ibid. p120.

6 – *Manitoba Free Press*, June 3, 1912.

7 – *Manitoba Free Press*, June 10, 1912.

8 – Knox, W (c1949) Notes for preparation of autobiography. Orillia Public Library, *Harold Hale Papers Collection*. 1912, p1.

9 – Ibid. 1912, p1.

10 – Ibid. 1912, p1.

11 – Knox scrapbook of newspaper clippings. Archived at Orillia Museum of Art and History, Orillia, Ontario. p121.

12 – Knox, W (c1949) Notes for preparation of autobiography. Orillia Public Library, *Harold Hale Papers Collection*. 1912, p1.

13 – Knox scrapbook of newspaper clippings. Archived at Orillia Museum of Art and History, Orillia, Ontario. p121.

14 – Ibid. p169.

15 – Ibid. p121.

16 – *Manitoba Free Press*, June 10, 1912.

17 – Ibid, June 14, 1912.

18 – Knox scrapbook of newspaper clippings. Archived at Orillia Museum of Art and History, Orillia, Ontario. p121.

19 – *Vancouver Sun*, April 24, 2010.

20 – Ibid. April 24, 2012.

21 – Black History Canada website. *Timeline 1900-Present*. Retrieved from http:// blackhistorycanada.ca.

22 – *Vancouver Sun*, April 24, 2012.

23 – Ibid. April 24, 2012.

24 – *Manitoba Free Press*, June 27, 1912.

25 – Ibid. August 5, 1912.

26 – Knox, W (c1949) Notes for preparation of autobiography. Orillia Public Library, *Harold Hale Papers Collection*. 1912, p1.

27 – Ibid. 1912, p2.

28 – *Manitoba Free Press*, August 24, 1912.

29 – Knox scrapbook of newspaper clippings. Archived at Orillia Museum of Art and History, Orillia, Ontario. p171.

30 – Knox, W (c1949) Notes for preparation of autobiography. Orillia Public Library, *Harold Hale Papers Collection*. 1912, p2.

31 – Ibid, 1912, p2.

32 – Knox scrapbook of newspaper clippings. Archived at Orillia Museum of Art and History, Orillia, Ontario. p171.

33 – *Manitoba Free Press*, August 6, 1912.

34 – Ibid. August 6, 1912.

35 – Knox scrapbook of newspaper clippings. Archived at Orillia Museum of Art and History, Orillia, Ontario. p171.

36 – *Manitoba Free Press*, August 24, 1912.

37 – Ibid. August 6, 1912.

38 – Ibid. August 6, 1912.

39 – Ibid. August 8, 1912.

22 – The Stockholm Olympic Games

1 – Ibid. July 6, 1912.

2 – Ibid. August 5, 1912.

3 – Knox scrapbook of newspaper clippings. Archived at Orillia Museum of Art and History, Orillia, Ontario. p116.

4 – Ibid. p139.

5 – Ibid. p131.

6 – Knox, W (c1949) Notes for preparation of autobiography. Orillia Public Library, *Harold Hale Papers Collection*. 1912, p2.

7 – Knox scrapbook of newspaper clippings. Archived at Orillia Museum of Art and History, Orillia, Ontario. p121.

8 – Ibid. p123. What an ironic comment. Merrick went gallivanting off in London, checking in with the team infrequently during the whole two week fracas of training camp. He had to know how Walter was losing control of the team and chose to continue his holiday, even missing the first two days of the Olympics.

9 – Paton, G.A. (2006) James GB Merrick (1871-1946): Sports Organizer, Negotiator, Canada's Second IOC Member. In *Cultural Imperialism in Action, Critiques in the Global Olympic Trust*, 8th International Symposium for Olympic Research. University of Western Ontario, London, Canada. p206.

10 – *Manitoba Free Press*, August 8, 1912.

11 – Ibid. August 6, 1912.

12 – Knox scrapbook of newspaper clippings. Archived at Orillia Museum of Art and History, Orillia, Ontario. p171.

13 – Ibid. p123.

14 – Ibid. p123.

15 – Ibid. p125.

16 – Ibid. p171.

17 – *Manitoba Free Press*, August 24, 1912.

Chapter 23 – Scottish Tours and Disappointments

1 – Knox, W (c1949) Notes for preparation of autobiography. Orillia Public Library, *Harold Hale Papers Collection*. 1912, p3. Forty years later, in recalling this episode, Walter said he remembered being "boiling mad". This episode stood out in his memory above all else. That's pretty remarkable, given the experiences he had.

2–Knox scrapbook of newspaper clippings. Archived at Orillia Museum of Art and History, Orillia, Ontario. p133.

3 – Ibid. p149.

4 – Ibid. p155.

5 – *Toronto Star*, April 4, 1913.

6 – Musil, Robert, *Der Mann ohne Eigenschaften: Roman*. Neu durchgesehene und verb. Aufl. ed. Reinbek bei Hamburg: Rowohlt, 1981. Quoted in Blom, P. (2008) *The Vertigo Years. Change and Culture in the West, 1900-1914*. McClelland and Stewart Ltd., Toronto, Ontario. p 34.

7 – *Toronto Star*, June 11, 1913.

8 – *Toronto Star*, June 11, 1913.

9 – *Toronto Star*, June 18, 1913.

10 – Knox, W (c1949) Notes for preparation of autobiography. Orillia Public Library, *Harold Hale Papers Collection*. 1913, p1.

11 – Knox scrapbook of newspaper clippings. Archived at Orillia Museum of Art and History, Orillia, Ontario. p169.

12- *Orillia Newsletter*, July 2, 1913.

13 – Knox scrapbook of newspaper clippings. Archived at Orillia Museum of Art and History, Orillia, Ontario. p227.

14 – Ibid. p160.

15 – *Orillia Newsletter*, July 2, 1913.

16 – Knox scrapbook of newspaper clippings. Archived at Orillia Museum of Art and History, Orillia, Ontario. p57.

17 – Ibid. p155.

18 – Elfers, J.E. (2003) *The Tour To End All Tours. The Story of Major League Baseball's 1913-1914 World Tour.* University of Nebraska Press, Lincoln and London.

19 – Knox scrapbook of newspaper clippings. Archived at Orillia Museum of Art and History, Orillia, Ontario. p175.

20 – Ibid. p156.

21 – Ibid. p153.

22 – Ibid. p119.

23 – Ibid. p173.

24 – Ibid. p182.

25 – Ibid. p187.

26 – Ibid. p172.

27 – Ibid. p172.

28 – Knox, W (c1949) Notes for preparation of autobiography. Orillia Public Library, *Harold Hale Papers Collection*. 1913, p1.

29 – Knox scrapbook of newspaper clippings. Archived at Orillia Museum of Art and History, Orillia, Ontario. p180.

30 – Webster, D. (1973) *Scottish Highland Games*. Edinburgh, Scotland: MacDonald Printers. p12.

31 – Knox, W (c1949) Notes for preparation of autobiography. Orillia Public Library, *Harold Hale Papers Collection*. 1913, p2.

32 – Knox scrapbook of newspaper clippings. Archived at Orillia Museum of Art and History, Orillia, Ontario. p213.

33 – Ibid. p169.

34 – Knox, W (c1949) Notes for preparation of autobiography. Orillia Public Library, *Harold Hale Papers Collection*. 1914, p1.

35 – Ibid. 1914, p1.

36 – Ibid. 1914, p1. Walter never commented on how his backers took the news that he was withdrawing. They had supported him for two months and had laid money down on him to win. It was a total loss for them.

Chapter 24 – Finally, Respect and a Legacy

1 – Knox scrapbook of newspaper clippings. Archived at Orillia Museum of Art and History, Orillia, Ontario. p174.

2 – Ibid. p175.

3 – Ibid. p175.

4 – Lovesey, P. (2002) Conan Doyle and the Olympics. *Journal of Olympic History*, vol 10(1), pp. 6-9. p8.

5 – *Manitoba Free Press*, Sept 5, 1914.

6 – Knox scrapbook of newspaper clippings. Archived at Orillia Museum of Art and History, Orillia, Ontario. p174.

7 – *Manitoba Free Press*, Sept 5, 1914.

8 – Knox scrapbook of newspaper clippings. Archived at Orillia Museum of Art and History, Orillia, Ontario. p175.

9 – *Manitoba Free Press*, Sept 5, 1914.

10 – Knox scrapbook of newspaper clippings. Archived at Orillia Museum of Art and History, Orillia, Ontario. p175.

11 – *Manitoba Free Press*, Sept 5, 1914.

12 – *Manitoba Free Press*, Sept. 5, 1914.

13 – Knox scrapbook of newspaper clippings. Archived at Orillia Museum of Art and History, Orillia, Ontario. p175.

14 – Knox, W (c1949) Notes for preparation of autobiography. Orillia Public Library, *Harold Hale Papers Collection*. 1914, p2.

15 – Lovesey, P. (2002) Conan Doyle and the Olympics. *Journal of Olympic History*, vol 10(1), pp. 6-9. p7.

16 – Knox scrapbook of newspaper clippings. Archived at Orillia Museum of Art and History, Orillia, Ontario. p174.

17 – *Manitoba Free Press*, Sept. 5, 1914.

18 – Knox, W (c1949) Notes for preparation of autobiography. Orillia Public Library, *Harold Hale Papers Collection*. 1914, p2.

Chapter 25 – New Directions
1 – *Health and Strength*, Jan 16, 1915.

2 – Knox scrapbook of newspaper clippings. Archived at Orillia Museum of Art and History, Orillia, Ontario. p179. In his notes, Walter doesn't even mention this episode in his life. Obviously it was a career move he was happy to forget.

3 – Ibid. p179.

4 – Ibid. p232.

5 – Ibid. p177.

6 – Ibid. p177.

7 – Ibid. p179.

8 – Ibid. p179.

9 – *Orillia Newsletter*, March 7, 1951

10 – Knox scrapbook of newspaper clippings. Archived at Orillia Museum of Art and History, Orillia, Ontario. p221.

11 – Ibid. p208.

Chapter 26 – Another Tour of Olympic Duty
1 - Knox scrapbook of newspaper clippings. Archived at Orillia Museum of Art and History, Orillia, Ontario. p213.
2 – Ibid. p189.
3 – Paton, G.A. (2006) James GB Merrick (1871-1946): Sports Organizer, Negotiator, Canada's Second IOC Member. In *Cultural Imperialism in*

Action, Critiques in the Global Olympic Trust, 8th International Symposium for Olympic Research. University of Western Ontario, London, Canada.

4 – Ibid.

5 – Knox scrapbook of newspaper clippings. Archived at Orillia Museum of Art and History, Orillia, Ontario. p205.

6 – Ibid. p207.

7 – Ibid. p188.

8 – Ibid. p188.

9 – Ibid. p203.

10 – Ibid. p188.

11 – Ibid. p207.

12 – Ibid. p200.

13 – Ibid. p194.

14 – Ibid. p197.

15 – Knox, W (c1949) Notes for preparation of autobiography. Orillia Public Library, *Harold Hale Papers Collection*. 1920, p2.

16 – Knox scrapbook of newspaper clippings. Archived at Orillia Museum of Art and History, Orillia, Ontario. p193.

17 – Ibid. p201.

18 – Ibid. p191.

19 – Ibid. p201.

20 – *Calgary Herald*, Apr 26, 1920.

21. Knox scrapbook of newspaper clippings. Archived at Orillia Museum of Art and History, Orillia, Ontario. p197.

22 – Canadian Sports Hall of Fame website. *Tommy Thompson*. Retrieved from http://sportshall.ca

23 – Knox scrapbook of newspaper clippings. Archived at Orillia Museum of Art and History, Orillia, Ontario. p203.

24 – Ibid. p202.

25 – Ibid. p202.

26 – Ibid. p202.

27 – Ibid. p202.

28 – Ibid. p203, and Town, D. (2008*) Building Character: Stories From Orillia's Remarkable* YMCA*, 1872-1955*. Self-published by the YMCA of Simcoe-Muskoka, Orillia, Ont. p40. In 1911, Boyle won three gold medals at the Canadian Junior Championships and later was inducted into the Northwest Ontario Sports Hall of Fame for his efforts in developing the minor hockey program in Port Arthur (Thunder Bay).

29 – Knox scrapbook of newspaper clippings. Archived at Orillia Museum of Art and History, Orillia, Ontario. p203.

30 – Ibid. p206.

31 – Ibid. p207.

32 – Ibid. p207.

33 – Ibid. p207.

34 – Ibid. p207.

35 – Knox, W (c1949) Notes for preparation of autobiography. Orillia Public Library, *Harold Hale Papers Collection*. 1920, p2.

36 – Knox scrapbook of newspaper clippings. Archived at Orillia Museum of Art and History, Orillia, Ontario. p205.

27 –The Antwerp Olympic Games
1 – Ibid. p207.

2 – Ibid. p206.

3 – Ibid. p205.

4- Ibid. p195.

5 – Ibid. p203.

6 – Ibid. p206.

7 – Ibid. p206.

8 – Ibid. p207.

9 – Ibid. p206.

10 – Ibid. p203.

11 – Knox, W (c1949) Notes for preparation of autobiography. Orillia Public Library, *Harold Hale Papers Collection*. 1920, p2.

12 – Knox scrapbook of newspaper clippings. Archived at Orillia Museum of Art and History, Orillia, Ontario. p207.

13 – Knox, W (c1949) Notes for preparation of autobiography. Orillia Public Library, *Harold Hale Papers Collection*. 1920, p2.

14 – Knox scrapbook of newspaper clippings. Archived at Orillia Museum of Art and History, Orillia, Ontario. p207.

15 – Ibid. p206.

16 – Ibid. p206.

17 – Ibid. p206.

18 – Ibid. p206.

19 – Ibid. p245.

20 – Paton, G.A. (2006) James GB Merrick (1871-1946): Sports Organizer, Negotiator, Canada's Second IOC Member. In *Cultural Imperialism in Action, Critiques in the Global Olympic Trust*, 8th International Symposium for Olympic Research. University of Western Ontario, London, Canada.

Chapter 28 – Putting Ontario on the Right Track

1 – Knox scrapbook of newspaper clippings. Archived at Orillia Museum of Art and History, Orillia, Ontario. p207.

2 – Ibid. p207.

3 – *Toronto Star*, Nov 21, 1921

4 – Kidd, B. (1996) *The Struggle For Canadian Sport*. Toronto: U of T Press. p107.

5 – Ibid. p110.

6 – Knox scrapbook of newspaper clippings. Archived at Orillia Museum of Art and History, Orillia, Ontario. p228.

7 – Kidd, B. (1996) *The Struggle For Canadian Sport*. Toronto: U of T Press. p111.

8 – Skeaff, B. (1978) *The Complete Centennial History of Orillia and District Collegiate Institute After 100 Years On "The Finest Position in the Dominion."* Self-published by ODCVI high school, Orillia, Ont.

9 – Knox scrapbook of newspaper clippings. Archived at Orillia Museum of Art and History, Orillia, Ontario. p215.

10 – Ibid. p228.

11 – Ibid. p209.

12 – Ibid. p214.

13 – Ibid. p207.

14 – *Montreal Gazette*, Oct 22, 1920.

15 – Ibid. p212.

16 – Ibid. p214.

17 – Kidd, B. (1996) *The Struggle For Canadian Sport*. Toronto: U of T Press. p112.

18 – Knox scrapbook of newspaper clippings. Archived at Orillia Museum of Art and History, Orillia, Ontario. p222.

19 – Ibid. p210.

20 – Ibid. p214.

21 – Ibid. p214.

22 – Ibid. p216.

23 – Ibid. p216.

24 – Ibid. p228.

25 – Ibid. p216.

26 – Ibid. p216.

27 – Ibid. p220.

28 – Ibid. p219.

29 – Ibid. p210.

30 – Kidd, B. (1996) *The Struggle For Canadian Sport.* Toronto: U of T Press. p113.

31 – Ibid. p215.

32 – Ibid. p215.

33 – Orillia Collegiate Institute. (1925) *The OrCollegist.* Orillia: Calvert and Maynard. Vol #1, #1. Orillia Museum of Art and History, Orillia. pp. 35-41.

34 – Knox scrapbook of newspaper clippings. Archived at Orillia Museum of Art and History, Orillia, Ontario. p217.

35 – Ibid. p228. Walter certainly did walk the walk of amateurism now. He commented in the paper once that on a visit to the Picton fair in the mid-20's he found a tent where "frame-up wrestling matches" were being staged, the fake, costumed shows that had become so popular but were the antithesis of everything the OAC stood for. Walter marched in and, under the authority of the OAC, which he said he represented, shut the whole affair down.

36 – Ibid. p209.

37 – Ibid. p209.

38 – Ibid. p209.

39 – Ibid. p220.

40 – Ibid. p220.

41 – Ibid. p220.

42 – Ibid. p221.

43 – Ibid. p228.

44 – Ibid. p244.

Chapter 29 – Developing Olympic Champions

1 – Knox scrapbook of newspaper clippings. Archived at Orillia Museum of Art and History, Orillia, Ontario. p219.

2 – Ibid. p224.

3 – Ibid. p216.

4 – Ibid. p223.

5 – Ibid. p224.

6 – Kidd, B. (1995) Making the Pros Pay for Amateur Sport: The Ontario Athletic Commission 1920-47. *Ontario History*, 87(2): 105-27. p113.

7 – Ibid. p113.

8 – Knox scrapbook of newspaper clippings. Archived at Orillia Museum of Art and History, Orillia, Ontario. p224.

9 – Ibid. p224.

10 – Kidd, B. (1995) Making the Pros Pay for Amateur Sport: The Ontario Athletic Commission 1920-47. *Ontario History*, 87(2): 105-27. p116.

11 – Ibid. p116.

12 – Hall, A. (1999) Creators of the Lost and Perfect Game? Gender, History and Canadian Sport. In White, P. and Young, K., eds, *Sport and Gender in Canada*, pp. 5-23. Don Mills: Oxford University Press. p16.

13 – Hall, A. (2002) *The Girl and the Game — A History of Women's Sport in Canada*. Toronto: Broadview Press.

14 – Knox scrapbook of newspaper clippings. Archived at Orillia Museum of Art and History, Orillia, Ontario. p218.

15 – Ibid. p229. Walter never commented on how much he was paid to coach at these private clubs.

16 – Ibid. p229.

17 – Ibid. p229.

18 – Ibid. p218.

19 – Ibid. p218.

20 – Ibid. p224.

21 – Ibid. p229.

22 – Kidd, B. (1995) Making the Pros Pay for Amateur Sport: The Ontario Athletic Commission 1920-47. *Ontario History*, 87(2): 105-27. p113.

23 – Knox scrapbook of newspaper clippings. Archived at Orillia Museum of Art and History, Orillia, Ontario. p214.

24 – Ibid. p227.

25 – Kidd, B. (1995) Making the Pros Pay for Amateur Sport: The Ontario Athletic Commission 1920-47. *Ontario History*, 87(2): 105-27. p116.

26 – Knox scrapbook of newspaper clippings. Archived at Orillia Museum of Art and History, Orillia, Ontario. p209.

27 – Ibid. p209.

28 – Ibid. p209.

29 – Kidd, B. (1995) Making the Pros Pay for Amateur Sport: The Ontario Athletic Commission 1920-47. *Ontario History*, 87(2): 105-27. p116.

30 – Ibid. p116.

31 – Ibid. p116.

32 – Ibid. p116.

Chapter 30 – Some Final Flings Before Retirement

1 – Knox scrapbook of newspaper clippings. Archived at Orillia Museum of Art and History, Orillia, Ontario. p230.

2 – Ibid. p218.

3 – Ibid. p230.

4 – Ibid. p231.

5 – Ibid. p231.

6 – Ibid. p230.

7 – Ibid. p239. The appeal of this position for Walter was that it allowed him to spend three weeks in the fall with Mary at their cottage in nearby Wellington. By 1930, Walter was finally paying attention to his new wife, finding ways to spend more time with her. Of course, there had to be some sporting angle too, so this coaching position was perfect.

8 – Ibid. p230.

9 – Ibid. p232.

10 – Ibid. p231.

11 – Ibid. p233. She lived in Uhthoff.

12 – Ibid. p234. In the now famous story, the champions of Canada, the US, Ireland and England were entered in that 1885 Canadian Championship. With the four top shot putters in the world competing, it was deemed the contest for the world championship. The rural 20 year old from the backwater of Coldwater, Ontario who showed up without a proper entry form, was allowed to compete only after the American champion, Flanigan, goaded the officials to "let the boy have a throw". Gray was not that big, under 190 pounds, but was athletic, soon to be the runner-up at the North American All-around Championship. He was the first to put the shot with his whole body, not just his arm, using the science of mechanics to his advantage. Over the next 17 years, he freely explained his technique to any and all of his competitors (including the young Walter Knox) but still beat them all. He was a superb athlete. Later he became a leading lumber man in northern Ontario, taking over the family business.

13 – Ibid. p233.

14 – Ibid. p235.

15 – Ibid. p240.

16 – Ibid. p242.

17 – Ibid. p242.

18 – Ibid. p242.

19 – Ibid. p247.

20 – Ibid. p243.

21 – Ibid. p232.

22 – Frost, W.S. (1934) A Century of Sport. In *Orillia Annual Week of Sport* booklet, French, F. ed, Orillia YMCA Archives. pp. 9-54.

23 – Orillia Public Library Orilliana collection newspaper clipping, likely the *Orillia Packet*, 1947.

24 – Knox, W Letter to Fred Town of Orillia, June 10, 1942. Personal Collection. Nineteen year old Fred Town had just beaten Walter's Orillia YMCA record of 48 feet in the 12 lb. shot put, with a heave of 50 feet, one inch. Walter wrote to congratulate him and sent him one of his medals as a souvenir (his silver in the shot put at the 1903 Conference Championship meet where he represented the University of Illinois, and where he had a badly sprained ankle, causing his loss to Archie Hahn in the sprint).

25 – Knox scrapbook of newspaper clippings. Archived at Orillia Museum of Art and History, Orillia, Ontario. p246.

26 – Ibid. p247.

27 – Ibid. p245.

28 – Ibid. p241.

29 – Ibid. p241.

30 – Ibid. p247.

31 – Ibid. p235.

32 – Ibid. p232.

33 – Feb 11, 1949, St Petersburg, Florida newspaper clipping, found in Orillia Museum of Art and History, Knox file.

34 – Knox scrapbook of newspaper clippings. Archived at Orillia Museum of Art and History, Orillia, Ontario. p245.

35 – *Hamilton Spectator*, Jan 21, 1939.

36 – Knox scrapbook of newspaper clippings. Archived at Orillia Museum of Art and History, Orillia, Ontario. p246.

37 – Ibid. p246.

38 – Ibid. p246.

39 – Ibid. p247.

40 – *Orillia Newsletter*, March 7, 1951.

41 – Town, D. (2008) *Building Character: Stories From Orillia's Remarkable YMCA, 1872-1955*. Self-published by the YMCA of Simcoe-Muskoka in Orillia, Ontario. p134.

Chapter 31 – Epilogue
1 – *Orillia Newsletter*, Sept 20, 1950.

2 – Newspaper clipping found in the Orillia Museum of Art and History, Knox file.

3 – *Toronto Star*, March 5, 1951.

Appendix 1: Walter Knox's personal best performances
1 – Knox, W (1951) *Hot Foot*. Unfinished and unpublished autobiography. Complete copy in Orillia Museum of Art and History, Orillia, Ont. p1.

Acknowledgements

There are many people I must acknowledge who assisted me with this book. First, I'll mention the organizations.

This whole project started at the Orillia Public Library, specifically the crowded, bursting-at-the-seams Orilliana Room in the old Carnegie building (which has since been replaced with a state-of-the-art room in the glorious new city library). Kelli Absalon, the Director of Reference Services, and her crack staff, allowed and assisted me in rifling through all the historical materials the library stores on behalf of the city of Orillia. That's where I found, buried in the Harold Hale papers, Walter's notes on his life. From that teaser, they directed me to any and all related materials they had. I became a familiar face in the library and could not have completed this book without their expert services.

My search continued and struck gold at the Orillia Museum of Art and History. First Marcel Rousseau, the diligent volunteer who knows everything about Orillia's history, spent many hours with me investigating the Knox file there and generously scanned all their photos for my use. The collections staff, now led by Sheena Westcott Sykes, introduced me to the Walter Knox scrapbook, which contained over one thousand newspaper clippings Walter had collected over his lifetime. You can imagine my expression when I first laid eyes on that! Marcel photocopied the whole book and gave me a copy. Then they gave me my own photocopy of the Walter Knox draft biography written in 1951 but never published. These two sources were the roadmap for my book. The staff and volunteers at OMAH have been patient and thorough in their support of my project, which never could have been done without them.

The staff at the Canadian Sports Hall of Fame also generously supplied me with critical materials. Before I knew there was a complete copy of Walter's biography at OMAH, I found the CSHF had six of the chapters and several other Knox recollections in their collection. The staff promptly scanned and emailed all of it to me. They also provided images for this book.

From there, my search became more academic and elusive as I educated myself on Canadian sports history, the history of gambling, the Highland Games tradition, the mining boom in northern Ontario and more. The staffs at several additional libraries were very helpful. First, the Lakehead University Orillia campus librarians helped me navigate the academic literature, sending many journal articles down from the Thunder Bay campus for me. We are most fortunate to have access to their collection in our small city. My brief visit to Elk Lake (on my way to a canoe trip) proved worthwhile in supplying me with materials from the Elk Lake library. I have to thank my daughter Jaina and her two friends, Kaitlin and Jessie, who patiently slept in the car (and then endured my regaling them with Walter Knox stories for half an hour) while I excitedly ran into the library. Finally, I have to thank Gail Priddice at the Inverness, Scotland library for generously scanning and emailing me several pages from David Webster's new book, *World History of the Highland Games*, that was not available in North America.

The Woodstock Genealogical Society provided me with a key document. They were able to hunt down the 1936 newspaper interview of Alby Robinson, the professional runner in the generation before Walter. This was the only other extended description of the life of the professional I found.

One final institutional source was the Orillia YMCA. I am the curator of their historical collection so I knew exactly what they had. The Y was the center of sports in Orillia in Walter's day and after he died someone donated a beautiful glassed case with all Walter's medals mounted for display, the Y being the obvious place to display them. It hasn't hung on the wall for over 20 years now and I'm probably the only person who knows it exists, but I'll change that when this book comes out. The Y archives have many diverse pieces of information that were very helpful to my research, most importantly a copy of the Orillia Week of Sport program with a three page biography of Walter. I thank the Y for going to the trouble to archive their historical artifacts.

There are also a number of people I need to thank. Foremost is Claudia Courtney, Walter's great-niece. She is the last member of Walter's extended family living in Orillia. Claudia graciously invited me into her home and granted me an interview. I gleaned much important background information from her. It was Claudia who donated Walter's scrapbook and the full copy of his biography to the Orillia Museum of Art and History just after I had started this project. I have to commend her on her timing. I am happy to know this important piece of Canadian history is in the hands of professional curators. Claudia also provided the majority of the photos for this book, either by donating them to OMAH or allowing me to copy them after our interview.

Two professional historians gave up many hours of their time to read my draft manuscript and assure me that I was making no grave errors in history. Bruce Kidd of the University of Toronto is the only historian I found who had done any primary research on Walter Knox, a 20 page paper on the Ontario Athletic Commission. I was very happy he consented to read my manuscript and offer his comments. At the same time, Todd Stubbs of Lakehead University also agreed to go over my manuscript in detail. Both very busy historians came back with positive comments and encouraged me. I thank them both; their input was greatly appreciated and reassuring.

My first proofreader was my mother, Mary Town. She was my valuable research assistant on my first book, *Building Character: Stories from Orillia's Remarkable* YMCA, *1872-1955*. She corrected a myriad of spelling and grammatical errors for me.

I cannot thank enough my editor, Sara Davison, at Cutting Edge Editing Services in Orillia, who made this book what it is. Her knowledgeable copy edit not only corrected uncounted grammatical errors and many examples of weak writing, but she helped me re-organize the information in the book, making it flow better. My book is significantly better thanks to her hours of toil on what she called "the big book".

My wife, Leslie, is responsible for the photos in this book. As she is a professional photographer (of horses mostly) I naturally dumped all my roughly scanned photos (many of 100 year old newspaper clippings, no less) on her lap to be cleaned up for publication. After working on a computer all day, I know how tiring it was for her to sit down again at night to do this for me. Thank you.

Finally, my daughter Keltie is the graphic designer responsible for the cover art. She was able to change my preconceived ideas and found a better way to present the book.

Bibliography

Black History Canada website. *Timeline 1900-Present*. Retrieved from http://blackhistorycanada.ca.

Blom, P. (2008) *The Vertigo Years. Change and Culture in the West, 1900-1914.* McClelland and Stewart Ltd., Toronto, Ontario.

Bouchier, N. (2003) *For the Love of the Game: Amateur Sport in Small Town Ontario,1838-1893.* Montreal: McGill/Queen's University Press.

Canadian Sports Hall of Fame website. *Walter Knox*. Retrieved from http://sportshall.ca.

Cosentino, F. (1973) *A History of the Concept of Professionalism in Canadian Sport.* Doctoral Dissertation: University of Alberta. CJHSPE 6, no.2 (Dec 1975) pp. 75-81.

Cosentino, F. (1998) *Afros, Aboriginals and Amateur Sport in Pre-World War One Canada.* Canadian Historical Society Booklet, Roberto Perin, ed. Ottawa.

Craig, J. (1977) *Simcoe County: The Recent Past.* Canada: The Bryant Press.

Elfers, JE. (2003) *The Tour To End All Tours. The Story of Major League Baseball's 1913-1914 World Tour.* University of Nebraska Press, Lincoln and London.

Evensen, B.J. (1993) Jazz Age Journalism's Battle Over Professionalism, Circulation and the Sports Page. *Journal of Sports History*, 20(3), pp. 229-247.

Farmiloe, D. (1994) *The Legend of Jack Munroe*. Windsor: Black Moss Press.

Frost, W.S. (1934) A Century of Sport. In *Orillia Annual Week of Sport* booklet, French, F. ed, Orillia YMCA Archives. pp. 9-54.

Gillespie, G. (2000) Roderick McClennan, Professionalism and the Emergence of the Athlete in Caledonian Games. *Sport History Review*, 31, pp. 43-63.

Hall, A. (1999) Creators of the Lost and Perfect Game? Gender, History and Canadian Sport. In White, P. and Young, K., eds, *Sport and Gender in Canada*, pp. 5-23. Don Mills: Oxford University Press.

Hall, A. (2002) *The Girl and the Game — A History of Women's Sport in Canada*. Toronto: Broadview Press.

Howell, C.D. (2001) *Blood, Sweat and Cheers: Sport and the Making of Canada*. Toronto: University of Toronto Press.

Hughes, Lorrie. (2005) *Elk Lake and Back: The Guts and Glory*. Published by Township of James, District of Temiskaming, Ontario.

Hurst, A.M. (1947) *The Canadian YMCA in World War II*. Goodfellow Printing Company Limited.

Hyde, F. (Sept 11, 1936). Professional Sport a Half Century Ago. *The*

Woodstock Daily Sentinal-Review, pp. 2-3.

Jarvie, G. (2004) Lonach, Highland Games and Scottish Sports History. *Journal of Sports History*, 31(2), pp. 161-175.

Jones, K.G. (1975) Developments in Amateurism and Professionalism in Early 20th Century Canadian Sport. *Journal of Sport History*, 2(1), pp. 29-40.

Kidd, B. (1995) Making the Pros Pay for Amateur Sport: The Ontario Athletic Commission 1920-47. *Ontario History*, 87(2), pp. 105-27.

Kidd, B. (1996*) The Struggle For Canadian Sport*. Toronto: U of T Press.

Knox, W. (1939) Scrapbook of collection of personal newspaper clippings 1898-1939. Held in Orillia Museum of Art and History, Orillia, Ontario.

Knox, W. (1951) *Hot Foot*. Unfinished and unpublished autobiography. Complete copy in Orillia Museum of Art and History, Orillia, Ont. Partial copies: Orillia Public Library, chs. 1-6 in the Harold Hale Papers collection; Canadian Sports Hall of Fame, Toronto, chs. 7-13.

Knox, W. (c1949) Notes for preparation of autobiography. Orillia Public Library, *Harold Hale Papers Collection*. Orillia, Ont.

Knox, W. (1949) "I Got a Run For My Money". Canadian Sports Hall of Fame Museum, Toronto, Ontario. Paper, 4 pages.

Knox, W. (c1949) Notes for preparation of autobiography. Orillia

Public Library, *Harold Hale Papers Collection*. "Johnson, Hahn and Walker Stories", 2 pages.

Lovesey, P. (2002) Conan Doyle and the Olympics. *Journal of Olympic History*, vol. 10(1), pp. 6-9.

Manitoba Sports Hall of Fame website. *J. Army Howard*. Retrieved from http://halloffame.mb.ca.

Marks, L. (1996) *Revivals and Roller Rinks: Religion, Leisure and Identity in Late Nineteenth Century Small-town Ontario.* Toronto: U of T Press.

Metcalf, A. (1970) Physical Education in Ontario During the Nineteenth Century. *Canadian Association For Health, Physical Education and Recreation.* 37(1), pp. 29-33.

Metcalf, A. (1987) *Canada Learns to Play: The Emergence of Organized Sport, 1807-1914.* Toronto: McClelland Stewart.

Metcalf, A. (1988) Leisure, Sport and Working: Some Insights from Montreal and the Northeast Coalfields of England. In *Leisure, Sport and Working Class Cultures.* pp. 65-76. Toronto: Garamond Press.

Mewett, P. G. (2000) History in the Making and the Making of History: Stories and the Social Construction of a Sport. *Sporting Traditions*, 17(1), pp. 1-3.

Mikkelsen, G. (1996) The Sport of Kings in Victorian Canada. *Beaver*, 76(4), pp. 18- 21.

Morrow, D. (1986) A Case-Study in Amateur Conflict: The Athletic

War in Canada, 1906-08. *British Journal of Sports History*, 3(2), pp. 173-190.

Morrow, D. (2005) *Sport in Canada: A History*. Don Mills: Oxford University Press.

Orillia Collegiate Institute. (1925) *The OrCollegist*. Orillia: Calvert and Maynard. Vol. #1, #1. Orillia Museum of Art and History, Orillia, Ontario.

Paton, G.A. (2006) James GB Merrick (1871-1946): Sports Organizer, Negotiator, Canada's Second IOC Member. In *Cultural Imperialism in Action, Critiques in the Global Olympic Trust*, 8th International Symposium for Olympic Research. University of Western Ontario, London, Canada.

Quercetani, R. L. (1990) *Athletics: A History of Modern Track and Field Athletics (1860-1990)*. Milan: Vallardi and Associates.

Richmond, R (1996) *The Orillia Spirit*. Toronto: Dundurn Press.

Robinson, A. (1936) Professional Sport a Half Century Ago. *Woodstock Sentinel-*

Review Anniversary Edition. 11 September, 1936.

Ross, M.G. (1951) *The YMCA in Canada*. Toronto: Ryerson Press.

Schwartz, D.G. (2006) *Roll the Bones: The History of Gambling*. New York: Penguin Books.

Scully, F and Sper, N. (1943) You Must Let Jim Run. In *Reader's Digest*, August 1943, pp. 7-10.

Scrapbook of Walter Knox newspaper clippings saved by the Knox family. Orillia Museum of Art and History, 30 Peter St. S, Orillia, Ont. L3V 5A9. 278 pages.

Skeaff, B. (1978) *The Complete Centennial History of Orillia and District Collegiate Institute After 100 Years On "The Finest Position in the Dominion."* Self-published by ODCVI high school, Orillia, Ont.

Smith, R.A. (1993) History of Amateurism in Men's Intercollegiate Athletics: The Continuance of a 19th-Century Anachronism in America. QUEST, National Association for Kinesiology and Physical Education in Higher Education journal, 45, pp. 430-447.

Sports Reference website. Olympic Sports. Retrieved from http://www.sports-reference.com.

Town, D. (2008*) Building Character: Stories From Orillia's Remarkable* YMCA, *1872-1955.* Self-published by the YMCA of Simcoe-Muskoka, Orillia, Ont.

University of Wisconsin Badgers website. Celebrating UW's African-American Olympians: *George Poage.* Retrieved from http://uwbadgers.com.

Walmsley, K.B. (1998) State Formation and Institutionalized Racism: Gambling Laws in Nineteenth Century Canada. *Sport History Review*, 29, pp. 77-85.

Walmsley, K.B. (1999) The Public Importance of Men and the Importance of Public Men: Sport and Masculinities in Nineteenth Century Canada. In White, P. and Young, K., eds,

Sport and Gender in Canada, pp. 24-39. Don Mills. Oxford University Press.

Willis, J. and Wettan, R. (1976) Social Stratification in New York City Athletic Clubs, 1865-1915. *Journal of Sport History*, 3(1), pp. 45-63.

Webster, D. (1973) *Scottish Highland Games*. Edinburgh, Scotland: MacDonald Printers.

Webster, D. (2011) *World History of the Highland Games*. Edinburgh: Luath Press

Zarnowski, F. (1989) *The Decathlon: A Colourful History of Track and Field's Most Challenging Event*. Champaign: Leisure Press.

Zarnowski, F. (2005) *All Around Men: Heroes of a Forgotten Sport.* Scarecrow Press.

About the Author

The city of Orillia, with its dynamic sports and cultural history, was an apt place for David Town to grow up. As an athlete himself, formerly a National Swim Team member and currently a record setting masters swimmer, it is not surprising he chose perhaps Orillia's greatest athlete as the subject of his book. In tackling track and field, Walter Knox's sport, David can speak knowledgeably: his older brother was Canadian decathlon champion. Though David is a chiropractor by profession, he has always had a love of Canadian history and has found a wealth of material to write about in his hometown. His first book, *Building Character, Stories from Orillia's Remarkable* YMCA, covered a broad range of cultural history. *Hot Foot* is his biography of one nationally important local hero. When not in the office or writing history, David is a swim coach, YMCA volunteer and avid canoe-tripper. He lives in Orillia with his wife, Leslie and two daughters, Keltie and Jaina.

Index

A

AAA of C 56-60, 136
AAFC 137-9, 173, 179, 187, 194, 196, 469
AAU of C 139, 236, 279, 281, 337, 346, 349, 365, 386, 389, 391, 392, 397, 399, 400, 413, 425, 429
Aberdeen 308
Aboyne 248, 285, 288, 362
Antwerp 337, 338, 340, 343, 345-7, 349, 351-4, 359, 362, 485
Archibald, Ed 17, 18, 141-5, 152, 153, 173, 178, 179, 196, 273, 440
Athens 144, 145, 152, 178
Athletic Wars 57, 133-5, 139, 172, 173, 176, 187, 194, 236, 256, 278, 337, 413, 461

B

Batson, Henry 154-8, 169, 201, 384, 440
Bawlf, Nick 388
Baxter, IK 32, 37, 39, 438
Baxter, Jim 130, 237, 239, 241
Beaches Olympic Club 413, 416
Beeton 237
Belland, Dave 81-6, 128, 142, 194, 202, 439
Bellduger 228
Bell, Jane 394
Beloit College 6-8, 70-2, 77, 84, 86, 107-9, 142, 434, 435, 439
Bessemer 183, 184, 185
Blairmore 121, 123, 201
Boer War 151, 162
Boston 91, 135, 156, 182, 227, 231, 292, 293, 441
Boyce, Mary 381, 445

Bozeman 171-4, 195, 196, 440
Braemar 248, 256, 362
Bricker, Cal 173, 178, 196, 266, 275, 276, 440
Bridge of Allen 290
British Amateur Athletic Association 309
Broderick, Jack 389
Buffalo 41, 42, 175, 296, 438

C

CAAA 35, 38, 60, 113
CAAU 135-9, 142, 172, 173, 187, 194, 196, 198, 205, 440
Caledonian Games 48, 56, 74, 75, 78, 140, 231, 238, 291, 293, 441, 502
Cameron, AA 247, 287, 290, 429
Cameron, John 341, 348, 350
Campbellford 231, 254
Canadian Championships 25, 33, 39, 83, 142, 144, 152, 176, 177, 179, 272, 273, 275, 284, 311, 393, 410, 413, 430, 438
Canadian Olympic Association 138, 194, 396, 420
Canadian Olympic Hall of Fame 426, 447
Canadian Sports Hall of Fame 409, 426, 447, 450, 467, 484, 498, 501, 503
Catherwood, Ethel 39-7, 445
Central YMCA, Toronto 142, 144, 151, 152, 174, 178, 181, 413
Charlie Boyle 347
Churchill Mining and Milling Company 384
Church, Wes 253, 325
Cleverley, George 229, 230, 253, 325, 441
Coaffee, Cecil 342, 348-51, 355, 358, 399
Coalinga 219
Cobalt 164-6, 168, 169, 225, 229, 331
Cobourg 238
Cochrane 229, 427
Coldwater 19, 20, 23, 25, 36, 65, 90, 209, 365, 438, 493

Cook, Myrtle 393, 394, 396, 409
Cooper, Alf 111, 190, 191, 459
Corkery, Jim 266
Cornelius, JR \ 379, 380, 400
Cornell, Dean 199, 200, 223, 377
Corry, PA 154, 155, 156, 158, 169, 201, 384
Cramb, Findlay 290, 300, 305, 306, 314, 315, 316, 443
Cranbrook 105, 106, 118
Creamer, Dallas 408, 446
Crieff 302, 303, 304
Crocker, JH 174, 175, 176, 413
Cropley, Charles 231, 254
Crow, Norton 5, 70, 118, 120, 257, 266, 267, 269, 270, 279, 284, 338, 350, 360, 365, 449

D

Davidson Lake 224, 227, 230, 237, 320, 326
Dooley 188
Douglas, Kirby 96
Drury, EC 365, 366

E

Earlton 151, 163, 165, 169
Edinburgh 131, 237, 243, 248, 285, 286, 307, 361, 472, 480, 507
El Centro 211, 212, 215, 217
Elk Lake 167, -9, 171, 183, 189, 193, 223-7, 230, 233, 236, 241, 250, 253, 291, 298, 299, 307, 317, 325, 331, 441-3, 498, 502

F

Federation Sportive Feminine Internationale 391, 392

Ferguson, HW 125, 126, 146-9, 435, 440
Fernie 100-5, 117-9, 150, 190
Fesserton 18, 20-3
Flanagan, Tom 255, 295
Freeman, EC 348, 349, 358
Fresno 219, 382

G

Gaudaur, Jake 19, 38, 327, 328
Gerhardt, Pete 206, 221, 222
Giddings, Harry 143, 144, 152
Gilles, Duncan 277
Gill, Harry 19, 21, 23, 38-41, 65-71, 73, 81, 85, 92, 98, 107, 110, 136, 152, 175, 274, 291, 295, 296, 415, 417, 434, 435, 439, 446
Glarner, Andrew 206, 222
Glover, Jessie 375
Goderich 400, 445
Godson, Jean 408, 410, 446
Golden 123, 125, 130, 198
Goulding, George 259, 272, 273, 349, 370, 371
Gowganda 224, 227, 253, 321, 331
Grant, Leslie 124, 130
Gray, Ab 36
Gray, George 19-21, 36, 38, 68, 78, 209, 410
Grosse, Rosa 375, 392, 394, 409

H

Hahn, Archie 71, 72, 155, 171, 172, 184-8, 429, 439, 440, 449, 468, 470, 471, 494, 504
Haileybury 164, 165, 167-9, 228, 253, 325
Halpenny, William 141, 160, 179, 265, 273, 274

Hamilton 77, 152-4, 158, 169, 176, 177, 179, 207, 211, 255, 266, 273, 337, 346, 370, 376, 379, 399, 400, 407, 410, 411, 440, 451, 495
Hancock 188
Hanlan's Point 173, 254, 294, 442
Harrison, Bob 87
Hein 189, 190
Highland Games 219
Hodgson, George 271, 272, 276, 277, 278
Hot foot 434, 435, 450, 451, 456-61, 463-73, 496, 503
Howard, Army 257-66, 269-72, 278-84, 347, 353, 406, 413, 442, 504
Hughes, Elwood 263, 266, 267, 270, 282, 409, 502

I

International Athletic Federation 391, 392
Inverness 243, 247, 289, 498
Ironwood 185, 189
Ishpcming 186

J

Jane Bell 394, 395, 397, 445
Jedburgh 301, 304
Jeffries, Jim 13, 165, 166, 226
Jerome, Harry 284
Jerome, Valerie 284
Johnson, Jack 4, 6, 9, 13, 80, 165, 200, 203, 264, 429, 449
Johnstone, Jack 299-301

K

Keane, Tom 91, 156
Keeper, Joe 265

Kerr, Bobby   152, 153, 159, 160, 173, 176-8, 196, 230, 255, 258, 337, 370, 426, 440, 464
Kiely, Tom   84, 175, 204, 292
King, Tom   150
Knox, Jack   24, 25, 162, 165, 167-9, 224, 329, 333, 440

L

LaRose, Fred   163, 164
Latremouille   180
Lawrence, Edward   348-50
Lawson Township   224, 226, 236
Lethbridge   117
Liginger, Walter   84
Livingston   186
London   13, 86, 145, 162, 178, 194, 196, 198, 205, 266, 267-9, 272, 274-6, 279, 280, 282, 283, 309, 337, 338, 353, 354, 380, 392, 476, 477, 479, 483, 486, 501, 505
Longboat, Tom   135, 138, 139
Long, Erastus   30
Los Angeles   220, 382, 412
Lovering's Grove   19, 20, 50
Lukeman, Frank   265-7, 269-1, 273, 279, 281, 282, 353, 426

M

MacDermid, Archie   348-50, 358
MacDonald, Dan   78
MacDonald, John A   231, 293, 439, 442
Madill, W   152, 158-60
Maple Creek   126, 127, 129-31, 142, 237
Marquette   189, 407
Marsh, Lou   187, 292-4, 322, 415, 468
Matchless Six   393, 396, 397, 399, 445

McClelland, Walter 95-7, 99, 197, 454, 455, 461, 462, 466, 478, 501, 504

McEachern, John 349-51

McFarlane, Bob 425

McKenzie 248, 290

McMillan 114, 129, 141, 228

McTavish, Bob 112-4, 125

Merrick, James 257, 258, 264, 266, 267, 269, 270, 278, 279, 282-4, 337-9, 343, 350, 353-5, 357, 360-3, 365, 379, 476, 477, 482, 486, 505

Mexicali 210-3, 219, 220, 384, 441

Michel 118, 119, 124

Midland 25, 34-6, 38, 81, 374, 376, 378, 389, 438

Milwaukee 67, 69, 70, 72, 74, 77, 83, 84, 142, 155, 171, 175, 186, 407

Mitchell, Fred 100, 101, 103-5, 118, 150, 190, 191, 378, 439

Monroe 125

Montana Agricultural College 171, 174, 184, 440

Montesena 197, 201, 441

Montreal 39, 42, 56, 57, 59, 83, 84, 87, 129, 137, 140, 160, 167, 168, 172, 173, 176, 179, 238, 256-8, 270, 273, 277, 279, 280, 282, 343, 345-7, 356, 360, 362, 364, 380, 389, 407, 415, 441, 444, 452-6, 465, 488, 501, 504

Montreal Amateur Athletic Association 56, 58, 137, 281, 345, 347

Morris, Tom 112-4, 142, 439

Mulqueen 366, 371, 379, 380

Munroe, Jack 165-9, 224-7, 229, 398, 465, 466, 471, 502

N

Nanaimo 145-7, 149, 211, 270, 440, 464

Nelson 98-106, 111, 112, 117-120, 125, 126, 146, 149, 190, 342, 439, 459

New York Athletic Club 32, 199, 221

O

OAC 199, 366-77, 379-91, 393, 394, 396- 404, 406-8, 417, 420, 422, 426, 429, 430, 444-46, 489

Oakland 4, 207, 217, 218, 432

Olympic Athletic Club 199, 205, 206

Olympic Team 254, 256, 258, 261, 264, 266, 269, 282, 309, 336, 340, 341, 344, 347, 349, 350, 355, 379, 389, 393, 395, 399, 400, 412, 420, 424, 430, 443, 444

O'Neil, Dorothy 375

Ontario Athletic Commission 366, 398, 417, 429, 444, 499

Ontario Championships 25, 34, 142, 392, 409, 411, 412, 438

Orillia 3, 9, 18, 19, 21-5, 27, 28, 30, 31, 33-41, 43, 44, 57, 65-68, 81, 83-5, 87, 88, 93, 95, 98, 99, 111, 121, 128, 141, 150-2, 159, 160, 162, 163, 165, 169-71, 177, 193, 195, 200, 204, 207, 208, 210, 223, 227, 231, 233, 237, 240, 250, 254, 275, 288, 291, 294, 295, 299, 303, 315, 316, 321-7, 330, 333, 344, 347, 350, 355, 367, 368, 371, 373, 377, 383, 388, 395, 400-3, 408-11, 415-7, 420-2, 426, 429, 430, 435-8, 440, 443, 446, 447, 449, 450, 451, 456,-61, 463-92, 494-500, 502, 503, 505, 506

O'Rourke, Tim 43, 157, 173, 179, 180, 196

P

Pan American Exhibition 41, 438

Parry Sound 34, 37, 44, 65, 438

Parsons, Charles 206

Penman Games 150, 154, 440

Peterborough 81, 83, 84, 87, 128, 142, 194, 322, 376, 439

Phillips, Hec 356, 413

Picton 322, 323, 329, 374, 381, 412, 421, 443, 444, 489

Poage, George 70, 71, 435, 439, 456, 506

Ponton, Alex 346-50, 355, 358, 370

Port Arthur 111, 149, 189, 191, 194, 375, 376, 440, 484

Powderhall Sprint 131, 141, 237, 239, 242, 250, 291, 306, 307, 310, 443

Q

Queen's University 407, 446, 453-5, 465, 501
Quinn, Sandy 76, 77, 79

R

Regan 127-30
Robinson, Alby 55, 454, 457, 498, 505
Rosenfeld, Bobbie 392-5, 409-11
Rose, Ralph 206, 208, 222, 429, 433, 441
Rossland 99, 106, 114, 149
Rowntree, Arthur 85, 86

S

Sanders, George 90, 91
San Francisco 4, 198, 200, 203, 204, 206-8, 210, 217-9, 222, 223, 225, 226, 382, 430, 432, 433, 441
Santa Clara 218
Sault Ste. Marie 73-5, 142, 163, 183, 385, 387, 414, 439
Schneider, Bert 359, 360
Schoolboy Provincial Championship 386
Scott, Bryce 247, 300, 301, 303, 304, 442
Seattle 198, 222
Shancy, Harry 389
Sheridan, Martin 175, 204, 292
Shotts 241
Shrum, Mamie 409, 410, 412, 446
Slocan 95, 97, 98, 100, 439
Smith, Ethel 397
Smith, JC 378
Smithson, Forest 218, 432, 441

Smoke, Art 355
Southbridge 91, 92, 439
Speedie, JA 242, 244, 247, 249, 290, 300
Spokane 112, 117, 129, 141, 142, 228, 439
Stevens, George 81, 82, 83, 84
Stevenson, NJ 181
Stewart, A 343, 346, 348, 454, 455, 461, 462, 466, 478, 501, 504
Stockholm 178, 254, 257, 260, 264, 267-70, 273, 274, 276, 279, 283, 287, 289, 290, 292, 297, 309, 337, 338, 353, 424, 476
St Petersburg 447, 495
Sullivan, James 188, 222

T

Tait, Jack 263-5, 280, 370
Teddy Oke 393, 396
Thompson, Jean 393, 394, 396, 397
Thornton Junction 286, 288
Thorpe, Jim 12, 136, 165, 271, 292-4, 296-301, 316, 442
Tommy Thomson 346, 347, 356, 359, 398, 426
Toronto 16, 18, 20-2, 32, 34-6, 38, 43, 50, 54, 57, 59, 60, 80, 87, 129, 137, 140-3, 151, 163, 173-5, 178-81, 187, 189, 195, 196, 205, 207, 222, 231, 237, 255-8, 261, 270, 275, 277, 280, 282, 283, 292, 299, 322, 330, 331, 337, 338, 341-3, 345, 354, 358, 360, 364, 365, 370, 375-8, 385, 391-3, 397, 407-9, 412, 414, 415, 420, 421, 435, 436, 438, 440, 442, 446, 447, 450-2, 454-6, 461-3, 465, 467, 469, 478, 487-9, 491, 496, 499, 501-5
Town, Fred 430, 431, 494
Town, Tommy 341, 348, 350, 355, 356
Trivett, Walter 266, 267, 280
Turner, George 325-8, 359, 360, 429, 443

U

University of Chicago 69
University of Illinois 68, 107, 142, 152, 295, 417, 439, 494

V

Vancouver 125, 145, 146, 149, 261, 296, 305, 341, 399, 435, 464, 474, 475
Verner 30-2, 65, 210, 412, 438

W

Walker 211, 212, 215-17, 384, 441, 449, 468, 470, 471, 504
Walmsley, Charley 100-7, 111, 112, 114, 116, 125, 126, 342, 452, 453, 456, 506
Weller 291, 293
West End YMCA 144, 152, 174, 175, 177, 178, 181, 196
West Shining Tree Lake 321, 329, 330
White, Ron 36, 38
Williamson, Charles 184, 185, 467
Williams, Percy 358, 399, 425
world record 3, 32, 37, 68, 69, 78, 130, 144, 145, 160, 172, 187, 190, 206, 209, 213, 215, 218, 219, 222, 269, 271, 273, 276, 284, 290, 344, 347, 348, 356-8, 375, 392-6, 399, 426, 432, 433, 439, 441, 461, 470

Y

YMCA League of Canada Championships 158

Printed in Canada